Exploring Nightlife

Exploring Nightlife

Space, Society and Governance

Edited by Jordi Nofre and
Adam Eldridge

ROWMAN & LITTLEFIELD
INTERNATIONAL

London • New York

Published by Rowman & Littlefield International Ltd
Unit A, Whitacre Mews, 26-34 Stannary Street, London SE11 4AB
www.rowmaninternational.com

Rowman & Littlefield International Ltd. is an affiliate of Rowman & Littlefield
4501 Forbes Boulevard, Suite 200, Lanham, Maryland 20706, USA
With additional offices in Boulder, New York, Toronto (Canada), and Plymouth (UK)
www.rowman.com

British Library Cataloguing in Publication Data
A catalogue record for this book is available from the British Library

ISBN: HB 978-1-78660-328-9
          PB 978-1-78660-329-6

Library of Congress Cataloging-in-Publication Data Available
ISBN: 978-1-78660-328-9 (cloth : alk. paper)
ISBN: 978-1-78660-329-6 (pbk. : alk. paper)
ISBN: 978-1-78660-330-2 (electronic)

∞™ The paper used in this publication meets the minimum requirements of
American National Standard for Information Sciences—Permanence of Paper
for Printed Library Materials, ANSI/NISO Z39.48-1992.

Printed in the United States of America

Contents

Acknowledgements ix

List of Figures xi

'Shaken, Not Stirred': An Introduction to *Exploring Nightlife* 1
Adam Eldridge and Jordi Nofre

**PART 1: NIGHTLIFE AND URBAN CHANGE
IN THE NEO-LIBERAL CITY** **17**

1 Precarious Gentrification: Dreading the Night While
'Taking Back the City' in Johannesburg 19
Chrystel Oloukoï

2 Civilising by Gentrifying: The Contradictions of Neo-liberal
Planning for Nightlife in Sydney, Australia 35
Peta Wolifson

3 Night-Time Economy and Urban Change in Post-War
and Post-Socialist Sarajevo 53
Nihad H. Čengić and Jordi Martín-Díaz

4 Amusing Ourselves in Athens's 'Ghettoes of the Mind' 68
Penny-Panagiota Koutrolikou

PART 2: POWER, CULTURE AND IDENTITY

83

5   Mashhad, Iran: Challenging the Concept of a
Twenty-Four-Hour City   85
Atepheh Amid

6   Cairo Nights: The Political Economy of Mahragan
Music   99
José Sánchez García

7   Young People, Alcohol and Suburban Nightscapes   114
Samantha Wilkinson

8   Reviewing Night-Time Economy Policies through
a Gendered Lens: Gender Aware or Gender Neutral?   129
Marion Roberts

PART 3: GOVERNANCE OF THE URBAN NIGHT

145

9   Consumption Patterns of Erasmus Students in Lisbon:
Circulating between Mainstream and Alternative
Nightscapes   147
*Daniel Malet Calvo, João Carlos Martins and
Iñigo Sánchez-Fuarros*

10   Nightlife and Urban Change in Southern European
University Cities: The Case of Montpellier   163
Emanuele Giordano and Dominique Crozat

11   The Transformation of Amsterdam's Red-Light District
and Its Impact on Daily Life in the Area   177
Irina van Aalst and Ilse van Liempt

12   Nightlife as an Educational Setting: The Harm Reduction
Perspective   192
*Helena Valente, Cristiana Vales Pires and
Helena Carvalho*

13   Policies for Nightlife and the Democratic City: From
Urban Renewal to Behaviour Control in Rio de
Janeiro, Brazil   207
Marcos Paulo Ferreira de Góis

PART 4: AFTERWORD **223**

Afterword: Night Mayors, Policy Mobilities and
the Question of Night's End 225
Will Straw

Bibliography 233

Index 273

About the Editors and Authors 281

Acknowledgements

We are indebted to a number of friends, colleagues and loved ones for their support and immense patience over the course of compiling this anthology. First and foremost, Martina O'Sullivan, formerly with Rowman & Littlefield International, responded to our first proposal with nothing less than her complete support and encouragement. In those early stages Martina's help was invaluable. Since then, Michael Watson, Natalie Bolderston and Holly Tyler from Rowman & Littlefield International have been equally encouraging and have lent us their expert advice throughout. Adam would like to say a very special thank you to colleagues in the Department of History, Sociology and Criminology at the University of Westminster, and Jordi would like to thank the Interdisciplinary Centre of Social Sciences from the New University of Lisbon and the Foundation for Science & Technology of Portugal (SFRH/BPD/108458/2015) for their support. Finally, without the commitment and trust of all the contributors this anthology would not have happened, and to them we owe our greatest thanks.

List of Figures

1.1   Lit but deserted, deconstructing Maboneng nocturnal
self-presentation, Auret Street. *Source*: Juliette Garms.   27

1.2   Map of the expanding and retreating dynamics of
the gentrification process in relation to temporalities.
Production: Chrystel Oloukoï. *Source*: © OpenStreetMap
contributors.   32

2.1   Map locating the 'CBD Entertainment Precinct'
(i.e., 'lockout zone') in inner Sydney. 1. Star casino,
Pyrmont; 2. Crown Sydney development, Barangaroo
(due for completion in 2020); 3. Kings Cross Precinct.
Source: Esri, DigitalGlobe, GeoEye, Earthstar
Geographics, CNES/Airbus DS, USDA, USGS,
AEX, Getmapping, Aerogrid, IGN, IGP, swisstopo
and the GIS User Community.   43

6.1   Youth cultural consumption in Egypt (2016). *Source*:
SAHWA Project. Graph constructed by author.   101

11.1   Red-light district, Amsterdam (Wallen area).
Source: Authors.   182

12.1   Frequency of use of different psychoactive substances
among partygoers in Viseu and Lisbon. *Source*: Authors.   203

'Shaken, Not Stirred': An Introduction to *Exploring Nightlife*

Adam Eldridge and Jordi Nofre

Thomas Burke's *English Night-Life* begins with a reflection on the state of British cities after dark. Written in the midst of the Second World War, a picture is drawn of dark empty streets, curfews and blackouts, and a 'dim, subdued kind' of night (1943, 142). According to his extensive review of nocturnal leisure, the past offered ample opportunity for night-time festivities, pleasures and transgressions, and not only for the elite. Like today, various forms of inclusion and exclusion existed, and the night was similarly organised around class, gender and space, but the war led Burke to wonder whether British nightlife would ever quite recover. Two points become clear from Burke's discussion. First, late-night leisure is not new. Van Liempt et al. note that 'city centres have always had late-night amenities in some form' (2015, 411), and, indeed, Amin and Thrift (2002) have argued that a distinctive nightlife emerged sometime in the nineteenth century (see also Erenberg 1984). Koslofsky's (2011) *Evening's Empire* also refers to a 'nocturnalisation' of European cities from the Enlightenment onwards, a period marked by the emergence of street lighting, a new urban culture and expanding opportunities for both work and pleasure after dark. But there is another way of interpreting Burke's commentary. While the conditions under which he was writing are vastly different from today, many contemporary reports of nightlife paint a similar picture, one where all the joy and fun associated with the night has been extinguished or is under threat.

Claims about the imminent collapse of nightlife in London, Sydney, New York or elsewhere are perhaps overstated, but they speak of a similar anxiety about nightlife to that expressed by Burke (1943). This is not an anxiety about crime, danger or antisocial behaviour, though these fears continue to circulate. It is instead a belief that the night and consumers of nightlife need protection. Overzealous authorities who wish to stamp out, over-regulate or control nightlife play an important role in Burke's history as they do in our present. Neighbours complaining about noise from late-night revellers are also not new, as Ekirch (2006) demonstrates. Added to these now-familiar concerns about immorality, noise, crime and disorder, however, new problems have emerged, which equally threaten late-night pleasures: new forms of exclusion, gentrification, commercialisation and mass tourism in particular. Whether these will entirely kill off nightlife is doubtful, but the question as to how we might save nightlife or whether it will ever offer the promises through which it is so commonly understood resonates as much today as it did in the past. How might we make nightlife in our twenty-first-century cities more sustainable, inclusive and secure?

Two questions linger in our minds as we finish this volume: what exactly is under threat here, and why does it matter? Why should we care about the night, least of all nightlife? As night-time scholars, it is perhaps our own failing that these questions have yet to be convincingly answered. Fears about the loss of the night sky due to excessive illumination, the loss of nightlife venues or the muddying of the boundaries that separate night and day (Crary 2013) have become common subjects of debate and tell us as a good deal about what it is we think the night should be and for whom: a time of play, rest, work or darkness are all equally competing discourses about cities after dark. At the very least, as Henckel (2016) has argued, there is little evidence that nightlife even exists beyond a few central streets in most cities, and his own research has found surprisingly little evidence for a clear expansion in night-time employment. As night-time scholars we have perhaps been guilty of assuming that town and city centres in so-called developed Western economies are uniformly open and buzzing twenty-four hours a day and that simply because we can drink, dance or shop at all hours we do so. As Gwiazdzinski suggests, 'As we advance into the night, the options on offer decrease, and the city shrinks and seems to condense itself into a few clusters of streets where we find concentrations of illumination and animation' (2014, n.p.). As Evans (2017) has also suggested, cities often characterised as 24/7 would be more accurately referred to as 24/2. In many cities, it is perhaps true that the night is a time when most people sleep or conduct domestic tasks. The night, as Gwiazdzinski goes on to argue, 'is expensive, and any sense of social and generational diversity is illusory' (2014, n.p.).

We are confident that Henkel, Evans and Gwiazdzinski would agree, however, that the urban night is not as it used to be. In the time it has taken us to compile this anthology, London, inspired by the Night Mayor post in Amsterdam, has appointed its very own Night Czar to champion the capital's nightlife. Paris, Toulouse and Zurich also have Night Mayors (Roberts 2016), as does Shibuya in Tokyo. In 2017, New York City Council approved the creation of a Nightlife Advisory Board, motivated by similar concerns as elsewhere about threats to small, independent nightlife providers (Delgadillo 2017). Just in the past two years the editors of this volume have met up at no less than four international conferences and symposiums to discuss nightlife. We have also met with other international academics, planners, city promoters, festival and cultural managers, entrepreneurs, politicians, journalists and representatives from various government and non-government organisations to discuss the nocturnal city.

van Liempt et al. (2015) argue that the night has been neglected in urban studies, but while this continues to ring true, the 'night-time economy' is now recognised as an important feature of city branding and a means of stimulating the local economy (Schwanen et al. 2012). Many of the chapters in this volume speak of change. As editors, it has been our task to push them on this point; if cities are changing, what are they changing from? Would the bars, taverns and gambling halls of the eighteenth century really be that recognisable to us today, or have urban centres at night changed beyond recognition? Perhaps so. It is hard to image any major city now failing to offer some form of nocturnal infrastructure or entertainment. Typing the word 'cities' into a search engine reveals images not of industry or commerce or even many cities in the daylight at all but of skylines lit up, sun setting on the horizon or artfully lit motorways and signature buildings. A buoyant, varied, diverse and cosmopolitan night-time is increasingly sought, promoted and enabled by government policies and urban regeneration strategies.

The urban night remains articulated with fear and risk, but it has equally become articulated with modernity, progress, cosmopolitanism and urbanity. London has had a night-bus service for just over a century, but when the city's Underground tube network opened throughout the night on weekends in 2016, there was a sense of pride, a feeling that London had finally joined other important modern cities like Tokyo or New York. The ability to shop, visit the gym, attend a night class or have a haircut seems to have become contemporary markers of progress and modernity (Kreitzman 1999; Crary 2013). While it might be unclear what exactly cities are changing from, the night is an optic (Straw 2015a) to think through what we think cities should or could be, and indeed what we think the night should be. Studying the night is not simply about researching clubbing, deviancy or subcultures, though such studies continue to reveal important and fascinating results (Malbon 1999; Riley et al. 2010, 2012), but it also offers the opportunity to think through emerging forms of governance, economic and social transformation, new urban identities, the blurring or indeed stubborn distinctions between night and day and the shifting anxieties and pleasures through which the night is so often framed. As many of the chapters make clear, the night is now as much about pleasures and fears as it is about city branding, regeneration policies, tourism promotion, business and market expansion.

'Neo-liberalism' is a term that has become much used in the past few decades, and it is equally relevant here. Brown (2006, 693) defines neo-liberalism as 'the explicit imposition of a particular form of market rationality'. And while she argues this occurs well beyond just the economic realm, it is worth starting here. The value of the night-time economy is subject to much debate, not least because of the often-vague ways the night is defined. Do we begin at 6:00 p.m. or later? Of course this matters, as we explain later, but when promoting the new night-time economy perhaps it doesn't matter in the ways we might expect. The specificities, scale or inclusions and exclusions of the nocturnal city often seem secondary to market-led and economic language. Will a new bar reduce the price of nearby housing or add value? This way of framing leisure and the night spills over into privileging economic benefits and economic costs. The cost of nightlife to the public sector, such as health services and policing, is offset by the value the night-time economy brings in terms of employment figures, job growth, council rates and tourists. New late-night infrastructure is justified on the basis of how it might enable new markets to open or add value to existing ones.

The chapters here point to a similar economic rationality underpinning much night-time expansion and urban redevelopment. However, it is important that we do not sentimentalise the night and recognise from the outset nightlife has typically entailed some form of commercial exchange. Following Schivelbusch (1988), the expansion of lighting in the nineteenth century was driven by industry and harbour commerce, that is, by an increasing drive towards productivity into the night rather than simply providing more opportunities for leisure. Nonetheless, there is a sense of both urgency and anger in many of the chapters included here. The night is important for reasons beyond whatever market benefits it might entail; there are spaces, places and networks that operate at night to which we feel a sense of belonging, places that are crucial to the formation of our identities (Smith 2014), to emerging political movements, to socialising and leisure. Whether referring to the Take Back the Night marches, LGBTQ+ clubs and bars, venues associated with black and minority ethnic communities, or our own local pub, nightlife serves as a context for a range of social, political and cultural movements (Talbot 2007; May 2014; Campkin and Marshall 2017). When venues or even entire areas are threatened, it feels as if a part of our own biography is being erased. Without wanting to paint an overly romantic picture of the night, maybe there was a time when it did not feel so commodified and so reducible to market-led discourses and rationales.

Though we have no desire to sentimentalise the night, nightlife has undoubtedly changed, as have the ways that cities function after dark. The night has moved up the policy agenda and not only in terms of strategies for better managing crime or antisocial behaviour. New policies, recommendations and branding campaigns have appeared; Night Mayors, good practices guidelines and city marketing campaigns circulate across and between different cities and countries not only in Europe (e.g., Lisbon, Paris, London, Berlin, Belgrade) but also across the globe (e.g., Sydney, New York, Buenos Aires, Tokyo). As we have also established, the night is already understood as crucial to the economic sustainability of many cities. On the one hand, this has led to greater opportunity for nocturnal leisure, socialising and employment. On the other hand, it has led to an increased framing of the night in terms of costs and benefits. More important, these policies, investments, regulations, deregulations and government interventions challenge one of the more romanticised perceptions of the night, which is that it is, or at least should be, a time and place free or somehow different from the more regulated and 'capitalist' daytime.

Having established these broad themes of the collection, it is worth pausing and exploring them in more detail. In doing so, we introduce some of the rationales and the histories of contemporary debates about urban nightlife, many of which continue to shape the examples explored in this volume. While the selection of chapters here challenge the Anglophone-centred approach to the study of the urban night, it has become somewhat customary when discussing modern nightlife, particularly from a European perspective, to begin in post-war Britain (Laughey 2006; Fowler 2008; Marwick 2011). Of course, leisure at night is not unique to Britain, but the idea of a night-time economy, one where regeneration, creativity and leisure intersect, is often attributed to a unique set of conditions in post-war Britain. In one of the first papers to document Britain's expanding evening and night-time economy, Lovatt and O'Conner (1995) recount the now-familiar story of how post-war deindustrialisation, urban decline, suburbanisation and domestic leisure activities such as watching television left many town and city centres vacant by nightfall. The regulation of retail and leisure hours further contributed to what was termed 'the 5:00 p.m. flight', at which time city-centre workers would return to their homes, only to return to the city the following morning (Bianchini 1995). Nightlife continued to take place, but the perception was that cities after dark were dangerous, exclusionary and welcoming to only a small minority of people. Comedia Consultancy (1991), again working in the United Kingdom, identified further problems with British cities after dark from inactive street frontages and poor transport to 'lager louts' and a lack of anything to do. Its report *Open All Hours: A Study of Economic, Social and Cultural Life in Twelve Town Centres in the UK* was influential in not only articulating the problems with evening and night-time opportunities across Britain; it also provided solutions. Comedia called for an *18-hour city*, one that was less of a 'nine-to-five retailing and employment centre' and instead more of an 'economic, social and cultural centre' (Roberts 2004, 11). The relaxation of licensing laws in the United Kingdom, and a greater mix of uses including residential, was called for.

This was not a uniquely British phenomenon. Bianchini (1995) recounts that the first time he heard the phrase 'night-time economy' was in Rome in the late 1970s. The phrase was used by Renato Nicolini, organiser of the city's programme of summer events from 1977 to 1985. In terms that would echo later in the United Kingdom, Nicolini argued that 'city centres in the West are becoming, in many cases, day-time office and shopping districts, almost a wilderness after the afternoon rush hour' (Bianchini 1995, 122). While this trope of the abandoned urban core resonates across a range of different post-war studies, by the 1980s and 1990s attention turned to how cities were being transformed into creative, consumer and cultural hubs. The emerging study of urban tourism (Law 1993; Page 1995; Judd and Fainstein 1999), for example, explored the extent to which post-industrial cities were being transformed from centres of commerce and industry to culture and entertainment. Particularly from the United States, a new urban economy was being recognised and developed, which again centred around the narrative of post-war urban decline and urban growth on the back of culture and leisure from the 1980s onwards (Zukin 1991, 1995; Sorkin 1992; Hannigan 1998; Eckardt 2003; Florida 2005; Lloyd 2010; Hyra 2017).

Hadfield (2015) has referred to the study of the night-time economy as having followed distinct waves and the first very much engaged with the themes identified here, particularly the story of decline then rediscovery of Britain's post-industrial cities in the 1980s onwards. O'Conner and Wynne (1996), for example, bring together two threads of research prominent at this time: urban regeneration and the new postmodern citizenry. Cities, they recognised, had become less about production than consumption and afforded citizens new ways of experiencing, developing and doing urban identities. Milestone (1996) focused this line of enquiry on Manchester's deindustrial urban core in the 1970s and 1980s, which, she argues, provided the space for new forms of nightlife and entrepreneurialism to flourish. The abandoned warehouses, department stores and factories of the city allowed for young entrepreneurs to transform the commercial landscape and develop their own clubs, bars, rehearsal spaces, housing and retail stores.

What makes Milestone's (1996) work especially notable is this explicit connection between the emerging urban, creative economies others had previously identified, with a recognition that the night was central to this narrative. The devalued urban core transformed by consumption was not an explicitly new argument by the 1990s, but by articulating it with night-life, Milestone and others (Lovatt 1996) identified how the newly anointed night-time economy followed the familiar pattern of urban centres being re-orientated towards cultural and consumptive purposes. This is by now a familiar argument and finds accord in many other accounts of post-industrial cities, or parts of cities, where it is not just culture but nightlife culture that is driving regeneration, such as Sheffield (Frith 1993), Temple Bar (Montgomery 2003), New York (Hae 2011a, 2012), Berlin (Evans 2012), Lisbon (Nofre et al. 2017a) and Hoxton (Eldridge 2010; Harris 2012). However, not all cities now associated with nightlife followed this same trajectory. Some of the examples of nightlife discussed in this volume, such as in Sarajevo (Bosnia and Herzegovina), Mashhad (Iran) and Cairo (Egypt), can be more accurately understood in terms of war or religion than post-industrial decline. It is equally important to note that deindustrialisation has different histories, and its outcomes are not linear or predictable (Waitt and Gibson 2009). While culture-led entrepreneurialism and gentrification appear common to Manchester, Lisbon, Montpellier, Amsterdam and Athens as discussed in this volume, their unique cultures, policies, histories and geographies lead to singular, if not unique, outcomes.

Something that is shared across the examples explored here, and many accounts of nightlife, is a concern about its effects. As alluded to in the beginning of this introduction, anxiety about nightlife is not new and indeed by the 1990s both new and more dated 'problems' with the night were being discussed (Roberts 2006). No longer was the issue abandonment or the 5:00 p.m. flight. The second wave of night-time research identified by Hadfield (2014) engaged explicitly with the negative consequences of rapidly and seemingly haphazardly emerging night-time economies. Fears of abandonment and decline might have abated, and in many cities a new urban renaissance had started to emerge. New concerns were raised, however, especially around drunkenness, antisocial behaviour, noise and the expansion of a decidedly alcohol-focused urban night-time economy (Lister et al. 2000; Thomas and Bromley 2000; Hobbs et al. 2003; Winlow and Hall 2006). Shaw (2010) identifies that working-class people were, in particular, singled out for having failed to live up to the promise of a sophisticated, urbane, alternative nighttime economy.

From a comparable perspective, Chatterton and Hollands (2003) questioned the homogenous, de-territorialised nightscapes that had come to characterise many urban centres by the millennium, especially in Western post-industrial cities. Rather than the alternative, youth-driven nightscapes explored by Milestone (1996) and others, nightlife had seemingly become dominated by large pub chains and corporate interests. Many of the changes that had occurred in urban centres were a result of the laws specifically designed to deregulate the industry (Hadfield 2006). Young people's *determined drunkenness* (Measham and Brain 2005) was aided by an industry concerned with profit and expansion, as well as by governments encouraging new venues on the one hand and developing strategies for people to better manage the consequences of their own consumption patterns on the other (Haydock 2014). Elsewhere, as documented in some of the chapters about southern Europe in this anthology, governments actively courted new and emerging youth tourism markets as a way of propping up failing econo-mies. As per the neo-liberal framework, citizens were cast in crude terms as productive, rational night citizens 'whose moral autonomy is measured by their capacity for "self-care"' (Brown 2006, 694) versus the 'urban savages' (Eldridge and Roberts 2008) much mocked in the mainstream press. Other voices added to the concern that the new night-time economy was but a pale imitation of the much-lauded urban renaissance of the 1980s onwards. Greed (2003), for example, noted that much of this new urban economy was male dominated and alcohol based. The urban core might have become revalued, and the discourse of the creative industries had been clearly articulated with the urban core, but the belief that nightlife-led regeneration would herald an urbane, cosmopolitan urban renaissance had, as noted by Davies and Mum-mery (2006), 'soured'.

This is a very UK-based picture, but while some critics of Britain's new night-time economy were wondering why we could not be more like Bar-celona, Lisbon or Rome, these other cities were experiencing comparable concerns. Again, it came back to a shared anxiety that nightlife and nightlife districts had become almost too successful and too commercialised and were losing the more authentic and convivial characteristics of the past. What we see here then are quite different problems with the night. Expanding retail and leisure opportunities into the night-time was initially promoted as an answer to post-industrial decline. Instead, urban centres became quickly characterised as dominated by alcohol-related establishments with associated problems of drunkenness, violence, noise and antisocial behaviour. From a slightly different perspective, and as is well documented in many of the chap-ters here, the night had seemingly lost whatever critical or authentic edge it was once believed to possess. Rather than local bars serving local residents, the marketisation and commercialisation perceived to be a problem in the United Kingdom is now equally felt in many other cities, Lisbon, Sarajevo, Montpellier, Johannesburg, Athens and Sydney being some of the examples explored in this anthology.

It is worth emphasising here that some of the terms dominant in these accounts warrant further reflection. To speak of the night as *commercialised* ignores preexisting forms of economic exchange in the night. Equally, to speak of the loss of authenticity can unwittingly lead to further questions about whose authentic nightlife is privileged. While not discounting the effects of violence and antisocial behaviour at night, it is also notable that a great deal of the moral panic about late-night revellers centres on the working class and women. We should also be mindful that critiques about tourists or students populating urban venues do not replicate simplistic ideas about who does and who does not belong. It is precisely through addressing these questions that we come to a point raised earlier about why we study the night; the discourses that circulate about the night, especially those that mobilise notions of threat or loss, reveal much about our desires and what we think cities at night should be. They also, in turn, reveal underlying tensions and assumptions about who does not belong, what is the *right* type of city at night and what fears and desires continue to circulate at night. In thinking about these, we are attempting to address a critical question about the nocturnal city, that is to say, how we might manage simultaneously the right to leisure and the right to the city in an inclusive and sustainable manner.

Thinking about how discourses, representations and policies of the night circulate leads us to a final and perhaps overdue question. What is the night? When critics lament the loss of a favourite nightclub or the blurring of night and day, whose and what sort of 'night' are they referring to? We started this introduction asking why we might want to study the night at all. For the authors in this volume, the night is a way of thinking through a range of topics such as access and inclusion and associated issues of power and social justice – homophobia, racism, classism and sexism at the very least. Others are concerned with how the night has developed over recent decades and what those developments reveal about capitalism, neo-liberalism, gentrification and the urban policies and indeed stakeholders that drive or resist them. Studying the night also allows for a critical engagement with terms such as authenticity, the local and global, place identity and what these mean when thinking about a space as deceptively simple as a neighbourhood bar or pub. As a phrase, 'the night-time economy' and, in particular, the term 'night' have caused much debate. In some cases, as shown in this volume, both terms are strongly affected by geopolitical factors. Despite evident differences found within northern and southern Europe, and between Anglophone, Asian and Arab countries, a further distinction between the evening and the night remains important in Western post-industrial cities. At one point, the night-time economy referred to 21:00 p.m. onwards, with the evening economy characterised as 18:00–21:00 p.m. and largely entailing restaurants and families. This has more recently given way to a more important debate about using the term 'economy' at all and whether other terms should be used instead (Shaw 2014). While these distinctions might seem unimportant, they are necessary for a range of reasons. In northern Europe, it might be dark by 16:00 p.m. in the winter, but this would not be referred to as evening or night. Perhaps, then, the night is less about darkness than attitude, an orientation, an atmosphere, a set of practices or a way of inhabiting social space.

Critical work has tended to frame the night largely in terms of crime, exclusion, antisocial behaviour and threat. It is for many people also time to relax, even if in theory more than practice. In everyday discourse, the night is conceived as a space of transgression, freedom, pleasure and escape. While these accounts need acknowledging, the familiar conception of the night as transgressive or purely hedonistic needs to be challenged however. The night, just like the day, is subject to multiple forms of inclusion and exclusion (Schwanen et al. 2012) rules, norms and regulations. Class, race, gender, sexuality, disability, religion and age all impact on the ways that we experience the night, if indeed we have access to it at all. To speak of the night only in terms of transgression or fun obscures fundamental questions about for whom it offers such promise and upon whose labour this trope is dependent.

If we can't fully define the night, we can at least identify, as we do here, the policies and the actors that have shaped it. We can also identify that *who* defines, manages and controls the night is equally important. As argued elsewhere (Roberts and Eldridge 2009), the night remains dominated by certain voices, in terms of representation, management and planning as well as definition. Significant voices remain absent, however. Particularly in the case of Europe (but not only), this is of crucial importance in the current period of uncertainty, austerity and societal challenges derived from both the No-Future Scenario for younger generations (Feixa and Nofre 2013) and the recent flow of migrants and refugees escaping from war, misery and poverty.

A kaleidoscopic approach to the study of the urban night should provide us with different tools for thinking about how the night is lived, experienced, managed and understood. In doing so we come to a simple definition. The night is, for us, a means of thinking about urban landscapes after dark and how they have become a source of new and sometimes quite predictable forms of employment, leisure, identity, policy management and, most of all, power (Williams 2008). We hope this anthology provides a step forward in thinking about fostering an inclusive, egalitarian, community-centred conception of the urban night by taking into account specific geographical, social, cultural, political, and local contexts. In sum, this volume on global nightlife intends to bridge a gap between strategic research, decision makers, nightlife actors and the public towards thinking about more sustainable, inclusive and safer nights in our cities and, in doing so, recognises such debates tell us a great deal about our own desires and fears of what the urban night can be.

THE CHAPTERS

Bringing together case studies from across the globe, the chapters explore a set of topics, including nightlife and urban development, race, gender and youth culture, alcohol and drug use and urban renewal. We begin in South Africa where nightlife plays a key role in the urban redevelopment and socio-economic revitalisation of central areas of Johannesburg. In this chapter, Chrystel Oloukoï argues that the night has an ambivalent status in the context of Johannesburg's inner-city gentrifying spaces, revealing the precarious-ness of the gentrification process. Shaw (2015b) has examined the frontier metaphor that frames our understanding of the night. Crary (2013) suggests that in our 24/7 economy, we have moved on from this metaphor, and Melbin (1987), who is most strongly associated with the frontier analogy, was the one to argue in the 1980s that it was being chipped away. But Oloukoï reminds us that at night, processes of racialisation might deepen rather than dissolve any border between the day and night. The night in Maboneng (Johannesburg) is envisioned by developers as an empty space, but they typically overlook the rich and varied culture that already exists there after dark. The area has subsequently become subject to regeneration and gentrification, as is all too common in areas associated with race and poverty.

The consequences of radical changes in the regulation of night-time leisure activities are then explored in chapter 2. By taking Sydney, Australia, as her case study, Peta Wolifson analyses the embedded contradictions within and between the two levels of government most active in regulating Sydney's night-time economy – the City of Sydney Council and the New South Wales Government. Wolifson argues that their contrasting neo-liberal strategies have bolstered class inequality in Sydney through gentrification, despite both levels of government having attempted to 'improve' nightlife through the controversial lockout laws. In doing so, Wolifson discusses whether the pervasiveness of neo-liberalism, particularly in relation to Sydney's nightlife and the status of the city as 'global', has muffled and muted public critique.

In chapter 3, Nihad H. Čengić and Jordi Martín-Díaz provide an analysis of the role of nightlife transforming the city of Sarajevo in Bosnia and Her-zegovina. Čengić and Martín-Díaz start with a short retrospective review of a vibrant, multicultural, nightlife scene in Sarajevo in the 1970s and 1980s. This is not, as documented in many night-time studies, about the effects of post-industrialisation. Instead, they provide an account that places subculture first, as well as the small cafes and venues available across parts of the city at that time. The disintegration of the former Yugoslavia and subsequent war, of course, radically changed nightlife across the city, and they recount the cen-tral role of nightlife in fostering the leisure-led revitalisation of the historic centre of the city, the functional and social transformation of the city centre and the enormous complexity of the 'nocturnal geography' of the city in the current post-socialist period.

Chapter 4 provides further evidence of the complexity and variation in contemporary nightlife, the policies that guide it and the often transformative power it has on vulnerable people in certain neighbourhoods. Penny-Panagiota Koutrolikou takes us to Athens's neighbourhood of Metaxourgeio. Using media discourse analysis, she examines the contradictory ways that nightlife has developed in Metaxourgeio since the early 2000s. While the area has become a creative hub for theatres, galleries and bars, it remains subject to a highly racialised 'ghetto narrative', and much of the development rests on the erasure of existing communities. Koutrolikou's chapter echoes the work of Lloyd (2010) and his account of 'grit as glamour': those working-class areas characterised by graffiti, poverty and decline that are recast through the lens of bohemian chic. But the winners here are predictable, and it is not the asylum seekers, drug users and sex workers who populate the area.

Amid's account of Mashhad in Iran, the subject of chapter 5, acts a punctuation point in the volume. Until now, the contributors have focused largely on Western examples, or on examples where Western forms of nightlife shape and inform local contexts. But despite the pervasive belief that the twenty-four-hour city is relatively new, Amid demonstrates that there were numerous activities occurring in Mashhad in Iran and other Middle Eastern cities well before our current discourse of the night-time economy. Conducting various kinds of routine activities at night is historically part of the social fabric of the city of Mashhad, and Amid starts the chapter by exploring the religious and cultural context of the night in Iran. After doing so, she turns to a more detailed focus on the Imran Reza shrine area where various services cater to both residents and the millions of pilgrims who arrive in the city across the day and night. Amid also warns that while the city currently has an active and vibrant late-night culture, recent plans to develop the area echo other concerns explored in this volume about gentrification and the erasure of existing late-night cultures. This is again a nightlife under threat, but not through punitive measures. Instead, it is about expanding further the opportunities in the area which, in doing so however, have damaged the fine-grained and intricate character of the urban form.

Chapter 6, by José Sánchez García, takes us to Egypt. Exploring the politics of *mahragan* music, Sánchez García argues that this musical genre has become an important media form through which to critique local politics. Focusing on the neighbourhood of Dar as Salam, a deprived area of Cairo, the chapter explores how *mahragan* has both risen and declined in popularity across the country. For working-class young men, however, it has remained an important way of voicing their discontent, as well as serving as a backdrop to parties and gatherings. Sánchez García argues that after the Tahrir Revolution in 2012, *mahragan* became increasingly politicised, and the lyrics not only spoke about the marginalisation of its performers and fans but also challenged the neo-liberal politics that have come to characterise Egyptian society. But this is about more than just fandom, or the politicisation of young people. The chapter also demonstrates how *mahragan* enables self-empowerment and the formation of new spaces in which to perform new subjectivities.

Chapter 7 again takes up the theme of youth culture but provides us with an entirely different context. Samantha Wilkinson explores the practices and experiences of teenagers and young people from the suburban areas of Wythenshawe and Chorlton, in Manchester in the United Kingdom. Wilkinson demonstrates that suburban drinking for young people from these areas is a diverse and heterogeneous practice where there are clear classed spaces that young people move between for their drinking experiences. Rather than framing young people as overtly subject to commercialisation, Wilkinson draws on one of the more recent strands of nightlife theory research by exploring the atmospheres and materiality of street and park drinking. She provides a rich account of how young people's active production of their own drinking atmospheres is co-constituted through the non-representational such as sound, smell, lighting and mobility.

Chapter 8, by Marion Roberts, remains in the United Kingdom but moves from a case study approach to the broader question of gender mainstreaming. Roberts focuses specifically on heterosexual spaces and the ways that they might produce and reproduce gender inequalities. Nightlife in the United Kingdom remains strongly gendered, but recent years have seen both the expansion of women's participation in night-time leisure and new policies designed to challenge gendered inequalities and hegemonic masculinity. Roberts subsequently examines shifts that have occurred in the management and consumption of nightlife, focusing on new partnerships, gender-sensitive local initiatives and attempts by venues to eradicate specific forms of gendered violence and harassment.

Daniel Malet Calvo, João Carlos Martins and Iñigo Sánchez-Fuarros, in chapter 9, develop an equally important thread in nightlife research, focusing specifically on students. They examine the differentiated nightlife practices, experiences and discourses of Erasmus students in nocturnal Lisbon. This chapter exemplifies many of the debates we discussed earlier: the globalisation of commercial nightlife, the threat nightlife is believed to pose to existing working-class areas and the effect of nightlife-led gentrification on existing communities. Malet Calvo, Martins and Sánchez-Fuarros raise issues about the socio-economic backgrounds of those different groups of students and their distinctive forms of consumption in Lisbon's nightscapes. The authors argue that class, subcultural lifestyles and national and linguistic identities have emerged not only as boundaries between mainstream and alternative students but also as intersections to negotiate their consumption practices in Lisbon's gentrified nightlife spots as mobile, middle-class European students.

Also focusing on university students, chapter 10 explores the nightlife of Montpellier, in southern France. The picture drawn by Emanuele Giordano and

Dominique Crozat resonates with Malet Calvo, Martins and Sánchez-Fuarros's discussion earlier, but it points to a quite different set of influencing factors and outcomes. While recognising the effects of studentification in the city's historic core, the chapter also explores how the city had already undergone an intense period of gentrification from the 1970s onwards. This has led to tension between the existing first wave of gentrifiers and the newer students who popu-late the numerous bars and clubs in the city centre. Giordano and Crozat extend critical work on studentification and articulate it with both gentrification and nightlife, providing insights into the importance of local context.

Irina van Aalst and Ilse van Liempt, in chapter 11, also examine the impact of recent gentrification processes, urban regeneration policies and the increase in urban tourism on residents and entrepreneurs living and working in the Amsterdam's red-light district. In this chapter, we see further the spa-tial and social effects of the current transformations in one of Amsterdam's most famous quarters and the resulting complex balance between partying, working and living in this rapidly changing neighbourhood.

Safer partying is the focus of chapter 12. The night as documented here entails 'submitting every action and policy to considerations of profitability [and] the production of all human and institutional action as rational entre-preneurial action, conducted according to a calculus of utility, benefit, or satisfaction' (Brown 2005, 40). While deregulating the market and allowing for greater freedom and choice in night-time leisure, governments have also framed consumers as able to make rational, individual choices. Drug test-ing at parties and clubs is a crucial component of this, allowing consumers to make informed choices. By focusing on three Portuguese cities (Lisbon, Porto and Viseu), Helena Valente, Cristiana Vales Pires and Helena Carvalho explore the implementation and development of CHECK!N, a community intervention project based on harm reduction policies. In their chapter, the authors analyse partygoers' behaviours and the impact CHECK!N's interven-tion has on them.

In the final chapter, Marcos Paulo Ferreira de Góis explores Rio de Janeiro in Brazil and discusses the role of public policies for nightlife in the carioca city, especially the actions taken by public officials to renew and regulate public spaces. de Góis argues that after a decade of urban projects and public policies aimed at changing the urban environment, the city has developed a new night-time offer. Much of the preexisting culture of the city continues to reverberate, however, and de Góis provides a fascinating account of how gentrification and a decidedly culture-led policy for renewal have panned out across the city. Finally, Will Straw, author of numerous works exploring nightlife, provides some concluding thoughts to the collection.

As with any volume, one can look back at the end and see gaps; the night markets of Southeast Asia, employment practices late at night and cities such as New York, Tokyo and Berlin, each famed for their nightlife, seem conspicuously absent. As we identified earlier, there is also a real paucity of research about specific aspects of nightlife, such as nightlife and disability, and much more still needs to be said about gender, race, religion, sexual orientation and class and how these intersect, shape and are shaped by nocturnal leisure. On that note, there is also much to be said about *ordinary* nightlife and the ways in which our everyday domestic lives are enfolded into and shape our nocturnal lives. Highlighting these gaps is not intended to detract from the work here, however. Each chapter provides insights into important themes about the management, representation and lived experience of cities, both during the day and after dark. At times they might appear to contradict each other; in some cases gentrification has expanded and enabled new forms of socialisation, while in others it has led to new forms of punitive restraint. In some cases, creativity appears to be little more than a marketing tool for an already-privileged elite, while in others we see new and unexpected opportunities. What the chapters really speak of is the incredible diversity of nightlife and indeed the ways the night is understood across quite distinct sites. They demonstrate the extent to which nightlife reproduces some forms of power, while also providing opportunities for resistance in others. Most of all, and while there is a common theme about contemporary forms of urban governance across the chapters, they individually and together reveal the complex ways the night is understood and what these contrasting accounts reveal about our current desires, hopes and fears for urban life more generally.

Part 1

NIGHTLIFE AND URBAN CHANGE IN THE NEO-LIBERAL CITY

Chapter 1

Precarious Gentrification: Dreading the Night While 'Taking Back the City' in Johannesburg

Chrystel Oloukoï

'Why study the night? Nothing happens at night here', said the first resi-dent of the Maboneng Precinct that I met when conducting my fieldwork. Many others asked the same or similar questions. What raised my interest in Johannesburg's nocturnal spaces was the widespread idea that they were mostly deserted spaces, supposedly because of a fear of crime. At the same time, marketing images of the city were riddled with nightscapes, reveal-ing a paradox between repulsiveness and attractiveness towards nocturnal spaces. From that starting question about deserted spaces at night to that startled question that I encountered many times ('Why study the night?'), my research was guided by the feeling that nights actually had a lot to tell us about Johannesburg.

Until recently, cities at night had been notoriously understudied. A *daytime approach* has been dominant in the study of both urban activities and geogra-phies of everyday life (van Liempt et al. 2015). Yet, when night falls, we are often faced with very different cities that deserve their own reading (Horn-berger 2008). This is particularly the case in inner-city Johannesburg, where night spaces, at the exclusion of the commodified, enclosed, secured and private spaces of the clubs, are uniformly dreaded and avoided by middle- and high-income populations due to fears of criminality. In the middle- and upper-class imagination, the inner city at night is considered the emblematic space where crime unfolds. At the same time, both inner-city spaces and night-time itself arouse an ambivalent feeling of fear *and* desire, fear *but* desire (Oloukoï 2016b).

In the lower-class neighbourhood of Jeppestown, which has been under-going a process of gentrification since 2008, in the gentrified space being renamed Maboneng[1] (Nevin 2014; Oloukoï and Guinard 2016) the night emerges as the main point of tension between the lower-class residents and the new upper-class residents. This class phenomenon is also heavily racialised in a context where the lower classes of the urban centre of Johannesburg are predominantly black, while the suburban middle and upper classes that try to 'take back the city', supposedly against crime, are predominantly white (Bremner 2010; Murray 2011). This class and racial phenomenon, the two being to a large extent intermingled in South Africa (Seekings 2008; Seekings and Nattrass 2008), brings out the symbolic importance of nocturnal spaces. While the process of gentrification is undeniable during the day, it is affected by dynamics of retreat and contraction at night, demonstrating the fact that gentrification is temporal as well as spatial.

In this chapter, I argue that the night has an ambivalent status in the context of Johannesburg's gentrified inner-city spaces. Being a time-space over which the new residents' claim over space is less tangible and less controlled, the night reveals the precariousness of the gentrification process. On the other hand, precisely because of the challenges they pose, nocturnal urban spaces are being targeted as the main focus of a new and ongoing gentrification phase in Maboneng (Oloukoï and Guinard 2016).

The night-time economy refers to a transformation of urban nightscapes in a context of heightened competition between cities, with the promotion of city centres as 'sites of mass consumption at night' and 'a proliferation of leisure, entertainment and drinking spaces . . . [which] are increasingly corporatized and monopolized' (Gallan 2015, 556). Turning away from the consequences of that shift to the night-time economy in terms of spatial fragmentation and exclusion at night, I analyse in this chapter the origins of that shift and what leads to the identification of night spaces as the main stakes in the *reconquest* of the city by a cosmopolitan, young, middle-class and mostly white new elite. If the impacts of the night-time economy on class relations are well documented, the relationship of the night to race appears underexamined in this scholarship (Talbot 2004, 2007; May and Chaplin 2008; May 2014), especially seen in the light of the post-apartheid cities of South Africa. Through the use of various ethnographic methods, participant observation, semi-structured interviews and urban walks (Anderson 2004; Evans and Jones 2011; Oloukoï 2016a) conducted from January to April 2015, I argue that the destabilising impact of the night on the gentrification process in Maboneng has turned nocturnal spaces into an urban frontier; no longer being at the margins of the gentrification process, they have ended up constituting its core.

My analysis is threefold. First, I give a brief overview of the gentrification process in Maboneng and how it differs from other contexts. Then, I insist on the place the night occupies in a series of discourses and images produced by the developers or the residents to legitimise the existence of the Maboneng Precinct. Finally, I move to explore the dynamics that belie the developers' and residents' self-legitimising discourse. This last part concludes with a critical analysis of the way the night is envisioned as a frontier (Turner 1921; Smith 1996; Shaw 2015b) and a stake of the gentrification process in Maboneng by developers.

GENTRIFYING MABONENG: AN OVERVIEW

Jeppestown is undergoing a process of gentrification, the reclaimed space being renamed Maboneng. By gentrification I mean not merely a change in residents but more accurately an entire remodelling of the urban space (pavements, lighting, security, building renovations, etc.). Such a colossal enterprise is not the doing of isolated individuals whose converging actions ultimately lead to social change, as in Ruth Glass's now-canonical story (1964). Gentrification in Jeppestown resembles more Smith's (2002) depiction of a reinvestment by capital before people, in the sense that while 'the key actors in Glass's story were assumed to be middle and upper-middle-class immigrants to a neighbourhood, the agents of urban regeneration thirty-five years later are governmental, corporate, or corporate-governmental partnerships' (ibid., 439). Gentrification has evolved from a marginal and random phenomenon to something 'increasingly systematized' (ibid.).

Three main characteristics singularise the urban regeneration process in Jeppestown. First, instead of being the convergence of multiple individual initiatives (Ruth Glass's version of gentrification), this process is led by a unique actor. In 2007, Jonathan Liebmann,[2] the mastermind behind the Maboneng Precinct, created the urban regeneration company Propertuity, a wordplay on 'property' and 'perpetuity'. In 2008, Liebmann acquired his first building in Jeppestown, bought from DF Corlett Construction,[3] and named it Arts on Main. From then on, he expanded his territorial hold over Jeppestown and, to a lesser extent, Doornfontein, a neighbouring area to Jeppestown. Both neighbourhoods are characterised by a landscape of dilapidated industrial buildings, which echoes Kolko's argument (2007) about the importance of older housing stocks in the gentrification process.

Second, instead of confining itself to housing, this model led to taking charge of the urban environment in a holistic manner: landscapes, commercial spaces, residential spaces, leisure spaces, security. Most of the buildings were first rehabilitated by Propertuity and changed to a set of specific purposes (retail, offices, accommodation). It was only then that they were leased or sold to other developers. Through Propertuity, Liebmann participated to an unusual degree in urban production. While Harvey's entrepreneurial city (Harvey 1989) blurs the lines between public and private by incorporating private tenets into fields that are the prerogative of public actors, Propertuity blurred them in the opposite direction, taking charge of public prerogatives but with a discourse that rearticulated tenets of public intervention. Complementary to the figure of the entrepreneurial city emerged a figure of a *city-maker entrepreneur*, that is, entrepreneurs who act as city planners and increasingly substitute themselves for public actors. Furthering this logic, Maboneng is going through a voluntary City Improvement District establishment process. This will allow Propertuity to raise an additional tax among the area owners to fund more services than those furnished by the municipality, mainly in regard to the cleaning of streets and improving security.

Third, far from being haphazard, this process is very intentional. From the start, it was not about a single building, or a single street, but about a whole precinct. As Liebmann (Pitnam 2013) states, 'I didn't want to just do my own apartment. . . . I wanted to become a property developer'.[4] Another sign of the intentional aspect of the process is the close collaboration between the private developers (Propertuity) and artists. Conscious of the role of artists in the image of a place (Zukin 1995), Propertuity actively sought their collaboration through various incentives, in a classic case of *art-washing*. In Liebmann's words:

> While travelling and in my time living near 44 Stanley I'd learnt that artists and creatives are often the best catalysts for change. They are the perfect first adopters. It's not in any way unique to Arts on Main. It's been proven in many cities throughout the world. It was important to get them in as they would become the foundation of the community.[5]

The use of the term 'foundation', which means both the origin of something and what allows its stability throughout time, reveals the developers' project of a new community, with different foundations than the existing community. This statement renders visible the process of erasure upon which is predicated the development of Maboneng. In addition, this statement elicits Liebmann's accurate knowledge of urban developments around the world and the way he uses them as benchmarks to improve his own localised project. It testifies to the circulation of urban models and best practices throughout the globe, circulation that largely undergirds 'the generalization of gentrification as a global strategy' (Smith 2002, 437).

Finally, despite the connections the developers made to various places across the world when they elaborated on their inspirations, the gentrification phenomenon in Jeppestown has also been significantly anchored in a larger South African, and more specifically Johannesburg, context (Garside 1993; Visser and Kotze 2008; Winkler 2009). The inner city occupies a special place in the collective imagination of the residents of Johannesburg suburbs. The early urban desegregation in the late 1980s was followed by a white flight phenomenon, the white residents leaving the inner city for the suburbs because they feared an increase in criminality and a decrease in property values (Crankshaw and White 1995; Guillaume 2000, 2004; Beall et al. 2002; Beavon and Orrock 2004). Like Liebmann himself, a white thirtysomething South African, the current residents of the Maboneng Precinct grew up in the suburbs of Johannesburg or other secluded neighbourhoods of various South African cities, estranged from the inner city. Having left the inner city in their early childhood or being born in the suburbs, they construe their attachment to Maboneng as being generated by a sense of loss.

The inner city emerges as a symbolic space that has structured and still structures familial narratives (Gervais-Lambony 2012). Therefore, it elicits a feeling of urban nostalgia, defined as 'a geographical sadness that associates time and space since it is as well the regret of a lost time than the regret of a lost space'[6] (Gervais-Lambony 2012, 1). 'Some people doing Critical Mass[7] have not come back in town since the fall of apartheid, since they were kids', said Loïc Bellet, one of the organisers of Critical Mass, during an interview. This feeling of nostalgia is all the more complex that it is associated with a time (the apartheid regime) and a space (the apartheid city) that is delicate to express regret for (Dlamini 2009). Thus, the inner-city space is the support of a project longing to resurrect a *golden age* in which images of a regretted past and images of desired contemporaneous urban locales that embody a specific vision of modernity are confusedly merged. A conflicted *regime of historicity* sprung from these imaginations and discourses, in Hartog's sense of a context-bound and localised articulation between past, present and future (2003). Here, both past and future are convoked by the middle and upper classes to erase a present inner city deemed worthless because it is populated by low-income residents.

Discordant voices exist in this erasure process, however. For instance, Melvin Neale, one of the organisers of Critical Mass, states:

> For a long time, our city has been viewed as a dangerous place and it is not. . . . But the slogan 'take back the city', I really think it is a really bad choice of words, the city has always been there, it is just that people don't use it, you don't have to take it back from anybody, so I don't like that comparison, Critical Mass is not about taking back the city, but about using the city.

For the populations who feel that they have something to *take back*, however, the night functions as a synecdoche of their lost relation to the city. Night-time, while it materially challenges the gentrification process by stressing precariousness, is nonetheless a privileged medium for gentrification because it plays on people's imagination and fantasies (Oloukoï 2016b) in the context of Johannesburg. Indeed, for a large part of the middle and upper classes from the suburbs, and predominantly for the white part of it, as the demographics of the Critical Mass event reflects, night spaces in the inner city are *no-go* areas. Therefore, the attempts, like Critical Mass, at reclaiming that time-space generate a strong symbolic message.

NOCTURNAL REPRESENTATIONS AS A FIELD OF POWER

Setting Up the Stage for *'Maboneng – Place of Light'*

Reclaiming space in Jeppestown is achieved through a self-legitimising discourse that articulates a sense of loss towards the inner city and a forged vision of inner-city nocturnal spaces as uniformly dangerous and deserted. It is mainly by contrasting itself to Jeppestown that Maboneng – which includes the developers and the residents – constructs its identity, positing itself, first, as fundamentally different from Jeppestown and, second, as an urban revival in a context of dearth. Watching one of the numerous promotional videos made about Maboneng for instance, we are told from the start:

> Downtown Johannesburg has at night the appearance of an abandoned movie set. The high crime rate keeps the streets empty and people out of the inner city. But there is one street where the lights are on day and night: a lively area full of art, creative people and entrepreneurs. It's called the Maboneng Precinct. (Janssen 2012)

This characterisation epitomises the imagery of the city centre as deserted and dangerous at night among middle and higher classes. Maboneng developers build on the myths surrounding central night spaces in Johannesburg. In that sense, the sentence also captures the *ethos* of the urban regeneration project. Maboneng, far from being an anodyne name, means *place of light* in *Sotho*. Through place naming, discourses and images, the developers set the stage for their urban redevelopment project, legitimising their enterprise. Indeed, Maboneng is supposed to 'bring back life into the inner city', according to their website. The dichotomy between life and death, redevelopment and abandonment, light and darkness is used ad nauseam.

In a previous work (Oloukoï and Guinard 2016), I have argued that symbolic violence is inflicted upon nocturnal practices and spaces in Jeppestown by both the developers and the residents of Maboneng. This symbolic violence can be deciphered in discursive acts of erasure. Comparing the city centre of Johannesburg at night to an abandoned movie set, for instance, is a blatant example of how the social uses of the nocturnal spaces in Jeppestown are rendered non-existent. In the same vein, I was repeatedly told during my fieldwork that in Jeppestown 'nothing happens at night'. In an interview, Alice Cabaret, the urban strategist of Propertuity, said: 'Joburg, there really is an issue, at 9 p.m., the city is dead'.

Whether nocturnal practices and spaces in Jeppestown are negated, discredited or criminalised, it is not that surprising if we consider the ambivalent relationship Maboneng residents entertain with night spaces. For the middle and upper classes, night spaces are rarely, if not ever, experienced directly. Nocturnal spaces are approached through a series of mediations and filters (Oloukoï 2016b). Their nocturnal experience, far from being continuous, is archipelagic, from secured places to other secured places through the use of cars, rarely walking. Yet it is in the light of these partial and limited experiences that legitimate and illegitimate nocturnal spaces and practices are defined and reconfigured.

Seeing Like a Developer: Valuable Buildings, Invaluable People

While they recognise the value of the architecture of Jeppestown's decaying buildings, the developers erase the people actually living there, their aspirations and uses of space. The multiple erasures that occur alongside the development of Maboneng are eased by the imaginary surrounding inner-city spaces. As evidenced by the quotation that opened this chapter, nocturnal inner-city spaces in Johannesburg are most commonly described as deserted and devitalised due to criminal activities. Abstraction is the best exemplification of the way Propertuity deals with the symbolic and material entanglements that produce Jeppestown, only preserving the structure of buildings to be rehabilitated. This is reminiscent of James Scott's analysis of how states, in order to make certain realities legible and at the same time capable of being acted upon, carve from these realities only the aspects that can be used for their own interests. State bureaucracies commonly 'dismember an exceptionally complex and poorly understood set of relations and processes in order to isolate a single element of instrumental value' (Scott 1998, 21). Similarly, in the developers' words and practices, Jeppestown appears as a blank space (Nevin 2014), populated by valuable old and spacious industrial buildings waiting to be filled. The developers deny that the rehabilitated buildings were previously occupied and that there were evictions. For instance, Alice Cabaret, urban strategist at Propertuity, stated in an interview with me:

> There are many opportunities. This is really a chance since part of this neighbourhood is a disaffected industrial space. So the buildings developed by Propertuity were empty industrial buildings. They were completely empty, completely filled with, you know, trash and everything. And I love the idea

of giving a new life to these buildings. That is regeneration too, transforming empty spaces in spaces that can be used for human purposes.

This statement of previous emptiness is hard to believe, knowing that in Jeppestown other buildings that were not part of the regenerated portion, renamed Maboneng, are all densely occupied. In an inner city where a place to sleep is very hard to find for disenfranchised individuals, and where so many buildings are *squatted*, a whole set of empty buildings waiting for developers to renovate them seems close to impossible. Another instance of Propertuity's erasure of previous occupants is even more striking. Jonathan Liebmann, while visiting an abandoned building that had seemingly been emptied, was asked to describe what he was seeing, in the documentary 'Place of Light' (Janssen 2012):

> I mean for me, I see absolute mess you know, I see sewage all over the place, human sewage, with no services whatsoever, all the lifts are broken, no windows. So I just see a complete mess, but I also see at the same time a vision of what it could become.

At the same time that Liebmann denies any previous human presence, he manifests it by alluding to 'sewage' and specifically 'human sewage' that litter the ground, referring to the probable possibility that the building was previously squatted by homeless people. Thus, Liebmann's discourse elicits how the denial of previous occupants legitimates the urban regeneration led by Propertuity: renovating empty buildings is far less controversial than renovating buildings from which people were evicted. In an extremely condensed manner, Liebmann's words illustrate how Jeppestown is perceived only as a set of degraded but valuable buildings. The vision of what these buildings *could become* is made possible only by the erasure of previous communities. This leads to the *narrowing of vision* (Scott 1998); taking certain aspects of Jeppestown into account while erasing others is what makes Jeppestown 'legible' for the developers.

PRECARIOUS GENTRIFICATION: NOCTURNAL WITHDRAWALS AT THE PERIPHERIES

Theory and Practice: Jeppestown as a Resource at Night

According to the developers, and even the residents, the urban regeneration project is bringing the city back to life, especially after dark. Tikhe's statement about how Maboneng has changed her relationship to night-time is a case in point. The young, middle-class, black executive at Maboneng explains:

> Maboneng looks beautiful at night, especially with the lights lit, so it is a place of light. Different lights lit, and the business of the street at night, now, because I can imagine in my mind, ten years ago, what the impression of Jeppestown was: no street lights, dark roads, no people, no cars, no one, you know. That was before Maboneng. Everything shut down at a certain time and everything opens at a certain time. So now, Maboneng looks beautiful, I can walk at night now, I wouldn't then, but now I can.

Tikhe's discourse evinces the fact that Maboneng presents itself as a beacon of light among a sea of darkness. Figure 1.1 illustrates all the ambiguity of the image constructed around Maboneng.

The borders of the precinct may be well lit and thus highly visible at night, but they are, nonetheless, deserted, in part due to the absence of shops or places open late into the night. The practices of the residents of the precinct belie this light and darkness dichotomy and even reverse it. At night, since Maboneng's few grocery shops close early, Jeppestown becomes a centrality. Most residents of the Maboneng Precinct limit their incursions to Jeppestown

Figure 1.1. Lit but deserted, deconstructing Maboneng nocturnal self-presentation, Auret Street. *Source*: Juliette Garms.

shops situated at the outskirts of Maboneng, such as Fox Den, a bar, and the grocery next to it, on Main Street.

These places function as spaces of nocturnal sociability for locals in Jeppestown but are mostly used by the residents of the precinct as places to buy alcohol and food at night when everything else is closed. Compared to Maboneng, Jeppestown is characterised by a thick tissue of formal and informal shops (mainly grocery shops, sometimes hair saloons) that are open or semi-open far into the night. These shops have at night a larger function than their classical commercial functions (food provision, house provisions and hair services): they become spaces of sociability, and the manager or owner and client relationship shifts. Some of the clients still entertain a utilitarian relationship to the shops, but others come just to buy a product or a service than to socialise with friends.

When night falls, shops have functions that are larger than their diurnal utilitarian ones. Similar to the Marseille snacks studied at night by Bouillon (2000, 48), about which she argues, 'the snack is more than a place where you come to eat, it is a place where you come to spend time', the formal and informal shops animate Jeppestown at night. The managers or owners of the shops have developed very strong relations with their clients, mostly low-class black residents of Jeppestown, and often enough to be noted, clients act in these commercial places as they would in a familiar domestic setting, coming with a portable folding chair, for instance, to sit and converse in the shop. With the edges of residential buildings, where neighbours socialise until late at night, formal and informal shops are invaluable spaces of animation and diversity at night in Jeppestown in terms of age and gender. Children or adolescents in the shops late at night are a frequent sight. Being sent for an errand, they take advantage to meet with friends inside or in front of the shop. Because they are open late at night, Jeppestown commercial spaces have at night a reassuring function for the residents, which belies Maboneng's depictions of Jeppestown. This reversed relationship at night is the first contestation in the set of discourses and images that construct Maboneng in opposition to Jeppestown, as a place that reinvigorates the city. Another contestation is what happens at nights when power outages occur.

Power Outages, Reclaim of Space and Power Inversion

Nights when power outages occur happen frequently in the inner city. Light is an essential component of the management of security in Maboneng, to the same extent as security guards and CCTV cameras. When the lights go out, their importance strikes all the more. Indeed, the absence of light illustrates to which point all the components of the Maboneng security complex function synergistically. When the lights go out, despite the continued presence of security guards and CCTV cameras, the whole system has to be reconfigured. The security guards insist on accompanying the few residents who venture outside on such nights to their destinations. A movement of withdrawal towards interior spaces can be observed: for instance, the tables of the restaurant and cafes situated outside are moved inside. A similar attitude could be observed at night against evictions in Jeppestown, where Maboneng residents were advised to stay home. Nights without lights spark the same attitudes as nights of protest. The precinct residents literally disappear from public space in both cases, and the streets are then occupied by other populations, mainly black and young, low-revenue people from Jeppestown, with a majority being men. While on lit nights Maboneng seems to gain space over Jeppestown, on dark nights, it is the opposite that happens. Vaughn Sadie, a South African artist who performs in the Museum of African Design in Maboneng and in the streets, grasps accurately the extent to which our relationship to night and light is a social construct, a class construct and a historic construct:

> So infrastructure, when it works and when it doesn't work really define our relationship to the city. But it depends, if you are middle-class it changes your relationship, but poor people are used to it, there are streets that are never lit, and people live there anyway, and children walk on those streets, not running, not panicking. But on Fox Street when there is a shortage, everybody is running.

For the residents of Jeppestown, light does not always equal safety, contrary to its signification for Maboneng residents. The apartheid legacy of lighting policies that had a *prison-like effect* (Hornberger 2008, 288) can still be felt in Jeppestown residents' ambivalent feelings about lighting.

One could argue, however, that these are rather exceptional nights, which do not entirely disrupt the gentrification process unfolding in Jeppestown. But in reality, what happens during power shortages is an exemplification of what happens at a lesser scale on ordinary nights. Outside of extraordinary nights, with specific events that push further the nocturnal limits of the gentrified space (e.g., public performances and outdoor screenings), it is rather a retreating dynamic that characterises the nocturnal gentrification process.

The Core and the Periphery: Retreating Gentrified Spaces at Night

Looking at gentrification with an eye for short-term temporal variations can be a useful lens for analysis. To be able to do this, however, one must depart from classical characterisations of gentrification. While gentrification has long been defined as a change in residents (Glass 1964), others (Johnston et al. 2000; Lees et al. 2008) advocate for a more inclusive definition than the one centred on housing. Gentrification is a multidimensional process for which housing is an important dimension, but by no account the only one (Johnston et al. 2000; Clerval 2008). This allows the focus to shift from housing and residents to central urban spaces as sites of struggle in times of increased competition over space (Smith 2002). As stated by Anne Clerval, gentrification is about 'a material and symbolic reclaiming of popular spaces (of residence but also of work and leisure) by a more affluent class of people'[8] (Clerval 2008, 63).

Putting housing aside, I have chosen to concentrate on aspects of gentrification that are subject to short-term change and can thus reveal differences between night and day, such as practices and activities (artistic, commercial, etc.). During the day, the gentrified space is expanded by various activities and events – such as markets, pop-up shows and shops, street performances and other similar events, beyond the space delimited by more stable components of gentrification (e.g., housing). The urban landscape of Maboneng, but also parts of Jeppestown, is thus transformed, both in a visual and an acoustic sense by activities that push further the borders of the gentrified space. At night, one can observe the reverse phenomenon. Indeed, in Maboneng, night is a time of retreat of the gentrification process. The market at Arts on Main, the first reclaimed building of Propertuity, that happens every Sunday morning and early afternoon for the daytime market and every first Thursday of the month for the night-time market, is a striking example of this.

Initially held inside the building itself, the market at Arts on Main has progressively extended to the street (Boichot and Guinard 2013). At night, however, the market is confined to indoor spaces, inside the building and the interior yard. It is interesting to note that this yard is designed to resemble outdoor public space, with the delimitation of alleys and sidewalks. Privately owned, this space is made public but only to an extent (Staehell and Mitchell 2016). The profile of the users also shifts: while the daytime market attracts a diversified public in terms of age (with the presence of families) and geographical origin (with residents from distant suburbs), the night market attracts mostly residents and regulars. The occupation of space at night is thus more restrained and less tangible, illustrating a side of gentrification not stressed enough: its temporal precariousness.

While in other contexts the process of gentrification can be slowed or hidden by the visibility of popular activities in the urban space (Clerval 2010; Chabrol 2011), in Maboneng, however, the material and symbolic reclaiming of space by diverse actors (developers, residents, users) is curbed not by visibility but by the very invisibility of criminal practices, which makes them so suitable for rumours, fantasies and myths. Crime marks space in a particular manner. The least suspicion of a criminal presence is enough – in middle- and upper-class views and practices – to turn nocturnal public spaces into no-go zones. The changing occupation of night spaces in Maboneng is less – contrary to power outage nights – about popular classes reclaiming space than about residents and users of Maboneng relinquishing it. In a country still deeply marked by racial prejudice combined with the growing importance of social prejudice, the criminal other is always presumed masculine, black and poor (Dirsuweit 2002, 2007; Houssay-Holzschuch 2010). The nocturnal outposts of gentrification, in that logic, can only be spaces where such a presence is controlled or even suppressed. On ordinary nights, the segment of Fox Street going from Arts on Main to the Curiocity Backpacker is the only portion of Maboneng in which such a mastering of nocturnal time-space is assured (cf. figure 1.2). Therefore, this is also the only portion of Maboneng where the diurnal and nocturnal maps of the gentrification process overlap completely.

The spatial and temporal dissociation between different components of the gentrification process in Maboneng is crucial, since it stresses the areas and times in which the process is completed and the remaining areas and times in which it is still somewhat challenged. Night-time challenges the gentrification process in more than one count. It underscores the contradictions lodged at the core of the Maboneng discourse. The developers would have us believe that Maboneng brings back life at night in the neighbourhood, while a thorough ethnographic analysis highlights that life was always already there. Moreover, it appears that Maboneng shuts down early on ordinary nights, making Jeppestown a resource space for food, alcohol and sometimes leisure provision. Finally, while the developers project their imprint on the neighbourhood through maps that exaggerate the real limits of the precinct, night-time reveals the weakness of that imprint at night, the gentrified space being reduced to a segment of the street (cf. figure 1.2). Night-time curbs the process of gentrification in the sense that it slows it down but also in the sense that it threatens it, by exposing its fragility. Therefore, night occupies an ambiguous position in the Maboneng project; being identified as an obstacle, it has been converted into a new field of neo-liberal predatory conquests, in order to answer the challenge it poses. A limit and possibility at the same time, the night is a 'frontier' in the eyes of the developers, a time-space to be conquered, with all the colonialists' and Eurocentric implications of that metaphor (Shaw 2015b).

CONCLUSIONS

Succeeding in transforming a portion of Johannesburg's inner city into a place physically and mentally available for suburban residents was impressive

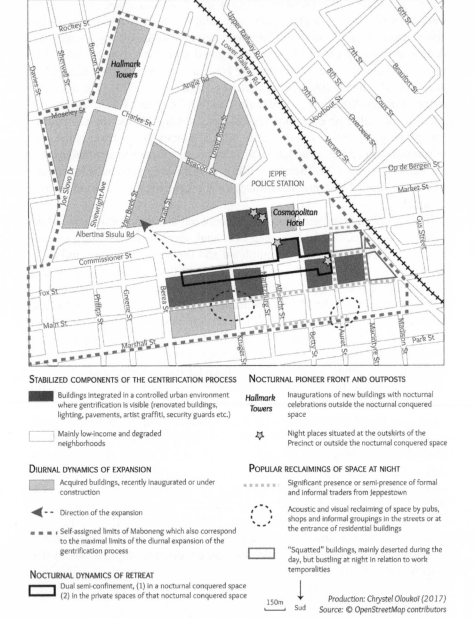

STABILIZED COMPONENTS OF THE GENTRIFICATION PROCESS

Buildings integrated in a controlled urban environment where gentrification is visible (renovated buildings, lighting, pavements, artist graffiti, security guards etc.)

Mainly low-income and degraded neighborhoods

DIURNAL DYNAMICS OF EXPANSION

Acquired buildings, recently inaugurated or under construction

Direction of the expansion

Self-assigned limits of Maboneng which also correspond to the maximal limits of the diurnal expansion of the gentrification process

NOCTURNAL DYNAMICS OF RETREAT

Dual semi-confinement, (1) in a nocturnal conquered space (2) in the private spaces of that nocturnal conquered space

NOCTURNAL PIONEER FRONT AND OUTPOSTS

Hallmark Towers — Inaugurations of new buildings with nocturnal celebrations outside the nocturnal conquered space

Night places situated at the outskirts of the Precinct or outside the nocturnal conquered space

POPULAR RECLAIMINGS OF SPACE AT NIGHT

Significant presence or semi-presence of formal and informal traders from Jeppestown

Acoustic and visual reclaiming of space by pubs, shops and informal groupings in the streets or at the entrance of residential buildings

"Squatted" buildings, mainly deserted during the day, but bustling at night in relation to work temporalities

150m   Sud

Production: Chrystel Oloukoï (2017)
Source: © OpenStreetMap contributors

Figure 1.2.   Map of the expanding and retreating dynamics of the gentrification process in relation to temporalities. Production: Chrystel Oloukoï. *Source*: © OpenStreetMap contributors.

enough. Maboneng developers have managed to capitalise on the fear, desire and nostalgia that the inner city inspires, but they have temporarily failed to make it true also at night. This is largely because of the different kinds of fear that characterise day and night spaces. During the day, specific places crystallise these fears, these are the no-go areas, for instance, the taxi ranks. At night, however, the spatial logic of fear shifts, as evidenced in the fieldwork I conducted. While most of the people I interviewed would mention specific places that elicited fear in them, during the urban walk at night, it appeared that it was not specific places but the night temporality itself that was fearful to the residents of Maboneng. Instead of a concentration in specific places, the spatial logic of fear at night is that of an extension. While during the day specific places inspire fear, at night, the whole urban space inspires it, and only a few specific places are considered reassuring. One can contrast the diurnal crystallisation of fear to a nocturnal diffusion of fear: delimited and circumscribed places are safe heavens in an environment considered as uniformly dangerous.

At night, other geographies of gentrification are uncovered in Maboneng, with their own outposts and logics, which need to be compared with those of the day. Night-time affects gentrification processes and is affected by them in return. Indeed, with the night acting as a *frontier* of the gentrification process, it needs to be put into order in the developers' eyes with a very neo-liberal vision of order. The subsequent bifurcation towards the night-time economy of Propertuity's urban strategy can be read through this lens, since the night-time economy goes hand in hand, in the developers' minds, with logics of securitisation and pacification. However, as elicited in some works, gentrification and the night-time economy entertain an ambivalent relationship (Hae 2011a). While the night-time economy is precisely the element that disrupts order in other contexts, in Maboneng it is mobilised to ascribe a certain order to a supposedly disorderly nocturnal city.

The implicit assumption in the *night blindness* (van Liempt et al. 2015) that characterised urban studies until recently was that it was enough to study daily realities and that the night didn't bring considerable difference in those realities. Doing a geography of the night is stating the exact opposite: nights are an interesting angle to capture urban realities. But it is more than that; it is also a political standpoint, yearning for a geography of the time-space margins in the neo-liberal global south city, giving back a voice to the narratives of those that are denied the lights in a context where the night is instrumentalised to further spatial processes of exclusion. I would like to finish on that note with reference to one of the people I interviewed in an abandoned building; when I asked him if he knew what Maboneng meant, he said: 'Place of light, yeah, we are blinded by the lights'.

NOTES

1. 'Maboneng' means 'place of light' in Sotho, one of the eleven official languages of South Africa. The light metaphor accurately illustrates the kind of light and darkness dichotomy upon which the developers have based their marketing strategy.

2. Liebmann is a white South African entrepreneur, originally from Durban.

3. The building built in 1911 was initially a bonded liquor warehouse for William McBain. Later, it was acquired by the construction company of D. F. Corlett, master builder and Mayor of Johannesburg from 1931 to 1932. With the demise of the neighbourhood in the desegregation era, the building became derelict. Economic activity had long ceased in the premises before Liebmann acquired it.

4. Pitnam, Juliet. 2013. 'Maboneng Precinct: Jonathan Liebmann. An entrepreneurial spirit revitalises downtown Joburg'. *Entrepreneur*, 27 March 2013.

5. Ibid.

6. Personal translation from the French.

7. Critical Mass is a global movement to promote ecological transportation occurring in various cities across the world. This international event takes on a very different emphasis in the context of Johannesburg. Both the discourses of the participants and organisers and the press coverage reveal that it is less about ecology and reclaiming space for cyclers than it is about reclaiming space in the inner city for suburban, affluent and white populations. The ride takes place throughout the inner city at night, every last Friday of the month, in order to take back the city. The route is punctuated by stops, often in gentrified parts of the inner city, such as Maboneng.

8. Personal translation from the French.

Chapter 2

Civilising by Gentrifying: The Contradictions of Neo-liberal Planning for Nightlife in Sydney, Australia

Peta Wolifson

In 2013, the City of Sydney Council introduced itself as a key player in global nightlife planning via the release of its 'world first' strategy and action plan, *Open, Future Directions for Sydney at Night*. Despite its claim of exclusivity, the plan largely followed the global trend in 'night-time economy' planning and extended the Council's established entrepreneurial strategy into the city's nightscape (Wolifson and Drozdzewski 2016). Since then, Sydney's night-life regulation has been thrust into the spotlight. Following the 'one-punch' killings of two young men in the Kings Cross nightlife precinct, Thomas Kelly on 7 July 2012 and Daniel Christie on New Year's Eve 2013, pressure mounted on the New South Wales (NSW) State Liberal Government to act.[1] Its response, in early 2014, was the introduction of a suite of regulatory changes that included the controversial 'lockout laws' (NSW Government 2014).[2] The subsequent laws, which stipulate no admissions after 1:30 a.m. and last drinks at 3:00 a.m. within a delineated inner Sydney zone, have had a dramatic impact on the nightscape.

This chapter explores the embedded contradictions within and between the two levels of government most active in regulating Sydney's night-time economy – the City of Sydney Council and the NSW Government – which, despite contrasting ideologies and visions for Sydney, have each sought to employ nightlife for economic growth. While both levels of government have attempted to 'improve' nightlife, their contrasting neo-liberal strategies have bolstered class inequality in Sydney through gentrification, particularly mobilised through the surrender of civic spaces to private interests (Lees et al. 2008). Despite much public debate around the lockout laws, there have been only minor shifts in policy since their introduction, and the debate has neglected to effectively engage with the issue of state-sanctioned gentrification. In this chapter, I argue that the pervasiveness of neo-liberalism in a discursive sense (Foucault 1991; Springer 2016), particularly in relation to Sydney's 'global city' status, has muffled and muted public critique. This chapter demonstrates how neo-liberal discourse has variously infiltrated these three key mechanisms in Sydney's nightlife; nightlife planning by both the NSW Government and City of Sydney Council, and the surrounding public debate. Gentrification is drawn out as both an outcome of planning born out of this discourse and an intentional mechanism of it.

Sydney has long struggled with issues of metropolitan governance, with a lack of coordination between and within levels of government and the private sector (McGuirk and O'Neill 2002; MacDonald 2015). Since the high of the 2000 Olympics, the city has grappled with contested aspirations for its (global) future (Rowe and Lynch 2012; MacDonald 2015). Eager to present itself as a progressive and innovative council, under Lord Mayor Clover Moore, the City of Sydney projects new urbanist, sustainable ideals with an entrepreneurial approach appealing to the growing, socially liberal middle class of its constituency. The state government, on the other hand, has long been perceived to advocate for developer interests, and its privatisation agenda has only ramped up in recent years. Despite their demonstrable differences, both the council and its state counterparts are complicit in exacerbating gentrification through neo-liberal governmentality (Foucault 1991). The council's focus on 'civilised' hospitality, for instance, through its 'nighttime economy' and 'fine-grain' strategies, encourages upmarket small bars, cafes and restaurants, while large-scale events and high-end retailing make up elements of the tourism and business investment focus (McNeill 2011). This approach has done little to counter rampant gentrification and co-opted well-meant intentions of an inclusive and diverse nightlife (Wolifson and Drozdzewski 2016). Meanwhile, the NSW Government has pursued regulatory change as a moral agenda with a core message of public safety. Combined with its continued appeasement of vested interests including powerful lobbyists, from gambling industry groups to property developers, this morally imbued message has, too, become co-opted. While its stated prioritisation of public safety fails to coalesce with the government's public image of favouritism towards liquor and gaming interests, its targeting of businesses in a 'lockout' zone also conflicts with its deregulatory mantra of economic liberalism. Changes in the commercial landscape of this lockout zone have, intended or not, provided new development opportunities likely to equate to gentrification in an area already under pressure by Sydney's high property values.

The lockout laws appeared amid a coalescing of seemingly contradictory discourses around morality, entrepreneurialism, neo-liberalism and desires to boost the night-time economy. Public responses to the lockouts have been significant and divisive. With their implementation viewed by many as a proactive response to widespread calls for action, a position championed by the two major Sydney newspapers (Wadds 2015; Homan 2017), they have had significant public support. High-profile medical professionals and police leaders have backed the pro-lockout lobby for the impact it has had on hospital admissions and crime rates. They have been further supported by Ralph Kelly, who started the Thomas Kelly Youth Foundation to improve the safety of young people out at night.[3] At the same time, activist groups, *Keep Sydney Open* and *Reclaim the Streets*, have held well-attended protests opposing the laws, citing economic and cultural losses from associated business closures and damage to the global city's reputation. Opponents also criticise the lockouts' geographical specificity, pinpointing the non-inclusion of *The Star* and (under construction) *Crown Sydney* casinos and a lack of consultation prior to the laws being introduced.

NIGHTLIFE TO NIGHT-TIME ECONOMY

The trend that saw a shift from nightlife as a liminal and diverse space to an economic policy priority in many global cities is now well documented (e.g., Talbot 2007; Roberts and Eldridge 2009; Hadfield 2015). With the shift to post-industrial urban economies, maximising economic output has become a priority for global city governments. From the twenty-four-hour cities concept, developed by 'creative cities' think tank Comedia, came the emergence of the night-time economy (Montgomery 1994). This now-ubiquitous urban strategy justified an increased consumer tax base (Bianchini 1990) through the mantra of regeneration and the mal-adoption of Jacobs's (1961) notion of vibrant streets. This notion was used to espouse the theory that a busier nightlife meant improved safety that would, in turn, attract a more diverse population and engender a more civilised nightlife (Hadfield 2015). Rather, the drawing of neo-liberal thinking into nightlife planning, via a competitive creative cities agenda (Florida 2002), spawned both undesirable criminogenic outcomes of deregulation, including increases in alcohol-related violence (Hobbs et al. 2003, 2005), and the homogenising effects that frequently accompany gentrification (Talbot 2006; Hadfield 2015).

The shift from managerialism to entrepreneurialism in urban governance (Harvey 1989) has unfolded through internationally and regionally competitive place-making strategies. The creative city model is dependent on changes in consumer behaviour and demographics, deindustrialisation and subsequent gentrification, with night-time economies promoted as vital to the appeal of cities to the so-called creative class. This has led to deregulation to boost the economic capacity of the city at night through a more fertile local economy and efficient tax base (Talbot 2007; Hae 2011b). As these benefits arise largely through increases in alcohol sales, there has been substantial criticism of the 'naivety' with which this type of governance has consolidated the influence of the alcohol industries (Hadfield 2015). Permissive licensing practices have also led to inevitable alcohol-related problems, stakeholder conflict and re-regulatory measures (Hae 2011b). Despite problematic local outcomes, these practices have continued to inform urban place-making strategies.

Ill-fated 'creative city' strategies have persisted despite substantial empirical evidence of their exclusionary outcomes. As within other creative cities' strategies, night-time economy policies have served to commodify and homogenise urban cultural resources, 'suturing them as putative economic assets to evolving regimes of urban competition' (Peck 2010, 218). As Blum (2010, 80) has noted, Florida's (2002) vision serves to normalise and thereby constrain creativity within the realm of what is acceptable and mainstream, thereby eroding its inherent cultural value and essential 'creativity'. Global shifts to a more 'genteel' or 'sanitised' night-time economy have created urban playscapes that undermine, uproot and eradicate spaces of subcultural deviation, cultural resistance and political radicalism (Chatterton and Hollands 2002; Talbot 2007). The increasing forfeiture of these civic spaces to commercial interests encourages gentrification and the creation of leisurescapes of *sameness* for the creative class (Griffiths 1998).

PROHIBITION TO 'POKIES' IN SYDNEY'S NIGHTLIFE: REGULATION AND RHETORIC

Sydney's nightlife has evolved in tandem with the city's historic geography of production and consumption or, as discussed by Rowe and Lynch (2012), the changing patterns of work and play. As such, the inner city's recent history of deindustrialisation and subsequent gentrification is not atypical when compared with other global Western cities. In particular, however, the *oscillation of sentiment* (Wadds 2013) and regulation around alcohol consumption and night-time leisure have been tied to the city's social and political contexts. 'Moral panics' (Cohen 1972) have long been illustrations of discrimination against the 'folk devils' of the day – be they poor, queer, working class, indigenous, migrant, 'Westie',[4] women, youth, sex workers, addicts or subcultural – translating into prohibition (Homan 2003). Sydney's relationship to alcohol and nightlife since colonisation in 1788 can be seen to mirror more contemporary struggles with regulating the night-time economy (such parallels are explored later). While alcohol taxation revenues have held significant value for NSW since the early days of colonisation, economic gains have been increasingly prioritised to the detriment of social and cultural benefits in Sydney's nightlife. This neo-liberal underpinning of nightlife governance has been cemented by the city's shift to night-time economy planning. Contradictions have marred this transition as images of a vibrant, culturally diverse and safe nightlife meet long-standing alcohol industry resistance to regulation. This anti-regulation sentiment has been bolstered by a socially liberal public response to the regulation of alcohol and leisure, reinforced by a colonial Australian myth linking heavy public drinking with perceptions of masculinity and national identity (Room 1988; Tomsen 2014).

Drawing from Britain's stratification of drinking practices, Sydney's Temperance targeted 'disrespectable working-class leisure' (Sturma 1983; Wadds 2013; Tomsen 2014, 463), mirroring the civilising intent in contemporary night-time economy strategies (Talbot 2007; Hae 2012). The *six o'clock swill* resulting from trading hour restrictions[5] paradoxically marked a shift to *vertical drinking* due to changes made to pubs and made Australia's uncivilised drinking 'the wonder of the world' (Phillips 1980, 251; see also Wadds 2013). Public rejection of the religious and moral influence on public policy ensured a thriving *sly-grog* trade throughout the 1920s.[6] The (now-dwindling) nightlife zone and red-light district of Kings Cross in the city's inner-east developed its notorious reputation off the back of *sly-grogging* profits, stimulated by the nearby naval base from the Second World War which later boomed with American Vietnam War soldiers on rest and recuperation (Wadds 2013; Van den Nouwelant 2017). As opening hours were gradually extended after a 1954 referendum, a growing, socially liberal middle class supported a shift towards promoting civilised drinking, while the 1980s' mantra of market liberalism reawakened negative public rhetoric around nightlife regulation.

Alongside the deindustrialisation of the inner city, this political setting spurred the development of the nightlife industries, and gentrification became a key tourism strategy to counter the inner city's economic decline. The development of the Darling Harbour leisure precinct in the 1980s on the edge of the Central Business District was Sydney's clearest case of this (Bounds and Morris 2006), only perhaps matched now by the nearby Barangaroo development (ongoing as of 2018). This night-time economy expansion was bolstered by alcohol's classification as an *ordinary commodity* under the National Competition Policy by then Prime Minister John Howard (Wadds 2013). Resulting stakeholder tensions that emerged, particularly around noise complaints, were exacerbated by post-industrial demographic shifts and reflected in a 'cycle of license, repression and containment' (Turner, in Homan 2003, ix). Moral panics over some important nightlife spaces, from the pubs of 1970s 'Oz Rock' to the AIDS epidemic politicising employment and recreation spaces for the gay, sex worker and drug-user communities around (Sydney's gay capital) Taylor Square and Kings Cross (Midwinter-Pitt 2007; Race 2016), set the scene for 'politicisation of control' (Homan 2003, 153) around these key areas. In the 1990s, dance music's resurgence saw *out-of-control* youth become the latest 'uncontrollable other' (Homan 2003, 153).

Poker machines in licensed clubs, then extended into pubs from 1997, saw exponential growth in gaming profits (and associated government revenue) in NSW and perhaps the most significant (and ongoing) impact on the landscape of Sydney's licensed venues and their cultural offerings. The normalisation of gaming in drinking venues helped develop 'a very problematic relationship between drinking and gaming in Sydney', one that encouraged the expansion of organised crime and political and police corruption in NSW (Wadds 2013, 58). Business adoption of lucrative *pokies* in place of live music was facilitated by an increasingly complicated and expensive regulatory landscape; the state's desire for 'manageable' *cultural citizens* (Homan 2003) meant the demise of live music in pubs and other smaller venues.

'GLOBAL SYDNEY': A NEW ERA
IN NIGHTLIFE GOVERNANCE

Against the backdrop of inner Sydney's revalorisation and the rise of strategic planning (Kornberger and Clegg 2011), an increasingly laissez-faire attitude to Sydney's planning (Punter 2005) saw the *twenty-four-hour city* concept, then emerging in Europe, promoted in the Sydney City Council's (1994) Blueprint for Sydney, *Living City*. Driving this change was the strategic targeting of the 2000 Olympics as a showcase for Sydney as a dynamic global city, which meant a relaxing of licensing regulations in the lead-up to the games. Later, Sydney attempted to reinforce its cosmopolitan global city status. Championed by Clover Moore,[7] the NSW Liquor Act 2007 aimed for a Melbourne-like laneways culture in the inner city with a more affordable small bar liquor licence (McNeill 2011). In 2009, restrictions on entertainment in venues were also removed (NSW Government 2009) in an attempt to address over-regulation and encourage live music. The same year, venue saturation concerns also meant a temporary freeze on new liquor licences which has remained in place since (Van den Nouwelant and Steinmetz 2013). These changes sought to civilise and diversify Sydney's nightlife, where the deregulation-led drinking culture was increasing public debate around alcohol-related violence. Public outcry came to a head after the killings of Thomas Kelly and Daniel Christie (Wadds 2015). In early 2014, amid widespread moral panic about Sydney's nightlife, the lockouts were introduced, less than a year after the City of Sydney's night-time economy plan, *Open* (City of Sydney 2013; Wolifson and Drozdzewski 2016).

SYDNEY'S NIGHT-TIME ECONOMY: OPEN LATE FOR EVERYONE?

Open was posited as an international blueprint for night-time economy policymaking (City of Sydney 2013). The council emphasised the plan's grounding in evidence and consultation, however, adapted it to fit into the neo-liberal framework of its strategic plan, *Sustainable Sydney 2030*, measuring non-economic concerns by economic output (City of Sydney 2008; Wolifson and Drozdzewski 2016). *Open*'s development reflects both the 'constructed unity' (Peck 2010, 180) of neo-liberal urban planning and the ubiquity and depoliticisation of neo-liberalism, its normalising as a discursive regime (Birdsall 2013; Prince 2016), embedded in night-time economy planning (Hae 2012). The council's plans assume that both cultural diversity and social inclusion would result from economic growth and define creative culture as a component of a competitive economy (Kornberger and Clegg 2011). Such notions of global competitiveness were central to *Open*, with a key objective for Sydney to become a 'world leading night-time city' (City of Sydney 2013, 7).

In defining the acceptable spaces and demographic for a civilised nightlife, *Open* exemplified the embeddedness of gentrification within night-time economy strategies. *Open* placed young people as the folk devils of Sydney's nightlife, misusing the city's own figures to exaggerate the numbers of people aged eighteen to twenty-nine out at night. Its goal for more civilised, over forties served the City of Sydney's gentrifying ambition for more upmarket small bars and night-time retailing. This strategy reflected the assumption that such an economic shift would improve urban subjectivities and foster more civilised consumption in the city at night. It was in large part a response to previous (de)regulatory failures by the NSW Government that led to perceptions of a violent drinking culture and the decline of the pub as a social and leisure space. Competition with Melbourne was also a factor, mimicking calls in early nighttime economy planning for a more European nightlife scene (with Melbourne considered the cultural capital of Australia) (Tierney 2006; McNeill 2011).

Open emphasised the risk of perception, framing Sydney's drinking culture as a reputational concern risking visitor numbers, rather than public health (Wolifson and Drozdzewski 2016). The solutions were relatedly targeted. Despite the impact of pro-gaming and gambling regulation on the social and leisure aspects of Sydney's pubs, the City of Sydney framed and encouraged the proliferation of small bars as an antithesis to inherently problematic pubs. Where 'quirky', 'boutique' bars (City of Sydney 2008, 176) would add 'depth and sophistication' (Moore 2013), 'unsophisticated' (City of Sydney 2008, 176) 'beer barns' (City of Sydney 2012) were characterised by 'blaring sports screens' (Moore 2013) and drunken revellers. The council's assumption that small bars would provide opportunities for live music was complicated by NSW's regulatory history.

As a local Australian example of the global trend in night-time economy planning, *Open* reflected the mobility of this policy script, despite appearing at a time it had been heavily critiqued elsewhere. In particular, the City of Sydney case highlights the ubiquity of culture as an agent for civilising and gentrification as a panacea for alcohol-fuelled violence. Despite being constrained by the framework of *Sustainable Sydney 2030*, *Open* unashamedly espoused public 'wants', and although boasting a 'world first . . . public consultation about NTE' (City of Sydney 2013, 6), it failed to address many concerns of the limited public sample (Wolifson and Drozdzewski 2016). Despite this limitation, *Open* was undoubtedly a success for Lord Mayor Clover Moore's City of Sydney in terms of public political gain (or at least public placating), from participatory planning rhetoric, and set out actions grounded in the existing policy setting.

LOCKOUT: MORAL PANIC AND NEO-LIBERAL GOVERNANCE

Within a year of *Open*'s publication, NSW Premier Barry O'Farrell dramatically shifted this policy setting and initiated widespread debate with the introduction of the lockout laws. While media concerns about alcohol-related violence had been building in Sydney for some time (Wadds 2015), editorial on this issue had escalated in the months prior. Sydney's major newspapers championed an *enough is enough* rhetoric that put pressure on O'Farrell to act (Wadds 2015; Homan 2017). The subsequent 1:30 a.m. venue lockout and 3:00 a.m. last drinks were applied to licensed venues within a delineated zone labelled the CBD Entertainment Precinct (see figure 2.1). This large area contains more than 1,300 licensed venues and includes within it the Kings Cross Precinct that had been a designated management area since December 2012. Both *The Star Casino* and *Crown Sydney* casino (due for completion in 2020) sit outside the lockout zone. Indeed, as mentioned, the spatial targeting of the laws has been a key criticism against them. Negative impacts on businesses within the lockout zone and perceptions of flow-on business to the Star have fuelled these criticisms, particularly given that the selective regulation appears at odds with the government's ideology of market liberalism. Within the zone, the lockout was applied regardless of venues' regulatory compliance records, clashing with the government's previous strategy[8] and effectively priming certain areas for development as a result of business closures. The lockouts also heightened long-standing resentment of

Figure 2.1. Map locating the 'CBD Entertainment Precinct' (i.e., 'lockout zone') in inner Sydney. 1. Star casino, Pyrmont; 2. Crown Sydney development, Barangaroo (due for completion in 2020); 3. Kings Cross Precinct. *Source:* **Esri**, DigitalGlobe, GeoEye, Earthstar Geographics, CNES/Airbus DS, USDA, USGS, AEX, Getmapping, Aerogrid, IGN, IGP, swisstopo and the GIS User Community.

the opacity and influence of political donations in NSW and apparent special treatment of the casinos and other gaming venues.[9] Despite significant social and economic problems resulting from the unprecedented proliferation of gaming machines in NSW,[10] the government has shown no desire to forgo the associated revenue in attempting to address the problem. The high violent incident rate at *The Star* compared with lockout venues has further driven resentment, as have the cultural and economic shifts in nearby nightlife areas since the lockouts were implemented (Donnelly et al. 2017).

Despite two new Premiers since O'Farrell introduced the lockouts, they have continued to be supported by an NSW Government demonstrating a neo-liberal agenda and autocratic behaviours. They have faced significant backlash, including by the City of Sydney Council, over controversial and mismanaged developments and infrastructure projects. Controversial plans include the WestConnex Road project; public building and infrastructure sell-offs, including public housing and transport services; forced mining and fracking; and the removal of civil liberties, including anti-protest legislation and increased police powers (Blanks and Burke 2016; Farrelly 2016). Also controversial have been forced amalgamations and administrations of several local councils, highlighting the local council's ultimate lack of autonomy from the state government.[11]

Taken alongside the history of corruption at the NSW Government level (Australian Broadcasting Corporation 2016), the actions outlined earlier have spurred theories of the lockouts as a pro-development scheme. With Sydney's uncontrolled property market driving stamp duty revenue, property has become far more significant to the NSW Government in recent years. Although certainly not immune to the escalation of inner Sydney's gentrification over the past twenty years or so, the Darlinghurst and Kings Cross areas, most dramatically affected by the lockouts, have been more resistant to the blanket gentrification experienced by some neighbouring inner-city areas. There is a complex and contested history behind this unable to be explored in this chapter (see Iveson 2014), but it is important to note that a significant factor here is their role as specialised community and service hubs, notably for the gay population in Darlinghurst and for homeless, sex-worker and drug-user groups in Kings Cross (DeVerteuil 2015). Valuable services include the long-fought-for (and against) Medically Supervised Injecting Centre and the Wayside Chapel in Kings Cross, which provide crisis accommodation for vulnerable people. Government attempts to socially and morally sanitise this area (Nofre 2013), whether intended to boost development or not, have undoubtedly punctuated the unremitting displacement pressures against such services and those they help.

While the moral panic that ensued following the one-punch deaths in Kings Cross appeared to serve the O'Farrell government's value-judgement-laden efforts to 'clean up' the area (Hills 2011), the controversy-ridden *Crown Sydney* development was approved with alarmingly little scrutiny (Wilkinson et al. 2017). While violence in Kings Cross had been dropping prior to the introduction of the lockouts (Menéndez et al. 2015), *The Star* remained NSW's most violent venue, despite not appearing on the biannual violent venue list (and so not subject to its restrictions).[12] In April 2014, with debate raging about the newly introduced lockouts, O'Farrell resigned amid a corruption inquiry. As Mike Baird stepped in to replace him as Premier, questions were raised about the influence of his religious beliefs on his politics (Nicholls 2014). As the lockout debate raged, and apparent special treatment of the casinos was highlighted, the nickname 'Casino Mike' took hold.

In late 2016, following the release of the Callinan review into the laws, although prior to the government's response, it was revealed that *the Star* had been significantly underreporting violent incidents (Branley 2016), renewing pressure on the government to correct its special treatment of the casino. Separately, but relatedly, a growing mountain of evidence that highlighted the detrimental impacts of gambling and especially poker machines was emerging, with clear links shown between machine numbers and domestic violence (Markham et al. 2016). Less than six weeks later, however, the government adopted the minor alterations suggested by the review, with no changes to the casino. While Baird (2016) appeared to take pride in accusations of moralising by what he too touted as an attempt to clean up Sydney's nightlife, the government's reliance on alcohol and gambling revenues not only problematised its stated intention to reduce alcohol-related violence but contradicted its moralising rhetoric.

Undoubtedly, the lockouts have had a drastic impact on the commercial landscape, especially within the lockout zone. While directly resulting closures are difficult to state with certainty, more than forty nightlife businesses have reportedly closed from their impacts (Barrie 2016), from restaurants and small bars to pubs and nightclubs, with associated job cuts. Flow-on closures and impacts on the daytime economy (Darlinghurst Business Partnership 2015) counter suggestions of an antithetical relationship between the commercial day and nightscapes that were used to support the case for the lockouts. Somewhat ironically, given O'Farrell and Baird's pledges to 'clean up' the area, one who appears to have adapted well is so-called King of the Cross, John Ibrahim; the long-time alleged organised crime figure has taken advantage of development opportunities left in the wake of the lockouts to transition from nightclub boss to property tycoon (Harris 2016).

A shift in nightlife activity to Newtown, an inner-west area outside the lockout zone, prompted several local businesses to take self-regulatory steps, including a 3:00 a.m. lockout (with pass outs) (Koziol 2015). Known for its acceptance of diversity, Newtown had a rise in reports of harassment and anti-queer abuse (James 2015). In response to the bashings of Isaac Keatinge and Stephanie McCarthy in particular, Reclaim the Streets held a protest, calling to Keep Newtown Weird and Safe to 'reassert . . . Newtown's identity as a beautiful community of queers, weirdoes, freaks, hippies, goths, punks, ferals, migrants and everyone else who doesn't fit in elsewhere' (Reclaim the Streets 2016a). In Double Bay, a predominantly quiet and upmarket area not far from the lockout zone, a lockout-driven spike in nightlife activity prompted the local council to reshape the nightlife economy into a more genteel one (Moran 2014; Keulemans, in Bastians 2016) through new upmarket development (with unprecedented height approval). The NSW Bureau of Crime Statistics and Research confirmed the long-observed displacement of recorded incidents (Donnelly et al. 2017). While an agglomeration of Newtown, Double Bay and the beachside suburbs of Coogee and Bondi Beach were collectively labelled the *distal displacement area*, the Newtown Liquor Accord labelled the suburb's inclusion misleading, citing that its local management strategy coincided with a drop in incidences in Newtown when viewed separate from the other *distal displacement* suburbs (McNab 2017).

In centring on the intention to reduce alcohol-related violence within the lockout zone, the Callinan review was largely able to avoid giving due consideration to the effects of the lockouts on nightlife as an important space of social and cultural development, expression and belonging (Quilter 2016; Race 2016). 'Views of the opponents' (to the lockout) are outlined in Callinan's (2016) report in seven sections, none of which overview these effects in a detailed way. Rather, opponents' views are framed in economic terms, with sections: the night-time economy, 'Sydney as a vibrant international city' and 'adverse effects upon business'. The 'live entertainment' section also lacks a more nuanced discussion; in Callinan's (2016, 116) (limited) observation, 'Entertainers are unfortunate casualties of the amendments'. As Tyson Koh (2016) of *Keep Sydney Open* reflected, '[Others'] spurious claims were treated as fact, while facts such as the impact on live music and business were either overlooked or treated with suspicion'. Even despite significant evidence of impacts on the night-time economy, the review's tunnel vision on violence rates within the lockout zone meant it failed to adequately consider costs, economic and otherwise, of the lockouts. As Quilter (2016) has noted, the review's recommendation to relax the statewide take-away alcohol restriction from 10:00 p.m. to 11:00 p.m. came with the acknowledgement that it would likely increase domestic violence rates. The review's persistent justification for the lockouts on violence grounds effectively preferences targeting (mostly male victim) nightlife violence over (mostly female victim) domestic violence.

THE ACTIVIST RESPONSE

Scholarship examining pro-nightlife activists has asserted that they have largely failed to challenge drivers and proponents of gentrification (Hae 2011b). The relative traction of activist responses to the 'lockouts' by *Keep Sydney Open* and *Reclaim the Streets* broadly reaffirms this observation and points to the difficulty of this challenge. Notable differences between the rhetoric and methods of these two groups provide a telling elucidation of the impact of neo-liberalism on urban activism and on the public receptivity to activist messages. Depoliticisation of night-time economy rhetoric is a key mechanism shaping ineffective responses to problematic nightlife regulation. This normalised neo-liberal discourse presents a crucial, yet largely unknown, barrier to attempts to gain political traction and affect change. Historic parallels of the promotion of a civilised nightlife highlight that rhetoric palatable to the middle class may serve rather than resist gentrification. Such rhetoric supports regulation beneficial to upmarket spaces that appeal to the so-called creative class, while stifling alternative venues.

The rhetoric of *Keep Sydney Open* (2016a) embodied in its tagline 'We support safe nights in a global city. We support Live Music. Our mission is to Keep Sydney Open!' reflects the pervasiveness of the *global city* mantra. In defence of Sydney's nightlife, the group has often stressed its (potential) economic outputs, mimicking the City of Sydney's (2013) night-time economy plan, *Open* (Wolifson and Drozdzewski 2016):

> As a growing, diverse and vibrant city, Sydney nightlife has much to offer its residents and visitors. The city's night-time offerings have made it a leading tourist destination in the Asia-Pacific, contributing to its international reputation as a Global City and bringing considerable economic opportunities to the state. (Keep Sydney Open 2016b, 4)

The group's focus on business impacts of the lockouts, particularly in Kings Cross, is evidenced in its submission to the Callinan review:

> The economic impact of the lockout laws includes venue closures, decreased tourism and increased unemployment which conflict with the overall objectives of the Act 'to contribute to the responsible development of related industries such as the live music, entertainment, tourism and hospitality industries'. The lockout laws are not contributing to the development of these industries because they have made them financially unviable. (Keep Sydney Open 2016b, 10)

In responding to the government's economic focus, *Keep Sydney Open* has forced itself to frame its criticism of the lockout laws based on economic and reputational concerns. While the broad appeal of *Keep Sydney Open*'s rhetoric has helped maintain public debate, its focus on Sydney's damaged reputation has arguably meant further reputational damage. Indeed, as the fight against the laws stretches on, a key question for the group is whether its persistence is doing more harm than good to Sydney night-time vibrancy. This outcome speaks, in part, to the stifling of creativity within the night-time economy model, extended it seems, into activist approaches.

In contrast, *Reclaim the Streets* has focused on issues of power and access to space. Its concerns with the lockouts align with its goals of 'community ownership of public spaces and [opposition] to the dominance of corporate forces in globalisation' (Reclaim the Streets 2016b). As stated in its submission to the Callinan review, 'The great public outcry against this suite of laws stems not only from the absurd injustice of a curfew affecting responsible adults, but also from a fear of loss of critical public space and community. This fear became justified with the closure of many significant venues' (Reclaim the Streets 2016c). There are key contrasts in *Reclaim the Streets'* and *Keep Sydney Open*'s rhetoric around business closures. The former group's submission emphasises the significance of many of these spaces, particularly for certain vulnerable, marginalised groups, for whom it provides connection and counters discrimination (Tomsen 2014; Race 2016). On economic impact, its main concern is for musicians, who, it stresses, need to be paid for their work. While both groups have addressed the exclusion of the casinos from the lockout zone, *Reclaim the Streets* has focused more keenly on the context of this special treatment. Its first anti-lockouts protest, in September 2015, stressed: 'The decay of [Sydney's] nightlife is a visible symptom of a much bigger problem: the influence of money upon policy'. In March 2016, protesters left the memorable image of giant faeces on the sign for *The Star*, pointing to the 'stink' of corruption in the casino's special treatment. Protesters were called on to 'demand a better nightlife. Demand an end to political donations. Blow up the pokies[13] and Reclaim the Streets' (Reclaim the Streets 2016d).

Notwithstanding considerable opposition to the anti-lockouts movement, *Keep Sydney Open*'s popular impact has been much greater than *Reclaim the Streets'*. Koh has been a frequent guest speaker and spokesperson for the anti-lockouts movement, as well as taking part in government roundtables on the issue. The slogan 'Keep Sydney Open' has been widely adopted, including by several high-profile performers. While the message of *Reclaim the Streets* appeals particularly to queer-identifying people and those concerned with the right to the city, many who simply want to 'fight for their right to party' have been attracted to the depoliticised message of a vibrant night-time economy, one long sold to the growing, socially liberal, middle class. Indeed, the group's appeal is a hardly surprising follow-up to the City of Sydney's promoting of the night-time economy over several years. The enormous popularity of Matt Barrie's (2016) article 'Would the Last Person in Sydney Please Turn the Lights Out?' points to this trend. Barrie reignited an anti-regulation, *nanny state rhetoric*, promoting the free-market perspective of nightlife regulation, arguing that the failure of the lockouts lay in the government going against its own liberal mantra. In addition to the lockouts, frustrations with the ban on take-away alcohol after 10:00 p.m. (now 11:00 p.m.), and limits on straight spirits and cocktail alcohol content, highlighted the difficulty the government faced in attempting to regulate a city intent on both a civilised and liberalised nightlife, simultaneously promised and feeling denied of both. The nanny state rhetoric was only inflamed by comments made by the new (and current as at January 2018) NSW Premier, Gladys Berejiklian, who, in supporting the continuance of the lockouts, stated that 'mums and dads in the suburbs are worried about what their young kids are doing when they're having a good time. . . . You want [a government] that's really thinking about what we can do to keep kids as safe as possible' (Mackinnon 2017). These reignited perceptions of the much-hated moralising paternalism are seen in Baird's rhetoric around nightlife, harking back to prohibition.

NEO-LIBERALISM CO-OPTING NIGHTLIFE:
A CITY GENTRIFIED

Neo-liberalism is rife with contradiction, both within and between its ideology and its many practical manifestations (Peck 2010; Springer et al. 2016). The pervasiveness of neo-liberal governmentality (Foucault 1991) has been reinforced by the City of Sydney Council's approach to the night-time economy. Despite the council's progressive image, this framework, with its focus on economic growth and global city competitiveness, has undermined creativity and diverse cultural expression in the inner city's nightlife. In doing so, it has embraced gentrification as a strategy for a more civilised nightlife, appeasing a long-held desire of the city's growing middle class. While attempting to correct past NSW Government regulatory failures that have bolstered a night-time culture of drinking and gambling, the council has perpetuated stigmas that emerged from such failures, only further fuelling drivers of gentrification. The NSW Liberal's efforts at nightlife governance have highlighted the shape-shifting character of neo-liberalism. In succumbing to ever more powerful private interests, the (ideologically) deregulatory Liberals have instituted targeted regulations that manifestly benefit those interests. The increased government revenue that has come from Sydney's unrelenting property market in recent years has come at a disastrous cost to the city, with housing affordability at an all-time low. The government's ostensible inability or unwillingness to act against influential industries points to an urgent need for structural political reform to re-democratise the city, protecting governance for the best interests of the state and limiting governance led by populism and sensationalism. While the incoherence of nightlife policies between the council and state government reflects a structural failure of communication and collaboration between (and within) them (and is likely exacerbated by the latter's long-running feud with Clover Moore), it also reflects the failure of their neo-liberal approaches. The council's image for a thriving live music scene, for instance, will, for the foreseeable future, be limited by state gaming regulation, while its insistence on economic outcomes for the city's cultural scene only reinforces this barrier.

Amid moral panic about 'antisocial behaviour' at night, the stigmatisation of Kings Cross has served the state government well, with support for the laws arising from concern about violent incidents there (Wadds 2015; Robertson 2016). These concerns have received legitimacy based on declines in hospital emergency admissions and recorded crime rates that are, of course, positive. Whether an accelerated decline in violence in the lockout zone justifies the myriad of other outcomes both there and elsewhere, however, remains a pertinent question for the government. Sydney's problematic drinking and gambling practices have emerged in the context of rhetoric that pits civilised middle-class leisure practices against uncivilised working-class leisure, a dualism that continues today. Through the socio-spatial divisions resulting from Sydney's (poorly managed) global city planning, this dualism is now, more than ever, reflected spatially. The state-sanctioned gentrification of the inner city, enflamed by substantial recent public housing sell-offs and underlined by the city's exorbitant property prices, has seen to this division. The City of Sydney's (2011) hopeful image of Sydney in 2030 as 'open late for everyone' seems far less likely in 2017 than when first suggested. The lockouts have primed significant areas of Kings Cross and (already upmarket) Double Bay for more gentrification via residential development, while Newtown has needed to adjust to changes imposed on its subculturally significant nightlife by lockout flow-on effects.

Through the case of *Keep Sydney Open*, the depoliticisation of night-time economy rhetoric has been shown to have infiltrated activism not best served by the underlying capitalist goals of this message. Whether the group, therefore, truly represents the broad group it has attracted, from various business situations, political persuasions and lived experiences of Sydney's nightlife, is questionable. Nonetheless, the popularity of its rhetoric is hardly surprising; alongside historically sentient nanny state arguments is the middle-class appeal of the cultural-economy growth mantra, encapsulated by Florida's creative class theory (Krätke 2012). Of course, the inherently flawed development and implementation of the lockouts has also played a role in its popularity. The popularity of *Keep Sydney Open* compared to *Reclaim the*

Streets, however, indicates how neo-liberalism has created an environment more hostile to, and challenging for, more progressive movements (Mayer 2012). The redundancy of existing modes of participatory planning is one such example of this environment (Schatz and Rogers 2016; Wolifson and Drozdzewski 2016).

Through the ever-changing case study of Sydney's nightlife governance, and the surrounding debate, this chapter has exposed Sydney's night-time economy planning as a contemporary process of gentrification by misdirected efforts towards a more genteel and civilised nightlife (Hae 2012). While the difficulty in balancing the regulation of nightlife activity in Sydney goes back to colonisation, the many, often-contradictory efforts to shape Sydney's night-time economy glaringly avoid acknowledgement and meaningful defence of the city's nightlife spaces as both remarkable and mundane political spaces of resistance and subcultural belonging, of creative communication and evolution. The effects of neo-liberalism on Sydney's nightlife have been shown here as a series of (poor) governance choices rather than as an inevitability within a particular, increasingly global, 'ideological atmosphere' (Peck 2010, xi). In ostensibly attempting to alleviate alcohol-related violence, the NSW Government has capitulated to political donors whose interests lie elsewhere, namely with their own profits. The drastic economic impact of the lockouts is, at least in part, indicative of the significance of alcohol to Sydney's night-time economy, emphasising the need for a more dynamic and diversified nightlife, one in which the desired cultural citizen is not sitting at a poker machine or placing a bet. The willingness of the NSW Government to so drastically impact Sydney's night-time economy (and the liquor industry it has long supported) shows the fickle character of its embraced neo-liberalism. In many ways, Sydney has adapted and will continue to adapt to the regulations reshaping its nightlife. What remains to be seen, though, is whether it will be a city whose spaces incubate creativity, diversity and joy. While changes announced following the Callinan review meant a loosening of some of the 2014 regulations, Sydney's property prices are unlikely to allow for a reclaiming of creative civic space where such nightlife businesses have already shut.

To 'bring neoliberalism to earth' (Peck 2010), the public must be cognisant to regulatory shifts that broaden the discretionary powers of government and restrict civil liberties. There is a clear need for governments to strengthen transparent policymaking structures that reveal the utility of technocratic knowledge and necessarily avoid undemocratic influence. Outcomes of better collaboration between the City of Sydney Council and its state counterparts via the Night Time Economy Taskforce remain to be seen. If public consultation is to continue as an element of planning, it must include legitimate and consequential pathways for consideration in policymaking that enhance, rather than undermine, technocratic expertise. Evidently too, efforts should focus on a shift away from the conceptualisation of 'the night-time economy' and neo-liberal creative city planning more broadly. This structural change is a tremendous challenge. It requires reimagining and reframing the narrative of what we value as urban dwellers and reflection on the genuine, messy value of urban nightlife, for everyone.

NOTES

1. The Liberal Party is Australia's major conservative party, named for its platform of individual freedom and free enterprise.

2. The lockouts were introduced on 24 February 2014 as part of the Liquor Amendment Act 2014, while the majority of other measures were introduced on 18 July 2014.

3. The foundation's Take Kare Safe Space programme has been running since December 2014 with the support of the NSW Government and City of Sydney, among others.

4. Politically charged term denoting persons from western Sydney. 'Westie' 'became shorthand for a population considered lowbrow, coarse and lacking education and cultural refinement' (Gwyther 2008, 1).

5. The result of the NSW Government's Early Closing Act 1916.

6. Prostitution, cocaine and sly-grog thrived in the time of the 'razor gangs' of Sydney's underworld (Upton 2016).

7. Moore was then also the State Member of Parliament representing the electorate of Sydney.

8. The *three strikes rule* punished non-compliant venues, while the violent venues list imposes conditions on venues based on incident numbers. Level 1 restrictions (nineteen or more incidents) include a 1:30 a.m. lockout.

9. Majority of venues exempted from the lockouts have poker machines. From 2017, some venues have been granted half-hour extensions to the lockout and last drinks when providing live entertainment after midnight.

10. NSW's gaming machine numbers are second only to Nevada (Safi 2015) and vastly exceed the other Australian states and territories.

11. The City of Sydney Council survived the recent round of amalgamations, but there is well-known, long-term hostility between Independent Lord Mayor Clover Moore and the state government, with several attempts to remove her from office over many years, including most recently allowing businesses two votes in the council election. In 2012, her right to be both Lord Mayor and State Member of Parliament was removed, forcing her to step down from the latter role.

12. This was related to its regulation by the Independent Liquor and Gaming Authority (ILGA) separate from the Office of Liquor, Gaming and Racing (OLGR, now Liquor and Gaming NSW, incorporating ILGA).

13. 'Blow Up the Pokies' is a song by Sydney band *The Whitlams*. Lead singer Tim Freedman wrote the song to comment on the destructive influence of *pokies* on the band's original bassist, Andy Lewis. Lewis took his own life in 2000.

Chapter 3

Night-Time Economy and Urban Change in Post-War and Post-Socialist Sarajevo

Nihad H. Čengić and Jordi Martín-Díaz

The evening and night-time economy in post-socialist Sarajevo has expanded and developed since the end of the Bosnian War (1992–1995). This is due to a combined effect of socialist economic practice and liberalisation policies promoted by international actors who have intervened in the peace-building mission (Martín-Díaz 2014). The Bosnian capital hosted the majority of international organisations operating in the country throughout and after the war, and the presence of numerous international soldiers, diplomats, policymakers and other foreign actors has favoured the expansion and commoditisation of nightlife. By taking the urban night as a case study and analytical lens simultaneously (Straw 2015b), this chapter explores urban changes derived from the transition of the city from state socialism into one marked by capitalism and specifically neo-liberalism. The first part of the chapter explores the flourishing of a vibrant, multicultural, nightlife scene in Sarajevo in the 1970s and 1980s. This period witnessed the emergence of a lively, kaleidoscopic Yugoslavian subcultural scene such as New Primitivism, a punk subculture that appeared as a complex form of cultural expression alongside the disintegration of former Yugoslavia. The second part explores how foreign and middle-class-oriented nightlife facilities appearing after the war in the city centre have played a central role in fostering the leisure-led revitalisation of both the Stari Grad and Centar quarters. In exploring the city both before and after the war, the chapter traces the ways that state-led interventions, followed by a more recent entrepreneurial and commercialised approach, have encouraged specific forms of nightlife to develop. While we argue that the city has now been transformed from an earlier, more inclusive nightlife, even today the case of Sarajevo demonstrates multiple forms of resistance, as well as the deeply political and politicised nature of urban leisure after dark.

NIGHT-TIME LEISURE IN SOCIALIST SARAJEVO
(1970S AND 1980S)

The 1970s and 1980s witnessed a flourishing of night-time leisure in Sarajevo. While in many western European capitalist cities there was a rapid and
intense process of expansion and commoditisation of youth leisure during
the *Swinging Sixties*, socialist cities showed profound differences in the conception, meaning and semiotics of 'leisure time'. In Western cities, specific
practices and activities have long been subject to their own appropriate place
and time (Bourdieu 1980), such that what we might refer to as urban day-
scapes differed quite remarkably from nightscapes throughout late modernity (Lefebvre 1974). However, under Tito's socialism in Yugoslavia, such
segmentation was not so clear, as 'work, recreation, family life, culture etc.
[were] just forms of integral human time' (Martinić 1965, 112). In contrast to
capitalist societies, leisure time under the socialist system in Yugoslavia was
not simply an evasion from the oppression of labour. Instead, leisure time had
a decisive role to play in human development. Work time and free time were
conceived as interdependent and thus functioned as a whole (Martinić 1965).
The aim of this discourse was to create a society where work could be understood as a 'joy and primary life need' (Ignatiev and Ossipov 1959, quoted in
Martinić 1965, 110). In stark contrast to the 'work as oppression' and 'leisure
as escape' binary that continues to shape Western models for understanding
leisure, the socialist concept of free time played a decisive role in the development of Sarajevo's nightlife during the 1970s and later. There was neither
the perception of nor practices associated with Western models of Fridays and
Saturdays as expressed by *J. J. Cale* (Friday, Friday evening/Come on Friday,
I wanna go home) or *The Cure* (I don't care if Monday's blue/Tuesday's grey
and Wednesday too/Thursday I don't care about you/It's Friday I'm in love).
In the urban night of socialist Sarajevo, every day was Friday.

Mass media significantly contributed to the growth of youthful nightscapes
in cities such as Sarajevo, Zagreb, Ljubljana, Novi Sad and Belgrade from
the 1970s onwards. At this time, local/national subcultural scenes intersected
with the rapid transnational expansion of pan-European youth subcultural
scenes. As Ramet argues, 'Rock music spread to every corner of Yugoslavia'
and, in a certain sense, 'it was an urban phenomenon' (2003, 176). However,
the connection between mass media, globalisation and the cultural industries
had profound roots in the first decades of Yugoslavia. In the late 1950s and
early 1960s Yugoslavia's popular music industry experienced rapid growth.
On the one hand, the promotion of music, theatre and film festivals, new TV
services, music magazines (like *Rock*, *Disco Selektor* and *Ritam* in the late
1970s and the 1980s) and record companies led to a cultural expansion that
strengthened the public visibility of the then government's achievements in

economic growth and the modernisation of the country (Vuletic 2011). As Vuletic also argues, the Yugoslavian administration 'broadly acknowledged the impact of popular music in terms of its political and social power and recognized that it was an important form of entertainment for Yugoslavia's citizens, especially young people' (Vuletic 2011, 271). Under direct influence – and assistance – from the United States and some western European countries like Britain and France, a number of domestic record and film companies and radio and television services emerged (Vuletic 2011), permitting Yugoslavia to create the foundations for the later emergence of a vibrant youthful nightlife in the country's largest cities.

By the late 1970s and early 1980s, nightlife in Sarajevo was of a mixed nature, including socially owned and privately owned venues.[1] In general, the socially owned venues were hotels and restaurant chains, express-restaurants, buffets, wine bars, nightclubs, student clubs and cultural and artistic associations. Small restaurants, coffee bars and sweet cafes were often run by individuals. However, a much more particular kind of venue stands out above all, the *kafić* (*cafettes*).[2] Though they appeared in the socialist period, because of their association with fashion, coffee consumption and a refined selection of fine music, *cafettes* were rapidly attributed to a certain Western form of capitalist cultural consumption. *Cafettes* could be described as a modern form of the traditional coffee bar that in some way brought back the once-popular cafes that rapidly spread over the city from 1534 onwards, similar to the rapid expansion and popularisation of the *caffe-room* that had occurred in early Ottoman Istanbul.[3] The ways of practising free time that they enabled, and being marked by a certain 'philosophy of life' that took place at night, made *cafettes* unique. Moreover, they were a unique cultural invention of Sarajevo and became the place where young Sarajevans expressed their politics and political curiosity through art and philosophy, shaping and reflecting a new movement that started with Sarajevo's student protests in 1968.

In the early 1970s, two *cafettes* were established – Gong and Evergreen (registered as buffets). These *cafettes* came from nothing but a wish to produce an indoor public space where it was possible to share information with others and enjoy company and music 'in a way we want', as one of our adult informants argued.[4] The space, of 26 sq.m., could accommodate 135 people and serve almost 1,000 people standing in the courtyard next to Maršal Tito Street (the city's main street) or on the sidewalk (Slobodna Bosna 2012). Over time, *cafettes* became a very serious issue. They gave way to the rise of a new culture, and the city centre of Sarajevo became one of the main nightlife hot spots in the country, attracting many guests from across the region. Streets like Tabašnica, Bravadžiluk, Nemanjina (Čekaluša) and Gabelina would be crowded with young people and almost entirely blocked to traffic.

The rapid expansion of *cafettes* in the 1970s also brought the expansion of particular subcultural scenes to the city: *šminkeri* (fancies), *hašišari* and *pankeri* (hashisees and punkers), *boemi* (bohemians), *raja* (urbans) and *papci* (the pejorative term for a peasant) could be easily identified by their dress sense, their music choices, how they expressed their philosophy of life and the specific *cafettes* they usually frequented. But the most important factor of self-differentiation, and therefore distinction, for both *cafettes* and their attendees was the music. Music was important, and the quality of the coffee was crucial. When people discussed *cafettes* there were two motifs that could make people move to another *cafette*: a new kind of music playing in the *cafette* and the existence of a very good coffee. These factors made a *cafette* worthy of visiting once again in a few days or even hours.

What was then the newly emerging 'nocturnal urban culture' of Sarajevo developed at the limits of the city centre in dark residential quarters on the left bank of Miljacka River (Evergreen, Gong, Čenga, Bijelo Dugme, Scotch, Mod, Gaj) as well as in the historic core of Baščaršija (Rock, Ada, Đerdan, Dibek, Bene, Arkada, Nava, Orijent, Slavuj, A, Stari Sat, MP, Charlie). Still, it was uncommon to find this new kind of nightlife existing elsewhere other than side streets or inner courtyards. The main streets were usually reserved for state-owned venues (Dubravka, Hotel Zagreb Cafe, Collegium Artisticum, Ski, Park, Istra, Galerija, Korzo, Hamam Bar, Dalmacija, Hotel Central Cafe). Parallel to these developments in the historic city centre, some nightlife venues (Korali, Ruža, Jesenjin, Mis) also opened at the Novo Sarajevo District, a new urban centre of the city built during Tito's administration. It was in this district where the first international public disco club (Dancing 77) opened in 1977.

By the mid-1970s there were approximately twenty *cafettes*, which played a central, revolutionary role in becoming sites for women's leisure. While traditional cafes were male-oriented places where alcoholic drinks were often served, *cafettes* rapidly became attractive, modern places frequented by women, who, consciously or unconsciously, participated in critiquing socialist forms of patriarchy. As Dević (1997, 51) argues,

> The permissive authoritarianism of the Yugoslav League of Communists in the late 1970s, lasting until the mid-1980s, allowed for the emergence of a Yugoslav brand of intellectual feminism, focusing on the place of women in the public arena and the detrimental impact of patriarchy that was discovered to have persisted in socialism.

Jancar (1988) further points out that the new feminists that emerged in the former Yugoslavia challenged the dogma that 'the woman question' had been solved in Socialist Yugoslavia, arguing that, in fact, the new industrial patriarchy was more pervasive and dominating than the old, traditional form.

By the early 1980s, *cafettes*, discotheques and bars led to a vibrant (and very profitable), youth-oriented and relatively inclusive nightlife. A place with five tables or less could serve up to 3,000 drinks in one night (Slobodna Bosna 2012). Leisure time was extended to after hours, and it partially contributed to many venues usually opening until 10:00 p.m. at which point proprietors locked the door and continued the night. A vibrant nightlife was by this stage emerging in the city and, paradoxically, the crisis of 1981–1991 and the later disintegration of the former Yugoslavia took place simultaneously with a golden decade for nightlife and various subcultural scenes in Sarajevo. The 1980s were subject to an urban and social renaissance that largely contributed to the flourishing of a vibrant, multicultural, kaleidoscopic nightlife culture in the Bosnian capital. The period between 1980 and 1992 was marked, in particular, by the rise of New Primitivism, a movement originally created by Sarajevo-based performers and rock bands (Zabranjeno Pušenje, Elvis J. Kurtović and His Meteors, Bombaj Štampa, Crvena Jabuka) that would 'advance an exuberant exploration of identity politics through performative play with the ideological and formal excess of Yugoslav mainstream cultural products' (Bahun 2010, n.p.). In others words, Sarajevo's New Primitivism was 'primarily a punk subculture that originated in the early 1980s . . . whose main principle [was] an alleged anti-intellectualism, the use of local iconic and lexical properties, [and] the manipulation of prejudices about Bosnians, with a particularly productive use of elements from the Muslim milieu in the Sarajevo suburbs' (Homer 2009, quoted in Levi 2007, 63).

New Primitivism became mainstream not only in 'nocturnal Sarajevo' but in the then-vibrant cultural life of the city's music scene, theatre and radio and television plays (*Primus*, *Top Lista Nadrealista*). New Primitivism rapidly spread across the country at that time. Although many scholars often see it as a complex cultural expression of the early years of the disintegration of the former Yugoslavia, some of our informants argued that ordinary people at that time saw New Primitivism as a way of 'reviling real life, including a political one, and making fun of it'.[5]

After the Winter Olympic Games, held in Sarajevo in 1984, nightlife in Sarajevo continued to expand. However, many initiatives to open new nightlife venues (especially disco clubs) came up against a 'spatial factor': most spaces that could be potentially transformed into new nightlife venues were small, and the growth of the number of new large-sized disco clubs was therefore limited. The recognised economic, cultural, social (and even political) importance of the vibrant nightlife culture in Sarajevo in the mid-1980s resulted in converting existing premises like the old TV House (both the TV and radio studios), Scouts House, blue-collar restaurants, football stadium premises or cellar warehouses into new disco bars (Evropa, Babilon, FIS, Sloga, Holiday, Monument, SGL, CDA, BB, Teatar, ABC, Koliba, Bambus,

Šaran). Some venues introduced live music and entertainment programmes by following new trends, mainly coming from European nightlife capitals such as Manchester, London, Amsterdam or Paris.

Much of this growth appears to have been the result of an almost *organic* expansion of nightlife, but the role of urban planning needs to be accounted for. The further development of the night-time economy in the city of Sarajevo during the second half of the 1980s had much to do with specific development goals discussed in the Urban Plan for Sarajevo, approved in 1990. The concept of urban planning is widely accepted as a legacy of the first modern urban plan designed in 1965, which promoted balanced development of the centre and periphery. On the one hand, the Plan was carefully designed to ensure well-balanced urban development between both central and peripheral areas through the creation and implementation of a polycentric urban system structured along the Miljacka River. More interestingly, the Plan also regulated the quantity and, in a general way, the typology of drinks and food venues per inhabitant, in five categories of centres, from local community to city core. That is, facilities related to free time and nightlife in Sarajevo were planned and regulated as a core element of the sustainable urban planning of the socialist city. Nightlife facilities were standardised at 0.85 sq.m./inhabitant for the whole city. In the city core area, it was 0.18 sq.m./inhabitant and 0.20 sq.m./inhabitant for local community venues. These rules about capacity resulted in the creation of a vibrant, dense, lively nightlife scene in the city centre while encouraging the spatial expansion of other nightlife facilities in other areas of the city.

Although the major concentration of nightlife was in the flat area of the city centre, new and relatively distant agglomerations of venues appeared in the hillside residential quarters of Džidžikovac-Bjelave and Ciglane (S.O.S., Milk, Bugati, Piramida, Miris Dunja, Gogo, No.1, Bulldog, Ciao, Kućica, Austrijska kuća). This spatial distribution of nightlife followed the balanced urban development of the city, as previously mentioned. While the city core became crowded with various nightlife facilities, the western parts of the city core and new urban areas developed during the 1960s and 1970s along the Miljacka River were rich in food-led venues (Galeb, Capri, Maestro, Stari Krovovi, Lav, Šentada, Koštana, Bard, Aroma) but lesser marked by bars, pubs, clubs and discos (Flamingo, Cappuccino, Papagaj, Pjetao, Bell, Bel Ami, Blue Point, Cabaret night-bar, ABC disco-bar).

The rise and further expansion of nightlife beyond Sarajevo's city core since the mid-1980s is therefore not surprising. Since the 1970s, and especially during the 1980s, policymakers reshaped the urban matrix of the historic core by proposing clearing up, engaging and connecting inner courtyards of Austro-Hungarian residential blocks. However, only some planned actions took place (Glass City), while others were mostly carried out in a bottom-up manner. Furthermore, some private venues, unlike before, started to occupy the main streets as well (Kogo, Ribica, Crvena Galerija, Kinema, Bambus), and some existed within hidden terraces. Open-air parties and concerts that took place in terraces that extended cafe bars (Kišobran, Crvena Galerija, FIS) became the great novelty and attracted a large number of people.[6]

HAVING A DRINK UNDER THE SIEGE: BETWEEN ETHICS AND RESISTANCE

The *Golden Eighties* in the nightlife scene of Sarajevo ended with the violent dismantling of the Yugoslav state. The Bosnian War (1992–1995) and the 1,425-day siege of the city brought, among many abrupt changes, a complex, nonlinear redefinition of the meaning of *normality* in the everyday lives of Sarajevians (Maček 2000). Regarding nightlife, the siege of the city led to the rise of a crucial ethical question: is nightlife an activity that should be practised at all? Previous decades, especially the 1970s and 1980s, had clearly shown that nightlife, such as any other daily or ordinary activity, played an important role in strengthening social relations (even building new ones) and provided immaterial benefits for the good life of citizens. But although social links established before the war, as well as the multicultural, kaleidoscopic nature of the nightlife scene in Sarajevo, were broken once the war started, nightlife during the war also appeared as an opportunity for socialisation where besieged citizens could learn and share ideas and experiences as well as build social capital.[7]

The presence of dozens of foreign actors in the city (i.e., UN soldiers and staff, diplomats, journalists) helped keep some nightlife venues alive. Around 150 *cafettes*, restaurants, discos, ice-cream stores, cake shops and other facilities were registered in Sarajevo during the siege (Halilović 2014). It is interesting to note that the spatial mobility patterns of nightlife participants were much the same during as before the war. That is to say, nightlife facilities were differentiated between the city core and periphery. In turn, the urban dynamics of the city continued to be structured by following a polycentric system structured along the river. For example, one had to walk 2.5 km from the central quarter of Marijin Dvor to the SSH Bar, both on the so-called Sniper Avenue, or Merkur in order to play billiards (and sometimes accompanied by Ismet 'Ćelo' Bajramović, a controversial Bosnian soldier who became the symbol of the city's resistance). Nightlife facilities under the siege had an important role to play in enabling the sharing of information and ideas, and creating 'social nods', which allowed one to express resistance to siege. An ethnographic account by the first author of this chapter explains:

[Sharing nods] could be expressed with modest – *akšamluk* (drink but not to get drunk and food in sunset with quiet conversation and music), regular or hedonist nature. There were no Fridays then, no days, nor even time, nor technology supported communication, but information was flowing. It is hard to say the frequency of going out during evening and night-time hours. Due to the fact that the movement distance is directly proportional to life threat, nightlife based on local community level was strengthened. Since the curfew was on the power, it is expected that nightlife facilities did not operate after 10 p.m. All venues were squeezed until curfew. But it was not like that always. Sometimes it was rationally risked to spend a night in police station, or to continue partying until morning. Due to number of limitations in nightlife production and consumption, all types of venues should be considered as its descriptors. . . .

Nightlife in times of siege was composed of simple socialisation, consuming music, drinks, food or dope, live guitar play performed by Nihad and Čizma or fashion show in front of Youth Theatre, billiard competition in Miris Dunja and Loto Club, *Hair* musical theatre play in Chamber Theatre, Beauty Competition that send message to the world 'Don't let them kill us', Sarajevo International Film Festival, disco nights in BOCK, SS and Cocktail or simple home parties. Nightlife in that time of siege was important in creation of practice kind of normal-like life. It was night economy with amplified emotions. . . .

A significant role in defining night-time economy has been played by international citizens in Sarajevo – UN militaries, newspaper and TV reporters, NGOs like Journalists Sans Frontiers, and individuals, some predefined and some opened. Some were enjoying the city in the maximum of her potential, e.g. food, drinks, drugs, prostitution and money. There were also those internationals that were making this kind of city life under the siege possible, smuggling all supplies needed. One NGO van could smuggle 75 litres of brandy easily. Unexpected selection of food and drinks could be found on the menu in some restaurants. On the other hand, there were those who enjoyed newly discovered culture, concept of life and love for life and way of expressing it, and stood up for like Bono Vox and Susan Sontag.[8]

NIGHTLIFE IN POST-WAR AND POST-SOCIALIST SARAJEVO

The post-war period brought a number of changes in terms of the ethnic composition of this city, and this was reflected in the available social and cultural life of the city as well as its property development (Filipović 2003; Puhalo 2009; Hodžić 2013). The state of post-war Sarajevo is often described as a social and cultural breakdown. Urban life was forcedly reshaped in the city into something that makes prewar Sarajevans feel uncomfortable. Stefansson (2007) analyses the social and cultural transformation of Sarajevo, arguing that the distinction between people from Sarajevo and migrants does not follow an ethnic pattern but falls along the lines of people originally from the city versus newcomers.[9] In a parallel way, a neo-liberal economy was further developed, with the international administration deployed in Bosnia and Herzegovina (BiH) after the signature of the peace agreement.[10] During the post-war period, the neo-liberal economic model of BiH produced a further destruction of social cohesion and a deepening antagonism between work and capital (Grabovac 2015, 136), exploitation, inequity and disempowerment, leading society into a monstrous fall, social injustice, mass humiliation and the destruction of human dignity and hopelessness (Zgodić 2015, 31) – a world opposite to the one developed during Tito's socialism.

All this affected nightlife facilities in terms of an emerging reinforcement of the socio-spatial segregation of night-time leisure activities in the city. Nightlife appears to have lost its more inclusive nature and given way to social, class and nationality-based distinction and stratification. This is most apparent in the restaurant business.[11] Though the post-war evening and night-time leisure 'economy' has emerged as a significant and productive economic activity for the city, the opening of dozens of new middle-class-oriented nightlife venues in the Stari Grad and Centar quarters of the city centre should be seen as epiphenomenal to the process of leisure-oriented urban, residential and functional changes of the city centre that have occurred since the late 1990s and early 2000s. Recent research on inner-city attractiveness (Čengić and Hodo, 2018) shows that Stari Grad and Centar city core quarters are the most attractive areas of the city for nightlife business.[12]

The number of new nightlife venues and the privatisation of the former socially owned ones; the (re-)construction of hotels and hostels; and the opening of new shopping malls, banking offices and international decision-making organisations in the city centre after the war are some examples of the most visible urban spatial changes in post-socialist Sarajevo (Martín-Díaz 2014).[13] No less important, public space has been progressively privatised as a result of the installation of restaurant and bar terraces in some urban parterres. This initially occurred in Radićeva Street, Branilaca grada, Skenderija, Trg Heroja, Grbavica, Zlatarska ulica and Muvekita Street as well as in many sidewalks of the city centre like those belonging to Radićeva, Ferhadija and Štrosmajerova streets. The terraces were introduced after the war and produced a change in the street atmosphere. Urban planning guidelines conducted in 1997 established that terraces could occupy one-third of the pedestrian area, but, in practice, much public space has been occupied over this limit. This new tendency for occupying public space was well illustrated in the case of Štrosmajerova Street, in Baščaršija. This pedestrian street placed in the axis of the Cathedral, connecting Ferhadija and Zelenih Beretki streets, was largely occupied by terraces until 2016 when the municipality authorities decided to remove them.

Of course, the development of nightlife venues is not the result of private initiatives alone. Urban changes are also prompted by the state planning institutions such as in the case of Radićeva Street, where the Arts Quarter plan was inaugurated with the construction of a pedestrian bridge. It is a relatively isolated and quiet residential area in the very centre of the city, next to the city prison. Rich in greenery and located on the axis of the Fine Arts Academy and the bridge, the area is being converted into a lively and attractive area with cafe bars, restaurants, an art gallery and a book shop, with terraces covering the sidewalks.

In 1975, only 35 percent of all night-time venues in the central part of the city were private. In 1999 the share of private night-time venues was 65 percent, while today there are no socially owned venues remaining (ZPUPPS 1977, 60; Kanton Sarajevo 1999). Once nightlife venues become increasingly private domains, terraces appear, and these urban parterres and terraces rapidly turn into lively and attractive places, playing a central role in the distinction-oriented (Bourdieu 1984) place-making of Sarajevo city centre. The development of nightlife in the city centre post-war mainly encompassed seven streets of the city centre, namely Ferhadija, Strosmajerova, Saliha Hadzihusejnovica, Zelenih Beretki, Branilaca Sarajeva, Kundurziluk and Bazardzani. During fieldwork conducted by the authors, informants argued that some aforementioned venues of the city centre such as Hacienda, Caffe Club Havana (located in Baščaršija's old town), Café Alfonso, Kozor, Cheers, Downtown Cafè, City Lounge, Galerija, Central Café, Club Jez, Café Opera, Cheers and Mash were popularly seen among both local young people and young adults as spaces for exhibiting social distinction and for demonstrating social status. These venues were indeed designed to attract, first, the new local middle classes that emerged after the war and, second, the foreign young adult population who were mainly working as diplomats or NGO staff in the region. In these nightlife venues, an Italian style of dress is seen as one such example of exhibiting social distinction, and the consumption of such a 'distinguished' nightlife would therefore appear as one of the most important strategies for the accumulation of social distinction for local young people in post-socialist Sarajevo.

The expansion and commodification of this youth-oriented, Western-styled (and sometimes) alcohol-fuelled nightlife in the city centre has taken place in parallel with the rise of new halal nightlife facilities. This is the case of two venues, among others, Restoran Kolobara and Damask Bar near the two main mosques of Baščaršija (Gazi Husrev-beg and Havadza Durak). Damask Bar, which is covered during the winter season, is frequented by young Bosniak middle and lower-middle classes, most of whom are high school and university students aged between sixteen and twenty-five years. They typically spend the evening smoking *shisha* (hookah) and drinking fruit juices or other nonalcoholic drinks. No alcoholic drinks are served in these establishments. On the other side, while Damask offers a youthful lively atmosphere, Kolobara is mainly oriented to young and adult middle classes as well as to some members of the international community. In one of its two entrances, the menu is accompanied by innovative and official certification (in official Arabian language), saying Kolobara meals are halal. The night-time industry therefore recognises a growing number of guests and has responded accordingly. In the same neighbourhood, it is possible to find halal and alcohol-led venues side by side.

However, for some of the educated middle classes from Sarajevo, 're-Ottomanised' Baščaršija's nightlife and re-Westernised-like nightlife in the city centre are not representative of the 'authentic soul of the city', as a thirty-five-year-old informant from Sarajevo emphasises. He adds: 'I don't like to go there [pubs and coffee bars of the city centre]. It's just for local posh people and Americans working in their embassy'. Another informant aged twenty-nine years also points out: 'I usually meet friends in Tito's Bar [officially called Marsal Tito], because it sounds Yugo-rock . . . it's a way of remembering good times when we were children . . . we don't like this country and we want to come back to be Yugoslavia. I think it's still possible . . . but politicians don't want it . . . it's a shit'. One of his friends, a thirty-seven-year-old fervent defender of the former Socialist Yugoslavia from Dobrinja, argues: 'Now the pubs and clubs are full of "sponsored girls", you know? They're looking for machos with a lot of money, expensive cars and that kind of fucking stuff. But before the war, girls weren't such materialists, they were different, with other values, other attitudes . . . they were much more open-minded. This city has changed'.

The changes explored here in post-socialist Sarajevo have resulted in the rise of some social and political resistance, and the socialist-nostalgic style of urban nightlife deserves our attention. Nostalgia should not be confused with the absence of criticism of both socialist and capitalist democracies and economies (Čengić 2013, 92). For a small minority, the consumption of these 'socialist-nostalgic' nightscapes in Marsal Tito Bar (19 Bihacka Street) or Nostalgija Bar (10 Mukevita Street) becomes one of the few means of expressing social and political resistance in neo-liberal Sarajevo. Equally, the consumption of such *socialist-nostalgic-retro urban nightscapes* could be seen as merely an inoffensive and naïf *bohemian activism* against the social, economic and political order established in post-socialist Sarajevo. Indeed, *socialist-nostalgic nightscapes* may be understood not only as a radical contestation of neo-liberal capitalism but also as an alternative, *distinguished* way of social distinction for local college-educated young-adults and adults, who often dislike the presence in *their* socialist-nostalgic-style venues of 'those masses who love turbo-folk, that shit commercial music morally degrading the individual', as a thirty-eight-year-old informant from Sarajevo states. The discreet presence of turbo-folk aficionados in nostalgic-socialist-style nightlife venues or even the presence of clients who do not identify them-selves with the socialist cause would devalue the *authentic* and *prestigious* nature of the consumption of such nostalgic-socialist nightscape in post-socialist Sarajevo.

Resistance to Western nightlife in the city centre is not exclusively appro-priated by socialist nostalgics, however. The second author of this chap-ter sometimes visited Aqua Diskoteka with local friends. This discotheque is located at Ilidza, a suburban neighbourhood of Sarajevo. Although currently closed, Aqua Diskoteka was mostly oriented to the young working classes who were mainly aged between sixteen and thirty-five years. A twenty-nine-year-old informant from Sarajevo working at the university confirmed to us that the youth and young adults who regularly party in Aqua Diskoteka 'are low-skilled teens and some young adults who love that kind of music [turbo-folk]'. However, her sister, a twenty-four-year-old client of Aqua Diskoteka asserted that 'turbo-folk is broadly listened to among not only young and young-adult Bosnian Serbs working classes but also among young middle-class university students, although they usually listen to American and Latin commercial music'. Turbo-folk has gained centrality in Sarajevo's nightlife over recent years. Club Jez, Club Boemi and Davor are the most important turbo-folk clubs in the city centre, although other turbo-folk clubs are located in some suburban towns such as Bachus, in Lukavica. However, an adult infor-mant explained to us: 'Citizens strongly relate it [turbo folk] to dis-urbanity and names the followers as "square heads" or "peasants" expressing their discomfort and repulsiveness to [its] idea, music, lyrics and dressing style'.

Ethnographic fieldwork included attendance to some turbo-folk live ses-sions. It enabled us to confirm that the mainstream turbo-folk imagery is based on the celebration of physical, symbolic and sexual violence; sexism; misogamy; hyper-masculinity; homophobia; and the over-adoration of easy money, jewellery and luxury cars. It is very much embedded within a stereo-type of Latino warrior-chic and *macho* imagery (Kronja 2004). However, the lyrics, aesthetics and semiotics of most turbo-folk pieces contain interesting subtexts, which, in some cases, show a profound sense of *emotional-nostalgic* brotherhood. Indeed, it is about not only reinterpreting the Balkan identity but also claiming a 'return to the Balkan world of emotions and passion, away from the "boring" European lifestyle . . ., an escape into an emotional world, free of neoliberal, rational, and individualistic Western reality' (Volčič and Erjavec 2010, 111, 114).

In short, turbo-folk in Sarajevo's urban night can be seen as a collective reaction (and fear) of the neo-liberalisation of the city and its harsh everyday consequences for the younger population. In celebrating turbo-folk songs, young people and adults from Sarajevo refuse the background of contradic-tions and political tensions that characterise life in the neo-liberal climate of post-socialism in former Yugoslavia (Volčič and Erjavec 2010). In parallel to the development of turbo-folk, venues that were initially oriented towards the middle-class or university students also attracted international community members – such as in the case of City Pub, Underground Club, Barhana, Ćulhan, Babaloo, Nostalgija, Lora, Clou, Ribica, Opera and Sloga Club. These venues have preserved and celebrate cross-social, cross-generational and cross-ethnic meeting points in Sarajevo's nightlife. Thus, Bosnia's *strait-jacket*, that is, 'geoethnopolitical' boundaries imposed during and after the war, is continuously challenged and questioned by Sarajevo's youth through a variety of social practices and behaviours.

CONCLUSIONS

Sarajevo, especially since the 1970s, developed a vibrant and unexpected nightlife through an expansion of *cafettes*. This expansion was propelled by the social concept of free time in Socialist Yugoslavia, that viewed every-day life in a much less segmented way than in western European cities. It also resulted in an urban night that did not differ between Fridays and other weekdays. The expansion of *cafettes* both at the limit of the city centre, in the left bank of the Miljacka River, and in the city centre resulted in a diverse subcultural scene marked by such subcultures as fancies, punks, bohemians or urbans. During the 1980s, and concomitant with the demise of Socialist Yugoslavia, nightlife and subcultural scenés lived a golden age in the city marked by the rise of New Primitivism, which rendered the city as the cultural referent for the whole country. This golden decade saw an expansion of nightlife beyond the city's core following specific urban planning goals that sought to create a balanced urban development. There was an increase in newly developed western areas of the city in food-led venues, but also disco bars and *caffetes*.

The golden decade ended dramatically with the siege of Sarajevo, which broke social links established before the war and the previous multicultural and kaleidoscopic nature of the nightlife scene in the city. Nightlife under the siege suffered serious constraints, and participation became a means of resistance for besieged citizens who learned and shared ideas and experiences in a context in which daily experiences had many challenges. However, nightlife was also marked by some continuity during the siege. Along with general forms of sociability, spatial mobility was maintained despite threats to one's life, with nightlife facilities being differentiated between both the city core and periphery. But the war and siege produced a social and cultural breakdown in the city, with an acute distinction later produced between people from Sarajevo and newer migrants.

During the post-war period, nightlife facilities were transformed into private domains that resulted in the privatisation of physical public spaces and reinforced socio-spatial segregation along economic, rather than just subcultural, lines. As manifested in the restaurant business, nightlife lost its more inclusive nature to give way to less subcultural distinction and instead distinction based on class and international-based stratification. The post-socialist transformation of Sarajevo is not only illustrated in the loss of the inclusive nature of nightlife venues. The opening of new, middle-class-oriented nightlife venues in Stari Grad and Centar quarters, sometimes driven by city planning or municipality offices, highlights the process of leisure-oriented urban, residential and functional transformation of the city centre that has occurred since the late 1990s, making these quarters first-tier centres and now the most attractive areas in the city.

NOTES

1. Socially owned property was created under both Law on Enterprises and Law on Associated Labour of Yugoslavia in the 1950s. It is a collective form of ownership that differs from state property. It is owned by the broader social community, by all citizens, and never ceases to be owned by the broader social community.

2. *Cafette* is a diminutive of cafe and describes a small cafe where alcoholic drinks and sandwiches are served.

3. Consuming opium was also introduced in Sarajevo at this time.

4. Practicing 'a way we want' form of nightlife resulted in a court decision to close Evergreen for one year due to certain styles of dancing and 'possession of two record players and two loudspeakers' (*Start Magazin* 2016).

5. New Primitivism was officially terminated in 1987 by a common declaration by the founding members in the presence of their friends, although their work continued even in the time of the siege.

6. Terraces were a privilege of socially owned venues, so, generally, terraces were allowed only in these premises. It was very rare to find a private venue with a terrace in the street but only inside inner courtyards. The exception in the privately managed venues was some venues in the new parts of the city.

7. About 350,000 citizens were locked in a territory about 8×2 km in total, under constant shelling and snipering and brutally reduced sources of existential needs. If someone were asked where his or her friends were, all would answer that they left the city. New social links and networks subsequently emerged.

8. Self-ethnographic description of nightlife in Sarajevo carried out by the first author of this chapter.

9. In this sense, there is a powerful distinction between 'locals' and 'newcomers' in post-war Sarajevo. The related stereotypes of urban/rural and 'cultured/noncultured' were already very much present (e.g., Simic 1973).

10. A neo-liberal model was introduced to Bosnia and Herzegovina with the war under the veil of 'transition', which was the most frequent word used next to 'democracy' in political speeches about our promised bright future at the turn of the century. It will be shown later that democracy was a 'candy-word' that stood for 'predatory neoliberalism' (Zgodić 2015, 31), which was uncritically adopted in BiH (Grabovac 2015, 11). The manifestation of privatisation and deregulation is conditioned by local 'parochial, ethnoclerical and nationalist interpretations' (Ćurak 2015, 10).

11. Importantly, international actors involved in the peace-building efforts were very numerous in Sarajevo after the end of the war. According to estimates, 11,000 apartments in Sarajevo were lived in by non-Bosnian people working in international organisations (Omeragić 1998).

12. These quarters are ranked first-tier centres. The second-tier centre is not yet differentiated, while Novo Sarajevo is the third-tier city centre that acts as an extension of the city core.

13. Who the 'privatisers' are is not still clear since international people may be the only visible people who pursue leisure in local venues. The overall process was termed 'transition', as an argument and explanation for any decision shaping our new reality. The main tool of installing the new economy was privatisation of socially owned properties. A new perception of rights as based on private property ownership has also since been constructed – 'it is mine so I can do whatever I want'. Chaos has entered into the city again, just as was stated in the Athens Charter almost 85 years ago (Le Corbusier 1973, 49). The privatisation process has become an opportunity for many selected local and international individuals, including those in nightlife businesses.

Chapter 4

Amusing Ourselves in Athens's 'Ghettoes of the Mind'

Penny-Panagiota Koutrolikou

The urban night represents a time of shadows and emotions, of pleasure and danger, of things deemed inappropriate for daily life. The night is a time of mystery, for some providing the opportunity to transgress boundaries, for others a time of work or sleep. All these elements that have long fascinated artists sit in contrast to the *moral entrepreneurs* (to paraphrase Stanley Cohen 1972), who instead focus on threats to moral values and the dangers to the structure of an ordered society. Regulating night-time activities and places associated with nightlife has long concerned city managers, who have made tremendous efforts to control vice and *illegal* economies. As Williams argues, urban nightlife is mediated by social values, and 'night spaces are neither uniform nor homogenous. Rather they are constituted by social struggles about what should and should not happen in certain places during the dark of the night' (Williams 2008, 514). As such, night-time places and neighbourhoods become entangled in discourses, representations, policies and narratives concerning both the dangers nightlife is said to represent and the fears and pleasures associated with nightlife areas.

Neil Postman's (1985) *Amusing Ourselves to Death: Public Discourse in the Era of Show Business* explores the ways that mainstream media, especially television news, influence and, to an extent, shape our lives. This phrase, 'amusing ourselves to death', is especially relevant when thinking about Metaxourgeio, an area at the centre of Athens and the focus of this chapter. The reason for this is twofold; first, the Metaxourgeio area has long been part of the *ghetto narrative* that characterises several inner-city neighbourhoods of Athens, framing it as dangerous and crime ridden. Equally, the area has become a hot spot for nightlife since the early 2000s. The parallel *truths* concerning this area reflect numerous studies concerning the stigmatisation of inner-city neighbourhoods in Athens. These studies highlight the significance of media discourses in establishing and perpetuating territorial stigma and geographies of fear that often 'are better seen as ghettos of the mind rather than ghettos of reality' (Simpson 2007, 17).

The discussion presented in this chapter draws on findings from a broader research project concerning the mobilisation of 'ghetto discourses' conducted for the Centre of Athens (see Koutrolikou 2016). The research was based on a critical discourse analysis of newspapers, political statements and policy documents. Focusing on the area of Metaxourgeio, the research entailed a critical review of newspaper articles concerning the area in two influential newspapers: *Vima* (centre-right) and *Kathimerini* (conservative) between 2007 and 2015. The analysis was structured around three key narratives: ghettoisation/downgrading, potential regeneration and, finally, art and entertainment, while recognising the latter two were often intertwined. Particular attention was also focused on major local stakeholders, who featured frequently in these articles and who were well known to the broader public such as artists, designers or developers. Additional data for the area was collected by drawing on comparable studies (e.g., Kaouni 2009; Alexandri 2013) as well as by the permits' registry for businesses with *health concerns* (which includes bars, restaurants and cafes). Moreover, it is important to note that I have been involved in the area for the past twenty years, not only as a researcher (through area mapping, semi-structured interviews, participant observation and discourse analysis) but also as a client and through personal relations with venue owners and employees. As such, I have closely observed how the area has transformed over the years and experienced personally the contradictions of the dominant narratives concerning nightlife, gentrification and *fear* in Metaxourgeio.

NIGHT-TIME ENTERS THE URBAN POLICY ARENA

While scholars have been interested in urban nightlife since at least the post-war period, it has been of marginal concern for urban planning, geography and urban studies beyond the occasional foray into debates about noisy or *improper* activities, or when exploring concerns about safety and security (van Liempt et al. 2015). However, since the 1980s the night has entered the policy arena in different ways. Intensified competition between cities has focused attention not only on attracting international capital but also on the rebranding of cities as sites of and for leisure, tourism and consumption. The *return* to city centres, which has been strongly associated with gentrification (Lees et al. 2010) or what Smith (1996) refers to as *revanchist urbanism*, has come together with a growing interest in increasing liveliness, both during the daytime and night-time. The allure and marketability of *creativity* (Florida

2002) has further emphasised the significance of a lively local nightlife to enable people to meet, network and socialise outside of their daily lives.

In post-industrial city centres, the night-time economy has been represented in terms of its economic potential and the opportunities it affords for regeneration, as well as a means for attracting the 'creative class' (van Liempt et al. 2015). In addition, the expansion of youth lifestyles (Chatterton and Hollands 2003) and the increased demand for places to *go out and play* have provided the necessary rationale for supporting a diversified night-time economy. The night subsequently entered into local policy strategies, particularly in North European and North American cities, not only in regard to regulations about proper uses and behaviours but also as an economic and revitalisation strategy, a strategy that had the added benefit of being relatively cost-effective to implement since it was largely privately driven and financed.

Florida's (2012) well-known argument about the significance of the creative class in the new economic competitiveness between cities was often translated into a checklist of (municipal and/or regional) actions in order to attract this loosely defined and volatile demographic (or 'class'). His three Ts – technology, talent, tolerance – were spatialised in urban environments characterised by social mix, by liveliness during the day and night and by controlled edginess. Yet simultaneously, as many critics have pointed out (Peck 2005; Prichard et al. 2006; Atkinson and Easthop 2009), this turn towards the creative class may well facilitate another wave of gentrification and displacement. While talent and tolerance (as well as exclusions) are interpreted according to contextual preferences, more *traditional* agendas of welfare and redistribution have been pushed aside in favour of a more neo-liberal agenda (Brown 2006).

Nevertheless, the traditional approaches towards dealing with nightlife, namely that of regulation and control, have not entirely disappeared; rather, they have intensified (Chatterton and Hollands 2003; Crawford and Flint 2009). Crime, fear of crime, *out-of-control* behaviour and informal/illegal activities have always been associated with the night in the West. As such, a number of technologies have been employed in order to control night-time behaviours as well as assure those seeking nightlife entertainment that they are safe. Police patrols, private security and surveillance and stricter licensing laws are some of these technologies. Through them, further distinctions have been made between night-time entertainment and cultures that are privileged and supported and those that fall off the regulatory framework and become excluded and often prohibited (Hadfield 2015).

The night-time therefore continues to embody multiple and often-contradictory narratives entailing desire, fear and economic potential. When these are focused around deprived or stigmatised areas, as is often the case with emerging nightlife destinations, then further contradictory narratives concerning these areas emerge. Nightlife is often seen as a vehicle for revitalising an area, bringing together not only economic profits but also potential residents and regeneration. However, this expected revitalisation cannot take place without ensuring potential investors of the area's safety (or sense of it). Subsequently, further policing measures tend to be introduced, this time in the name of nightlife, often resulting in the targeting and displacement of those perceived as potential *threats*.

Contextualising Metaxourgeio through Urban Transformations and Migration

Metaxourgeio is part of the historic centre of Athens, located at the western edge of the inner, historic core. Although it is legislatively defined as one area, it is typically understood as two neighbourhoods: Metaxourgeio, which is close to Omonoia Square, and Kerameikos, which is to the south and borders the fashionable neighbourhood of Gazi. Although the character of these neighbourhoods differs, the precise border between them is rather vague. Like many of the nightlife areas discussed elsewhere in this collection, for much of its history Metaxourgeio has been a working-class and lower-middle-class neighbourhood. It took its name from the silk factory located on its central square and has since housed many small-scale manufacturing units and car-repair businesses (Agriantoni and Hatziioannou 1995).

From the 1960s to the 1980s, Athens became densely (re)built, mostly with blocks of flats, through the process of *antiparochi* (Emmanouil 2014). From the mid-1970s in particular, an extensive process of suburban expansion resulted in a significant number of households moving from inner-city neighbourhoods to nearby or outer suburbs. Across a range of socio-economic categories, people moved in search of what was perceived to be a better quality of life. Air pollution, particularly smog, was a significant problem at the time and played a part in the suburbanisation trend. As a result, and along with an over-provision of new houses, the number of empty properties rose (Maloutas et al. 2013). While this pattern of inner-city decline was common in other Western cities, Athens city centre was never really abandoned, however, and as Emmanouil (2013) observes, the demand for housing did not entirely drop until the 2000s.

The suburbanisation of the 1970s resulted in a population loss of 5,000 people, from 15,495 residents in 1971 to 10,250 in 1991, although it did rise slightly again to 11,010 in 2001 (Kaouni 2009). In the 1980s, Muslim-Greeks from the northern region of Thrace settled in the area, mostly in the small houses, as did many Roma. Around 1990 a well-known squat moved into the area, strengthening its political character. The cheap rents and its proximity to areas of employment also attracted migrant groups living in Athens. By 1991, the more numerous migrant communities were of Polish, Albanian and Egyptian origins. By the end of the 1990s, a number of people of South Asian and of Arabic origins (including Egyptian), and a significant part of the Chinese community of Athens, also moved there and opened businesses.

Throughout this period, many small houses in Metaxourgeio were redeveloped into blocks of flats, though a significant number of small houses remained. This, together with its many small pedestrian streets, gave Metaxourgeio a distinct character. Due to its proximity to one of Athens's central squares, Omonoia, the northern part of the area was much more densely developed and hosted more commercial and office uses. Land-use laws from 1998 banned manufacturing activities and promoted leisure uses and the protection of housing, thus promoting the government's future wishes for the area. In terms of its informal economy, informal brothels started moving into the area in the 1980s (Hatziotis 1999), and their number steadily rose until recently, especially after the 1999 earthquake that significantly impacted on the neighbourhood. Moreover, at its northern side, and close to Omonoia Square, an infamous drug-dealing *piazza* appeared and has remained since the 1990s.

Due to the way Athens was built, instead of socio-spatial segregation spread across neighbourhoods, its neighbourhoods have been shaped by vertical differentiation (Maloutas and Karadimitriou 2001), where the lower-floor flats are inhabited by the poorer residents and the top-floor ones attract a wealthier class. This has also been the case with migrant housing in Metaxourgeio, where the blocks of flats were shared by migrants and non-migrants alike. This pattern of socio-spatial organisation has contributed to the relatively low levels of singly deprived communities, despite the fact that the greatest percentage of migrants traditionally settle in the city centre (Vaiou 2007; Arapoglou and Sayas 2009; Kandylis et al. 2012). Despite discourses of criminality and institutional gaps regarding integration and discrimination, local everyday life in the area has been characterised by its social mix.

Several interventions have nonetheless occurred, which have resulted in significant redevelopment in central Athens. The 1990s saw a focus on 'rebranding the city centre' and re-charting its cultural terrain. In light of the then forthcoming 2004 Olympic Games, an array of flagship projects were instigated in the city and transformed specific inner-city neighbourhoods. Simultaneously, the economy grew, which further boosted investments in construction and redevelopment.

Metaxourgeio, however, did not immediately follow the path of neighbouring areas such as Psirri and Gazi. By the late 1990s a number of theatres and performing arts spaces were established in the area, and some well-known artists moved there. The 1999 earthquake significantly impacted on the area, however, especially the small houses that were already deteriorating. Many of these small houses were deemed unfit to live or in need of major repairs, resulting in a gradual displacement of people, especially the most vulnerable. Considering the broader development expectations for the centre of Athens, along with gentrification pressures from nearby neighbourhoods as well as plans to highlight and promote the area's historic past, there were clear pressures to transform the area.

Slowly but visibly, from 2000 onwards Metaxourgeio began to change. A few *kafeneia*[1] catering for an alternative crowd appeared, while older ones were renovated to appeal to a new emerging clientele. Prices, especially for buying small houses, increased, and new development initiatives emerged along with galleries and art spaces. New high-profile development projects also took place. The development company Oliaros,[2] one of the major stakeholders in the area, started operating there in 2006 and now owns thirty-nine properties and 10,000 sq.m. of land.[3] By 2007, Oliaros started organising a highly promoted, albeit controversial, arts festival (ReMap) in the area with local and international guests. The event took place every two years until 2013. In 2008, the company also established KM Model Neighbourhood, a not-for-profit association (often confused with the local residents' association) that became very active in local projects and in lobbying for the area. Simultaneously, it started cooperating with architectural schools and well-known architects from Greece and abroad, becoming involved in architectural competitions and more established in the architectural scene.

By the end of the 2000s, Metaxourgeio was definitively 'on the map' of fashionable neighbourhoods in Athens, in terms of both art and nightlife and everyday life. Many cafe bars opened during this time, while equally small-scale art projects as well as more well-known ones settled in the area. In 2010 Metaxourgeio's Carnival was established and is still going. Although initially the area's clientele could broadly be defined as *alternative*, its reputation soon grew much broader.

Metaxourgeio has now become part of the architectural and creative representation of the city, especially since it has been a subject for many architectural workshops and competitions. It is also frequently featured as a 'working area' for architectural design projects and, conversely, in research projects examining gentrification in Athens. As research conducted in this area frequently points out, change in the area's population is small, albeit visible (Alexandri 2013, 2015; Katsaouni 2014). And although displacement of certain social groups, such as the Roma and Muslim Greeks, and the influx of newer residents are evident, the area remains socio-economically mixed. Ethnic businesses continue to exist in the area, and, in some cases, they have expanded through attracting a more diverse clientele, as do more gentrified stores and expensive restaurants.

At the same time, the implementation of the Dublin II Agreement concerning asylum-seeking in European countries, in conjunction with Greece's economic crisis, has significantly impacted on the lives of migrants and asylum seekers in the city. A number of migrants and asylum seekers have become trapped in the country with very limited asylum provision and with an economy in recession. Hence, many people have found themselves living in cramped accommodation, often rented per head, in empty properties in the broader area of the city centre, in squatted houses or on the streets, while the unfolding financial crisis further exacerbates their situation. Although limited in scale and duration, such conditions have been encountered in parts of Metaxourgeio. Policing measures have harshened, and the infamous Operation Xenios Zeus stopped and detained any migrant perceived to be without papers (Koutrolikou 2015). At the same time, many old houses remain abandoned, while the number of sex establishments is still significant and the drug-use problem that was present in adjacent neighbourhoods of Athens has fluctuated in and out of the area. Thus, while displacement and urban population change are difficult to quantify through data, the area is now marked by competing claims and representations. Art-led establishments, migrants and asylum seekers, new developments and gentrification have become visible through the new users, uses and aesthetics of the area, including its nightlife.

METAXOURGEIO: BECOMING A FASHIONABLE NIGHTLIFE DESTINATION

Whereas significant residential gentrification may be difficult to substantiate due to the small population change, broader transformations in Metaxourgeio are visible primarily through the area's local nightlife and nightlife businesses. 'Trendyfication' (Kidd 2008) is a term that is suitable for describing the economic, cultural and spatial transformations that have occurred and continue to occur. As already mentioned, Metaxourgeio is currently one of the more fashionable nightlife destinations in the city centre. Yet this transformation has taken place gradually over the course of more than a decade. Although theatres existed there for some time, only in the beginning of the 2000s did new performing arts spaces and galleries emerge. Around the year 2000 several kafeneia and a bar opened in the area, attracting a mostly 'alternative' clientele from different parts of the city. As the data from the Municipality of Athens demonstrates, fifty-six venues for food and/or drink have opened in the area since 2008 (including bars, restaurants and kafeneia). For a relatively small area such as Metaxourgeio, this large number of food-and-drink venues is obviously catering not only to locals but also to many visitors, reaching beyond its initial *alternative* clientele. These places differ in terms of clientele as well as in their ways of operating. Some of them follow a popular trend in Athens and operate as a form of a cooperative, mostly with lower prices but without necessarily catering only for a politically oriented or alternative clientele, although some still do more than others.

On the other end of the spectrum, there are now more upmarket restaurants, even one specialising in molecular cuisine, that attract a wealthier clientele. In between, there are many other places that cater to a very diverse clientele in terms of income, age, sexual orientation and self-identification. Most of the kafeneia, bars and restaurants tend to be located at the south part of the area (Kerameikos), which is also the part much more affected by trendyfication. Nevertheless, while the southern area continues to be a popular destination, new places have appeared on the northern side. Although the gallery scene is different, most venues are relatively small and privately run, with no corporate chains or large-scale nightlife entrepreneurs operating there. Contrary to other areas, there are also few nightlife places that have private security.

While not as visible as its nightlife, the art and theatre scene also contributes to the area's growing attraction to residents with social and cultural capital. At present (2017), with the international exhibition *Documenta 14 Learning from Athens*, the area's nightlife recalls Lloyd's notion of *grit as glamour* (2010) in terms of both neo-bohemian cool and a fetishisation of diversity. But there is also a genuinely darker side to Metaxourgeio nightlife. A significant number of informal brothels exist in the area, located mostly in rundown houses to the north. Although street criminals tend to avoid these places, serious questions arise regarding sex trafficking, the working conditions of the sex workers and organised protection rackets operating in the area.

TERRITORIALISING NOCTURNAL CONTESTED NARRATIVES OF CRISIS IN METAXOURGEIO

As discussed earlier, urban nightlife has often been used as a tool for economic development and to assist in the revitalisation of post-industrial areas. Since it is mediated by social values and practices (Williams 2008), implicitly or explicitly the night becomes part of the wider narrative about an area where nightlife develops. In cases where nightlife areas are stigmatised, specific nightlife practices may be employed as an excuse for measures to be taken in order to facilitate increased policing and redevelopment. In other cases, nightlife might become a means for challenging neighbourhood stigmatisation. The presence of expensive restaurants and fashionable bars would be examples of this. Such contradictory discourses of danger, development and entertainment have shaped much of Metaxourgeio's recent identity.

The emergence of Metaxourgeio as a fashionable area coincided with the beginning of what was termed as the 'crisis of the centre' of Athens and, later, with the unfolding of the sovereign debt crisis which officially started in 2010, with the first Memorandum of Understanding. The dominant discourse about the crisis of the centre of Athens mainly employed representations of specific neighbourhoods (or at times the centre as a whole) as dangerous *ghettoes*, overrun by migrants without papers (the term used was '*contraband* migrants'), crime, drug use, sex work and health hazards, places where idealised residents would not dare to venture out of their houses and where the police could not enter (Maloutas et al. 2013; Koutrolikou 2016). However, even before the financial crisis, Metaxourgeio appeared in the *ghetto discourse*. By 2010 the belief that Metaxourgeio was a kind of 'ghetto', with all the strong racialised overtones of this term, had become an established truth, which was rarely challenged and which prescribed its own remedies. This was exemplified by a high-profile conference that took place at the new Benaki Museum, where ministers, municipal politicians, professors of architecture schools and experts debated 'Athens in Crisis' with the support of the Oliaros company.[4]

For Metaxourgeio, the ghettoisation discourse focused mostly on fear of crime and rising criminality, second on migrants living in deprived conditions, as well as on issues of sanitation – all of them associated with migrants, intravenous drug users and sex workers. Although its northern part had been associated with drug dealing for a long time, when the police started operations in the nearby area of Gerani targeting intravenous drug users and migrants, many, without any other option, crossed into Metaxourgeio. As a result, the issue of drug users using the streets or abandoned houses in the area, as well as the informal occupation of such housing by migrants, became key concerns in the developing politics and geographies of fear (Shirlow and Pain 2003).

The role of some prominent local stakeholders was pivotal. The development company Oliaros, through its CEO, had a very significant presence in the media, as well as in whatever concerned the area. Although rarely referring to criminality and fear himself, he mostly discussed regenerating the neighbourhood, or about gaps or the inability of the authorities to deal with the situation. In contrast, he was often presented as on the other side of the area's decline (see, e.g., Lialios 2010). However, the related KM Model Neighbourhood often joined calls and initiatives of residents' associations of the city centre calling for measures to be taken[5] and came up with its own proposals, which it lobbied to the municipality. The KM Model Neighbourhood proposals included a redesign of Kerameikou Street into a minor traffic street with enlarged pavements in order to designate its cultural significance; a redesign of Salaminos (pedestrian) Street in order to highlight its *archaeological significance*; the initiation of an ideas competition for the reuse of the abandoned IKA building; the introduction of tax and other incentives for attracting students, young couples and creative businesses and for retaining existing residents, improving the sense of safety in the area; strict control or amendment of land uses in order to control Chinese business activities and to control and regulate the brothels; a redesign of the central Avdi Square; the diversion of metropolitan bus lines from inside the neighbourhood; and the immediate construction of an approved state kindergarten.[6]

Other well-known local stakeholders were influential in pinpointing the area's problems and in demanding particular strategies. For example, a well-known theatre representative sent and publicised two separate letters to the Mayor and relevant ministers (in 2008 and 2011), the second ending with the claim 'the city has been captured'. The problems identified included sex workers, drug users, homeless persons (who were associated with specific health hazards) and the lack of sanitation. In 2010 a meeting of artists and entrepreneurs of the broader area of Metaxourgeio along with the police authorities received significant media attention, as did their calls for action to be taken against sex work, drug use and the abandonment of local buildings. One of the newspaper articles, referring to these events, *aptly* titled 'The Ghetto of the Centre Drives Theatres Out', prominently featured several well-known local stakeholders (Kleftogianni 2010). Less than a month later, another article, 'They Push Us to a Civil War' (Ismailidou 2010), also featured many of the previously mentioned stakeholders, although it referred to the whole city centre and painted a much bleaker picture. It appeared that the grit of the area (Lloyd 2010) was in many respects either too gritty or simply not the correct type.

At the margins of this discourse, other well-known residents painted less of an emergency picture, however. As mentioned (Tsantaki 2012), one such resident argued that 'criminality is the pain of those living and working here. We are not talking about criminality that makes your hair stand, but petty thefts. The small-time dealer/user who hasn't sold heroin and breaks into a car, steals a bag or a chain from one's neck'. Undoubtedly, Metaxourgeio and other neighbourhoods hosted, and to an extent still do, a significant number of people in dire need of help and support. Albeit, as often observed (Wacquant 2007; Peach 2009), the way that problems are represented also predefines their solutions, solutions that more often than not end up with repression, extreme policing and displacement, or detainment rather than actual care of those in need. This has been the case with drug users and sex workers in the area.

As expected, the repercussion of the broader discourse of fear that circulates through the centre of Athens has had multiple repercussions. Apart from the well-documented normalisation of racist discourses and stigmatisation of migrants and asylum seekers, it has paved the way for large-scale sweep (and detainment) operations by the police (Human Rights Watch 2012). Moreover, for the areas of Gerani and Metaxourgeio, it has established financial and tax incentives for the so-called rehabilitation of buildings and for property owners who rent them, while a broader urban regeneration plan for the centre of Athens has been announced (YPEKA 2011). Besides fighting crime, an overarching aim of the announced plans was, as stated, the return of residents to the centre of Athens, albeit desirable residents meaning young, professional, creative and non-migrant.

THE NIGHTLIFE EXPERIENCE

'Where do you think we should go out tonight? Should we go to Metaxourgeio? You're kidding me'. This would be many people's reaction if they suggested to them to have a night out in the area of Metaxourgeio. Foreigners' ghetto, drug-users' hangout, prostitution centre; these and many other gritty things one can hear about the area and as expected to get scared. However, the truth is somehow – or very – different. . . . Metaxourgeio is a neighbourhood, people greet each other, the shops communicate and if need arises they help each other. The residents discuss their common problems and solve them collectively. . . . And it's not the only one [café-bar]: around the square and in the adjacent streets during the past 3–4 years many similar shops have opened, rejuvenating and significantly contributing to the rise but also to the safety of the previously much blighted area. (Harmpis 2014, n.p.)

This sort of news commentary quoted is not infrequent (Fragkos 2011; Kounadi 2012), especially since 2013. It is occasionally joined by articles from foreign newspapers describing the renaissance of the centre of Athens as a destination rich with history, creativity and a lively nightlife, a *new* Berlin (Khemsurov 2010; Drake 2014). At the same time, in many articles of this kind some of the area's most well-known residents, especially actors, designers and gallerists, share their views. Nevertheless, it is not only since 2010–2011, as the aforementioned article claims, that kafeneia, bars and meze places have opened in the area. Rather, while the dominant discourse about the area has been about crime and fear, these kinds of businesses, celebrated as changing the area, have been increasingly appearing over a number of years.

Taking a closer look at the news articles published about the area from 2010 onwards, read in terms of the aforementioned discourse of crisis, one will also come across, often in the same newspapers, articles concerning the development potential of the area, especially praising private development and arts entrepreneurs in such a *difficult territory* as well as the new creative initiatives taking place there. Emphasising creativity (in discourse rather than strategy) resonates with Florida's (2012) recommendations about attracting and supporting the potential of the creative class. In this case, creativity with selected (limited) tolerance is used as a *facade* for rebranding the area and for facilitating the development investments that were already under way (but also future ones). As expected, such articles often combine what they see as positive initiatives for the area with the need for greater security and policing, as well as for economic/investment incentives in support of the daring, pioneer gentrifiers (Smith 1996), often accompanied by arguments for *controlled diversity*. Central to these accounts are some of the key actors operating in the area, who also seem to have preferential relations with media organisations and who voice very specific concerns as well as solutions and proposals for the area's future.

These accounts of Metaxourgeio's flourishing nightlife and potential juxtapose, and to an extent challenge, other dominant media representations of Metaxourgeio. This does not mean that in many people's minds these representations of danger do not hold some truth or that the area's nightlife does not go together with the still-existing sex work, hidden sex trafficking or drug use and poverty. Rather, it becomes a starting point of discussing the influence of the media in establishing negative socio-spatial representations and what the implications of such dominant representations might entail.

These contrasting narratives about Metaxourgeio, where on one hand newspapers stigmatise the area by emphasising concerns about migration, criminality and sanitation while promoting it as an appealing area full of potential and creativity, at first glance seem to contradict each other and to negate each other's 'truth'. However, another reading of this contradiction might see it as a carrot-and-stick tactic whereby these representations of socio-spatial danger and fear along with 'cries for help' in dealing with the area's problems become not only an excuse for harsh repressive measures but also an 'implicit contract', arguing that since the stakeholders already there have invested in the area, if the authorities clean it up from *undesirables*, then these private stakeholders will redevelop it along with the preferred plans for bringing new and desirable residents in the city centre. It is therefore important to keep in mind that while Metaxourgeio's flourishing nightlife might challenge negative stereotypes, these stereotypes serve to facilitate and enable its gentrification.

CONTRASTING REPRESENTATIONS AS 'GAPS' IN THE AFFIRMATION OF 'TRUTHS'

In the broad field of urban studies, exploring the role of discourse in colonising, legitimising and de-legitimising places, social groups and/or actions has been growing in popularity since the 1990s (Lees 2004). This body of research is mostly concerned with how place meanings and representations are constructed, how discourse about particular places and groups affects them and their future and how socio-spatial stigmatisation and discrimination is deepened and functions (Hargreaves 1996; Martin 2000; Mele 2000; Wacquant 2007; Slater and Anderson 2012).

Representations are powerful in regard to their meaning-making potential as well as in their affirmation of 'truths' and 'blame' (Foucault 1972; Hall 1997). As discussions about the politics of fear have illustrated, this is particularly pertinent for representations that appeal to popular fears, which construct the 'perpetrators' and thus provide 'solutions' that target particular groups and areas (Shirlow and Pain 2003). One ever-popular representation is that of the ghetto, a representation rooted in the popular imaginary through wildly circulated and often racialised images and texts rather than experience. In terms of urban politics, the representation of the ghetto often works as a signifier of emergency and threat, a stigmatisation process 'that can only be understood in relation to broader notions of power and domination' (Parker and Aggleton 2003, 16) and one which can be used for fostering certain measures and development prospects. Metaxourgeio is one area that has found itself in the midst of such discourses.

Metaxourgeio has followed a rather predictable path of urban transformation. In the post-industrial/manufacturing era, it has gradually transformed into a nightlife destination, primarily alternative in the beginning but much more diversified at present. Since the late 1990s, leisure and the night-time economy were perceived by the planning authorities as its future, while its central location and its specific urban character made it a lucrative place for development and for developers' and gentrifiers' aspirations. Although the popularity of its nightlife could have resulted in its complete gentrification, it seems that it mostly contributed to its trendyfication. However, the analysis of the area's dynamics and relations would be incomplete without considering the role of significant local stakeholders: investors who tried to mobilise different elements of the area, including its nightlife, for their own benefit.

By juxtaposing dominant discourses along with data and personal accounts, everyday experiences and contradictory representations, an intricate network of actors, aspirations and contestations emerge, which provides an in-depth understanding of the area per se, as well as the locally specific power relations operating there. In the case of Metaxourgeio, nightlife becomes the 'joker' through which a gap in the dominant discourses emerges, challenging certain truths. However, besides offering a different analytical lens, just as with the joker it entails risks, risks of further displacement of the less powerful. When amusing ourselves to death, it is necessary to consider exactly who is amused and who becomes excluded from the joke.

NOTES

1. *Kafeneia* are the traditional coffee houses. Since the mid-2000s the term has also been used to describe relatively cheap places serving drinks and small food dishes and often bears a more 'alternative' connotation.

2. For further information, see http://www.oliaros.com/kerameikos-metaxourgeio/.

3. For further information, see https://mitarakis.gr/drasi/ypan/766/766. Also see http://www.oliaros.com/?lang=en&p=374&title=KM-Properties-a-step-forward.

4. For further information, see http://www.oliaros.com/?lang=en&p=202&title= Athens-in-Crisis-Symposium-in-Benaki-Museum.

5. See, for example, http://prokopisdoukas.blogspot.gr/2012/02/blog-post_23.html.

6. See also http://www.imerisia.gr/article.asp?catid=26510&subid=2&pubid= 99573157.

Part 2

POWER, CULTURE AND IDENTITY

Chapter 5

Mashhad, Iran: Challenging the Concept of a Twenty-Four-Hour City

Atepheh Amid

The literature exploring the twenty-four-hour city concept, and the night-time economy more generally, has focused primarily on the West, western Europe, the United States and Australia in particular (Melbin 1978; Schivel-busch 1988; Kreitzman 1999). It is commonly argued that, with the advent of new technologies in the late nineteenth and early twentieth centuries, new forms of social activities emerged (Roberts and Eldridge 2009). Now, in the early twenty-first century with these technologies firmly embedded, Western societies have experienced a blurring, extension or reconfiguration of traditional time patterns (Koslofsky 2011), enabling everyday activities to take place at night. Hospitals, police stations, service stations and television and radio broadcasts as well as many shops, gyms and other forms of infrastructure now operate twenty-four hours or at least have extended opening hours (Crary 2013). Various factors, beyond simply technology, play a role in how we experience or develop cities at night, of course. The economic, social, political, climate and urban facilities influence the way people use cities, both before and after dark. In turn, age, social class, race and gender affect people's experience of the night-time city. A less-examined aspect is religion. As also documented in chapter 6, religion not only shapes the type of activities available after dark and who accesses them but also informs more general discourses about the night.

This chapter focuses on Mashhad, Iran, a city where the boundaries between day and night are perhaps less stable than in the West and where people perform commonplace activities late into the night. The discussion intervenes within some of the common tropes that have come to dominate studies of the night. Melbin's (1978) understanding of the *night as a frontier* is a case in point. He argues that the night which has developed in the United States 'may appeal to developing countries with meagre treasuries and

teeming populations of unemployed' (ibid., 20). Kreitzman's (1999) argument about twenty-four-hour chemists as 'an American phenomenon which
has not yet [in 1999] crossed the Atlantic' (ibid., 15) similarly stands out. In
these and similar accounts the night is cast as a decidedly Western phenomenon, bound up with equally Western discourses relating to technological
progress, economic expansion and 'freedom' to shop, consume and pursue
leisure at all hours. However, despite this pervasive belief that the twenty-
four-hour city is relatively new, and largely unique to the West, numerous
late-night activities have been taking place in Mashhad and other Middle
Eastern cities much earlier than the 1990s, including the opening of late-night
chemists. Conducting various kinds of routine activities at night is historically part of the social fabric of the city, as it is in many cities in developing
countries (Brunt 2003; Barrett 2010).

While nightlife in developing countries has been relatively under-examined
compared to the West, it does not mean that it does not exist. All cultures
have unique forms of time management, but the boundaries between daytime
and night-time activities are perhaps more visible in Western societies due
to a distinct relationship between time and moral order (Nottingham 2003).
In Iran and other Middle Eastern countries, this moral framework functions
quite differently such that 'normal' or everyday activities might seem as
equally normal taking place at night. As Scott (2009) argues, the definition of
'mundane' and 'ordinary' depends on the norms of each society, and what is
deemed everyday life in one society might be extraordinary in another. Urban
life in highly time-regulated Western cities (Rowe and Lynch 2012) stands in
sharp contrast to cities such as Dubai (Barrett 2010), Singapore (Su-Jan et al.
2012; Su-Jan and Kiang Heng 2013) and Mumbai (Brunt 2003) where commercial businesses and small-scale industries occur with a less-clear border
between daytime and night-time or work and leisure time (Brunt 2003). These
are examples of what Melbin calls *incessant communities* (Melbin 1978, 7)
and challenge assumptions about the conventional use of time in Western
societies.

This discussion begins by exploring the religious and cultural contexts
of the night in Iran. I then turn to a more detailed focus on the Imam Reza
shrine area in Mashhad where various services cater to both residents and
pilgrims across the day and night. While the city currently has an active and
vibrant late-night culture, mostly around the shrine, recent plans to develop
the area echo other concerns in this volume about gentrification and the
erasure of existing late-night cultures. In conclusion, I turn to some preliminary thoughts on nightlife from a non-Western perspective, arguing for a
more contextual understanding of how late-night areas work and the need to
examine how different practices, behaviours and the built environment come
together to produce distinctive late-night cultures and spaces.

NIGHTLIFE IN IRAN

The differences between daytime and night-time activities first appeared to me on a family trip to Yerevan in Armenia in 2008. As was our usual habit, my family and I went for a late-night walk to do some window-shopping. We went to the city centre but were surprised when we found it quite empty with all the shops closed apart from a few supermarkets and a few people walking on the streets. We started asking each other, 'Why is everywhere closed? Is there something wrong tonight? Maybe it's a public holiday and everybody has gone home early?' My experiences in London as a PhD student several years later were not altogether different. Despite its growing reputation as a twenty-four-hour city, my own experiences, such as being declined entry to shops that were soon to close, led to further questions about the ways that time is culturally contingent. Having been raised in Iran, where shops are routinely open until or even past midnight, London's relatively early closing times forced me to reconsider a whole range of customary behaviours, such as shopping late into the night.

Before exploring Mashhad in more detail, I want to start with a general overview of Iranian culture and how the night functions quite differently from the West. As chapters elsewhere in this collection demonstrate, to speak of the West in the singular ignores tremendous differences between and among Western cities. Roberts and Eldridge (2009) argue that there are multiple night-time economies operating in different cities and indeed different parts of the same city which can further support or be in opposition to one another. There are equally significant differences between Western cities and Western suburban or rural areas, especially in terms of how they function temporally. To speak of nightlife in the West does not, therefore, imply the West is singular or that there is a single nightlife or indeed single conception of the night. There are, nonetheless, several notable social, economic and religious aspects that allow a broad comparison to be drawn between the Middle East and more secular Western cities. For example, and as alluded to earlier, the ways in which time is linked to morality in Christian countries is a case in point. There are many other differences between the night in the West and elsewhere. In Iran, in common with other Middle Eastern countries, there are less visible boundaries between what are considered appropriate daytime and night-time activities due to a range of social, cultural, religious and climatic reasons (Brunt 2003; Barrett 2010). The terms *Shab-neshini* (soirée) and *Shab-zende-daari* (vigil) have their roots in Iranian literature and mean having meetings until midnight or until the next morning with families and social groups. In cities located in the warm climate of the Persian Gulf in the south of Iran, various forms of everyday activities such as shopping also take place at night when it is cooler. Night-time activities in Iran, while excluding activities not permitted in Islam such as consuming alcohol, gambling and going to nightclubs, will often include more everyday services. Climatic, religious and cultural habits therefore distinguish typical everyday and nightlife activities in Iranian and other Middle Eastern cities from many of the Western examples explored in this collection.

SOCIAL AND RELIGIOUS CONTEXTS

Iran is an Islamic country, with Islamic rules having been imposed since January 1979. Certain leisure activities, including any that are alcohol related, gambling and going to nightclubs, have been officially prohibited since this time. While these activities used to be common in Iranian cities before the revolution, now there are other practices and opportunities, some secular, some Islamic, that keep cities active at night. Shopping or visiting relatives late at night, for example, is fairly common. The official working hours in Iran are 8:00 a.m. to 2:30 p.m. with an optional second shift in the afternoon (BMI 2010; Aftab 2011). While this clearly suggests there is a daytime economy with specific norms around working hours, it does not mean the entire city follows suit. Shopkeepers and the self-employed, for example, have their own timetables, which vary across different times of the year and different parts of the city. They may work until 11:00 p.m. (Almas-e-Sharq 2012), and shops may stay open twenty-four hours a day. In summer, many shops extend their opening hours until midnight. This is greatly influenced by the type of facilities they provide. Convenience stores and newspaper kiosks are typically open until midnight or operate twenty-four hours. Restaurants and fast-food outlets close later than any other shops, and it is generally possible to have dinner at 2:00 a.m. or an early breakfast at 5:00 a.m. Bazaars are also an important component of Iranian culture (Kheirabadi 1991) and function as leisure spaces as much as providing necessary consumer products: clothes, home appliances and many other items. It is common to arrange to meet friends while shopping, turning the event into a wider social practice that might include meeting in cafes, dining out or going for a walk to browse late into the night.

The hours that we eat are subject to historical and cultural variations (Koslofsky 2011), but as Scott (2009) argues, family mealtime has remained an important time for social interaction, bringing people together and producing social order. One important feature of nightlife in Iran is visiting relatives and friends for various reasons and on different occasions. Family meals at night are arranged at least once a week, serving a similar function to Sunday lunch in many Western countries. While late dinners remain fairly quotidian, one of the most popular and at times controversial events at night is

Shab-e-Sher (poetry night). At these meetings poets, or people interested in poetry, meet up seminar-style to read poems (Rezvani 2005). More broadly, different kinds of ceremonies, including official receptions and also wedding ceremonies, are also held at night. Wedding ceremonies typically begin in the afternoon, the main part taking place in the evening, with a late dinner finishing around 2:00 a.m., followed by a private party.

While these practices demonstrate how participating in nightlife is fairly common, there are deeper, more historical events that continue to influence and structure perceptions and experiences of the night. Ibrahim (1982), for example, recounts the extent to which religion and leisure are entwined within Islam. He further argues that there was never such a 'stern attitude' towards recreation in Islam compared to other Abrahamic religions. And while gender plays a central role in shaping and determining leisure opportunities, gardens, sports and the celebration of religious festivals were playing, and continue to play, a key role in Islam. There is, of course, considerable variation within the Islamic world, as Martin and Mason (2004, 7) suggest, but like Ibrahim they argue that the recreational experiences of Muslims are shaped by less 'presumption against leisure'. Moreover, they go on to suggest that many sacred festivals and times in Islam 'have an important, and distinctive, leisure component' (ibid.).

The most well-known religious event in the Islamic calendar is, of course, Ramadan. Ramadan is the ninth month of the Islamic lunar calendar and is a fasting month for Muslims. Nightlife in Ramadan is similar across Iran and in other Muslim countries and is when every Muslim, excluding the sick or travellers, is forbidden to eat, drink, smoke or have sexual relations from dawn until sunset. While official working hours in Ramadan are reduced in order to help people fast during the day (Tabnak 2012), they are extended at night. Restaurants, food services, shops and leisure facilities such as cinemas or swimming pools are open from sunset to sunrise in order to serve more customers (Aftab 2012; Azad-Del 2012). During Ramadan urban life, from sunset to sunrise, is typically more active than during the day. Ibrahim (1982) also refers to coffee houses, television and social gatherings, while children roam the streets singing.

Not all late-night leisure is so clearly tied to religion, however. While having religious origins, *Norouz*, the Iranian New Year, has been celebrated for over 3,700 years to mark the spring equinox on 20 or 21 March. People prepare for *Norouz* ceremonies almost a month in advance, replacing old clothes and home appliances with new ones to celebrate the coming of spring and nature's renewal (Enjavi 1973; Shakourzadeh 1984; Razi 1992; Encyclopædia-Iranica 1996c). This custom results in extended opening hours for shops, food industries and transport. Several customs related to cleaning and cooking also mean working until late. *Norouz* holidays last for fourteen days after the festival, and cities are active across the day and night as residents and tourists shop, celebrate and prepare for the new year almost a month in advance. During *Norouz*, shops, restaurants, food services, leisure activities and even museums and historic places in large cities such as Shiraz and Isfahan extend their opening hours. An especially important date is *Charshanbe soori*, the Wednesday before *Norouz*, which dates back to at least 1700 BCE. The ceremony starts after sunset and ends in the morning and entails different rituals for each member of the family. Another night festival is *Shab-e-Yalda*, which is celebrated in Iran on the longest night of the year at the winter solstice on 20 or 21 December. On this night, parties with friends and relatives are held to eat nuts, special dishes and fruits (Enjavi 1973; Shakourzadeh 1984; Razi 1992; Encyclopædia-Iranica 1996b).

What these disparate examples point to is not simply different uses of the night but a fundamentally different way of understanding it. As noted earlier, a key difference to Western cities is that the night in Islam is not as clearly articulated with sin or immorality (Edensor 2015b). This is not to say the Christian Church has uniformly denounced the night. Koslofsky (2011) argues that the night in the Middle Ages of the West was not entirely articulated with evil. Ekirch (2006) also explains how many Christian festivals and events have taken place at night for centuries. He also notes, however, that even in the 1700s Roman authorities opposed artificial lighting at night, believing it to be 'a sacrilege against the divine order' (ibid., 72). As Edensor (2015b, 424) explains, 'In times of widespread religious beliefs and superstitions, night was commonly conceived as the domain of Satan in which his powers magnified and assorted evil spirits lurked: night demons, imps, hobgoblins, ghouls, boggarts, elves and witches'.

In Islam, however, the Qur'an was first revealed in Ramadan during the *Nights of Qadr*. Now, Shiite Muslims stay awake on the *Nights of Qadr* until sunrise, conduct specific rituals and read the Qur'an, only going to sleep after dawn. The night, in effect, is strongly associated with reflection and the divine. It is recommended in Islam to take part in mass prayers rather than performing individual prayer, and Muslims try to attend mass prayers when possible. Dawn praying time, which varies between 3:00 a.m. and 5:00 a.m. during summer and winter, further shapes Muslim cities and their activities in the early morning. Visiting cemeteries and graves of deceased family members, friends and religious leaders is also an important ritual for Shiite Muslims (Kheirabadi 1991; Rokni 2007). Glazebrook and Abbasi-Shavazi (2007) note that visiting shrines is 'heretical' for Sunnis, but for Shias it is recommended by prophets and other religious leaders as *Mustahab* (Allame-Majlesi), which means that duties are recommended or favoured in Islam but are not essential. Visiting shrines might be to take part in mass prayers similar to what happens in mosques, or to recite special prayers for the Imam or the leader buried in the shrine and supplicating to God through them. The importance of prayer and visiting shrines at various hours has had a clear effect on the nightlife of Mashhad, which this discussion turns to next.

NIGHTLIFE IN MASHHAD

Mashhad is the second-largest city of Iran after Tehran and is located on the north-east of the country with the shrine of Imam Reza (eighth Imam in Shiite Islam) at the centre of the city. The city has almost 3 million residents and attracts over 28 million pilgrims annually (IRNA 2011). Mashhad is very much shaped, influenced and reliant on these millions of pilgrims visiting the shrine each year. Night-time activities take place in different parts of Mashhad, similar to other large Iranian cities, but the pilgrims who arrive in the city at all hours of the day or night searching for accommodation and food and to go to the shrine, keep the city working over twenty-four hours. Visiting the shrine is highly recommended in religious texts, and residents of Mashhad also go to visit the shrine alongside the pilgrims. It is among the most common night-time activity of Mashhad's residents, largely because the shrine area is more accessible at night-time. After 8:30 p.m. the local traffic congestion charge scheme ends, and along with offices closing for the day, residents mix with pilgrims visiting the area. The crowded nature of the area in the daytime, which is partly due to nearby offices, the lack of parking spaces and public transport, makes daytime pilgrimage for residents living far from the shrine difficult or even impossible, further encouraging them to visit the shrine in the later hours.

Mass prayer times are among the busiest times of the shrine area drawing people from all around the city. Dawn mass prayer, which is conducted between 3:00 a.m. and 4:00 a.m., is a clear example. The sunset mass prayer is also very crowded as it is performed when offices are closed, and many residents and pilgrims attend. As well as prayers, it is a common tradition to bless marriages in the shrine by performing an unofficial marriage. Throughout the day and night couples and their families enter the shrine to perform these ceremonies. While the ceremony must respect the holiness of the shrine and pilgrims and thus be held in silence, the ceremony continues afterwards on the streets with a common tradition known as *Aroos keshan*, a circumambulation of the shrine after the wedding parties to bless the marriage. The couple's car is followed by their friends' and relatives' cars, beeping their horns on the streets around the shrine. Although this musical carnival is joyful for participants, it is subject to numerous complaints by residents of the shrine area.

Although many pilgrims might only spend their time in the shrine area, others visit shopping centres and other services or leisure sites in Mashhad. The whole city is subsequently influenced by the presence of millions of pilgrims, much like the studies of other pilgrimage cities conducted by Belhassen and

Almeida-Santos (2006), Finney et al. (2009) or Leppäkari and Griffin (2017). Pilgrims play a significant role in influencing local populations, customs and indeed the spatial form in the places they visit.

MASHHAD'S URBAN FORM AND DEVELOPMENT

Earlier, I spoke of the numerous religious events, festivals and customs that influence Mashhad. These are crucial to understanding how the city functions at night, as are the discourses of the night and how they contrast to the West. Pilgrims, the climate, the absence of strict regulatory hours for shops and the influence of Islamic laws are also key. However, the spatial organisation of the area is in itself equally of utmost importance in enabling and constraining the city's nightlife, especially around the shrine. In other words, the links between nightlife and the night-time economy are intimately bound up with geography and the built form. Events, histories, cultural differences and regulatory frameworks are important, but nightlife is also oriented by and enfolded in the spatial.

In much of the Western literature about nightlife, it is the presence of abandoned buildings associated with industrialisation that are central to developing nightlife. Milestone's account of Manchester's Northern Quarter, for example, captures the ways that small businesses, market stalls and the 'non-corporate' character of the area facilitated its burgeoning nightlife. Warehouses and factories similarly provided the alternative spaces for local cultural entrepreneurs to develop unique, alternative spaces. The narrative of Berlin follows a similar logic, whereby affordable rents alongside empty warehouses support the growth of the city's night-time offer. From New York, Hae (2011a) also explores how bars, cafes and clubs offer the necessary spaces for young creative entrepreneurs to meet, create networks, share information and socialise. In this section, I turn to how the built form of Mashhad similarly plays a crucial role in creating the conditions for nightlife to flourish.

The city of Mashhad was shaped historically in the tenth century as a pilgrimage destination as well as a trading post. The town developed around the shrine and included bazaars and houses to provide for the needs of pilgrims. When the shrine attracted more pilgrims and immigrants, the city expanded, and the bazaars also became more active. The history of urbanism in Iran indicates that there was always a mutual close relationship between mosques or shrines and bazaars. Mosques were located at the focal point of bazaars, and the bazaars provided the materials needed for religious activities for studying at the mosque. This is reflected in the close relationship between Imam Reza's shrine in Mashhad and the commercial streets around it, which were previously bazaars.

The connection between the shrine and bazaars, hotels and restaurants clearly demonstrate that religious culture, pilgrimage and the built form are important factors in shaping the local culture spatially as well as temporally, culturally and economically. It is also not simply the surrounding streets that are shaped by the shrine. It is difficult to disentangle the economy and culture of the shrine area from the rest of the city; the whole city needs to be active in order to provide for and support pilgrims' and residents' requirements around the clock. The pilgrims who arrive in the city at all hours are constantly moving between the shrine, accommodation, the bazaars and restaurants. Moreover, and as is explained further, this occurs in a dense urban area where pavements, small shop frontages, markets, shops selling pilgrims' requirements and food outlets all combine to give the area its character.

While there is a certain degree of spontaneity in terms of how this all fits together, the area has not by any means emerged organically. In order to meet the needs of pilgrims, large-scale redevelopment in the shrine area initially started in the seventeenth century, gaining pace after the 1920s when the whole country was subject to rapid modernisation (Vezarat-Maskan-va-Shahrsazi 1971). In an attempt to tackle some long-standing problems with infrastructure around the shrine, developers took their cue from the West. Centralised planning authorities took over the redevelopment process of Iranian cities, largely with the support of oil revenues. The result was rapid changes to the urban form of many other Iranian cities irrespective of users' point of view and the context, potential loss of social life and public dissatisfaction. This process continued after 1979 during the Islamic regime with almost the same pace but with larger plans. In Mashhad, an attempt was made in the early 1970s to turn the city into 'the most interesting of religious and pilgrimage centres' (Borbor 1974, cited in Izadi 2008), a desire that saw the redevelopment of vast swathes of land around the shrine and many commercial buildings, workshops and historical buildings being destroyed or regenerated.

As it stands now, the shrine area is a mix of various users, serving workers, residents and pilgrims. Residential use is the greatest land use in the shrine area, but it is also the primary location for government offices, business and commerce (Sherkat-e-Omran-va-Behsazi-e-Shahri 1999). Of particular importance, as different studies and surveys demonstrate, more than 72 percent of pilgrims staying in the shrine area are low-income pilgrims looking for affordable accommodation near the shrine (Sharafi 2006; Fakoori 2010; Rezvani 2010; Sazman-Mojri-Tarh 2010). As a result, many pilgrims stay in semi-legal or illegal rooms that residents provide. These are not only an affordable alternative to official accommodation; they provide accommodation for pilgrims who might not possess certain documents such as marriage certificates. In the peak of pilgrimage over summer, schools are also used as pilgrims' accommodation (Sherkat-e-Omran-va-Behsazi-e-Shahri 1999), providing large empty rooms with basic facilities such as toilets.

The shrine area is, in short, a complex and entangled site of commercial, residential and tourist usage that has been subject to numerous attempts to redevelop and modernise the area. While clearly of considerable importance to Mashhad, and the wider Islamic world, the area also attracts as many people as it detracts (Sherkat-e-Omran-va-Behsazi-e-Shahri 1999). For example, the area lacks many important urban facilities, especially compared to other parts of the city (Vezarat-Maskan-va-Shahrsazi 1992). However, many residents still choose to live near the shrine, despite all the problems they have to deal with. These people mostly have pilgrimage-related jobs and are dependent on the presence of pilgrims in the area. These contradictions make the shrine area like a small town within Mashhad, dependent but somewhat separated.

IMPACTS OF RPIS ON THE NIGHTLIFE OF THE SHRINE AREA

It is within this context that 'Regeneration and Reconstruction Plan of Imam Reza's Shrine-area' (RPIS) has been proposed. RPIS was instigated in 2000 with the aim of again 'modernising' the area in order to attract and accommodate more pilgrims. The RPIS area covers 309 hectares and affects 52,000 residents and an estimated 120,000 pilgrims who stay in the area every night (Tash-Consultant-Engineers 2008). The aim includes replacing small shops, guest houses and residents' houses with new multilevel shopping centres and hotels as well as street widening to accommodate increased traffic flow. Like many regeneration plans happening under the guise of modernisation, pedestrians are secondary to cars. The fact that these plans seriously impact on the local specific culture and economic success of the area has been ignored. Based as it is on the centralised planning system in Iran, the opinions of local users, including the residents of Mashhad and millions of pilgrims who visit it every year from all over Iran, have also not been considered (Sazman-Mojri-Tarh 2010).

Of more particular concern for my purposes here, RPIS will have a significant impact on nightlife in the affected area. The results of my study in the shrine area (Amid 2013) identified that nightlife in the area depends on several factors. These factors include the presence of large numbers of pilgrims but also, and of equal importance, various pedestrian activities at night and high pedestrian permeability. These factors are supported by the availability of different types of accommodation for pilgrims, based on their budget, various twenty-four-hour small businesses with active frontages and the street layout, which is currently pedestrian dominant. Equally, with the area active twenty-four hours a day, users perceive the area as safe, which leads to more people using the area day and night. These factors are interconnected, and removing any one element might weaken the whole. The urban design interventions proposed by RPIS under the rhetoric of modernisation, therefore, pose a significant threat to how the shrine area works. Various interventions such as the reduction of pedestrian permeability and activities, displacement of residents and workers, financial exclusion due to gentrification, the exclusion of everyday uses and loss of the perception of safety in the area are all contributing to changing the character of this important centre. Building more vehicular roads, widening the current streets, enlarging block sizes, displacing residents and workers and replacing small businesses with large residential and commercial complexes and residents' houses with apartments will fundamentally reshape the area spatially as well as temporally.

A whole range of interventions are already having a negative effect on how the area works. As noted, modernisation typically prioritises vehicular movement (Gehl and Gemzoe 2001), and as it imposes a large amount of traffic movement (Barnett 2011), the social life of the streets is affected (Jacobs 1961; Whyte 1988; Gehl 1996; Varna and Tiesdell 2010). Where large-scale demolition has already occurred, activities, and specifically night-time activities, have already decreased (Amid 2013). Since residential homes and guesthouses have been demolished, fewer pilgrims now stay in the area and, accordingly, many shops have reduced their working hours due to fewer customers. The vacant construction sites, produced as a result of large-scale demolition, have also reduced the perception of safety in the area. The condition has worsened where demolition has taken place without rebuilding or where the rebuilding process has taken many years. The execution of RPIS is indeed taking much longer than originally planned. The project started in 2000, but by 2010 only 2 percent was complete (Sazman-Mojri-Tarh 2010), and various properties in different parts of the area have been demolished and left vacant. This condition, and the fact that the whole area is subject to demolition and redevelopment, echoes what Kelling and Wilson (1982) call a sign of decay, which results in an urban area that *no one cares about*. This example of *planning blight* (Ravetz 1983) is, of course, temporary, and when the project is completed, all of the vacant areas will be developed. However, the developments constructed to date have not been successful at all in attracting pilgrims, leading to a decline of the nightlife areas (Amid 2013).

Despite these emerging problems, large-scale redevelopment remains the preferred method proposed by RPIS for revitalisation of the shrine area. In short, the whole area is set to be demolished and rebuilt in order to supposedly raise the quality of life. Also as well as shops and other retail or commercial offerings, buildings, which previously had a mixed-use function, have been demolished. As Bentley et al. (1985) note, old buildings can serve several uses, including commercial, residential and temporary accommodation at different levels. Most of the buildings in the shrine area had a high degree

of flexibility: garages functioning as small shops selling everyday requirements to residents and pilgrims, and large houses divided up into spaces for
pilgrims, for example. Their replacement with large, single-use buildings
has impacted on entire streets, and despite evidence of falling footfall (Amid
2013), there have been increased rates charged in the regenerated areas leading to greengrocers, bakeries, dairies, shops, garages, hardware stores and
ironmongers and other small businesses such as cheap souvenir shops giving
way to expensive jewellers or offices.

   RPIS, similar to other betterment plans in many cities across the globe (Ley
1980; Greene 2003; Harvey 2006; Watson 2009; Zukin, in Sevilla-Buitrago
2012, 467), is being conducted in the name of raising the quality of the
shrine area as the main destination for pilgrims, providing central commercial
premises and facilitating traffic movement. These are all important goals;
however, as discussed by Izadi (2008), the plans have been mostly conducted
to seek profit by taking highly desirable land from small traders and raising
land value through redevelopment. RPIS, also in common with other betterment plans or tourism industry plans in global cities (Hamnett 1984, 1991;
Kaminer et al. 2009; Watson 2009; Lees et al. 2010), has resulted in pricing
out and marginalising the majority of local people. Further issues, including
spatially and culturally disconnecting users of the area from their neighbourhood, community and social ties, are also similar to other international cases
(Davidson and Maitland 1997; Greene 2003; Harvey 2006; Cabannes et al.
2010; Bouzarovski 2011).

   The consequences of the plans to erase much of the built environment
around the shrine have thus been far-reaching. For the purposes of the discussion here, perhaps one of the key factors has been the effect on public life.
Public life is developed in public spaces, and it is not possible to produce
a successful public space without considering its social or physical context
(Sennett 1974; Zukin 1995; Ehrenfeucht and Loukaitou-Sideris 2007). The
shrine area has been shaped throughout history by interaction among pilgrims
visiting it and residents who live or work nearby to serve them. Erasing
certain public areas, or moving key facilities off the streets and into covered
areas such as new shopping malls lacking active relations to the street, will
impact on the opportunity for active life, during the day and night. Certainly,
other people will move into the area; however, as my own work in the area
demonstrates (Amid 2013), diversity, in spatial terms, is being compromised
by the blanket approach to redevelopment.

   The existing area emerged as a result of cultural, spatial, religious and economic conditions, and the character of the area, echoing Massey (1997), is a
complex, four-dimensional time-space. Urban design is a four-dimensional
tool, with time as its fourth dimension (Carmona et al. 2010). In a twenty-
four-hour society buildings and spaces function in a 'poly-chronic' way
(Tiesdell and Slater 2006, 140), which means that they might be used at

different times for various activities. Carmona et al. (2010, 241) suggest that planners need to appreciate and consider 'time cycles and the time management of activities in space'. Planners may need to prohibit some activities at certain times to avoid conflicts, separate them in time to reduce congestion or bring them together to allow connection and sufficient density of usage (Lynch 1984, 452). Also planners need to consider that raising the quality of spaces and safety at night is as important as raising their quality in the daytime (Rogers et al. 2008), and provision of an active nightlife is necessary for creating a successful public space (Cullen 1961; Llewelyn-Davies 2000).

In many gentrified and gentrifying cities, the loss of certain public spaces and buildings such as bars and nightclubs is having a detrimental effect on nightlife. Equally, as many critics have explored (Hae 2011a), gentrification, which typically prompts this erasure of nightlife, results in tensions between newer residents and existing forms of culture. The situation in Mashhad echoes but differs from many of these accounts. In Mashhad, nightlife did not develop out of post-industrialisation. Its nightlife did not result from bohemians discovering traditionally working-class areas and opening small venues for like-minded people. It also did not emerge from a neo-liberal drive towards deregulation whereby permissible hours of operation or the number of venues allowed encouraged economic development at night. Nonetheless, like Manchester, Barcelona or Berlin, the nightlife of Mashhad owes much to the enfolding of culture with geography, a geography that, until now, has lent itself to multiple users and uses. The idea of a twenty-four-hour active area includes varying types of land use, building type and size, form, age, tenure and urban grain (Tarbatt 2012) and various users from residents and visitors of different age and social groups who will use the area at various times (Jacobs 1961). Social life increases in diverse public spaces through mixed use, active frontages (Whyte 1988; DCLG 2012; Tarbatt 2012) and small businesses in the context of residential areas (Talen 2009; Tarbatt 2012). The twenty-four-hour activities in the shrine area very much reflect this ideal model. The area allows different users including residents, workers and pilgrims to use the area throughout the day and night.

CONCLUSIONS

The boundaries between daytime and night-time activities are culturally specific, and Iran demonstrates that the night is not necessarily a 'wild frontier' (Melbin 1978) dominated by 'hedonistic consumption' (Gallan and Gibson 2011, 2514). While Shaw (2015b) has questioned the frontier metaphor in conceiving nightlife, it is still often conceived in the West as a Western phenomenon that finds roots in economic expansion and a discourse of freedom and free choice. In this account, the night is also understood as having been made possible by technological development, specifically street lighting (Schlör 1998) which, again, began in the West before being exported to other countries (Melbin 1978). However, some parts of the world experience different forms of everyday and every-night activities despite having a lower technological base (Brunt 2003). In these places, there is also a different awareness of daytime and night-time boundaries.

It is equally worth noting that the discourse of nightlife, the 24/7 society or the twenty-four-hour city is typically framed by a sense of linear progress. This characterisation ignores, however, that some interventions in urban planning or development might have a reverse trend on the nightlife of a city (Nottingham 2003), and nightlife developed in some time periods might be decreased in a later period (Brunt 2003). The people who use the city at night might also change at various historical times (Nottingham 2003) or indeed in different places. Again, the Western focus in much nightlife literature remains on young people, which does not entirely resonate in pilgrimage cities such as Mashhad. Although these common assumptions about the night might be true in individual cases, none of them are necessarily true and applicable to the whole world. Nor is it a given that the nightlife in a city will improve when it technologically develops. And, as this chapter has also demonstrated, when a city achieves something close to an active twenty-four-hour economy, it will not necessarily keep it forever.

The twenty-four-hour society has become a trope of modern life as much derided as it is celebrated, but there is no global prescription for producing a twenty-four-hour society since it is a dynamic context-based concept. This chapter, by revealing a significant gap in the literature of the twenty-four-hour society and night-time economy, has highlighted the importance of further investigation into the multifaceted set of *nocturnal lived experiences* in non-Western countries (Rowe and Bavinton 2011, 817). This chapter also underlines the importance of considering the durability of local night-time economies, which can be endangered by careless urban interventions. Future regeneration plans should be based on the local context, consider social and cultural factors and investigate the drivers of an area's local nightlife in order to discover the important factors that can provide potential improvements in the area's nightlife. These influential attributes are local and context based and cannot be internationalised and applied worldwide. This idea becomes more necessary in developing countries where large-scale redevelopment plans take place with less awareness and consideration of the local nightlife of cities. Mashhad remains an active and buyout city after dark, sometimes long after the shops of Berlin or London have closed, but recent developments in the area demonstrate how tenuous nightlife can be, and the extent to which it emerges out of a complex, multifaceted entanglement of culture, geography, history and religion.

Chapter 6

Cairo Nights: The Political Economy of Mahragan Music

José Sánchez García

'We made music that would make people dance but . . . also talk about their worries'. Alaa al-Din Abdel-Rahman, better known as Alaa 50 Cent, stated this to Ben Hubbard, a *New York Times* journalist, for his article 'Out of Egypt's Chaos, Music Rebellion' in May 2013. The quote, in part, explains the appeal of *mahragan* music, a genre popular among lower-class youth in Egypt. The discussion that follows explores the social, political, cultural and economic meaning of *mahragan*.

Dar as Salam is a popular neighbourhood of approximately 100,000 people located in front of the island of Dahab in Cairo. Every year, informal neighbourhood networks organise the *Sidi Al Agami mulid*, which is celebrated in the second week of the month of *Jumada al Thani*.[1] For the *mulid*,[2] informal youth networks in the quarter rent portable DJ equipment and hire disc jockeys such as those commonly found at local weddings. The DJ mixes *inshad* songs, *shabi* tunes and electric rhythms, and, echoing Alaa 50 Cent's quote beginning this chapter, will improvise lyrics about conditions related to their everyday life such as local social constraints and aspirations.[3] The result is a musical form that is informally produced and consumed by predominantly male, lower-class youth. Like kuduro in Angola, Raï in Algeria or rap in Palestine, this could be understood as *resistance music*. In this specific case, the music and lyrics denounce social and class inequalities in Egypt, as *shabi* singers did during the 1980s and 1990s. Its continuity from the *shabi* music legacy is crucial for understanding why the local dominant classes consider such music produced and consumed by Cairene male, lower-class youth as 'vulgar' and 'uncultured'. However, their disdain for this kind of music also has much to do with the fact that this musical expression – which is popularly called *mahragan* music – challenges the marginalisation of Cairene lower-class youth. It further challenges the local leisure consumption opportunities

99

and patterns (re)produced and controlled by both the locally and nationally dominant class. In other words, the main concern of the dominant classes in Cairo would be the disruption *mahragan* music represents to mainstream neo-liberal market rules in contemporary Egypt, and everyday life.[4] Following Schielke (2015), we find that everday life in contemporary Egypt is deter-mined mainly by global capitalism. While opening up horizons of hope for those who have 'adapted' to the new world, it provokes deep anxieties about the future for those considered 'misfits': as young men who live in certain quarters are represented.

For young men in popular quarters of Cairo, *mahragan* music has become an important media form through which to criticise their marginalised situ-ation since the mid-2000s. Recorded *mahragan* music was already popular with all social groups after the events of 2011, having spread across the city and becoming a cultural form associated with counterculture discourses. Its 'minute of glory' was in 2012, when some popular DJs and singers were taken to London where some Western journalists and documentary makers were looking for something akin to an Egyptian 'revolution rock'. Diverse social projects such as *Cairo Calling* were even funded by the British Coun-cil (see http://music.britishcouncil.org/projects/cairo-calling). Six years after 2011, however, *mahragan* has been marginalised once again as a result of its current association with secularism and the religious ideological orientations of Cairo's urban nightscapes.

This chapter examines how *mahragan* producers and consumers (re)pro-duce informal social spaces to organise their own night 'parties' – the literal translation of the term *mahragan* – in Cairo. The discussion argues that these popular raves represent an alternative to the otherwise-typical cultural marginalisation of Cairene young, lower-class men. The chapter provides an insight into how the independence that the *mahragan* represents and affords these young men embodies a direct challenge to forms of state sovereignty and neo-liberal governance in contemporary Egyptian culture.

CLASS MARGINALISATION, LEISURE TIME AND *MAHRAGAN*

According to Wacquant (2007), marginalisation processes are not residual, cyclical or transitional but are instead organically linked to the most advanced sectors of the contemporary political economy, and notably to the financiali-sation of capital. Marginalisation is understood here as a process in which certain attitudes, ideologies, values, practices, discourses and beliefs are *excluded* from the public sphere. That is to say, it is a process that entails symbolic, cultural and material elements that erase, deny and subordinate some groups, such as young, lower-class men in Egypt. As Saad remarks, we may consider two kinds of marginalisation processes affecting this demographic: cultural and social marginality (Bayat 2013).

An exploration of leisure activities of young people of Egypt provides insights into this marginalisation. The results of the SAHWA Youth Survey (2016) in figure 6.1 shows that the leisure time practices of young women and men in Egypt are mainly related to group activities and social relationships. The use of the Internet is also directly related to their sociability practices: a significant 64 percent use the Internet to participate in social networks, while 57 percent of the 9,860 SAHWA Survey respondents use it to chat with friends. In terms of other leisure practices and industries such as attending the cinema, theatres, concerts, clubs, sports spectacles or exhibitions, a wide range of difficulties mean youth cultural consumption is virtually nonexistent. Their lack of economic autonomy, labour difficulties and financial responsibilities to their family are the most significant reasons that explain social and class inequalities regarding the level of access to entertainment and cultural facilities. While beyond the scope of this chapter, poor transport and mobility options, issues with infrastructure and other governance issues also play a part in shaping leisure opportunities and constraints (Sánchez García and Feixa 2016).

This unequal access to leisure confirms one of the main theses argued throughout this anthology. As in many other global cities, nightscapes in Cairo are clearly segmented socially, racially and spatially. In the case of urban nightscapes in Egypt, this disjuncture is clearly associated with class. But while one can easily find night-time leisure activities oriented

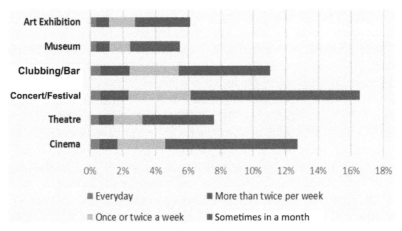

Figure 6.1. Youth cultural consumption in Egypt (2016). *Source:* **SAHWA Project. Graph constructed by author.**

to upper- and middle-class youth in central areas of Cairo or Alexandria, a number of other *hidden* nocturnal leisure activities take place in informal neighbourhoods and alleys across both cities. These more informal spaces are, importantly, where *mahragan* music plays a fundamental role in establishing politically alternative agendas for Cairene lower-class youth. This group creates at the same time a space where its own discourses about its everyday reality(ies) are freely produced and reproduced (and consumed). In other words, *mahragan* music allows Cairene lower-class youth to position (and sometimes self-engage) themselves politically in the Egyptian public sphere.

Beyond the difficulties lower-class young men in Cairo experience accessing other forms of leisure and cultural spaces, the marginalisation of *mahragan* music is typically based on lyrics directly referring to upper, middle-class Cairenes, who widely ignore the multiple, often-contradictory moral registers in Egyptian society and the complex desires shaping the everyday lives of (young) people. One could easily have the impression that the country is under a secular-liberal form of governance that de-emphasises political and economic constraints. However, state-led culture in Egypt aims to represent the nation globally as Arab, secular, liberal-oriented and free of complex cultural, social, generational or religious contradictions. This explains why, in the view of the dominant classes, *mahragan* music must be presented as simply a result of *ignorance* and *backwardness*. The Egyptian government seeks to base 'the truly Egyptian music' on the best of Western musical practice, mixed at the same time with local elements, thereby authentically embodying Egypt's specificity and cosmopolitanism. In turn, truly Egyptian music cannot include themes deemed vulgar or distasteful, that is, the third-party-banned trilogy of contemporary Egyptian cultural production: sex, religion and politics. This is a trilogy that *mahragan* players often use in a similar way to the Western rock music scene (sex, drugs and rock and roll). In these terms, the marginalisation of young, lower-class men is not related specifically to the lack of leisure structures available to them but a political marginalisation of the material culture they produce and consume.

Some informal expressions of social, political, cultural and even generational resistances carried out by youth from informal neighbourhoods of Egypt's largest cities such as Cairo and Alexandria have been long seen as 'dangerous' by most Islamic discourses in Egypt. That is to say, from official *shayks* to Salafist preachers (but with the exception of Sufi brotherhoods), the 'official' concerns are focused on counteracting the immorality of specific, informally produced, highly politicised youth-oriented film and music productions. Both *shayks* and Salafist preachers argue that such youth-led, informal, politicised cultural products could put at risk the process of building the *umma*.[5] Dominant Islamic discourses currently operating in Egypt about what constitutes good art and culture, and the potential of this good art and culture for civilising the nation, align with the dominant discourses of Egyptian cultural institutions, which also resonate with those of the European Enlightenment and Modernity. This long-standing cultural policy affiliation and orientation is akin to being 'cultured'. The opposite of culture (*thaqafa*) is ignorance (*jahl*), and this is how Cairene *mahragan* artists are stigmatised, as also occurred with *shabi* singers. This is the current political context of popular music in Egypt, which has often been used as a 'bargaining chip' between the state and Salafist groups, which dominated the political life of the country before the events of 2011 (Schielke 2006) but have since become marginalised once again.

THE AESTHETICS OF MAHRAGAN: SOME NOTES BEFORE ENTERING THE NOCTURNAL RAVE

The introductory section of this chapter has shown how *mahragan* can be understood as an informal creative practice that is produced and consumed in opposition to formal cultural circuits existing in Egypt, such as *shababiya*, which is the state-promoted music for young people. *Shababiya*'s songs performed by mainstream artists like Amr Diab or Cairokee (among others) sound very similar to global dance music and may be seen as an elite, state-led method for reviving *inshad* songs. In contrast, *mahragan* incorporates elements of both *shabi* music and traditional *inshad* songs that are rearranged and re-signified from a generational and classed perspective. The melodies acquire the atmosphere of Sufi spirituality, are full of emotional overtones and are enhanced with repeating known religious convictions and pious, deeply ambiguous formulas deployed by the DJs. In *mahraganscapes*, the love for the Prophet and the *wali* can be perceived as unrequited love, frustrated by the strict gender relations that are still in place today and imposed by the social order in Egypt. That is why most verbal and nonverbal expressions of *mahragan* are simultaneously associated with traditional *inshad* songs (Sánchez García 2010).

Mahragan is also connected with notions of *authenticity* and *heritage* for Egypt's young lower classes through the use of both *shabi* and *inshad* music mentioned earlier. Although the latter are related to events occurring in other places and to other styles across the Islamic world, both music styles are perceived as typically Egyptian and serve as markers of identity. Because such a cultural authenticity takes advantage of some local heritage (like using some elements of traditional *inshad* songs), *mahragan* is tolerated by adults of *shabi* classes, despite the profanity and vulgarity that can be heard in some songs. Through the use of electronics, sampling and remixing, *mahragan* creates genuine material with various vocal styles and themes such as sexual frustration, informal employment and the search for narcotics.

After what has been explained to this point about *mahragan*, it should not be seen as a form of Islamic culture that has shaken the Muslim world; neither is it a form of new World Music rooted in the Sufi Islamic tradition. *Mahragan* is, as a musical style without concessions to Western tastes, far from both the delicate ethnic melting tones of World Music and the new, refined, recently emerging Islamic music scene. In contrast, it is grim, sharp, playful and ambiguous, like the urbanscapes where *mahragan* players and consumers live, which are associated with bad taste, vulgarity and the poorer classes.

Mahragan is widely disseminated through the sharing of memory sticks and MP3 devices among its followers. It is also uploaded to social media platforms such as YouTube. In doing so, its followers become active agents of a certain complex, nonlinear, variegated but particular cosmopolitanism, which is further connected by re-signifying notions of authenticity and the heritage of local culture. Some *mahragan* recorded music has spread across other urban spaces of the city and other social groups as well – even when conducting fieldwork in a shopping mall, it was heard. This has allowed for the dissemination of its political message to non-marginalised groups in Egyptian society. In sum, the formal and informal dissemination of *mahragan* music and its increasing popularity, especially since 2013, have enabled it to go beyond its 'craddle': a tiny dance floor in an informal neighbourhood of Cairo until the presidency of el-Sisi. Despite this, *mahragan* is still conceptualised according to class hierarchies for young *shabi* groups in Egypt and continues to function as a kind of ethnic marker as *ibn al balad* (son of the homeland) (El Messiri 1977). This is of critical importance to the spread of counter discourses in post-Tahrir Egypt where young bloggers, football fans and any kind of youthful political critique are forbidden and violently repressed by the neo-liberal, G20-supported regime of General el-Sisi.

In sampling and remixing both traditional Sufi popular *inshad* songs (though not its 'cultured version' promoted by the Egyptian Ministry of Culture) and *shabi* music (but not the youth Arab mainstream music), *mahragan* followers, singers and musicians produce what Willis describes as a 'common culture' (1990). The creation of what one could call *mahragan*-grounded aesthetics, following Willis, allows for an understanding of this cultural form as linked to local semantics, constituting a response to other youth mainstream styles such as *Shababiya*. The aesthetic framework becomes visible in ways that also transform body image, dance forms and everyday behaviour in comparable terms to rap and hip-hop. Long hair, baseball caps and T-shirts of football teams may seem exotic to neighbours, and drug and alcohol use in their meetings can facilitate the belief that this is a deviant social order.

The lyrics of *mahragan* music also changed when the anti-Mubarak uprising erupted in January 2011. At that time, Abdel-Aziz, a *mahragan* player, sang a song called 'The People and the Government'.

> The people and the government, the machine guns and clubs Egypt rose up, and even those who didn't steal dove into it.
> I'll talk about those standing, the survivors and the dead.
> I'll talk about the church, the mosque and the Brotherhood. The people want the fall of the regime. The people want five pounds cellphone credit.[6]

After Egypt's Tahrir Revolution in 2011, *mahragan* lyrics were politicised and attracted different social groups and generations even if 'you don't understand three-fourths of the lyrics, but then you hear something good and realise the whole song relates to you', as a forty-seven-year-old coffee waiter explained. This raises the main danger for General el-Sisi's regime: the capacity of *mahragan* to extend a resilient political discourse like rap in the United States or Paris's banlieues, that is produced by *deviant* male youth in neighbourhoods of the largest cities of the country. In short, *mahragan* is simultaneously perceived as something intrinsically Egyptian, as was *shabi* music of the 1980s and 1990s and, like before, potentially dangerous by the Westernised middle and upper classes: 'We made music that make people dance but also talk about their worries', commented Alaa al-Din Abdel-Rahman, also known as Alaa 50 Cent, a twenty-three-year-old *mahraganian*, during my fieldwork: '[In] that way everyone can listen and hear what is on their minds'.

MAHRAGAN: POPULAR RAVES IN CAIRO NIGHTS

Mawālid, wedding nights and 'hypernights'[7] are the main popular spaces used to perform *mahragan*.[8] These festivities have a multitudinous character and, at the same time, they are ambivalent events. Sufis can be appreciated for the religious fervour of their rituals, while the neighbourhoods stage and perform a sense of collective identity during *mulid* carnivalesque street parades, where government authorities are openly criticised. As Schielke remarks (2003), the *mulid* is criticised by its own order, flexible and ambiguous, as well as by the kind of activities it entails, as described later. Its *uncultured* and *vulgar* character is widely claimed by state-led cultural actors, official institutions and several Islamist groups, who advocate for its prohibition, as an 'invention' (*bid'a*). The effect of these criticisms has led to different attempts to reform these festivities. First, state-led cultural institutions have made an effort to transform the festivities into events showing a more civilised, organised appearance. Despite this, their character has been considerably modified, especially in recent years, largely due to the introduction of new *shabi* practices, which have symbolically transformed the *mulid* into a place where there is a suspension of the quotidian order. The *mulid* is therefore opposed not only to the laicism of Western cultural hegemony as well as Islamic puritanism but also to the imposition of both kinds of moral values in the everyday life of local neighbourhoods.

Despite the dominance of Islamist opinion, and that contemporary Egypt considers *mulid* as religiously heretical, there is no doubt about its cultural authenticity – *asl'* – in terms similar to other types of manifestation of popular religiosity in the country. In addition, *mulid* is categorised as a *shabi* cultural activity that influences the participants beyond the rigorist understanding of religion among Salafist and other Islamist groups. During the festivities, the reign of the *shabi* is decreed, and participants are forced to follow 'correct' behaviour such as eating with their hands and showing solidarity and hospitality to pilgrims and indeed all people who might wish to participate in the festivities. Therefore, the *mulid* is a way of internalising the ideology and the symbolic referents that popular counterculture proposes. This is one of the main reasons why young men feel strongly attracted to participate in this festivity, in that it corresponds with the potential for political rejection of the hegemonic discourses of the current authoritarian regime and oppressive social order.

In festive periods, some young people in Dar as Salam take over an empty space in the neighbourhood and install portable sound and light systems. The informal networks established over the year allow for the collection of donations to rent the equipment which is similar to that used by DJs at weddings. In these time-spaces, young men dance an adapted *dhikr*,[9] with movements of the arms and hands similar to rap and breakdance. Young people move beyond the limits of what is normally allowed under the current social order in Egypt, blurring the division between the sacred and profane, and attempt to reproduce the states of mind achieved in the Sufi *mulid*, but with an original character. They join up *the irreverent* and *the serious* but within limits. In spite of its ambiguous approximation to spirituality, the youthful *mulid*'s festive atmosphere allows the young and adult shabi generation to usually consider the celebration as *hallal*.

In Egypt, *farah* is a word that describes the festive atmosphere of a local wedding. It is the same word that is used to describe the atmosphere in street celebrations like the youth-led *mulid*. The general perception among participants is that *mulid* allows for the breaking of social boundaries. Music, dance and the use of one's body challenge the separation between genres, between 'the sacred' and 'the profane', between 'the public' and 'the private', between *haram* and *hallal*. However, it preserves the spiritual character associated with traditional Sufi joyful demonstrations, making these youth-oriented *mawālid* a particular but intrinsic element of veneration to God, the Prophet and the *wali*. Without doubt, the ambivalence of youth-oriented *mawālid* can seem as if they are dramatically different to the Sufi *mawālid*. The young *mulid* represents a temporary transition from the profane to the abnormal and sacred order (Leach 1971). During the *mulid*, the world is good and free of oppression and greed, quotidian worries disappear and there is no anxiety about the future. These transgressions of the social order in relation to gender, generation and religious practices allow for the creation of a new, 'asecular discourse' (Agrama 2012), that is to say, the religious and secular simultaneously.

When the party progresses in these informal neighbourhoods' hypernights, *bango* (marihuana) and alcohol help young people to find the *tarab*[10] through trance rhythms like those used in *dhikr*. The presence of young women dressed in a way that is considered decent and modern at the same time (a head scarf to conceal the hair with wide blouses and jeans) is not uncommon. The young men dance and tease the young women by encouraging them to keep up with the sensual dances in the manner described earlier. The young women appear to be embarrassed, but at the same time they demonstrate pleasure at being an object of desire for their partners. It is a festive atmosphere, without restrictions, and young men dance in circles in which those occupying the centre enter into competitions. This is done to demonstrate their skills in front of the young women and involves exaggerating their virility. The DJs then improvise oral praise to the neighbourhood's saint, the Prophet, God and the main sponsor of the party. Dancers (men) respond to him in chorus while they follow the beat and the rhythm by letting themselves go, moving the trunk back and forth until they reach exhaustion. This young person's *dhikr* is enjoyed thoroughly, but it is not taken seriously as a mystical ritual. It becomes nothing more than a frantic game fuelled by the mixture of modern *inshad* music (*mahragan*), alcohol and *bango* (marihuana). Their simultaneous admiration and irreverence for the Sufi music is an ambiguity they incorporate into their everyday life, save it might offend the sensibility of any pious participant.

The celebration in the terms described earlier subsumes its participants, assuming a radical alteration of their ordinary life in neo-liberal Cairo. The festive delirium is such that participants appear to be in a trance, one where their ordinary personality has been supplanted by another. In these terms, the session functions in a manner similar to a vaccine, which injects into social life a controlled and harmless dose of transgression, inversion, orderly chaos due to the mixing of genders especially; it is situated in the plane of the utopian and the impossible in everyday life.

BEYOND THE RAVE: THE POLITICS OF MAHRAGAN

Mahragan recorded music is the genre resulting from the transformation of Sufi *mulid* music into dance music of varying rhythms that jumped to the Cairene musical scene in 2011. The previous section has shown how the marginalisation of *mahragan* music could be explained as a liminal space between secularism and religious ideological orientations that takes place in public nocturnal spaces during the celebration of a *mulid*. It is also where a complex and kaleidoscopic relationship between religion and politics is played out, which has become a key feature of currently *asecular* Egypt. Following Agrama (2012), the grammars and practices of *mahragan* players and consumers are expressed in secular or religious terms but embrace neither of them. As the author argues, 'In the sense that it stood prior to religion and politics and that it was indifferent to the question of their distinction, the bare sovereignty manifested by the initial protests stood outside the problem-space of secularism' (Agrama 2012, 29). *Mahragan*, in other words, provides young people from informal neighbourhoods new forms of understanding and seeing the(ir) world.

On the other hand, while it was after the Tahrir Revolution in 2011 that *mahragan* performers such as DJ Islam Chipsy could play in Al Azhar Park (a leisure complex between Muqattam and El Hourreya quarter in central Cairo), today *mahragan* music has turned back again to the alleys in the informal settlements on the outskirts of Cairo. Both secular and Islamic authorities still continue today to criticise *mahragan* music with the same arguments that were employed before the January 25 Revolution: it is still understood as bad taste, vulgar and Western influenced. Importantly, viewing *mahragan* as inherently secular or religious is analytically insignificant in exploring ethnographically how 'the secular', 'the religious' and the normative assumptions implicit in both terms are examined in the ways individuals identify practices, things and even themselves in shifting social contexts.

It was in 2011 when *mahragan* spread from the alleys of poor Cairo neighbourhoods to malls located in central areas of the city, high-class weddings and even television programmes. At the same time, young, lower-class men and followers of *mahragan* music disseminated their (somehow politicised) ideas through social media channels. In contrast, state-led cultural programmes – which remain created, implemented and managed by upper-class urbanites – are strongly oriented towards promoting the idea of the Egyptian nation through arts in which Islam is only one aspect among many others. This is because the post-Tahrir Egyptian regime continues to see 'culture' as a 'civilising process' (in Norbert Elias's terminology) for the Egyptian *shabi* classes. But as stated previously, these state-led, policy-cultural programmes ignore the multiple, often-contradictory, moral registers and desires shaping the everyday lives of lower-class youth in Egypt. One example would be the number of claims made by secular-oriented officials and intellectuals work-ing in (or working for) the Ministry of Culture, who have widely argued the urgency of tackling initiatives to combat the *ignorance* and *backwardness* that *mahragan* represents. For the official intelligentsia, a hegemonic culture drawn on a mix between local elements and the 'best' of Western arts should permit one to successfully build a new Egyptian cosmopolitanism, socially, morally and politically sanitised. In the case of music, as an art, it may sup-port the creation of public taste through teaching arts to school children, designing beautiful buildings or products, films, songs or theatre sets.

This section has shown how *mahragan* challenges the sensibilities of many religious-oriented and secular-oriented urban elites, who clearly ascribe to the idea of deploying state-led projects to prevent the vulgarity of this music by civilising not only *shabi* music but also its related performative events such as those previously described (*mulid*). One example of this state-led strategy of moral sanitisation of popular youth cultural practices would be the gov-ernment support given to some DJs belonging to the official music scene in Egypt, such as Amr Diab or Cairokee. The el-Sisi regime has recently facili-tated national and transnational investment in the construction of this new politically, socially and morally sanitised music scene, fostering the rise of a new body of young entrepreneurial artists supported (and controlled) by the state. Many preachers promote a 'peaceful' capitalist imaginary of entrepre-neurial cosmopolitanism and personal success. This 'peaceful capitalist imag-inary', together with the state-led, sanitised youth music scene mentioned previously, is oriented towards producing and reproducing the new image of 'the Muslim': internationally successful, cosmopolitan, entrepreneurial, com-petitive, urban, educated, civilised and wearing the latest in Western fashion.

However, the new image of 'the Muslim' is far away from the semiotic world of *mahragan* players, producers and followers. For the latter, the capa-bility of breaking the secularist/religious dichotomy means the capability of contesting the neo-liberal, repressive, social and political orders in post-Tahrir Egypt. That is why, in defining as asecular the grammars and practices that *mahragan* producers, singers and followers carry out in the informal urban nights of Cairo, we can better understand the very complex, kaleido-scopic set of significances that *mahragan* music – seen as a cultural creation of lower-class youth – has today in the Egyptian public sphere.

SOME FINAL NOTES ON INFORMAL LEISURE AND MAHRAGAN

This chapter has shown how *mahragan* music in Cairo can be seen as an innovative and creative practice that young people in informal neighbour-hoods of the Egyptian capital have produced in order to negotiate their social, cultural, generational, political and economic marginalisation. In their immediate day-to-day activities, they struggle with sharing urban services, alternative economic strategies, alternative means of production and alternative ways for communicating their feelings, expectations and frustrations. They are reclaiming their 'right to leisure', transforming the well-known words of Lefevbre (1968) and his sense of 'the right to the city'. Following Bayat, *Maharagan*, as a cultural artefact, is a kind of 'youth politics' that can be 'viewed in terms of the conflicts and negotiations over claiming or defending youthfulness; but this is a politics that is mediated by the position of the young in class, gender, racial, sexual and other involved social structures' (Bayat 2017, 16). *Mahragan* 'prosumers' in Cairo have been creating social spaces to establish and self-manage their musical compositions, which represent an alternative to their political and cultural marginalisation. In turn, new technologies of information and communication and social media allow young *mahragan* prosumers to disseminate more widely their feelings against the adult hegemonic classes. The millions watching *mahragan* songs on YouTube become aware of the worries, aspirations and discourses of young, lower-class men residing in informal and popular neighbourhoods of Cairo. The night parties celebrated in the social space represented by weddings, *mawālid* and other special nocturnal festive events challenge the mainstream market and spatialisation of leisure consumption in Cairo.

The economy of *mahragan* music has meant the distribution of millions of informal copies of songs produced by the principal figures of the genre. These copies are mainly sold in Cairo's informal markets that have become alternative economic channels for those escaping from the control of both the state and the currently dominant neo-liberal market. In parallel, *mahraganat* music played in Cairo's popular quarters during night-time hours and listened to during the day may be seen as an expression of the capability of these young, male producers to break the hegemonic secularist/religious dichotomy not only in their leisure consumption but Egyptian society as a whole. The collective, popular sovereignty that the production and consumption of *mahragan* music represent contrasts with the repressive state sovereignty or 'bare sovereignty' in Agrama's (2012) terminology. Therefore, it would not be risky to suggest we see *mahragan* music as a cultural counterpart to recent processes of economic neo-liberalisation undertaken in Egypt before and after 2011's Tahrir Revolution, Western cultural colonisation and dichotomies associated with modernity such as 'the secular' and 'the religious'. In this sense, *mahragan* music under the currently repressive period has become the main cultural means for lower-class men in Cairo's informal neighbourhoods to reclaim the plenitude of their life expectations and experiences and protest against state and 'adult' repression.

Mahragan music means much more than simply making its followers and artists political subjects. It permits the creation of new, informal, unrepressed spaces of (self-)identification as well as providing new opportunities for (self-)empowerment in order to find ways out of their social class and the subsequent marginalisation imposed by the social order in Egypt. The dominant classes see *mahragan* music as a 'subjugated' knowledge without the required level of erudition to become part of the current morally and politically sanitised national-cultural project of Egypt. Moreover, and simultaneously as a result of this 'civilising process' in Egypt, the resulting marginalisation occurring in informal neighbourhoods in Cairo has undeniable consequences for youth subjectivation and lifestyles. In particular, Egyptian lower-class youth seem to have internalised the negative representations that circulate about their lifestyles, ideologies and tastes dominant in the mainstream media, but this does not prevent them from being attached to virtual social networks and using it for their own purposes. Marginality seems to also favour the feelings of distrust they feel towards specific institutions, which is expressed by the distancing of youth by the government's cultural initiatives. It should be noted that *mahragan* music does not question the dominant pillars of Egyptian society. While labour, school and family remain privileged spaces in which young people anchor their (self-)identity and their (self-)recognition, *mahragan* and *mawālid* represent a challenge to Cairo's mainstream, marketised, upper-class nightlife. In sum, while *mahragan* challenges the official channels of leisure consumption and political hegemonic discourses, it does not reject the dominant social rules of *shabi* classes.

NOTES

1. The Muslim calendar is lunar, and months begin when the first crescent of a new moon is sighted. As a result, months change their position yearly compared with the Western solar calendar. In any case, *Jumada al Thani* is the sixth month of the Islamic calendar.

2. The term *mulid* (pl. *mawālid*) has two dominant meanings. First, it refers to the time, place or celebration of the birth of a person, although it originally refers to the birthday of Prophet Muhammad or a saint (*wali*) and, also, the panegyric in honour of the Prophet. Colloquially in Egypt and Sudan, the term *mulid* designates a festival in honour of a saint. The tradition of celebrating the anniversary of the Prophet dates back to Fatimid times, although the celebration had an officialist political character that had little to do with the pilgrimages of the Sufi orders that, from the seventh century of the Hegira (XIII), attracted crowds to the cenotaphs of their main masters such as the founder of Ahmadiyah, Sayid Ahmed al Badawi, in Tanta. From these early days, they were associated with *futuwa*, youth associations that defended the neighbourhoods in which they lived.

3. In general terms, the *inshad* is related to Arab urban music of the first third of the last century (Al Faruqi 1993). The instrumentalists maintain their personality by expressing it in rich arabesques, including improvisations, facilitated by the flexibility in the musical form. They incorporate all kinds of modulations floating from one mode (*maqam*) to another, supported by the melodic rhythms of percussion (*qafla*). The player, through his chanting, seeks to abandon corporeality, in conjunction with those assembled, dissolving each other of their daily limits and reason (*aql*) that governs human affairs. The *inshad* is considered by listeners to be the archetypal Egyptian art whose emotional force dominates them and compels them to participate in the *dhikr* dance. With its distinctive genre and religious context, *inshad* may seem more traditional than other forms of musical heritage or be easier to identify by borrowing rhythms and modes from the entire Egyptian musical spectrum. On the other hand, *shabi* music is an urban genre (despite its rural roots) with a strong rhythmic pulse made by singers often (but not exclusively) male. It has been usually compared to Greek *rembetika* and Portuguese *fado*. Its main themes are bad luck, informal squatting, illicit sexuality and crimes of passion. Until recently, these songs, many of which are officially prohibited, avoided an explicit allusion to politics. However, its very nature usually means there is a strong sensitivity to the *shabi*, denouncing social and economic discontent (Ambrust 1994). It is a music style oriented towards workers living in the outskirts of Great Cairo and is characterised by making use of the dialect of the streets. Some interpreters see *shabi* music as the only one unadulterated by the outside world, compared to music modernised by instrumental changes, joining drum machines, drums, organs, synthesisers or electric guitars that characterise contemporary Egyptian music. However, it creates the opportunity to allow individuals to 'contest' the state since *shabi* has been censored by the Egyptian state in order to make much more visible than before the 'inculturate nature' of the Egyptian (young, but not only) lower classes. Moreover, *shabi* derives from the noun *shab*, people, always with a collective meaning that implies a great political bearing. Its manipulation by the Egyptian ruling class and Islamist political groups has been consistent since the beginning of the independence process in the twentieth century. On the other hand, *shabi* also designates a social group and refers to a wide range of native practices, tastes and patterns of behaviour in everyday life that has given rise to a musical style of the same name.

4. The liberal politics started in Egypt with the Saddat government, and policies on privatisations were fully completed by the Mubarak regime. See Ayubi (1999), Mitchell (1988) and Schielke (2015).

5. According to *the Oxford English Dictionary*, *umma* is the whole community of Muslims bound together by ties of religion. In a post-colonial political context, the concept has become an important transnational identity marker for members of the Muslim diaspora.

6. Five Egyptian pounds is about €0.70 and is the minimum amount for a mobile money charge.

7. Following Schnepel (2006), in hypernights, in contrast to hyponights, 'we find that actors are seeking to turn the phenomena, things, beings and actions of the nocturnal chronotopos (Bakhtin) into something which is more intensive and vibrant

and which represents an alternative or even counterpoint to the day. "Hyper nights" are nights which offer spaces for rebellious and even revolutionary forms of behaviour, spaces in which the normal, diurnal form of life, with all its behavioural patterns norms and moral values, is questioned, mocked and even transgressed' (Schenpel 2006, 8).

8. The practice of *dhikr* consists of forming a circle or two rows and facing each other. Invocations are repeated and accompanied by rhythmic movements of the arms, body and head again and again until one falls exhausted. This is accompanied by one or more nay players, a double flute other times and percussions, accompanied by singers of religious principles.

9. The dichotomy *hallal* and *haram* categorises all the practices of Islamic believers according to if the action is allowed (*hallal*) or forbidden (*haram*) by religious jurisprudence traditions. By tradition, I refer to all that it is intended to present as typical of the early times of Islam. It is a manipulation of certain elements by different groups involved in the discussion to determine what is Islamic (*hallal*) and what is not (*haram*), legitimising some actions and condemning others. In general, all these discourses are based on an encounter between *fiqh*, the Islamic jurisprudence, and the 'spontaneous structures' of which Boudhiba speaks (2004).

10. As Frishkopf points out (2001, 67),

The aesthetic concept of tarab finds in the Arabic translation. Narrowly defined, it refers to musical emotion and the traditional musical-poetic resources for producing it, especially expressive only singing of evocative poetry, in an improvisatory style, employing the traditional system of maqam (melodic mode). . . . Tarab also depends on consonant performer-listener interactions, in which experienced listeners (sammica) react to the music by expressing emotion through vocal exclamations and gestures, especially during the pause which follows the *qafla*. The singer in turn is moved and directed by such 'feedback'. Moreover, it is an intense musical enjoyment felt both by the audience and by the interpreter.

Chapter 7

Young People, Alcohol and Suburban Nightscapes

Samantha Wilkinson

INTRODUCING WYTHENSHAWE AND CHORLTON IN MANCHESTER

Over the past two decades, much of the research into alcohol consumption has been written in the context of the expanding night-time economy, which itself tends to focus on urban inner-city areas (e.g., Lovatt and O'Connor 1995; Chatterton and Hollands 2002; Hollands 2002). While research has been undertaken into rural drinking geographies (e.g., Leyshon 2008; Valentine et al. 2008), holiday destinations (Bellis et al. 2000; Briggs et al. 2011) and drinking at home (Holloway et al. 2008), very little has been said about public drinking practices in suburbia, especially among young people. A notable exception is the work of MacLean and Moore (2014); however, despite focusing on the atmospheric mobilities of suburban young people, their work is primarily concerned with young people accessing the city centre for their alcohol-related leisure experiences. This chapter moves beyond the contemporary geographical imaginary of drinking and nightlife as an urban and city-centre practice (Holloway et al. 2008) and instead explores marginal/peripheral *drinkscapes*, including bars, pubs, parks and streets, in suburban areas.

Drawing on an ethnographic study exploring the alcohol consumption practices and experiences of young people aged fifteen to twenty-four years, this chapter shows how suburban areas provide a very different drinking and night-time experience to more urban areas. Authors such as Bancroft (2012) have noted that young people's transitions to adulthood are bound up with individual and group relationships with drinking spaces. This is of particular relevance in this chapter where I explore the suburban drinking practices of young people from Wythenshawe and Chorlton, two suburban areas of

Manchester in the United Kingdom. As well as being the setting for diverse and heterogeneous drinking behaviours, there are clear classed spaces in these case study locations that young people actively choose to move between for their drinking experiences. Moreover, and most important, I demonstrate that suburban drinking spaces are not simply passive backdrops to drinking (Jayne et al. 2008). While there is still a pervasive belief that young people drink only out of boredom or in parks because it is cheap, the argument developed here suggests that specific sensory atmospheres constituted by smell, light and darkness, sound and temperature are very important to young people's suburban drinking choices. Young people are not passive to such atmospheres; they are active agents with the capacity to craft their own drink-scapes, drinking practices and drinking experiences.

The two areas that constitute the focus of this discussion are located in Manchester, a city of almost 2.8 million people. Wythenshawe was created in the 1920s as a garden city in an attempt to resolve overpopulation and depra-vation in the city's inner-city slums. It continued to develop up to the 1970s; however, the 1980s and 1990s saw a steady decline, high unemployment, decaying infrastructure, crime and problems with drug misuse (Atherton et al. 2005). Wythenshawe is eight miles south of Manchester city centre and has relatively poor transportation links (Lucas et al. 2009). There are distinct neighbourhoods within Wythenshawe, along with a town centre with various shops, supermarkets, hairdressers, pubs and a club. Numerous pubs have shut down in recent years, and in the existing pubs, CCTV is in abundance (Pubs of Manchester 2012). In addition to commercial drinking spaces, Wythen-shawe has twelve parks and eighteen woodland areas, which provide young people with ample opportunities for outdoor drinking. Wythenshawe's great-est claim to fame currently is that it served as the outdoor filming location for the Channel 4 series *Shameless*, which included shots of the local tower blocks and housing estates.

Chorlton, on the other hand, is a residential area approximately five miles from Manchester city centre. It is a cosmopolitan neighbourhood with tra-ditional family areas alongside younger, vibrant communities. The area has good road and bus access to and from the city centre, and it is situated within easy access to the motorway network. Due to the increasing number of bars and restaurants in Chorlton, a Pubwatch has been initiated, a partnership scheme where licensees unify as an independent group to pre-empt crime and antisocial behaviour in licensed premises (Young 2011). Chorlton is renowned for having a more bohemian feel than other parts of Manchester; it has a large number of independent bars and pubs, yet no nightclubs. The drinking venues are popular with both students and young professionals and include a mix of traditional pubs and modern bars (Manchester Bars 2017). Bars often have some form of music and are considered to have a relaxed door policy. The distinct drinking venues existing in each of the two areas demonstrate first and foremost that suburban drinking spaces are neither uniform nor homogenous, and this heterogeneity warrants further analysis.

DRINKINGSCAPES: THE PRODUCTION, CONSUMPTION AND (IN)FORMAL REGULATION OF DRINKING SPACES

Before going on to recount young people's perceptions of the suburban commercial and outdoor drinkscapes in Chorlton and Wythenshawe, I want to start by exploring the literature about typically Western drinking spaces. In contrast to the case study locations discussed in this chapter, alcohol studies and night-life studies more generally are predominantly interested in city-centre drinking practices and experiences, typified by a large body of work on the night-time economy (Holloway et al. 2008). The night-time economy is a term used to describe an expansion in the number of bars and clubs operating with extended licences into the early hours of the morning (Roberts 2006). Work on Britain's nightlife has been particularly focused on issues relating to young people's experiences of alcohol, drinking and drunkenness and wider issues about safety, security and policing. Chatterton and Hollands (2002), for example, examine issues around safety and security as well as *urban playscapes* such as youth-orientated bars, pubs, clubs and music venues in Britain's night-time economy. While their work continues to be valuable to nightlife scholars, underage drinking in licensed premises in the United Kingdom has become much less prevalent over recent years. Unsupervised alcohol consumption by young people has instead become more concealed, occurring either in private homes or in public spaces such as parks (Townshend and Roberts 2013). Government measures prohibiting people under age eighteen entering pubs, bars and clubs have therefore been successful in terms of barring young people from entering licensed establishments but has moved youth drinking into other spaces (Roberts et al. 2012). Despite this being the case, the study of outdoor drinking cultures, especially involving young people, is rare, and the specificities of open-space drinking in suburban spaces are poorly understood.

An exception to this current lack of critical research on outdoor drinking is the work of Townshend and Roberts (2013), who argue that while engagement with open greenspace tends to be deemed positive for young people's health and well-being, drinking outdoors and unsupervised in parks is often considered a risky behaviour indulged in by teenagers. Further, Russell et al. (2011) highlight the importance of woods and fields for young people's drinking practices as they are out of sight of police and parents. Leyshon (2008) also notes that informal drinking spaces, such as parks, provide arenas of performance in which young women's identities are constructed, negotiated and reproduced.

Townshend (2013) argues, however, that while drinking in parks is a widespread practice among young people, many disapprove of this behaviour, labelling it 'trampy' or 'chavvy', a British term meaning rough and working class. Townshend and Roberts (2013) go on further to note that many young people deem drinking in parks to be pointless, or *trying to be hard* in an attempt to camouflage low self-esteem. Some of the participants in their study of youth drinking practices also commented on the perceived dangers of consuming alcohol in parks, asserting that it could result in attacks, injury or being sexually assaulted (Townshend and Roberts 2013). A common concern was that while parks afforded some privacy, such privacy also meant help would be difficult to summon. As a result, some young people, particularly young women, avoided drinking in parks due to the prevalence of street drinkers. However, and while there was a degree of fear and concern around drinking in parks documented in Townshend and Roberts's (2013) study, those who admitted to doing so claimed it was a relatively harmless activity for which they were often harshly judged. From this study, it can be seen that young people seem to have mixed opinions concerning consuming alcohol in parks, with some young people considering it to be an activity unlikely to offend others, while other young people criticise the 'types' of people who consume alcohol in such spaces.

Streets in the United Kingdom are also important drinking spaces for young people who may not be permitted to consume alcohol in their home (or others' homes) and are forbidden from consuming alcohol in licensed premises (Galloway et al. 2007). Streets may be popular with young people for drinking because licensed premises are restrictive in many other respects. This includes age constraints but also their size, smell, noise, permissible behaviours and the types of entertainment provided (Pennay and Room 2012). Further, Madriaga (2010) highlights that some students with Asperger's syndrome find that spaces where students tend to congregate, such as student unions and pubs, are difficult spaces due to their hypersensitivities to sounds, sights and crowds. In the context of the United Kingdom, Galloway et al. (2007) contend that, while various forms of exclusion do play a role in decisions to drink outside, outdoor locations, be those parks or streets, also offer a distinctive appeal to alcohol consumers. Street drinking enables young people to feel socially and physically unrestricted, for instance, by playing games such as football or listening to their own choice of music. Further, drinking in outdoor locations enables young people to smoke cigarettes, which is banned in UK licensed premises, or to take drugs while drinking (Galloway et al. 2007). Further, some young people may prefer to drink in open public spaces such as streets simply because licensed premises are open to the public and young people cannot therefore be selective about who they are drinking with (Pennay and Room 2012).

Pennay and Room (2012) note that despite offering some choice and freedom to young people, there have been numerous attempts to prohibit drinking in urban public spaces, such as via the implementation of street drinking bans. However, these enforcements can simply lead to displacement, often resulting in drinkers moving to covert, less-safe spaces in which to drink. The advantages of public drinking, as well as the restrictions of consuming alcohol in commercial premises, suggest that some young people may choose, and even prefer, to drink outside, whereas for other young people it can be a forced event.

Street drinking takes place in other European cities. In Spain, while street drinking (known as *botellón*) has been going on for a number of years, its popularity increased in the late 1990s; the practice can now draw anything between a few dozen to over 1,000 young people (Perez-Fragero 2008). Mobile phones and social networks facilitate the *botellón* existing at such a large scale. The reasons young people cite for participating in *botellón* include the excessive price of drinks in bars and clubs, current youth fashion and the possibility to drink in the open air (ibid.). Like street or park drinking in the United Kingdom, *botellón* causes some friction in Spain, partially due to the noise generated and the fact that young people are not spending money in local bars and restaurants. In 2002, the Spanish government introduced a law, backed by heavy fines, banning drinking in the streets (Chatterton 2002).

A final and crucial point to draw out here is that drinking spaces, whether indoor or out, should not be conceptualised as simply static backdrops against which drinking experiences unfold (Duff 2012). Demant and Landolt (2014) conducted research into young people's alcohol consumption in Katzenplatz, a square located in Zurich, Switzerland. They found that rather than the square being a pre-formed drinking space that determined drinking practices, it *became* a comfortable drinking space for young people due to the *thrown-togetherness* of disparate factors, including the square's location, the availability of alcohol and the privacy and intimacy afforded by the space (Demant and Landolt 2014). Demant and Landolt (2014) similarly explore alcohol consumption on the street within the vicinity of nightclubs. The authors recognise that, during a night out, young people often exit and (re)enter clubs to drink the less-expensive alcohol they have hidden outside on the streets. As the authors deduce, however, streets are considered to be more than 'going outside to grab a drink'; they also become part of the party zone, blurring the boundaries between inside and out. What these studies, and the earlier discussion of public drinking in the United Kingdom, attest to overall is that young people actively produce their drinking spaces. They intermingle with different young people and different subcultures at different locations, playing their own music and, in effect, creating their own drinking atmospheres. Equally, and as Demant and Landolt (2014) recognise, drinking spaces are not simply 'there' but are active agents with the capacity to influence, shape and enable drinking practices and experiences.

DRINKING ATMOSPHERES

One way of moving beyond the conceptualisation of drinking spaces as passive backdrops (Jayne et al. 2008) is by engaging with the sensory and affective atmospheres of drinking spaces. Atmospheres foreground the role of more-than-human elements to young people's alcohol consumption practices and experiences. As Böhme (2013) puts it, atmosphere is a *floating in-between*, something between things and the perceiving subjects. According to Reckwitz (2012), atmosphere denotes the affective mood that spatial arrangements evoke in the sensual bodies of their users. Anderson (2009, 77) has also referred to atmospheres as affective, arguing that 'to attend to affective atmospheres is to learn to be affected by the ambiguities of affect/ emotion, by that which is determinate and indeterminate, present and absent, singular and vague'. In order to get to grips with the concept of atmosphere, Bille et al. (2015) note that one must actively engage with colours, lighting, sound, odour and the textures of things, an approach that is thus inherently multisensory.

The alcohol studies literature has recently begun to consider this line of inquiry. An important outcome of this work is that drinking spaces and leisure practices are understood as not simply a result of price or some other determinant but are constituted and co-constituted by the coming together of a range of things, non-things, histories, practices and behaviours. Duff and Moore (2015) explore the atmospheres of mobility for young people residing in the inner city who take trams, walk or cycle to nearby venues, along with young people from periurban communities, that is, communities immediately adjoining an urban area, who also use trains, buses or taxis to travel to, and from, venues in the inner city. The more congenial atmospheres described by inner-city young people appeared to mitigate the likelihood of problems, whereas the atmospheres of boredom and unpleasantness described by periurban young people appeared to increase the potential for harm (Duff and Moore 2015). Furthermore, Taylor and Falconer (2015), in the context of the north-east of England, have gone some way towards engaging with the multisensual nature of queer leisure spaces, including bars. The authors incorporate an embodied, affectual analysis of *things* (e.g., food, drink and decor) and a sensual, affective articulation of *atmosphere* (light, dark, dirty, *seedy*). The authors highlight that material cultures and sensual atmospheres both seduce and disgust bodies, pulling people into and out of place. Women students in Bancroft's (2012) study echo this, noting the importance of heat and light to their drinking experiences. For instance, young women discussed the intense heat, and consequent sweat and body odours in clubs, highlighting that intoxication is a complex sensory and embodied experience shaped by multiple factors.

Shaw (2014) has also explored the night-time city centre as an affective atmosphere that emerges out of the coalescing (and dis-coalescing) of practices, materials, things, non-things and bodies. Shaw (2014) notes how taxis have a fundamental role in bringing people and objects into a particular area. Taxis enable people to make their way to the city centre late at night or in the early hours of the morning, having consumed alcohol elsewhere. Consequently, these practices contribute to the emergence of a bustling, flexible atmosphere, intensified within a small time-space. While Shaw's (2014) paper does not move beyond the night-time city centre, the author recognises that there is a need for more studies of places and spaces, which are not the city-centre streets or the bars that surround them. The following discussion goes some way towards addressing Shaw's (2014) plea by engaging with a range of 'atmos-spheres', to use Anderson's (2009, 8) phraseology, a term that encapsulates that atmospheres are inherently spatial, surrounding people, things and environments. In what follows, I pay attention to the atmospheres of drinking experiences in bars and pubs, along with streets and parks in a suburban setting.

COMMERCIAL DRINKING SPACES IN WYTHENSHAWE AND CHORLTON

This research is based on interviews, diaries, participant observation and mobile phone methods[1] (Wilkinson 2016) with forty young people. Participants' names, along with the names of streets, bars, pubs and clubs, have been anonymised, though to contextualise quotations I have noted young people's real ages and case study locations. What makes the research different to many of the other themes explored elsewhere in this volume is that suburban drinkscapes have tended to be neglected in the nightlife and night-time economy literature, with emphasis instead being placed on urban, central-city areas. Literature on the night-time economy is also often marked by a concern with regeneration and gentrification, especially in deindustrial locations. However, participants in my study demonstrate that a night-time economy is not entirely dependent on this link between gentrification and nightlife in an urban context. Suburban commercial drinking premises are also equally important for understanding the variety of experiences and developments occurring at night. While suburbia is often presented as homogenous, my research demonstrates that there are distinctive drinking practices, experiences and atmospheres both within and between the suburban areas of Chorlton and Wythenshawe.

Some young people in my study, particularly those from Chorlton, the more urbanised and connected area, enjoyed consuming alcohol in their local neighbourhood due to the slower rhythms and a more relaxed alcohol consumption experience. They would often consume alcohol here if they were not after a *big night out*. In other words, suburban drinking was believed to offer a different experience to consuming alcohol in city centres, which was associated with *going out out* rather than simply *going out*. In Chorlton, seating outside of bars is common, which gives the area more of a continental, relaxed, drinking feel. For many young people, this is alluring, and the ability to drink outside is seen to be liberating. The reasons for this are varied, but one notable argument for outdoor drinking is that there is less of an audience, compared to indoors, and therefore less pressure to censor what one wishes to say. This belief echoed a wider sentiment that the clientele in Chorlton are people who 'want to have a chat' (Louisa, 22, Chorlton) rather than seeking to achieve what Measham and Brain (2005, 258) have termed as 'determined drunkenness'.

Chorlton offers a range of affordable and more upmarket bars and pubs. It is notable, however, that affordable venues are not necessarily desired, and expensive places are not necessarily seen in negative terms. Rather, the ability to vary one's alcohol consumption practices is important and can be attributed to several factors such as the proximity to payday. Following on from this, *rough* venues were not seen as somewhere to necessarily avoid. Rather, consuming alcohol in such spaces was something that could be enjoyed. For young people in Chorlton then, suburban drinking is a diverse and heterogeneous practice, and while there are clear classed spaces, some young people moved between these in order to have different drinking experiences.

That said, other young people, from both Chorlton and Wythenshawe, articulated a variety of classed reasons as to why they did not enjoy consuming alcohol in bars and pubs in their local areas. Many young people expressed judgement about the kind of people that inhabited bars in Chorlton: 'pretentious', 'kooky' and 'special people' were commonly used. The notion that particular people can make commercial drinkscapes undesirable was also a theme in young people's accounts of consuming alcohol in Wythenshawe, which had 'old man pubs' frequented by the unemployed who 'shout and swear'. While some underage young people viewed consuming alcohol in pubs as holding personal kudos (Leyshon 2008), for those above the legal drinking age, pubs were also seen to be undesirable if many underage drinkers were consuming alcohol on the premises.

In addition to expressing disapproval over certain types of people, such as 'fag heads', meaning people who start fights,[2] young people highlighted that encounters with material culture and sensual atmospheres had the ability to pull drinkers out of place, similarly to what Taylor and Falconer (2015) argue. The notion that the atmospheres in commercial premises can alter young people's embodied feelings can be gleamed through a comment made by one young woman. Jenny, a sixteen-year-old from Wythenshawe, contrasts the feelings of drunkenness when sitting in a 'dead quiet old man's club' in her suburban area, where she would be 'bored and depressed', with being in a busy club in town, where she would feel more drunk. Jenny's words illustrate the argument made by Tutenges (2015) that proximity intensifies the interaction between bodies. The author says, in the context of bar crawls, that to be surrounded by numerous pub-goers is a strong experience, comparable to the effects of drugs (Tutenges 2015). The sensory atmospheres of bar space are comprised of lighting, the taste of drinks, the smell of the drinkscapes, the temperature of the drinking space and the music played. These factors are all important for young people when deciding where to consume alcohol, and have the potential to entice or repel, as I now explore.

The sonic geographies of suburban pub and club spaces have the potential to orientate people to feel and act in certain ways. For many young people, good music in the pub is important for enhancing their dancing mobilities, enabling them to transition from shy and reserved to someone who is out-going. That is, the affective atmosphere has the potential to prime young people to act in a particular way (Bissell 2010), temporally managing moods and movements (Forsyth 2009). Further participant observation revealed that, while low-lighting and upbeat popular music primed me and others to dance, the dance floor became scarce when lighting was brighter and when less popular music was being played, leading some young people to use this as a cue to go to the bar and get another drink. Forsyth (2009) explores this scenario and the role of music in the night-time economy, suggesting that it can alter moods and behaviour. He argues that an emotional response elicited by hearing a familiar song may encourage increased spending at the bar, for example. However, my observations found that young people are unlikely to leave the dance floor when familiar songs are being played. Rather, they use moments when unfamiliar or unpopular songs are being played to purchase drinks. Grayson and McNeill (2009, 525) suggest that managers mellow the music in bars in an attempt to keep customers purchasing alcohol. Indeed, the atmosphere of bar space clearly has an effect on customers and their decision-making processes (Grayson and McNeill 2009). Specifically, it can be seen that music plays a key role in shaping alcohol consumption at the micro-level (Forsyth and Cloonan 2008).

Olfactory elements of drinking spaces, such as the smell of people and the smell of alcohol, are also of significant importance for some young people when deciding where to drink. Coral, a twenty-four-year-old from Chorlton, described how the sensory atmosphere of a pub that accommodates what she described as 'council house people' was associated with the smell of 'proper horrible lager'. Coral exercises her *middle-class gaze* (Skeggs and Loveday 2012) and reveals her anxieties about consuming alcohol in this pub through statements of symbolic distinction designed to hold the working class at a physical and metaphorical distance. Unlike these *council house people*, Coral is put off by the smell of the pub and is thus secure in her boundaries that she is not them (Taylor and Falconer 2015). Smell 'is held to signal a dangerous proximity, which must then be guarded against, since to do otherwise would be to threaten the stability of middle-class claims of respectability' (Lawler 2005, 440). Here, then, the diversity of drinking practices and experiences in suburbia comes across; some young people enjoy moving between different classed drinking venues, yet other young people actively work to exclude themselves from working or middle-class venues.

With regard to the visual, young people in my study discussed how the lighting of commercial drinking spaces may either entice or repel them from accessing particular drinkscapes (Wilkinson 2017). For example, one participant noted that she preferred to access clubs in Wythenshawe when 'the lights are off . . . because then you can't tell how rough they [men in the pub] all look'. For her, light is a protective field, a boundary separating her from the 'rough' bodies present in the club space, holding these bodies at a distance. The darkness of the pub space, however, means these bodies are no longer held at a distance; they become hidden and unknown (Shaw 2015a). The affective power of darkness, and how it shapes experience of space (ibid.), is central here to producing not only specific atmospheres but different proximities to one's own and other bodies. Unhindered by multiple visual distractions of rough bodies, darkness cajoles our bodies into movement (Edensor 2013), motivating our bodies' dancing mobilities, for example. As Sumartojo (2015) contends then, darkness generates particular atmospheres; for instance, darkness can provoke people to move in different ways and has a role to play in people's decisions about where, and when, to consume alcohol. Moreover, darkness can influence people's embodied and emotional drinking experiences, all of which feed in to the production of affective atmospheres.

As can be seen then, young people's often voluntary inclusion and exclusion from commercial drinking spaces is bound up with the traditional identity markers of age, gender and class, alongside more performative, embodied, emotional and affective aspects; this theme continues when exploring outdoor drinking spaces.

OUTDOOR DRINKSCAPES

Not all young people are able to, or desire to, consume alcohol in commercial drinkscapes and, in what follows, I return to the importance of streets and parks for such young people. Consistent with the findings in Galloway et al.'s (2007) study, streets are important drinking spaces for many young people under the legal drinking age. In addition to consuming alcohol, the street offers a space where young people with different consumption preferences (alcohol and/or drugs) can mix. Further, the spatiality of the street makes it an appealing drinkscape for young people as it enables them to engage in playful fights and running races and to *claim space* by playing music loudly from their phones (Hil and Bessant 1999). In addition, the streets become the 'terrain of social encounters' (Gough and Franch 2005, 150), enabling young people to get *wired*[3] with friends.

Streets and parks can also provide a cheaper alternative, in comparison to consuming alcohol in commercial drinkscapes; there is no entrance fee, and the alcohol itself can be purchased from a corner shop or supermarket for a fraction of the prices found in commercial premises. By consuming alcohol in streets and parks, young people may be resisting the idea of leisure as a commodity, much like the young people who participate in *botellón* in Spain. In addition, drinking in parks and streets can be more inclusive; young people can consume alcohol with friends below the legal drinking age who are not permitted to access commercial drinkscapes. Parks and streets do not have a dress code; thus, young people do not have to deal with exclusionary door policies operating in many bars and clubs (Williams 2008), which can mean they are separated from friends who are denied access due to the perceived unsuitability of their outfits, for example.

While some of the women interviewed for this study did admit to drinking in parks, this space was more often recounted as a drinkscape by young men. Parks were presented as inclusive drinking spaces, as everyone could have fun together. While there was evidence of avoiding drinking in the home so as not to be seen getting *smashed*[4] in front of parents, public space afforded the opportunity to express one's drunkenness, such as through one's volume of speech. A notable tension emerges here around visibility and invisibility. Rather than keeping the volume down in order to avert the gaze of authorities, volume of speech could be a means by which one can affirm one's presence (Pennay et al. 2014). The park thus allows for what Lieberg (1995, 722) terms 'places of retreat and places of interaction'. Such spaces, on the one hand, provide young people with an opportunity to withdraw from the adult world and to be with one's own friends; yet, on the other hand, they provide young people with the space 'to meet and confront the adult world, to put oneself on display, to see and be seen' (ibid.). As White (1993) argues, parks can therefore provide a space where young people can spend their time among friends in an atmosphere of relative anonymity in which one can experience an excitement of the senses. Indeed, many young people suggested that the thrill of potentially *getting caught* for consuming alcohol in the park makes it even more *exciting* than consuming alcohol in other spaces.

Not all young people, however, spoke highly of the park as a drinkscape, as Townshend and Roberts (2013) similarly found. The reasons young people provided for not liking consuming alcohol in the park include the perceived lack of safety surrounding consuming alcohol in such an outdoor space. Surveillance was a key point here, especially in terms of someone hurting himself or herself and the possibility of finding help. Indeed, some young people considered it irresponsible to consume alcohol in a place without adult supervision. Others expressed disapproval towards the identities of those consuming alcohol in parks. Looming large against these concerns is the wider issue of how one is perceived. The figure of the *chav*[5] often expresses class-based disgust (Tyler 2008) and was deployed to describe park drinkers. The term was also used by a participant who is working class, to express a critical attitude to others of his social status (Valentine and Harris 2014) and those who consume alcohol in parks. It was important for some respondents to distinguish themselves from the *idiotic* people consuming alcohol in parks, who were seen as inferior.

As with the commercial suburban drinkscapes explored earlier, the sensory aspects of outdoor drinking spaces are equally important, particularly in regard to lightness and darkness. Dark and light are key components in the formation and emergence of atmospheres of varying intensity (Edensor 2015a). As Edensor (2013) suggests, there is a prevailing cultural understanding that darkness is a negative condition, a frightening, mysterious void; this was more commonly articulated by young people in my study from Chorlton, particularly young women. For example, walking in darkness while under the influence of alcohol was considered to be unnerving for some young people and associated with a fear of crime for others. One young male also preferred walking through Fallowfield (another suburban area in Manchester) than Chorlton, as it was better illuminated.

As was found with commercial indoor spaces, not all young people conceptualise darkness as a negative atmosphere. Some young people actively sought darkness, because it made drinkscapes exciting, alluring and mysterious (e.g., Edensor 2013, 2015b; Wilkinson 2017). Summer (16, Wythenshawe) felt that 'drinking in the dark [is] better, because I don't know what I'm going to do or where I'm going to end up'. Here, she suggests that the nocturnal landscape is visually apprehended in a different way to that of the day (Cook and Edensor 2017). Darkness allows for a temporary shift away from spatial, social and sensory norms (see Edensor and Falconer 2014). Due to a limited perceptible space, Summer's quote suggests that in darkness it is harder to judge depth and distance (Morris 2011), suggesting that darkness is not simply a background within which action takes place – it has the agency to alter this action altogether (Shaw 2015a). Vera (15, Wythenshawe) similarly felt that when in darkness, she is 'in [her] own world', finding both 'succour' and 'refuge' in the quiet and affective site of gloom, due to the imperceptible presence of others (Edensor 2013). This resonates with Shaw's (2015a, 590) assertion that 'night penetrates into our sense of self – it erodes the body and its independence from other objects'. While Edensor (2013, 463) contends that 'darkness offers opportunities to dream, mull over, remember and worry', for Vera, darkness has the allure of doing none of these things; she 'doesn't really think about anything'. This accords with Jayne et al.'s (2012, 221) argument that alcohol consumption often allows one to 'do nothing' and 'use up time'. Darkness then, echoing Edensor (2015a), is a key element through which the atmospheric experiences of space can be infused with qualities, including mystery, solace, intimacy and fun.

As I have illustrated here, parks and streets are not solely sought out by young people in the absence of anywhere better to go; rather, they have their own distinct appeals as drinkscapes and are thus 'deliberately sought out as places of action and incident' (Hall et al. 1999, 506). Young people are not passive to where and how they drink; they have the ability to craft drinking spaces so that they can consume alcohol in conditions of their own making. These spaces are co-constituted by their own agency as well as the materiality of the spaces concerned.

CONCLUSIONS

Throughout this chapter, I have illustrated that young people's alcohol-related transitions to adulthood are bound up with relationships with heterogeneous drinking spaces. I have argued that within nightlife studies, central, urban areas dominate the discussion rather than a recognition or acknowledgement of equally rich and nuanced drinking practices going on in suburbia. Moving beyond the contemporary geographical imaginary of drinking as a city-centre issue, the marginal/peripheral drinkscapes, including bars, pubs, parks and streets in the suburban areas of Wythenshawe and Chorlton, Manchester, pro-vide evidence of how, for some young people, suburbia is distinctly appeal-ing as a place to consume alcohol. In comparison to city centres, it provides a more relaxed drinking environment. Moreover, I have made clear that, rather than solely being a last resort, parks and streets have a distinct appeal as places to consume alcohol and drugs; such spaces enable young people to feel socially and physically unrestricted. For instance, young people are able to play the music of their choice, smoke, shout and play games. Young people reflected positively on the inclusive nature of such drinking spaces and the lack of surveillance. For some young people, the thrill of potentially getting caught by adults contributed to the excitement of drinking alcohol in such spaces. Drinking alcohol in parks and streets can also be linked with positive emotional and embodied experience while equally potentially dangerous spaces to consume alcohol, precisely because of the lack of supervision. Negotiating that tension between visibility and invisibility, danger and comfort, hiding and the threat of being caught marks these places out as sites where a complex range of affects, motivations and desires entwine.

Moreover, in this chapter I have highlighted that young people perceive clear classed drinking spaces exist. In line with existing literature about the urban night in Western cities, this chapter has demonstrated that some young people use moral judgements about the working class to justify socio-spatial processes of exclusion. For instance, some young people in this study perceived consuming alcohol in parks as *chavvy*, while, equally, others expressed disapproval over certain types of people frequenting specific commercial premises (e.g., *fag heads*). Interestingly, this study has revealed that some young people avoid certain commercial suburban nightscapes on the basis that they are *pretentious*, *kooky* or *posh*; thus, young people also exercise moral judgements about middle-class people and spaces, in an attempt to self-govern their nightlife experiences. Young people's perception of the 'classed other' then (Sutton 2009), both in human and more-than-human respects (including *soundscapes* and *smellscapes*), has a fundamental role to play in their desires to either access certain drinking spaces or purposefully exclude themselves from such spaces. Encounters with material culture and sensory atmospheres have the ability to pull young drinkers out of place, or draw them into other places, through specific smellscapes, soundscapes and *lightscapes*. Young people clearly view the suburban night through an atmospheric lens, and this may thus be a more appropriate way of viewing nighttime spaces as opposed to an *economy perspective* (Shaw 2014). Young people actively construct and express their identities through processes of inclusion and exclusion, the stereotyping and stigmatisation of certain drinkers and, most important, venturing into, and creating, certain drinking atmospheres.

NOTES

1. Mobile phone interviews involved young people taking photographs and videos on their nights in/out involving alcohol, using their mobile phones, and then using these photographs/videos as a prompt for further discussion in an interview scenario.

2. In a friendship group interview, Olivia (18, Wythenshawe) defined the phrase 'fag heads', used by Scott (18, Wythenshawe), as meaning 'people who always start fights'.

3. 'Wired' is a term young people use to refer to being high on stimulants.

4. 'Smashed' is a term used by young people to refer to the process of getting 'very drunk'.

5. The *Cambridge Dictionary* defines 'chav' as an insulting word for someone, usually a young person, whose way of dressing, speaking and behaving is thought to show the person's lack of education and low social class. See also Owen Jones's (2011) book on *chavs*.

Chapter 8

Reviewing Night-Time Economy Policies through a Gendered Lens: Gender Aware or Gender Neutral?

Marion Roberts

In July 2017, the Night Czar for London, Amy Lamé, hosted a Women's Night Safety Summit, the first of its kind to be held in the capital. The summit drew together over 100 women from different organisations, with a commitment to improve women's safety on public transport, in venues and at work. This commitment formed part of a 'vision' for London's night-time economy, articulated by the Mayor in ten broad aims, the first being the goal of making London the global leader in nightlife (Mayor of London 2017a, 2017b). This aspiration to enable women to move freely about at night and participate in nightlife constituted a significant and welcome shift in public policy, which, as this chapter elaborates, had previously been ambiguous in practice, despite legal and public claims to gender equality.

As a signatory to European legislation, specifically the Treaty of Amsterdam 1999, the United Kingdom has a duty towards achieving gender equality in its public sector policies, a duty made explicit in its Equalities Act of 2010. The act covers many categories of discrimination, including sex, sexual orientation and gender reassignment. Public policies cut across a wide range of statutory interests, which, in the context of UK night-time economy, includes licensing and planning, community safety, economic development and tourism, public space management, public health, transport and policing. This chapter focuses on the UK context and London in particular, drawing on a variety of secondary sources. In the final section, an excursion is made into other European countries with regard to the recent appointment of Night Mayors and their moves towards inclusivity, but as in 2017 little evidence existed, this final section is brief.

Nightlife has played an important role in the constitution of LGBTQ identities and communities (see, e.g., Hubbard 2012; Mattson 2015). This is a large topic that falls outside the remit of this chapter. For the sake of brevity and clarity, this chapter focuses on how policymakers have framed heteronormative concepts of gender throughout the expansion of nightlife (Hadfield 2015). Before turning to public policies, the first section reviews evidence as to the extent to which traditional versions of male and female relations are produced in nightlife spaces and places. In turning the spotlight on heterosexual relations, the chapter contributes to a relatively undertheorised area within night-time economy studies.

Public policy is analysed throughout drawing on the concept of European gender mainstreaming (Sánchez de Madariaga and Roberts 2013). As Moser (2016) points out, the form of gender mainstreaming which is required by the Treaty of Amsterdam has a dual implication. The first is to integrate women's and men's concerns into public policy, with equality as the expected outcome. The second is to carry out specific activities with the aim of empowering women. As such, this represents a social transformation. Of course, gender has to be conceptualised as intersectional and is calibrated by other axes of diversity, such as race, socio-economic status and disability. The author recognises the importance of these distinctions, for analysis, policy and political action. Where such distinctions are not highlighted, it is because the discussion turns to policy and legislation which refers to universal subjects, or the distinctions have not been brought to the fore in the studies cited.

In drawing on UK experience of nightlife, the chapter refers to the theme of economic liberalism, which had characterised public policies towards UK night-time economies. This was a theme set up through a loosening of licensing regulations during the era of the New Labour government of 1997–2010 and the reform of licensing in the Licensing Act of 2003. This administration, while pursuing *third-way* economic policies, charting a course between all-out laissez-faire capitalism and a *command and control* planned economy also championed progressive social policies. The Conservative-Liberal Democrat coalition that succeeded New Labour continued economic liberalism but rolled back state intervention, particularly by imposing severe budget restrictions on local government and to a lesser extent the police. Meanwhile, the night-time economy in many towns and cities in the United Kingdom has flourished despite the economic downturn. Although nightclubs have more recently been in decline and food-led entertainment has expanded, alcohol-fuelled nightlife in the form of bars, dance bars, clubs and pubs remains a dominant force in British nightlife (Roberts 2014).

NIGHTLIFE, 'HYPER-MASCULINITY' AND DIFFERENCE

A dominant theme in accounts of the recent development of heterosexual nightlife is its reproduction of traditional versions of masculinity and femininity. The extent to which this pattern has been historically embedded is unclear, though. Skeggs's (1999) observation that middle-class femininity is bound up with modesty, self-control and sobriety finds a deep contemporary resonance and accords with older women's perceptions of exclusion from local pubs (Holloway et al. 2009). As both authors demonstrate, for much of the twentieth century, middle-class norms of respectability placed many restrictions on where women could drink alcohol, with whom and in what setting. Nevertheless, a countercurrent of scholarship has documented the participation of women in nightlife, as workers and as customers. Within recent memory, certain class fractions of working-class women in northern cities took part in pub culture, even occasionally indulging in physical violence to express their aggression. In common with their male counterparts, these women valued a self-image of *hardness* (Day et al. 2003). These fractures at the intersection of class and gender have found a continuity in contemporary culture, through the figure of the ladette (McRobbie 2009), which stands in contrast to conventional norms of femininity.

As nightlife has expanded in the past two decades, so has women's participation. As has been extensively documented, the expansion of night-time entertainment has played a role in this (Chatterton and Hollands 2003). While it might have been anticipated that the decriminalisation of homosexuality in the United Kingdom in 1967, together with the second wave of feminism and the Sex Discrimination Act of 1975, would have transformed the masculinised cultures of nightlife, it seems that changes in the performance and embodiment of gendered roles and behaviours have not yet substantially materialised.

Researchers have drawn distinctions between the mainstream milieu of pubs, bars and clubs to more underground or alternative spaces (Hollands and Chatterton 2003). The mainstream is characterised as a hyper-masculinised space, the evidence for which is supported by a small number of ethnographic studies. Bancroft et al. (2014) point out that mainstream nightclubs are managed on the heteronormative assumption that men are the primary customers and are attracted by the atmosphere and female clientele. Door staff, for example, try to get a balance between genders and scrutinise young men more carefully for signs of intoxication. Young women are required to negotiate these spaces whose organisers produce an insistent sexual objectification of women, reducing young men to *gazers* and infantilising both sexes. Nicholls's (2016) research with young women in Newcastle, United Kingdom, points out how her young female respondents collude in their own subordination through conforming to stereotypical norms of sexualised femininity, featuring full make-up, a tanned body, either fake or real, erotically revealing outfits and high heels.

Where a sharper distinction between genders can be observed is in attitudes towards heavy drinking. Measham and Brain (2006) discuss how young people walk a *tightrope of intoxication* on their nights out, balancing the right amount of drink to loosen inhibitions but avoiding a level at which they lose control. For women, this *tightrope* is particularly fraught, due to the double standard with which they are judged, and judge themselves, as being disreputable and unfeminine if drinking heavily or suffering the effects of intoxication. Furthermore, unscrupulous managers and bar staff have been known to ply young women with alcohol in an attempt to keep them in a bar with a view to attracting male customers (Buvik and Baklien 2016).

Ethnographic accounts of alternative or underground venues offer a more muted and blended version of embodied gendered comportment. Going out is more likely to be in mixed-sex groups rather than the large single-sex groups of the mainstream. The atmosphere is more tolerant and less aggressive, with a friendlier set of interactions on the dance floor. Drinking to excess is less dominant, and drug use is more in evidence, albeit covertly. Nevertheless, the atmosphere still leads to a transgression of boundaries and unwanted touching. Hutton (2010) concludes that it is problematic for women to express their sexuality in a general sense, and club spaces, whether mainstream or alternative, are no exception.

Heterosexual male experience of nightlife is correspondingly deeply coded with regard to gender. Younger males may feel pressurised to approach women as predators, *hunting* for a mate, temporary or permanent. Here their self-consciousness is associated with a competition to perform (Grazian 2007; Waitt et al. 2011). Such predatory behaviour is not universal however. A smaller ethnographic study of a particular working-class, male subculture carried out by Nayak (2003) provides an interesting counterpart. His group of respondents seemed to be more focused on bonding together through joking, banter and building their own collective sense of identity in a hostile environment where their jobs and futures were under threat.

The relationship between drinking to excess and predominately male violence is well documented, in the public space of the street, in semi-public nightlife venues and in the private space of the home (Budd 2003; Finney 2004a, 2004b). Winlow and Hall (2006) in a study of the milieu of working-class young people in Newcastle, England, found a group of respondents who thought of violence as fun and part of the experience of a night out. More recently, when the Metropolitan Police in London carried out a detailed analysis of violence in the night-time economy in three different local areas in London, they found that 80 percent of perpetrators were male, and predominantly young, between the ages of twenty and thirty-three years (London Assembly Police and Crime Committee 2015).

There are also differences in the attitudes females and males take towards safety when going out at night. Some women cope by not going out at all at night (Scraton and Watson 1998), but as more women participate in nightlife, a variety of strategies are adopted. These include going out in groups, *looking out* for each other, taking taxis and being particularly aware of the type of venue, its atmosphere, the male/female ratio and levels of intoxication. Fileborn (2016) notes the paradox of young women restricting their own drinking as a safety measure in places they feel uncertain in, while drinking to excess in places in which they feel safe.

The association between women drinking to excess and vulnerability to sexual assault and rape is a particularly fraught area of debate. The suggestion that a woman *asked for it* by wearing revealing clothes or drinking to high levels of intoxication, even black out, has been hotly contested by feminists. The phenomenon of *SlutWalk* demonstrations emerged in 2011 in response to a Canadian policeman's comment that women should not dress 'like sluts' if they wanted to avoid being victims of rape (Leach 2013). This transnational movement reached six continents and brought together thousands of women who protested about a culture that blamed the victim rather than the rapist. The attitude that women are responsible for making themselves vulnerable to predatory men is deeply embedded, as evidenced in Sheard's (2011) research into drink spiking, the practice of putting a drug into a drink to make the consumer insensible. Even at the time of writing this chapter, a female judge[1] warned women that they put themselves in danger if they drank too much and were less likely to be believed.

While violent aggression is most commonly associated with men, this might apply only to a small minority. Focus group research with young men in employment and higher education in the United Kingdom and the Netherlands suggested a convergence between male and female attitudes towards violence, with a desire to avoid *trouble* (Brands et al. 2015). There is some evidence, however, that male attitudes to safety take a different form to women's. While there is a similar approach to 'looking out for friends', this may take the form of joining in a fight to protect friends (MacLean 2016). Fileborn (2016) reports that young men in her study did not respond clearly to questions that used the word 'safety' but preferred instead to discuss their 'anxiety' about particular venues or the presence of groups of other, intoxicated males. When prompted to discuss safety, references were frequently made to their own physical attributes, such as their height or level of fitness. Men also feel a sense of responsibility towards women friends, making sure they feel safe, to the extent that some men reported feeling burdened by this call to traditional chivalry.

The most vivid expression of embodied difference is represented by *gentlemen's clubs* and sex establishments such as lap dancing venues. Feminist objections to lap dancing and other similar premises centre around the objectification of female bodies inside the venues and a feeling of discomfort in walking past them (RTPI 2007). There are contesting voices as these objections are not shared by all women, and some sex workers have voiced their support for well-run clubs as a source of employment (Hubbard and Colosi 2015).

Alcohol-fuelled nightlife brings a further, more basic difference between men and women into view. Drinking heavily inevitably leads to a need to urinate or defecate, often at short notice. Public toilet provision has traditionally been rigidly divided along gender lines and is inadequate even in the daytime (Greed 2003). The increasing recognition given to trans rights challenges sex-segregated toilet provision, in the public sphere and within venues.

In summary, contemporary research has found the spaces and places of nightlife to be deeply gendered. Traditional versions of masculinity and femininity dominate clubs and bars, and these are inflected by social class, ethnicity and sexual orientation. The heightened and sexualised atmosphere in clubs and bars spills out into the streets of the micro-districts where nightlife entertainment venues are concentrated. The intense emotional background surrounding night-time entertainment brings differences of sex and gender into sharp relief and forms a contrast to the cool rationality of the legislative and regulatory environment that constitutes gender mainstreaming. It is to this divide that we shall turn to next.

NIGHTLIFE AND PUBLIC POLICY

Gender mainstreaming relies on gender-disaggregated statistics as a basis for coherent public policy (De Madariaga 2013). Analysis in a UK context is made difficult by the complexity of relationships between central and local governments and associated agencies. While central government sets the overall framework for planning, licensing and transport, local authorities make and enforce their own policies for their administrative areas.

Licensing in England and Wales has been the subject of controversial reform (Roberts and Eldridge 2009). Prior to the decade before the millennium, licensing was regulated by the local judiciary, who exercised tight controls over many aspects of venues, including the numbers of licensed premises, their hours of operation and whether they could offer food and opportunities to dance and play music. Controls were gradually loosened from the mid-1990s onwards, permitting an increased number of licensed premises and later hours of operation. The entire system was changed between 2003 and 2005, taking control away from the magistrates and giving it to local authorities, who have control within their local areas. The powers of local authorities are circumscribed by a national legal framework, which includes guidance that has been updated many times.

In contrast to many European countries, the United Kingdom does not have a strong system of regional government. This tier has been subject to constant changes. The most relevant for this chapter was the abolition of the regional authority for Greater London in 1986 and its subsequent reinstatement in 2000. In London, the Mayor and his council do not have responsibility for licensing as this is the responsibility of each London borough. The Mayor does have responsibility for transport, though, and makes an overall spatial plan that guides local planning policies in each local authority area.

Two major themes have dominated recent public policy towards nightlife since its expansion in the late 1990s in the United Kingdom. Crime and disorder has provided a persistent point of concern throughout, such that in 2004, doctors and other front-line specialists complained that the government was paying insufficient attention to the major issue of public health. From 2004 onwards the central government produced combined strategies towards alcohol (Cabinet Office 2004; HM Government 2007, 2012), seeking to make an integrated response, drawing together strategies for public health and crime and disorder.

Local authorities, who are the level of governance closest to managing nightlife in their areas, did not have responsibility for public health until 2013. Instead, health authorities were subregional bodies whose remit could cross local authority boundaries. The police, who represent one of the key stakeholders in regulating nightlife, are also organised in regional and subregional administrative areas. Local authorities have responsibility for licensing, planning, street cleaning, economic development, crime reduction and the promotion of safety. Transport is also complex, especially as train and bus services are privatised and profit making, although they are also regulated by central and local governments.

In the years since the millennium, many local authorities have pioneered partnership working between these different departments under their own authority and outside agencies and local businesses (Roberts 2004). Nongovernmental organisations have provided encouragement and support, sometimes with the backing of the central government and major players in the drinks industry. This formed part of the turn towards neo-liberal forms of governance, in a drive to reduce the reach of the state. Because these partnerships are subject to change, reliable data on the night-time economy is partial and time limited. An individual partnership or local authority may commission a report, which provides a snapshot of a particular area (see, e.g., Association of Town & City Management and TBR & MAKE Associates 2013; Hadfield 2017), but with the exception of health information, longer-term data sets are not available on public websites. In the absence of coherent data sets, it is unsurprising that public policies have displayed a limited degree of recognition of gender differences, ranging from complete neutrality to responses reinforcing stereotypes to a belated gender awareness.

Turning first to health, prior to the expansion of nightlife, drinking alcohol in pregnancy represented a key marker of difference, so that now it has almost become taboo for a woman to be seen drinking in a public place while visibly pregnant. With regard to non-pregnant women, the government, in 1992, had also publicly distinguished *safe consumption* levels between men and women, demarcating *safe consumption for males* (twenty-one units per week) as 50 percent more than that for females (fourteen units per week; House of Commons 2012). This guidance was revised further to equalise safe consumption between males and females at fourteen units per week in August 2016 (Alcohol Policy Team 2016). The increased participation of women in the evening and night-time economy in the late 1990s raised concerns for post-millennium health professionals on three counts. The first was that male and female drinking patterns could converge. As the Cabinet Office (2003, 6) points out, 'If the trends since 1993/1994 are simply extrapolated over the next decade, then the prevalence of drinking above the weekly recommended limits among young women will (around 53 percent) exceed that of young men (around 48 percent) by 2012'. While this fear might be dismissed as an example of *moral panic*, the impartiality of this report and the research summarised in the 2016 guidance provide ample evidence that alcohol consumption at high levels is associated with an increase in life-threatening diseases that particularly impact on women such as breast cancer, as well as the more *gender blind* diseases such as cirrhosis of the liver.

The second area of concern was the association between alcohol consumption and domestic violence. The relationship between domestic violence and public nightlife is more tenuous, if only because the bulk of alcohol consumption takes place in the home. The third gender-related concern highlighted the impact of intoxication on the behaviour of young people. Two issues were raised. One was an increase in unwanted pregnancies, citing a study that found young women were more likely to have casual sex while under the influence of alcohol. The other issue was the vulnerability to sexual assault. The evidence for this was provided by a study of male rapists, finding that 58 percent had been drinking beforehand (Cabinet Office 2004, 46).

Government policy towards the association between violent crime and increased alcohol consumption in the evening and night-time economy has been heavily criticised by criminologists and sociologists. Their argument is that, on the one hand, central government has encouraged increased consumption through a liberalisation of licensing legislation but, on the other, has penalised and demonised young drinkers (Hayward and Hobbs 2007). The plethora of offences and penalties introduced since 2000 have placed the responsibility on the individual. As would be expected, the legislation was framed in gender-neutral language.

The UK government's campaign in 2006–2007 to reduce young people's heavy drinking in nightlife situations was highly gender stereotyped. The 'Know Your Limits' campaign was targeted at local partnerships and authorities, and its resource pack included suggestions for a variety of means of communication, through mannequins, light projections and pavement stickers as well as more conventional media such as posters and advertisements. Its aim was to raise young people's awareness of the negative outcomes of binge drinking. In particular, it emphasised aggression and risky behaviour for men and young women's vulnerability to shame and vulnerability to sexual assault. The poster images were shocking, with true-to-life representations of young women with loosened clothing and, in one case, of being the victim of sexual assault. The government's own *Alcohol Strategy Report* commented that the campaign had reinforced women's sense of vulnerability on a night out (HM Government 2007). A gender-sensitive strategy might have focused instead on male responsibility for not being sexual predators, instead of which the posters targeted towards men highlighted the dangers of jumping in canals, fighting and climbing high buildings and feeling *invincible*. This was followed in 2008 by a television and print campaign. The strapline was 'you wouldn't start a night like this', with images showing a male victim of violence and woman with smeared make-up and vomit in her hair after a night out gone wrong (The Home Office 2008).

If the government's own campaign was a study in sexual stereotyping, industry was instead being persuaded to step back from overtly sexist advertising and promotions. The Advertising Standards Authority was tasked with extending its rules to bar adverts that associated alcohol with sexual success. The 2007 Strategy document noted the limitations of the authority's remit and suggested that a body with greater powers, OfCom, also be tasked. Meanwhile, the Portman Group, an independent industry group set up to promote social responsibility, had adopted its own Code of Conduct, which major industry retailers and suppliers had signed up to. Section 3.2(d) of the code bars marketing and advertising that associates drink with any social or sexual success (Portman Group 2015).

In 2010 the government finally intervened to reduce some of the worst excesses of alcohol-fuelled nightlife by introducing a mandatory code for alcohol retailers against irresponsible promotions. This code included in its clauses a ban on *women drink free* promotions. The overtly sexist component of many promotions had been raised previously, not least in the government's 2005 policy document in a section entitled 'changing the culture' (Department for Culture, Media & Sport et al. 2005). The culture that was in question was binge drinking. Research led by Hadfield, commissioned by the Home Office, demonstrated the extent to which a voluntary code was being disregarded to promote an association between drinking and sexual performance. The research team carried out observational research in eight venues in different locations. It found instances of DJs urging people to drink to loosen their sexual inhibitions, promoting a sexually predatory atmosphere, encouraging couples to dance together and to discard items of clothing. Women were encouraged to engage in sexually suggestive pole dancing, for the entertainment of male customers. Drink promotions repeated messages in the same vein, with suggestive names and slogans (Home Office and KPMG 2008). Nevertheless, the inclusion of this small phrase in the 2010 mandatory code was at least a small step towards a recognition that inequalities were being deepened, rather than denied, in nightlife.

A further statutory intervention was made into the private sector owned and managed spaces of nightlife. The deployment of female *bouncers* or door staff was initiated by the private sector and followed up by an update to the National Guidance to the Licensing Act 2003. Hobbs's research (Hobbs et al. 2007) found that the numbers of female door staff had increased, mainly in response to a market demand. In the *hyper-masculinised* world of nightlife, male bouncers could not be tasked to remove unconscious and partly naked women out of toilet cubicles, for a number of reasons. Female door staff were also observed to provide a calming influence in situations where aggression seemed imminent and for these reasons were favoured by club managers. At the local level, many local authorities now make a condition that female door staff are employed in premises of a certain size in the licensing policies for their area. Club owners are required to adhere to conditions in their licences, since licensing has a quasi-legal status and flouting licensing conditions can lead to revocation of the licence and, ultimately, closure of the business.

The background to these changes is provided by the Licensing Act 2003, which was conceived as 'light touch' regulation, formulated to respond to consumer demand and allow variation within local authority areas. In the decade or so following the act, venues have become more regulated through updates to Guidance to the Act. With the exceptions of the mandatory code on irresponsible promotions and the recommendation to employ female door staff, this tightening of conditions has been gender blind. Partnership schemes encouraged by the central government, such as Best Bar None, which promotes better-managed venues and Purple Flag, whose remit is to improve the environmental management of night-time economy areas have also adopted a gender-neutral tone.

Spatial planning policies are silent too on the gendered nature of nightlife. National policy favours economic development in town centres (DCLG 2012). Local authorities have a duty to reduce crime and to promote public health and an equality duty. Council planning departments are under severe pressure due to reductions in spending and the government's priorities to boost economic development and increase the supply of housing. Local policies vary, and without a detailed study it is difficult to generalise the extent to which spatial plans and development management schemes demonstrate gender awareness.

'GENDER-SENSITIVE' LOCAL INITIATIVES

It can be seen from the earlier account that public policy has been limited in its recognition of the deeply stereotyped nature of the evening and night-time economy. While recognition has been limited on the national stage, the most progressive initiatives and policies, as with many other aspects of the night-time economy, have come from the local and regional levels. Two examples stand out, both from London. This is not surprising given London's economic predominance in the United Kingdom as a whole and the significance of the West End as a world centre of entertainment.

Safer Travel at Night

Transport for London (TfL), the body that regulates the whole of and provides some of the transport services across the Greater London Region, launched the Safer Travel at Night (STaN) initiative in 2003. This came in direct response to a report by the London-wide police force that the number of sexual assaults against women in illegal minicabs had risen from 66 in 1997 to 212 in 2002. Fifty-four of the 212 offences were rapes. A more detailed study of the 2001–2002 statistics found that the attacks were targeted at women travelling alone, 91 percent of whom were under thirty-five years. The problem was symptomatic of a wider issue, that of taxi touting. At that point in London, there were two types of taxis, the emblematic black cab and minicabs, or private hire vehicles (PHVs). Both types are regulated by TfL. The key difference between the two types is that black taxis can be hailed in the street, whereas minicabs have to be pre-booked. The regulation system for minicabs covers the firms and the drivers, and the drivers are required to have a criminal record check. Illegal minicabs have unregulated drivers and 'tout', that is, look for trade directly from the street. The analysis also found that the majority of cabs involved in assaults had been hailed just outside or a street away from a nightclub or bar.

The approach adopted was multiagency and multifaceted. TfL, the Metropolitan Police and the Greater London Authority all worked together on four fronts. These were to raise awareness of the problem, to improve late-night transport services, to provide better information about late-night travel and to improve regulation of PHVs. The awareness campaign Know What You Are Getting Into, pursued through different media, provides a contrast to the central government's previous efforts. Of particular note was the short advert commissioned from Mike Leigh, an internationally famous film director. This film showed a middle-aged man, in a cab, recounting how he had been in and out of prison for several offences, including sexual assault. He complains of how hard it is to get a job and how he has to drive a taxi, illegally. The shot ends with him asking a young woman if she needs a cab. The framing of the driver as a potential offender, instead of focusing on the young woman as a potential victim, demonstrates a deeper and more nuanced understanding of gender relations.

The improvement to late-night public transport through extending the night-bus service has benefited all passengers. The number of routes was expanded to over 100, and the number of passengers using those routes has increased by 170 percent since 2000 (Volterra & TfL 2014). Overall TfL was able to claim STaN as a success, arguing London is one of the safest cities to go out at night (TfL 2006). There has been a worrying doubling in the numbers of incidents of sexual harassment on public transport to more than 2,000 since 2013, but it is unclear how many of these happen late night (Mayor of London 2017a). There have been other changes; for example, the use of smartphones has made it easier to record unwanted touching in crowded circumstances such as on the Underground system.

Women's Safety Charter

This was launched in December 2014 by a local council in south-east London. The London Borough of Southwark is home to an expanding night-time economy as part of its jurisdiction extends northwards to the Thames and takes in famous venues such as the Ministry of Sound and emerging nightlife areas such as Peckham. The charter is aimed at preventing sexual harassment inside nightlife venues. Managers who sign up to the charter agree to prominently display posters, explaining that there is a zero-tolerance approach to any kind of harassment, including verbal banter, unwanted touching and other types of intimidation. All house staff are trained by the feminist organisation Hollaback! to deal sensitively with customers who complain. Appropriate action is taken against perpetrators, and significantly, reports of incidents are not recorded in a way that would jeopardise the premises' licence. Staff are also trained to help victims to get home safely. The scheme continues as of 2018 and has over sixty-two venues signed up (London Borough of Southwark, no date). The Women's Night Safety Summit, referred to at the beginning of this chapter, has a brief to develop the Women's Safety Charter for London-wide application.

These examples provide exemplars of a gender-sensitive approach to nightlife. The STaN initiative, in avoiding blaming the victim and improving services, has created opportunities for all genders to benefit from access to public transport at night. Tourism and the visitor experience has also gained. The Women's Safety Charter offers a nuanced approach to the expansion of nightlife, which recognises difference and vulnerability but simultaneously is acting to overcome it.

AN INCLUSIVE HETERONORMATIVE NIGHTLIFE ACROSS EUROPE?

As the night-time economy in European cities has expanded, so has the interest of local government and local organisations of operators. The establishment of night-time champions, Night Mayors, has taken different, localised forms, from a nightlife industry-elected spokesperson in Amsterdam (Mirik Milan) to a local government appointee in London (Amy Lamé) to a fully elected Mayor in Paris (Clément Léon). Amy Lamé when starting her work for London's Mayor complained of having experienced harassment on the underground at night. The Chair of London's Night-Time Commission, Philip Kolvin's vision for nightlife includes a wish for it to be enjoyed by everyone, regardless of gender or sexual orientation. Mirik Milan's main focus of activity, as evidenced in speeches and interviews, is targeted at fostering creativity in twenty-four-hour clubs set on the periphery of Amsterdam.

The terrorist attacks on a rock concert and a street with crowded bars and on the Bastille Day festival in Nice, both of which happened in the evening, have had an impact on French policies and the visibility of night-time management. In Paris, a newly adopted set of rules or recommendations for the night (Maire de Paris, undated) urges people to stay with their friends, whether male or female, if they are not feeling well and to help them keep safe. An awareness campaign Take Care of Your Mates (Prends Soin de Tes Pôtes, in original) includes advice about going out in a group, not predrinking, and reminds participants that sex has to be consensual. The proposals for night-time include an action plan for venues to combat all forms of discrimination, including racism and sexism. Paris also hosts an annual event targeting sexism and other discrimination, entitled *A Nous la Nuit* (the night belongs to us), which includes a march, gigs and other events to raise awareness of sexism and other forms of discrimination. The Parisian authority has increased the number of public twenty-four-hour *sanisettes*, self-cleaning toilets, to 400, which are suitable for both male and female use. These policies display a degree of gender awareness and a willingness to combat overt discrimination, albeit on a voluntary basis for both operators and customers.

COMBATTING 'HEGEMONIC MASCULINITY'

Within the context of the night-time economy, the gender equality duty confronts some formidable forces. The first wave of the night-time economy's expansion crudely exposed the thin surface of social liberalism enshrined in equalities legislation. McRobbie's (2009) analysis of the 'raunch culture' of this period exposes the way in which young women have to make an individual settlement in negotiating their way through a conflicting and new set of demands. Young men who self-identify with gender equality find themselves confronted with traditional versions of comportment inscribed in nightlife. The response of public authorities has been patchy, to say the least. This has not been helped by the economic recession following the global banking crisis of 2007–2008, which led to an austerity programme in the United Kingdom, placing pressure on public services.

The police have an important role to play and can offer some progressive examples, such as the research by Operation Sapphire which provoked the STaN initiative. Nevertheless, this laudable piece of work has to be balanced against another example of action, or rather inaction by London's Metropolitan Police Service (MPS). Two young women were given ruling by the High Court against the MPS that their human rights had been breached through failures by the police to investigate serious sexual assaults on them by the driver of a black taxi in 2003 and 2007. The women were disbelieved because they had been tricked into drinking spiked champagne by the driver, had been out late and only had a hazy memory of the details of their experiences of rape (Laville 2017). Because of the MPS's failures the driver went on to commit over 100 similar offences and was apprehended only in 2009. In 2017, the MPS lodged an appeal against the judgement, supported by the central government. As one of the victims was reported to say, this shows the deep contradiction in government policy, which on the one hand promotes ending violence against women but on the other supports a case that will remove women's rights. It should be added, in parenthesis, that this case has led the MPS to seriously overhaul the way it deals with cases of sexual assaults.

CONCLUSIONS

As the United Kingdom prepares to leave the European Union, the legislation that is derived from the European treaties will be reviewed. It is unclear whether the Equalities Act 2010 will survive in its present form. This chapter, which has reviewed contemporary research into UK heteronormative night-time economy, demonstrates the extent to which it is a minefield for public policymakers. The heightened emotional environment of night-time spaces and places, combined with the economic drivers to maximise returns, exposes the fault lines of civil society and throws them into sharp relief. The traditional versions of masculinity and femininity embodied in the places of night-time entertainment require concerted and explicit action to challenge. There is a lack of evidence in the form of gender-disaggregated statistical information and a paucity of policy analysis from this perspective.

The thrust of public policies has been the neo-liberal concept of partnership, guidance and collaboration. The state's ambiguity towards gender equality has found its crudest expression in the treatment of rape and sexual assaults. It is only when guidance and partnership has been shown to fail that the state has intervened, as demonstrated in the discussion of overtly sexist promotions and the STaN initiative. The way forward promised by the Women's Night Safety Summit gives cause for hope that a new inclusivity and equality will be fought for.

NOTE

1. See   https://www.theguardian.com/society/2017/mar/11/judge-criticised-over-warning-to-drunk-women.

Part 3

GOVERNANCE OF THE
URBAN NIGHT

Chapter 9

Consumption Patterns of Erasmus Students in Lisbon: Circulating between Mainstream and Alternative Nightscapes

Daniel Malet Calvo, João Carlos Martins
and Iñigo Sánchez-Fuarros

THE ERASMUS PROGRAMME: EDUCATION, LEISURE AND IMPACT ON EUROPEAN CITIES

Mobility within Europe is an increasingly multifaceted phenomenon. One of its most important features is the circulation of higher education students taking part in the Erasmus Programme, a European Union–led student exchange programme. Since its launch in 1987, more than three million Erasmus students have circulated across thirty-three countries on an exchange studentship. The educational experience of going abroad has been publicised by its promoters as a knowledge-acquiring process that is enriched by travelling to a different country and getting along with the local culture and people, learning the local language and, finally, dealing with the everyday challenges of living independently in a foreign country. However, despite institutional claims about the intercultural experience enjoyed by these young students, several studies stress the low levels of participation between the Erasmus community and students living in the host countries (Waters and Brooks 2011; Mitchell 2012). Research suggests that most exchange students socialise primarily among themselves (especially with co-nationals) or with only a minority of local students, mostly ex-Erasmus or English-speaking individuals, gathering in bars, clubs and street areas that provide an international environment (Malet Calvo et al. 2017).

As in other European urban settings, Erasmus students are a growing presence in Lisbon's night-time leisure spots, having a visible presence in certain areas of the city every night. The small size of the city and the ability shown by some organisations (e.g., Erasmus Students Network [ESN] or Erasmus Life Lisbon [ELL], which will be discussed later) to disperse the most significant leisure events bring together most Erasmus students to share the same nightlife experiences in particular leisure areas. The process of commercialising the social life of exchange students (the organisation of parties, meetings and events for them) has caused their progressive segregation from night-time leisure spaces frequented by local youth and students. However, some Erasmus students in Lisbon reject both the mainstream international events (mostly drinking-oriented parties) and the same-country endogamy (especially among Spaniards and Italians) and seek instead contact with local residents, especially at night. These 'alternative' Erasmus students construct their identities while abroad in opposition to the standard Erasmus circuits and mainstream events by getting to know local students, speaking with them in Portuguese and attending underground parties and traditional nightlife areas that are otherwise invisible to mainstream Erasmus students. The consumption habits shown by these differentiated populations of Erasmus students in Lisbon's nightscape are illustrative as well as constitutive of urban change in Lisbon.

This chapter addresses the differentiated nightlife practices, experiences and discourses of Erasmus students in Lisbon, introducing some data from fieldwork conducted in situ from 2011 to 2016. The ethnographic insights, discussed later, include a discussion of the socio-economic backgrounds of those different groups of students and their distinctive forms of consumption and integration into Lisbon's nightlife. Social class, subcultural lifestyles and national and linguistic identities have emerged not only as boundaries between mainstream and alternative students but also as intersections to negotiate their consumption practices as mobile, middle-class European students. In this sense, the exchange students represent the increasing impact nightlife is having on urban change: considering their position as relatively wealthy nightlife consumers also allows us to better understand the transformation of contemporary Lisbon and the gentrification of its nightlife.

THE ERASMUS STUDENTS IN LISBON

Lisbon, located in the western part of the Iberian Peninsula in the north side of the estuary of the Tagus River, is the capital and largest city of Portugal with a population of 547,631 (INE 2011). Its location by the Atlantic Ocean was favourable for the colonial endeavours of the Portuguese Empire in the modern age. Now, as a global city, Lisbon still connects Europe with America and Africa (especially the Portuguese-speaking African countries, henceforth PALOP) as a geographically well-positioned hub for international trading and investment activities, start-ups in the information technology and communication industries, tourism, leisure and nightlife. In addition, the branding of Lisbon, which started with the proclamation of Lisbon's European Capital of Culture in 1994 and Lisbon's World Fair in 1998 and UEFA European Championship in 2004, has meant this once-quiet city has experienced an exponential growth in its tourism industry.

During 2012–2016, more than 44.1 million tourists have visited the Portuguese capital (according to the Global Destination Cities Index), drawn to its mild climate, gastronomy, its architectural heritage rooted in both Mediterranean civilisations and the Atlantic Age of Discovery and more affordable prices in comparison to other European capitals. At the same time, the neo-liberal turn in Lisbon's urban policies, which started with the creation of private partnerships driving urban regeneration in 2004, has been recently extended with the passing of the New Act on Housing Rent Market in 2012 (the 'eviction law' as known by its critics). The Portuguese Golden Visa for foreign real estate investors in 2012 also accords with a general drift towards privileging economic investments.

The rise in value of Lisbon's real estate market has prompted urban change throughout the city and has intensified the touristification of the city centre (Rodrigues 2010; Tulumello 2016). This has occurred alongside the post-crisis austerity policies that continue to impact negatively on working-class families (Carmo et al. 2015). As a result, 'old' and 'new' waves of gentrification continue to pressure and lead to the eviction of the most vulnerable populations: older residents and low-income workers. Because of increasing tensions over local house prices, with an increase of 33.5 percent in the period between 2013 and 2015, a growing number of local families are moving to suburban areas. As a result, an increasing number of inner-city properties are being purchased by national and international investors and converted into luxury residences, short-term rental homes for tourists and apartments intended for international students (Alves et al. 2015; Mendes 2016).

The attraction for international students (such as Erasmus students) can also be attributed to the international promotion of the city conducted by local institutions over the recent years. Lisbon's City Council has initiated a programme called Study in Lisbon to promote the city as a student destination, using specific images to attract tourists: surf, nightlife, cosmopolitanism, cheap prices and safety. Several authors have noted that international students often select their destination captivated by the images and attractions of the city or country they wish to travel to (Llewellyn-Smith and McCabe 2008), while recognising that their stay should be labelled as *educational travel* (van't Klooster et al. 2008) or *academic tourism* (Rodríguez et al. 2012).

Based on the most recently published data, during the 2015–2016 academic year 148,000 higher education students (HES) enrolled in the ninety-five higher education institutions (HEI) located in the Lisbon city area, the majority of them (and the most populated) in the city. Eleven percent of the annual student population (about 14,000) are not Portuguese citizens, and most of them (approximately 10,000) live permanently in Lisbon over their entire study period. The students are typically middle class and come from Brazil and PALOP (especially Angola and Cape Verde) and wish to graduate (bachelor's, master's or PhD) in the European education system.

While those students who spend their entire degree based in Lisbon warrant further analysis, the focus of this is the transnational young people (about 4,000) who come annually to Lisbon for a year at the most through several exchange programmes, most of whom are European students coming through the Erasmus programme. This population of European youth (led by Spaniards, Italians and Germans) has grown from 15 percent to 35 percent of the total foreign student population between 2008 and 2012, outpacing Brazilians, who grew from 20 percent to 23 percent in the same period. On the other side, PALOP students have declined from 62 percent to 37 percent due to increasing prices in Lisbon and the opening of several HEIs in their own countries.

The growing interest among European youth to visit Lisbon during their Erasmus stay should not be underestimated. According to European Commission reports, Portugal is the eighth most popular country in absolute numbers (academic year 2013–2014) but is ranked as the second destination as regards growth rate (59 percent in the past five years), with Lisbon and Porto leading the expansion. Only Poland exhibits a higher number than Portugal, but Poland is 3.4 times larger and 3.7 times more populated than Portugal. The marketing campaigns devised to advertise Lisbon as an inexpensive destination with a vibrant (and also bohemian) nightlife are certainly related to the success of the city among Erasmus students. Magazines and websites directed towards international students often place Lisbon at the top of their rankings of 'European cities for the perfect Erasmus experience' or 'most popular Erasmus destinations'. Lisbon, which has been receiving around 40 percent of the total number of Erasmus students in Portugal, has welcomed approximately 30,000 students between 2000 and 2013 (62 percent of them during the past five years).[1] But who are these young European students arriving cyclically in Lisbon's urban areas? Why are they important when seeking to understand the transformation of several urban economies (leisure, services and the housing market)?

International students have been considered a *migratory elite* (Musgrove 1963), given that their educational and socio-economic origins are wealthier than the average local college or university students (Windle and Nogueira 2015). Likewise, the subpopulation of Erasmus students described in this chapter comes from slightly wealthier family backgrounds than the HES in general (Souto-Otero 2008). As a consequence of their position in the class structure, Erasmus students are deeply involved in contemporary processes of urban change. Their practices and patterns of consumption represent an expansion of new, middle-class transnational youth culture(s) in European cities. Thus, these young students (22.5 years old on average) are often supported through parental financial assistance because the monetary grant awarded by the European Commission is very limited. Equally, as the duration of their exchange is typically quite short, they do not participate in paid employment, at least formally. In my own research, some worked as bartenders or public relations staff in Bairro Alto's nightlife venues, but this was typically without a contract and only for a few hours a week.

The Erasmus students are otherwise known for their dense networks of friends, which are made up of other international students, and for the emotional experience of transiting to adulthood experienced during their stay (Tse and Waters 2013). Moreover, they are the largest and most noticeable student community in European cities, exhibiting paradigmatic middle-class youthful and hedonistic aesthetics, consumption patterns and social practices, especially during night-time leisure activities. In summary, the seasonal arrival of Erasmus students in Lisbon can be seen as an annually replicated settlement of a particular urban territory by a new transnational, youthful, affluent class. This relatively privileged mobile population has a central role in producing and reproducing nightscapes in many other European cities like Lisbon.

MAINSTREAM NIGHTSCAPES: LISBON'S SEGREGATED NIGHTLIFE EXPERIENCES

Several actors, economic activities and institutional images converge in the creation of what we might call *mainstream nightscapes* to create venues and night-time circuits characterised by an international population of middle- to upper-class young people. The proliferation of these venues in Western cities is strongly associated with the transformation of industrial cities to service-based economies and what has been called the night-time economy (Chatterton and Hollands 2003; Roberts and Eldridge 2009). The emergence of these often youth-oriented mainstream nightscapes (bars, pubs, clubs, events and even entire districts like Bairro Alto and Cais do Sodré in Lisbon) varies throughout Western cities according to thematic, national and local tastes but presents a comparable social composition as a consequence of several ethnic, racial and class exclusionary practices (Schwanen et al. 2012). A mainstream nightscape offers comparable musical and behavioural languages and is recognised and enjoyed by a transnational population of relatively rich, young consumers (English-speaking locals, tourists and international students). These languages are characterised by specific rules and references that are transmitted through the dominance of Anglo-American mass media and their replication in the visual and musical cultures of other countries. These can be recognised through global aesthetic tendencies and styles (present in each venue's advertisings and decoration), the existence of a dress code (and, consequently, a bouncer as a gatekeeper to ensure the aforementioned aesthetic order), the predominance of social interactions based on heteronormative (and patriarchal) gender roles (with the obvious exception of mainstream LGBTQ+ venues) and the use of alcohol and other drugs as a social lubricant.

The musical language of these spaces is typically a mixture of pop, electronic dance music, all-time greatest hits and Latino music, and presents many other variations according to local inclinations. These behavioural and musical references are evident in other nightlife practices, such as ways of drinking, socialising, dancing and flirting – in several Western mainstream nightscapes. Finally, the presence of spoken and written English should be highlighted as the dominant language of communication. This takes place on a basic level among bartenders and many of the customers as well as through specific imagery; the musical and behavioural imaginaries are mostly in English.

As in many other Western cities, there is a circuit of mainstream nightscapes in Lisbon, which is promoted by several economic, political and educational actors as a commodity directed towards young locals, tourists and international students. The network of interests in the creation and maintenance of Lisbon's mainstream nightscapes goes beyond the tourism and leisure industries and includes the central role played by political institutions in sustaining a leisure-centred, neo-liberal development model for Lisbon, which exists in many other post-industrial cities (Campo and Ryan 2008; Shaw 2010; Eder and Öz 2014). Lisbon's leisure-centred agenda has been sustained by several urban policies (as previously mentioned) and also by favouring the association of Lisbon's brand, especially since the 2004 UEFA Euro Cup, with the idea of a low-cost, youth-oriented party and city-break destination.

After several years, which have seen the proliferation of new bars, clubs and other venues, Lisbon has become a top destination in the European nightlife scene due to its relatively affordable prices. The growing presence of Erasmus students in the city has led to the extensive use of the Erasmus label to identify and qualify the ambiance of bars, clubs, parties and events, which are also frequented by other members of the public such as young locals and other tourists. In addition to some isolated important clubs (e.g., Lux), three particular areas in the city of Lisbon can be identified as paradigmatic mainstream nightscapes in the Portuguese capital: Bairro Alto, Praça do Comércio and Cais do Sodré. These districts have in common their marginal characteristics, at least before the transformation of Lisbon's urban economy to a leisure-centred economy since the end of the 1990s. The Bairro Alto, for example, used to be a bohemian and countercultural district frequented by locals and some groups of alternative foreigners (Nofre et al. 2017a). The Cais do Sodré neighbourhood, a former harbour area in Lisbon's centre populated by working-class families, was frequented by foreign sailors docked in the city, who patronised the quarter to frequent brothels and strip bars (Nofre 2013). Finally, Praça do Comércio square was occupied by many homeless people who sought protection from the rain under the arches of several semi-abandoned ministerial buildings, which was originally without any nightlife activity. The opening of the city to growing tourist numbers has transformed the aforementioned urban areas into spaces of so-called gentrified nightlife (Hae 2011a; Nofre 2013; Straw 2015b; van Liempt et al. 2015). The transformation of these formerly deprived areas into mainstream nightscapes is strongly related to the nightly activities developed by some Erasmus-oriented organisations. Portuguese students who studied in other European countries often manage these events and associations.

The first non-profit organisation was Erasmus Lisboa (EL), established in 2004, which was also the first to organise and market international parties and trips around the country directly to Erasmus students. It also created for the first time in Lisbon a membership card and the so-called welcome kit, a package of useful items for those who recently arrived in Lisbon: a map of the city and the public transport network, a mobile phone card, several discount coupons and relevant information about the city. It is important to note that these packs are now widely distributed to attract students and contain similar items, the membership card, the welcome kit and the organisation of parties and trips.

In 2008 the Lisbon branch of the ESN was created by another group of former local Erasmus students. ESN-Lisboa became part of a European network of organisations devoted to receiving Erasmus students in different cities. It is supported institutionally by the European Union, although initially it received no funding from the European Commission. The emergence of ESN in Lisbon was the beginning of a marked rivalry to control the commercialisation of students' leisure in the Portuguese capital, thus inaugurating a new era also for nightlife venues that started to show an interest in hosting international parties to fill their venues during weekdays. From here on, the three urban areas aforementioned, Bairro Alto, Praça do Comércio and Cais do Sodré, began their transformation into leisure-based, night-time economy areas oriented towards both an international public (tourists and students) and local, middle-class and upper-class customers. In the following years two further stakeholders joined this arena: EOL (Erasmus Organization Lisboa) in 2010 and ELL in 2013, which comprised former members of ESN.

Today, considering the importance of the Erasmus economy, most Erasmus student associations have abandoned their former role as non-profit organisations to become instead small businesses specialising in housing

(EOL), offering welcoming packs for international students (EL) and organising parties (ELL). However, ESN, which continues to be a non-profit association tied to European institutions, still maintains a particular struggle against ELL, by setting competitive schedules of events, parties and travel opportunities. As a consequence, even in summertime when the majority of international students have not yet arrived, these two organisations offer a programme of daily activities, including an international party every night in one of the city's nightclubs. September and February (the two months in which students of the first and second semesters arrive, respectively) are the most important times of the year as this is when the new Erasmus students arrive and choose to attend events run by one organisation over another. For this reason, the programme of activities during September and February is completely overwhelming for the local area: pub crawls, surfing days, Erasmus barbecues, open bar nights, museum days, walking city tours, boat parties, movie nights, traditional dinners, sunset public drinking, language tandems, welcome parties and numerous excursions to other parts of the country occur across the week.

The most popular activities and those that attract the highest economic profits, both for the associations and for the nightlife venues, occur during night-time hours. In addition to some spin-off initiatives developed by these aforementioned Erasmus students' associations in providing housing to their clients, there is a hidden structure of gains inside the night-time activities of these associations, meaning they walk a thin line between being non-profit organisations and private businesses. Tiago Lopes,[2] who was a volunteer in one of these associations in 2013, explains how the structure of profits in his former organisation works:

> The agreement with the clubs varies between 20–30 percent of the tickets sold and 10–20 percent of the drinks served, so everything depends on how many people they can attract to a party. If PRs (public relations) bring 50 students the venue will pay an amount, but if they can bring 100 they will pay double.

The marketing operations for international parties are designed to attract the maximum number of students. They are marketed as must-do events that will be attended by *everyone* (especially young women). The organisers adopt three approaches. First, they advertise campaigns for parties through their social media accounts (especially Facebook), selling pre-order tickets, posting frequent reminders of the event and publishing a compilation of photographs from other parties, especially of young women in suggestive clothing or having fun with a drink in their hand. Second, public relations staff linked to various Erasmus associations encourage students to go to these *ultimate, crazy, amazing* parties with *special discounts*. And finally, the Erasmus students' associations organise a range of informal events before going to the clubs, such as pub crawls, all-you-can-eat-and-drink dinners and *Botellón* gatherings (drinking in the street) in order to draw big groups of students together and bring them to the clubs later on. In this sense, it is not fortuitous that most volunteers and leaders in these organisations are still studying or have recently graduated in business, marketing, tourism or economics. In fact, their internships with the Erasmus student associations centre around better understanding this niche market of international students.

According to the profiles of my interviewees and the observation of these events, the usual audience attending these parties are the youngest Erasmus students living away from their parents for the first time or those who interpret this experience abroad as the first moment of freedom in their lives. In addition, there are more mature attendees and groups of enthusiastic fans of the scenarios provided by the mainstream nightscapes (music, behavioural practices and norms, hard-drinking). But much more important than simply the events themselves is the cultural and linguistic element. Most central-European and Scandinavian Erasmus students who do not speak any romance language find Portugal a very arduous endeavour, especially those who studied little Portuguese before travelling. That is a key reason why they mainly choose to gather with English-speaking international students. The range of activities and parties proposed by these organisations are the few daily contexts they can do. These organisations utilise the initial isolation experienced by the foreign students, who can be seen as disoriented young people coming to live in a foreign country. In response to this situation, Erasmus organisations provide them several planned social activities for the entire week when they arrive as well as throughout the year. The first goal of these organisations has always been helping students to acclimatise in a new city in order to adapt to and understand the local context and people.

The commodification of activities promoted by the Erasmus organisations operating in Lisbon over the recent years has prompted a socio-spatial segregation between Portuguese and international students. This situation echoes Chatterton's (1999) depiction of the differences between traditional and non-traditional student lifestyles and identities in Bristol, United Kingdom. While the inclination of international students to socialise and organise their everyday lives among a group of foreigners (especially with co-nationals) has been widely recognised in the international literature (Bochner et al. 1985; Waters and Brooks 2011), the power of Erasmus as a label to identify and attract young, middle-class students to leisure activities has created a distinctive culture of consumption and socialisation in European cities. What Papatsiba (2006) has called the *Erasmus Cocoon*, that is, an ecosystem of friendship networks, leisure companies, nightlife venues and educational institutions that resembles holiday packages such as those offered in cruises, appears valid in the case of Lisbon. By trying to bring together all international students in the same place at the same time to maximise incomes based on agreements reached with the clubs, these organisations promote the separation of Erasmus students from local students. On the one hand, the use of English (even if young Portuguese are very proficient) and the cultural vernacular of these nightscapes are not engaging the majority of local young students. On the other hand, the prices charged to international students in these parties are higher than those offered to local students, discouraging a real diversified attendance. As a result, only English-speaking, middle-class and/or upper-class local students attend the international parties.

To summarise, the expansion of Erasmus students in Lisbon and the promotion of a range of activities by different student organisations have stimulated the transformation of three different urban areas of the city centre of Lisbon into night-time, leisure-centred areas mainly marketed to visitors. The logic of *commodifying* the isolation experienced by the students by bringing them to the same areas, bars and clubs has created a segregated nightscape between international students and the majority of local students. That is why the urban areas popular for these activities are now in an advanced stage of commercial and residential gentrification. However, this is not the only nightscape where we can find Erasmus students in Lisbon.

ALTERNATIVE NIGHTSCAPES IN LISBON, OR HOW TO AVOID INTERNATIONAL, NOCTURNAL AMBIANCE?

In order to understand the social worlds, identities and consumer choices of international students in Lisbon, it is necessary to recognise that they are social actors entangled in their own processes of becoming adults, even when living abroad (Tse and Waters 2013). During their short-term migratory experiences, they creatively adapt their identities and lifestyles to a new urban context where they are considered 'strangers' (Murphy-Lejeune 2002). As a consequence, some students wish to be differentiated from other groups and exhibit complex and individualised processes of distinction (Bourdieu 1979). Fieldwork conducted with these students has allowed us to shed light on the dominant discourses found among this group of international students, which is their rejection of the foreign student label. They often argue they are not the *typical* Erasmus student, a statement that lays the ground for the process of distinction that differentiates *mainstream* and *alternative* students in terms of their acquisition of cultural capital. In Lisbon, a significant number of Erasmus students construct their identities and everyday lives disregarding (and even disdaining) the cultural practices and the patterns of consumption built around the *Erasmus label*, considering typical Erasmus students as victims of a commercialised product. These 'alternative' students reject the idea of attending international segregated parties, speaking in English and frequenting venues that are only affordable for middle-class and upper-class students. We could group these students, their consumption practices and subcultural lifestyles as *alternative*, as they renounce the commodified model and propose a different way of living and enjoying the experience of being an international student in Lisbon. This is clearly a process of distinction that nourishes the cultural capital of alternative students, and their disdain and deliberate attempts to distance themselves from other students could be seen as a form of snobbery. By applying the typologies used to understand the tourism phenomenon (Smith 1989), one could argue that they could be the backpackers, explorers or drifters of studying abroad, who reject other modalities of travelling for being *uninformed* or *vulgar*. The cultural and economic logic underpinning the Erasmus party organisers discussed earlier attracts negative associations for these alternative students on the grounds that they resemble travel agencies with their all-in-one tourist packages. The small size of the city, and the ability of these associations to organise significant social events and to attract students to certain leisure areas, is critiqued for homogenising student experiences. Holding typically left-wing views that vary from new-age to revolutionary communism and anarchism, the alternative students reject the partying ways that take place in mainstream nightscapes and complain about sexist advertising in the venues, unrestrained alcohol consumption, the celebration of national identities and the exhibition of purchasing power by clothing and other means.

However, the main issue mentioned by alternative students when asked about their differentiated lifestyles is the lack of contact and communication between international students and the local reality. It is true that alternative students in Lisbon tend to strive to learn Portuguese and speak with the locals such as shopkeepers working in groceries or open-minded local students who have the predisposition to socialise with foreign peers. In this sense, the pursuit of the traditional and the typical in Lisbon by these alternative students involves a search for authenticity (Wang 1999) that travellers perform to differentiate their tastes from the mass consumption of tourists (Cohen 1979). As in the case of travelling, using the local language and acting as a connoisseur of Lisbon's cultural nuances and details is another form of distinction to differentiate themselves from other students, thus accumulating further cultural capital.

It is possible to differentiate two different, but intersecting, groups of alternative students in Lisbon based on their patterns of consumption, political identities and lifestyles: the neo-bohemian and the politicised. The first ones are the most numerous alternative demographic of international students in Lisbon. They study humanities, languages or fine arts; attend cultural and musical events and exhibitions; do yoga or other spiritual body trainings; and prefer *cafeterias* and tea shops instead of pubs and dancing bars. They also never go to clubs. Most of them live in particular neighbourhoods that they identify as typical and genuine, such as Alfama, Graça, Bica or Madragoa, which are in the early stages of gentrification. The second group is students who commit their leisure time to participating in local political activities such as assemblies, demonstrations and protests. They are also connected with political and/or social struggles in their home countries and partake in campaigns and protests against governments and private companies through digital media. They are typically students of the social sciences (political scientists, sociologists, anthropologists, geographers). Many are vegetarian or vegan and reside in poorer quarters of inner Lisbon such as Intendente, Anjos and Mouraria. These districts are associated with the presence of underprivileged Portuguese nationals and migrants from Brazil, Africa and Asia, a multicultural, working-class landscape with whom they sympathise as a result of their ideas of international solidarity.

These two groups of alternative Erasmus students comprise a variety of individuals coming from different countries, but two nations stand out: Spaniards and Italians. However, it is difficult to determine whether it is their cultural and linguistic proximity or the fact they are the largest Erasmus populations in Lisbon that makes them more prominent in alternative local cultures. By contrast, Polish students often speak good Portuguese; sometimes they take language courses before travelling to Portugal, but it is very unusual for them to be alternative students, even when they represent the third-largest proportion of Erasmus students in Lisbon.

Speculatively, this boundary between alternative and mainstream may also have a class component: a number of Spaniards and Italians come from the lower fraction of the middle classes, those who suffered the financial crisis of 2008 and witnessed the implementation of austerity policies. They can afford to travel to Lisbon because it is generally cheaper than Spain, whereas going to London would be impossible for them. In contrast, Polish students in Lisbon are coming from outside the eurozone, a move that suggests a relatively richer socio-economic background and a certain purchasing power. However, beyond national-based economic constraints, it should be said that alternative international students create cosmopolitan *universes of belonging* (Cuervo and Win 2014) opposed to the default homogenous Erasmus lifestyle mainly based on what they call the *typical Erasmus experience*, promoted by the various aforementioned associations. The country-oriented or language-oriented self-segregation of some friendship groups is also severely criticised by alternative students for disregarding the opportunity to experience an *authentic* or *multicultural* exchange, which is how they regard their own, culturally distinguished, lifestyles in Lisbon.

These strategies of distinction displayed by the young alternative international students are expressed through numerous nightlife behaviours. In Lisbon there are several venues and spaces devoted to offering an alternative to the dominance of mainstream leisure environments that we could identify as *alternative* nightscapes. These alternative nightscapes are essentially different from mainstream nightscapes commented on earlier because they are spaces that afford cultural capital for their customers. In spite of their heterogeneity we can find this kind of alternative places in almost every important city in the world, with global alternative music being played or performed, the same repertoire of aesthetic subcultural styles among the customers and underground or retro decorations which are inspired in the same cultural references (psychedelic new-age, classic UK punk, rockabilly or reggae). The customers of alternative spaces seek to recognise themselves in a deep way with the identity of the place, incorporating the cultural capital provided symbolically by the subculturally sensitive elements of the place (music, aesthetic, people's differentiated behaviour) and its correspondence with a particular worldview.

For example, DAMAS is a nightlife venue that attracts local, middle-class students in the Graça neighbourhood and usually offers live concerts and DJ performances until 4:00 a.m. on weekends. Access is free, but the prices of drinks are above average. Also, contemporary Portuguese food is served in the front section of a minimalist restaurant that also offers concerts in its basement, most of which are from the circle of Lisbon's alternative music scene. Disgraça is another alternative nightlife venue, supported by the anarchist and 'libertarian' community of Lisbon. It has a library of anarchist books and offers films, political discussions, hardcore and punk concerts and vegan food at very popular prices some nights of the week. The environment and the relationships established with the people (and with their ever-present dogs) are governed by anarchist ideologies. Finally, alternative international students also go to local neighbourhood associations such as Centro Recreativo de Anjos, which are popular places with a family and down-to-earth environment, and populated by a mix of low-income locals, migrants from Brazil and Africa and alternative students. These places do not have closing hours and do not offer specially selected music (sometimes there is no music at all), and the prices for drinks are extremely affordable for members, that is, people who dare to ring the entrance bell.

These types of alternative nightscapes are absent from the circuits promoted by Erasmus associations. However, it is possible to find alternative international students looking for alternative nightscapes in the events organised by Erasmus associations aiming to guide and attract new students to their own venues and activities. After spending a couple of hours in these venues, alternative students quickly realise that they are in the wrong environment, according to the processes of distinction that they have acquired and developed during the more general process of transition to adulthood (Murphy-Lejeune 2002). How these alternative Erasmus students find their place in the destination country in terms of meeting their expectations of having an alternative leisure space is notable. The most common way to hear about these places is establishing relationships with local students, specifically with similarly alternative local students, who eventually guide international students to these alternative nightscapes. According to our interviews, this was easier some years ago, before the growth of the Erasmus population, a trend that led them to interact more often among themselves (van Mol and Michielsen 2015). As stated before, the action of Erasmus associations to absorb the leisure demand of foreign students has caused the segregation of two differentiated night-time circuits: local students and Erasmus students. However, it is still possible for alternative international students to find the alternative nightscapes they wish to visit at night.

As previously noted, alternative nightscapes are mainly situated in areas characterised by a process of early or marginal gentrification, which is illustrated by the discovery and use of deprived urban spaces by populations with high cultural capital and low economic capital (Rose 1984), such as the alternative students. Low rental prices in old, central, non-regenerated buildings attract these cohorts of alternative and politically involved youth (locals and foreigners), who do not care about living side by side with an impoverished, mixed population of locals and migrants. As they have been educated in cosmopolitan and multicultural principles that shape their diversity-seeking propensity (Blokland and van Eijk 2010), artists, students, intellectuals and other creative classes feel attracted to living in these areas. Like other alternative nightscapes, these districts provide the cultural capital sought by these distinguished populations of (future) professionals that are shaping the cognitive-cultural urban economy (Scott 2014). However, despite being an interesting moment for urban social mixing, emancipation and cultural creativity (Caulfield 1989), marginal gentrification is the preliminary phase of discovery before the arrival of revitalisation projects promoted by the local government, and the expected commercial exploitation of property in the area carried out by major investors. The presence of a young, middle-class alternative population is a necessary step to clean up the image of the area and to increase the value of living and partying in what is now a *vibrant*, *diverse* and *exciting* neighbourhood. The nightscapes of several cities have followed this pattern: a formerly obscure and cheap area known for its rough nightlife frequented by low-income locals and middle-class alternative populations (who seek a culturally inspiring underground environment) is regenerated into an attractive area for middle- to upper-class, night-time users, displacing the former residents to other spaces. Usually, those middle-class alternative populations had already generated attractive lifestyles in these areas that were subsequently captured and commercialised to be sold to higher social classes, after a process of urban renewal. This is the case of nightscapes that are now part of the general trend described earlier: Bairro Alto and Cais do Sodré (Praça do Comércio did not previously have any significant night-time activity).

Alternative Erasmus students in Lisbon are undoubtedly marginal gentrifiers who take part in the recent tensions that have occurred in the housing rental market in central Lisbon since 2014. Integral to this process, the division of old, family houses into private rooms, or their conversion into modern apartments for students, indirectly results in processes of eviction, as similarly occurred in Britain (Slater 2006). The first Erasmus students in Lisbon, who once were labelled as alternative consumers, played a central role in the early gentrification of nightlife in Bairro Alto and Cais do Sodré at the end of the 1990s and the beginning of the 2000s when these areas were still dangerous and, as such, unvisited by the majority of the local middle classes (Malet Calvo et al. 2017; Nofre et al. 2017a). For this reason, alternative Erasmus students should be conceived as indicators for the progression of the urban frontier: after some time inhabiting deprived and typical areas such as Alfama, Graça, Mouraria, Anjos and Intendente, residential and nightlife gentrification processes are now expanding all over these neighbourhoods.

CONCLUSIONS: STUDENTS AS NIGHTSCAPE COLONISERS

A new, transnational, middle-class population of young people have arrived in Lisbon in the past few years: Erasmus students may be one of the few worthwhile elements still proudly promoted in this period of economic crisis inside the European Union. The success experienced by the Portuguese capital among Erasmus students should be connected to the more general process of marketing and promotion of Lisbon's nightlife, which is enjoyed by young tourists and students alike (within the following years some of these tourists will become Erasmus students, and many of these Erasmus students will return as tourists). All these young populations have contributed to transform Lisbon's nightscapes over the past ten years when most central nightlife neighbourhoods were still considered dangerous, rough areas to visit at night. The tireless action carried out by local associations of former Erasmus students, the bigger budgets of foreign students when compared with locals and the wish expressed by some nightlife venues to open on weekdays are the three elements that explain the rapid expansion of Lisbon's nightlife and its gentrification. However, some international students refuse to participate as consumers of mainstream nightscapes. They identify themselves as alternative and express neo-bohemian cultural and artistic tastes to far-left political positions. Following the local alternative trends and inclinations, they attend alternative nightscapes in order to find a place where they can accomplish their processes of distinction during their stay abroad, which includes above all contact with local alternative youth.

Both mainstream and alternative nightscapes should be considered as two different moments in the commodification of the student city (Chatterton 2010). Interestingly, today's mainstream nightscapes in Lisbon were, once, alternative nightscapes. Likewise, the current alternative nightscapes in Lisbon have the potential to attract wealthier populations in the night-time, as proven by the role of alternative students (both local and foreign) in improving the reputation of specific areas and publicising them through digital media as an *authentic* space, especially for international audiences. After that, local, middle- and upper-class young tourists and mainstream international students have started arriving in these areas, transforming the venues and the social composition of audiences in the neighbourhood, that is, transforming formerly alternative nightscapes into mainstream nightscapes. For that very reason, municipal authorities have recently planned urban reforms that have subsequently attracted major property investors and have created the conditions to commodify subcultural lifestyles and alternative leisure activities. Therefore, the *discovery* of these areas by a new, transnational, young middle class represented by Erasmus students has laid the foundations for the transformation of these neighbourhoods into gentrified nightlife areas in a few years. Further research is needed to understand how the commodification of alternative leisure activities and its transformation into mainstream nightscapes operate and to what extent the different Erasmus groups described in this text play a central role in this process of expansion and commodification of Lisbon's increasingly neo-liberal urban night.

NOTES

1. This date was retrieved from PORDATA, Study in Lisbon Platform, Erasmus+ National Agency (Portugal) and Eurostat, 2012.

2. The name was changed in order to protect the identity of this participant.

Chapter 10

Nightlife and Urban Change in Southern European University Cities: The Case of Montpellier

Emanuele Giordano and Dominique Crozat

Over the recent decades a number of social and cultural changes have profoundly altered the status of the urban night in most European countries. For many European cities in particular, nightlife has become an important component of the urban economy and an important drawcard in attracting new tourists, students and residents. However, the expansion of night-time leisure activities has also resulted in a steady rise in tension as a result of the simultaneous and antagonistic uses of urban spaces, particularly between long-time residents and other users. A growing number of scholars have paid attention to the role nightlife now plays in the urban regeneration of city centres and have proposed new policy-oriented actions are needed to limit negative impacts derived from the expansion of youth-oriented (Malet Calvo et al. 2017) and tourist-oriented nightlife (Ashworth and Page 2011). The urban night is thus now a key site through which to trace how the post-industrial city centre is being reshaped economically, spatially, socially, culturally and politically (Nofre et al. 2017a, 2017b).

However, scholarly attention has mainly focused on Anglophone case studies, with little attention paid to the evolution of the night-time economy in southern Europe. While the myth of a 'continental', southern European nightlife was often seen as a model for British cities and prompted some legislation such as extended opening hours (Roberts and Turner 2005; Roberts and Eldridge 2009), recent studies have revealed a more complex reality on the European mainland. Much like elsewhere, many European cities experience problems in terms of safety, violence and noise disturbances. At the same time, in recent years growing attention has been paid to how the expansion of the night-time economy in many southern European cities could potentially foster processes of neighbourhood change and processes such as gentrification, touristification and studentification. In order to contribute to this emerging discussion, this chapter focuses on Montpellier, in southern France. The objectives of the chapter are to analyse how the growing concentration of university students, and the consequent expansion of the night-time economy in the historical neighbourhood of the Ecusson, is contributing to the restructuring of the residential and commercial nature of the area.

After a short theoretical overview of the interplay between complex, multisided processes of urban change and the recent expansion of night-time leisure activities that have occurred in Europe over the recent decades, we analyse recent processes of urban change that have taken place in the historical neighbourhood of the Ecusson and examine the extent to which these recent changes are connected to the rise of new urban nightscapes. In particular, we examine how in the neighbourhood of the Ecusson the development of a student-oriented nightlife scene has contributed to a process of urban change that is transforming the historical quarter into *youthified spaces* (Moos 2016) characterised by small housing units that are not generally occupied by households with children.

Our discussion of the Ecusson, Montpellier, is based on fieldwork conducted between 2015 and 2016. At the outset, fifteen semi-guided and informal interviews were conducted with representatives from a vast range of local stakeholders (the so-called night brigade of the local police, those responsible for the city transportation services, bar and restaurants owners and members of the residential community). Twenty-five further Ecusson residents were then interviewed regarding their nocturnal experiences of the neighbourhood. Finally, sixty informal and semi-guided interviews were conducted with nightlife consumers (mostly university students) regarding their experiences and practices during their night-time leisure activities.

NIGHTLIFE AND TRANSNATIONAL PROCESSES OF URBAN CHANGE

The past two decades has seen the urban night emerge as a significant site for productive economic activity, as well as a key strategy in the urban regeneration of many cities (Chatterton and Hollands 2003). Concepts such as the *twenty-four-hour open city* or *party city* (Roberts and Eldridge 2009) highlight not only the importance of the urban night in the revitalisation of many post-industrial cities but also the growing nocturnalisation of everyday life in Western culture (Koslofsky 2011). The night-time economy has played an important role in (re)shaping how tourists, visitors and different segments of the local population (especially university students) experience the city today (Grazian 2008).

The concept of the 'night-time economy', understood here as a policy initiative articulated with urban regeneration, arose in the early 1990s in the United Kingdom. It was initially conceived as a strategy for socio-economic revitalisation of central areas of cities affected by deindustrialisation in the 1970s and 1980s, continuing suburbanisation that had occurred over the post-war period and the dramatic shift of retail to peripheral sites (Heath 1997). So-called big box retail outlets on the fringes of urban centres were particularly singled out for drawing consumers away from traditional high streets. The retreat of city-centre workers to suburban home-based activities after work played a further role in the urban night being a *dead time* with little economic potential or market value to central areas of British cities and towns. Urban areas were, as a result, increasingly perceived to be dominated by groups such as drug users and sex workers (Lovatt and O'Connor 1995). But it was under John Major's administration and thanks to the law to ban unlicensed raves (1990) that had spread across South England in the late 1980s that electronic music was driven back into cities and urban venues. In parallel, the deregulation and development of the alcohol and leisure industries at night were catalysts for the revitalisation of central areas, transforming them into leisure-led areas, which further helped to boost local economies after years of recession (Bianchini 1995).

While, initially, development of the night-time economy was related to specific conditions existing in the United Kingdom, it has become a global phenomenon since late 1990s, though with different effects depending on national, economic and social contexts. While Hae (2011a, 3450) argues that in the case of New York City 'nightlife establishments often constitute an important foundation for the rekindling of depressed property markets in derelict neighbourhoods by helping to generate an atmosphere of lively urban sociality', van Liempt et al. (2015, 409–10) note that

> originating in the UK's post-industrial cities, strategies to [re-]position the urban night in terms of economic opportunity and revitalise [parts of] city centres, which are underpinned by rationalities of urban competitiveness in a globalizing economy have steadily diffused through Europe, North America and Australasia and are now also pursued, albeit in modified form, in cities in the global South.

Today, in many world cities, the night-time economy has become not only an important part of the urban economy but also an important element of urban regeneration, branding and marketing distinction. Despite the initial optimism about the economic and cultural potentialities of the night-time economy, geographers and other social scientists have engaged critically with these developments. While many scholars argue that the night-time economy has become an important component of the lifestyle of urban populations such as middle-class cosmopolitans, tourists and students (Chatterton and Hollands 2002), others criticise mainstream nightlife as strongly marked by social inequalities based on gender, race, ethnicity, class, cultural and religious backgrounds and their intersections (e.g., Boogaarts 2008; Schwanen et al. 2012).

While this literature demonstrates the cultural as well as the economic outcomes and drivers of nightlife, and related problems, studies on the nighttime economy remain unevenly distributed. Existing literature has focused primarily on northern Europe, especially the United Kingdom, while southern Europe has received considerably less attention. This lack of interest is surprising considering how several British cities were attempting to model themselves on what, in the 1980s and 1990s in particular, was perceived as a more sustainable *continental nightlife*. This lack of critical works could be related to the long-standing perception of the existence of a peculiar continental style of alcohol consumption, allegedly produced by a more laissez-faire attitude in terms of licensing and control (Roberts and Turner 2005). Yet this simplistic vision has been increasingly criticised (Tierney 2006; Jayne et al. 2008).

Recent studies have started to reveal how the traditional vision of a southern European night-time economy based on cafes and characterised by a distinctive, diverse, wine-drinking and more *sensible* drinking culture does not correspond to the reality. As well as comprising as much diversity in drinking cultures as elsewhere, southern European cities also experience the same problems in terms of excessive drinking and concerns about safety that characterise British cities. At the same time, recent studies have explored how conflicts emerging in neighbourhoods due to gentrification have resulted in the rise of *gentrified nightlife* in formerly deprived historical quarters of the city centre (e.g., Malet Calvo et al. 2017; Nofre et al. 2017a). In a similar way, a number of complex, multisided tensions between different social actors of the urban night (consumers, residents, venue owners, municipals) are continuously being (re-)produced in nightlife districts of especially southern European cities. For example, this would be the case in Bairro Alto in Lisbon (Nofre et al. 2017a), the historical former harbour quarter of Barceloneta in La Barceloneta (Nofre et al. 2017b), or the city centre of Bordeaux, in south-west France. In this last case, Comelli (2015) has highlighted how, while the presence of a vibrant nightlife in central areas of this south-western French city has initially helped the revitalisation and gentrification of several neighbourhoods, once gentrification settles in nightlife businesses tend to be pushed out. As Comelli (2015, 224) also points out, 'There is a confiscation of the festive night which is poorly tolerated by the people of the upper class that have conquered neighbourhoods that were attractive areas in this temporality. These new residents, sometimes, carry a moral judgment and consider the nightly uses of their neighbourhood as deviances'. On the other hand, work on both La Barceloneta and Bairro Alto, as aforementioned, highlights the importance of the interplay between complex, multisided urban processes such as studentification and touristification and how these have socially and spatially (re)shaped the urban night in south European cities and towns. Researchers engaged in the study of the urban night in southern Europe have recently developed a growing interest in the effects produced by both studentification and touristification of urban nightlife in some south European cities like Barcelona and Lisbon.

Since the 1990s several European cities have encouraged the expansion of their nightlife. The night-time economy has increasingly become a central part of their tourism strategies, and several cities have adopted cultural and marketing policies to develop and communicate their status as *the* twenty-four-hour open city or party city (Roberts and Eldridge 2009). In southern Europe, this trend has been reinforced by the current financial and economic crises that, in cases like Portugal and Spain, have much to do with the recent challenges to national and urban economic systems (Janoschka et al. 2014). Facing such economic challenges, many city leaders from southern Europe have opted to strengthen the weight of tourism in local economies as short- and mid-term strategies to mitigate austerity policies. Therefore, the touristification of urban centres (Gladstone and Préau 2008; Ashworth and Page 2011; Knafou 2012) appears as a source of opportunities in terms of jobs for young skilled and unskilled workers, entrepreneurial opportunities and new forms of leisure (Scott 2006). For major urban destinations, tourist-led nightlife has thus become a key component of the urban economy. However, this process has not occurred without some negative social, economic and cultural consequences.

On the one hand, in many large cities such as Barcelona or Lisbon, the touristification of the urban night tends to affect residents' quality of life and leads to commercial gentrification. Traditional restaurants and bars have been progressively replaced by more tourist-oriented venues characterised by higher prices and different cultural sensibilities and aesthetic styles and codes (Cócola-Gant 2015). On the other hand, the expansion of youth-oriented and tourist-oriented nightlife in the city centre has often involved the rise of critical problems regarding the coexistence of residential communities and alcohol-fuelled nightlife entertainment uses, undermining community liveability during night-time hours (Nofre et al. 2017a, 2017b). In turn, the arrival of thousands of international university students to these cities since the inclusion of southern European countries in the Erasmus Student Exchange Programmes in the late 1980s has prompted the emergence of new nightlife spots in the city and the reorientation of traditional nightlife supply to newcomers, despite its often resulting in the marginalisation and spatial displacement of traditional working-class, night-time leisure activities (Nofre 2013).

Exploring the studentification of nightlife is of a great importance, and many Anglophone authors suggest the studentification of some neighbourhoods in European cities has led to the rise of 'student ghettos' (Hubbard 2008). In other words, studentification is the process by which specific neighbourhoods become dominated by student residential uses (Smith 2005, 2008; Smith and Holt 2007; Hubbard 2008, 2009; Chatterton 2010; Sage et al. 2012; He 2015). For Chatterton (1999), *traditional students* – white, middle-class and who have enrolled in a university in their late teens and left the parental home when entering a university – may be seen as perfect candidates to become part of the gentrifying class. In this sense, Smith (2005) and Smith and Holt (2007) have conceptualised *studentified spaces* as *gentrification factories* in which students, as *apprentice gentrifiers*, accumulate cultural capital and acquire the middle-class lifestyles and tastes representative of gentrifiers. According to this view, studentified spaces are *learning spaces* where students develop and express cultural capital and competencies and formalise (or reproduce) the values and beliefs of the new middle classes. As Smith (2005, 87) argues:

> While gentrification is linked to higher education as the gateway through which professional status (connected with economic capital) and cultural capital may be transmitted, the lifestyles within ghettoised studentified areas provide a certain kind of symbolic capital. This form of capital represents an attempt to find security in areas of 'people like us' and one which is likely to be repeated in future location decisions upon graduation.

While this account remains important, it does not consider diversification of the student body. The assumption that all students play an active role in gentrification is perhaps neither fair nor accurate. While the influence of social background in terms of access to higher education remains substantial, the number of students from disadvantaged backgrounds is increasing, placing them in a contradictory relationship to the forces critiqued here. According to Nakazawa (2017), 33 percent of full-time students under the age of twenty-one years whose permanent residence was in the United Kingdom and who were seeking their first degree had a working-class background (NS-SEC classes 4–7; statistical data in this paragraph relates to the 2014–2015 academic year and was obtained from HESA 2016, unless indicated otherwise). In addition, the composition of students in terms of race, ethnicity and age is changing, with a growing (but still marginal) presence of ethnic minorities. Among first-year students whose primary residence was in the United Kingdom, 21.2 percent were ethnic minorities, 65.0 percent of whom enrolled in a university in their teens. This is not to say black and minority ethnic or working-class students do not play a role in gentrification or studentification. That education allows for students to move up the social ladder should also not be ignored. However, as noted, their relationship to the marketisation of urban centres is often fraught and ambiguous. This would most clearly be the case in areas undergoing gentrification, which were already home to many black and minority ethnic communities. While existing studies have focused on UK universities, it is plausible to assume that the diversification of the student population is even greater in southern Europe. In the case of Montpellier, and despite the fact that university fees in France are less than €500 per year, in 2008, 30 percent of university students were in receipt of a scholarship, and this percentage has grown in recent years.[1]

While we should leave room for some ambiguity when discussing the relationship between students, studentification and gentrification, some recent studies have highlighted the role that the Erasmus students do play in changing the nature of the urban night in several southern European cities. Focusing on the case of Lisbon, Daniel Malet Calvo in the previous chapter and elsewhere (Malet Calvo 2017; Malet Calvo et al. 2017) has shown how the use of alternative and often deprived nightlife districts by Erasmus students is triggering broader urban processes that often involve gentrification. More particularly, Malet Calvo (2017, 10–11) highlights how 'Erasmus students that have been attracted to particular urban spaces, contribute with their presence to rising rents and eviction processes'. Crucially, the combination of studentification and the expansion of youth-oriented nightlife in a specific urban area often produces a multifarious process of neighbourhood change that entails economic but also symbolic and cultural transformations that could potentially affect former inhabitants' quality of life and so ignite the process of residential displacement (Cócola-Gant 2015). That is why a more kaleidoscopic approach to studentification in south European cities is needed, as it is much influenced by other complex, nonlinear urban processes.

To date, critical work on the role that students have played in reshaping nightlife in several cities has mainly focused on international students who represent specific and distinguished lifestyles when compared with their local peers. According to Malet Calvo (2017), international students could be seen as broadly a *migratory elite* (Musgrove 1963) because they tend to come from wealthier socio-economic backgrounds than the average local student (Souto-Otero 2008). The expansion of student-led nightlife and the rise of a vibrant nightlife spot in the city mainly frequented by university students are typically articulated with the production and consumption of aspirational, youthful lifestyles that at the same time have a central role to play in fostering processes of gentrification that in the long term can cause the displacement not only of former inhabitants but also of established nightlife establishments. In this process, tourists, visitors, international and national university students, or even *student-tourists* (Lesjak et al. 2015), young college-educated (often precarious) workers and creative young entrepreneurs are simultaneously central actors and beneficiaries of these urban, social and residential changes. In some recent cases like in Raval in Barcelona (Catalonia), these changes involve a more complex change of lifestyle and cultural identities that often entails forms of symbolic violence against life-long, working-class (and usually elderly) populations of the area (Fernández 2014). Cosmopolitan, youthful tastes and habitus come to dominate the nocturnal city. As such, traditional residents tend to experience an increasing *out-of placeness* (Wolifson 2016).

Exploring gentrification, studentification and spatial displacement leads to some pivotal questions about the nocturnal geographies of the student population. First, do nocturnal geographies produced by international students exhaust possible spatialities of the studentified nightlife or are other geographies possible? Second, how do local students interact with international university students, middle-class residents living in the city centre or tourists and visitors inside and outside the context of the night-time economy? To attempt to answer these questions, the second part of this chapter explores a specific case study, the neighbourhood of the Ecusson in the city of Montpellier in southern France.

STUDENTIFYING MONTPELLIER

Montpellier is located six miles inland from France's Mediterranean coast. It is the capital of the Hérault Department. Montpellier is the eighth-largest city of France and has also been the fastest-growing city in the country over the past twenty-five years.[2] The city population grew from 161,900 inhabitants in 1960 to 197,281 in 1982 and reached 272,082 in 2013. While during the 1960s and 1970s the growth of the city population was connected with the arrival of French immigrants (*les pieds noirs*) from Algeria after the end of the Algerian War, over recent decades population growth has been mainly related to the growing number of students living in the city due to the existence of two universities. The presence of university students is not a recent occurrence in Montpellier. The law school was founded in 1260, while the medical school was founded in 1289. In the beginning of the 1950s Montpellier was one of eight cities in France with more than 5,000 students (Vassal 1969). Traditionally based in the Ecusson, because of the growing number of students in 1960, and following the UK and US models, the universities were dispersed to the north of the city through the construction of two university campuses. In the city centre, only a few buildings, mainly fulfilling administrative duties, were left.

According to the traditional spatial perspective on studentification, the displacement of the universities to campus outside the centre should have caused the inflow and concentration of university students in those areas around the newly built campuses. Indeed, the existing literature on the process of studentification highlights how this process of clustering around campuses emerged prominently in the 1990s in the United Kingdom as a result of the country's expansive higher education policies. Due to the consequent growth of higher education students, several neighbourhoods adjacent to newly developed or expanding campuses started to receive a significant and seasonal migrant youth population. Some actors (house owners and small-scale capital investors) supplied student accommodation by converting family houses into flats shared by students. These are called houses of multiple occupancy (HMOs). At the same time, some investors started to construct new student-oriented developments (cultural and retail services for students, university-maintained accommodation). As a result, an increasing concentration of young people characterised by distinctive tastes and lifestyle started to reside in residential districts. The inflow of students restructured the local population and housing composition of neighbourhoods and prompted the transformation of retail outlets, services and entertainment venues. According to existing literature, in the case of British cities and towns, this process often fostered the displacement of low-income populations not otherwise in secure housing. Segregation between student and nonstudent populations was also exacerbated, causing the formation of *student ghettos* (Hubbard 2008).

Yet this UK-centred perspective on studentification (residential concentration of further education students in specific areas around campuses in the form of HMOs and the development of purpose-built student accommodation) that stresses proximity to the campuses as the main driving force in clustering (Sage et al. 2012) has been proven inadequate to explain the spatial distribution of university students in southern European cities. For instance, according to Malet Calvo (2017, 6) in the case of Lisbon, 'it is not possible to point to specific studentified areas because student accommodation (for both locals and overseas students) is more or less spread over the entire city. It also covers the most central neighbourhoods in spite of being far from the university, or college faculties, or being poorly connected to them by public transport'. Malet Calvo points to several factors that could explain Lisbon's peculiar student geographies. On the one hand, Lisbon is medium size, and its developed public transport system and the urban form all make the distances from home to education establishments less relevant compared with the UK case studies.

On the other hand, the concentration of students is reduced by the limited number of purpose-built student accommodation in the city. In several UK cities, these new developments have progressively reduced the supply of unregulated flats, considered a *risky business* for all parties involved (Smith 2009), and favoured the concentration of university students in certain urban areas. Yet in the case of Lisbon, rental and subleasing through informal agreements still dominate the housing offer for university students. While these elements explain the diversity and fragmentation of student housing in Lisbon in relation to the established literature exploring UK cities, they are not a peculiarity of the Portuguese capital but elements that Lisbon shares with several southern European cities.

Montpellier is no exception. The French city is half the size of Lisbon and possesses a well-developed public transport system that includes thirty-six bus lines and a fifty-six-km tramway network. At the same time, the city lacks purpose-built student accommodation (only 10 percent of students stay in this kind of accommodation). In turn, student accommodation is not concentrated in the areas around the campuses but is spread all over the city (INSEE 2012). As a result, since the 1990s, several neighbourhoods have experienced an intense studentification due to the growing number of students who attended the three universities. Indeed, while in the 1950s around 5,000 university students were living in Montpellier, according to the France Population Census Data, in 2014, 42,435 students were living in the city out of a population of almost 275,318.[3] Among the neighbourhoods that have experienced the most notable increase in student population is the historic neighbourhood of the Ecusson.

NIGHTLIFE AND STUDENTIFICATION OF THE ECUSSON QUARTER IN MONTPELLIER

The Ecusson represents the historical centre of Montpellier. Despite its origins as a residential area for the nobility and bourgeois families, during the nineteenth and twentieth centuries it was inhabited principally by the lower classes. By the beginning of the 1960s the Ecusson was characterised by the presence of marginalised populations and a strong deterioration of the housing stock (Ferras 1978). It was only towards the end of the 1960s that the situation started to change. The election of François Delmas as Mayor of Montpellier marked the starting point of a new urban project that aimed to transform Montpellier into a regional metropolis (Volle et al. 2010). In this context, the regeneration of the Ecusson became a key element of this strategy. Since the end of the 1960s a series of measures have been adopted to restore the decaying built environment. In 1967, a ministerial decree transformed the Ecusson into a *secteurs sauvagardés* (protected sector). Instituted with the Malraux Law in 1962, these special areas were created to restore the historical housing stock of central neighbourhoods. In the specific case of Montpellier, the goal was to restore the exterior appearance of the buildings and create comfortable lodgings within them, while preserving the neighbourhood's historic appearance.

While this intervention was focused on the physical layout, its social impacts were immediate. The law envisaged granting financial aid to owners for the restoration of the buildings, but this operation was not conducted on a voluntary basis; the owners were legally obliged to comply. Owners who were unable to financially contribute to the restoration of their buildings had two options: being evicted through a declaration of public utility and receive a financial aid for their relocation or sell their apartments, often to the public enterprise charged with the renovation. Crucially, this policy resulted in an intense process of gentrification. As Ferras (1978, 27) remarks, 'The restorations carried out in the centre justified a return of the bourgeoisie to the historical residences that they disputed with to offices of the liberal professions'. Alongside this process of residential change, the neighbourhood also experienced a process of commercial gentrification: 'Grocers, butchers, fruit seller, have been substituted by activities of different kinds, booksellers, jewellers, footwear, garment manufacturers, and so on' (Saltet, quoted in Ferras 1978, 18). As a result, the neighbourhood experienced a process of gentrification that led the population of the Ecusson to decline from 21,000 inhabitants in 1954 to 10,000 in 1975.

Yet since the end of the 1990s, due to its central location and the presence of both commercial and leisure activities, the Ecusson has experienced the greatest studentification. According to the France Population Census Data, in 2006 the young adult population aged between eighteen and twenty-four years represented 35.76 percent of the area. In 2013 they represented 37.84 percent (INSEE 2017). This data reveals a situation where students, rather than moving into a working-class area, have moved into a fairly well-established, middle-class location.

This concentration has caused growing tension between students and the first wave of gentrifiers, especially in relation to the development of a student-oriented nightlife scene. Since the 2000s the opening of student-led nightlife venues has led to the Ecusson becoming the main nightlife area of the city (Giordano et al. 2017). The development of the nightlife scene was not directly encouraged by local authorities, but they quickly appropriated this development as demonstrated by the marketing campaign Montpellier, The City on Which the Sun Never Sets. Indeed, the development of a vibrant nightlife was perceived as integral to the city's aspirations to present itself as a regional metropolis (Volle et al. 2010) and to attract university students. Yet the expansion of the night-time economy has resulted in tension between residents and nightlife consumers, who are mainly university students, due to litter on the streets and noise caused by hundreds of people drinking and talking outdoors.

Noise-related problems have increased over the years, as many informants confessed during our fieldwork, and nowadays the Ecusson is by far the

neighbourhood of Montpellier with the highest number of officially registered complaints about excessive noise (Louvet 2010). Moreover, noise
disturbances are also amplified by the physical layout of the neighbourhood.
As revealed by previous studies, historical neighbourhoods like the Ecusson,
which is characterised by narrow streets and small- to medium-sized blocks,
are more likely to experience problems related to noise and disturbance,
as also occurs in some British cities (Roberts and Eldridge 2009). These
disturbances do not affect all residents in the same way. Students, but also
young workers without children, tend to perceive noise disturbances less
acutely as they often do not share the same constraints on sleeping hours that
characterise households with children (Louvet 2010). The impossibility of
sleeping at night for them and/or their young children is the main reason why
a significant number of informants interviewed (some currently living in the
area and some now former residents) have left or are thinking of leaving the
Ecusson. This transformation of the Ecusson into a youthified space (Moos
2016) characterised by small housing units that are not generally occupied by
households with children is confirmed by the France Population Census Data.
While 329 families with children resided in the Ecusson in 2006, by 2013
only 254 remained (INSEE 2017). At the same time, while in 2006 there were
2,016 households comprising one person (representing the 62 percent of the
area's households), by 2013 this had increased to 3,317 single-person households, or 66.35 percent.[4] While the case of Montpellier confirms the role that
the night-time economy can have in triggering the social, cultural and residential transformation of urban spaces, it differs from the existing literature in
several ways. First, it extends existing studies on the changing nature of the
night-time economy in southern European cities by looking beyond deprived
and working-class neighbourhoods. In this sense, the Ecusson demonstrates
how the night-time economy can potentially develop in already-gentrified
neighbourhoods. Second, the case of Montpellier also points to the need to
extend the temporal perspectives of these processes.

  Existing literature has highlighted how once gentrifiers settle in, tensions
emerge between new residents and nightlife businesses due to the nuisance
caused by the latter (Hae 2011a). What typically occurs is the nightlife scene
becomes displaced. This has occurred with regularity where gentrification
has taken hold in existing nightlife areas. Battles between preexisting nightlife venues and 'new' gentrifying residents have been documented across a
number of areas. The case of the Ecusson shows a different dynamic due to
the fact that in the medium-long term the older gentrifiers, rather than the
nightlife venues, are being progressively displaced from the neighbourhood.
At the same time, the case of Montpellier shows the need to rethink the
relations between university students, tourists and the urban middle class in
the nocturnal city. Existing studies have highlighted how these populations

benefit from (and take part in) the evolution of the night-time economy and the processes of urban change it potentially triggers (Comelli 2015; Malet Calvo et al. 2017). Yet, while these populations are often said to easily coexist because they supposedly share similar cultural tastes and consumption patterns (Sánchez 2017; Malet Calvo 2017), the case of the Ecusson underlines how they do not necessarily share the same social and family constraints, such as sleeping hours. Crucially, these differences, as has happened in the case of the Ecusson, could potentially foster conflicts between these urban populations.

Finally, the case of Montpellier contributes to current debates, and expands current understandings, of studentification. It helps to rethink urban transformations resulting from increases in and concentrations of students and young people beyond the current focus on the dynamics of the housing market, revealing instead how urban changes are coproduced by a multiplicity of social process. On the other hand, it highlights the need to expand the scope of studentification studies beyond the epistemological constraints of gentrification (Nakazawa 2017). Crucially, the arrival of university students and the contemporary expulsion of the old gentrifiers from the Ecusson could not easily be conceptualised as a form of gentrification. Rather, it could be seen as a more general process of *youthification*, a dynamic that occurs as young adults (people in their twenties and early thirties) increase in terms of the total population in specific neighbourhoods. As Moos (2016, 4) highlights, 'The youthification process differs from gentryfication – an increase in social status of a neighbourhood – in that the former is not as explicitly a class-based process, although the two are not mutually exclusive'.

CONCLUSIONS

Focusing on the historical neighbourhood of the Ecusson in the French city of Montpellier, this chapter has analysed how the development of a student-oriented nightlife has actively contributed to tensions developing between students and older gentrifiers and has fostered a process of urban change that involves the progressive displacement of households with children. These homes have been steadily taken over by young people, mainly university students. Crucially, these dynamics highlight the need to expand the spatial, temporal and social perspectives that characterise the post-industrial city centre and how it is currently being reshaped spatially, temporally and socially. The case of Montpellier underlies the need to expand current understandings of the relationship between the night-time economy and processes of urban change from a spatial and temporal point of view. It highlights the need to expand the *spatial* focus on the development of a night-time economy in deprived neighbourhoods to other urban spaces. Temporally, it shows how in the medium to long term the older gentrifiers, rather than the nightlife scene, could be potentially displaced.

This case study also reveals how the urban night could be an interesting setting to extend critical thinking on the limits of studentification studies beyond its current framing as a form of gentrification (Nakazawa 2017). Indeed, while current literature has tended to highlight how students and gentrifiers tend to share similar consumption patterns and cultural tastes, the case of Montpellier highlights how their lifestyles still differ in several ways, for instance, in terms of sleeping hours. As such, like in the case of the Ecusson, tensions could increase between these populations, especially regarding the use of both time and space in the contemporary city.

The Ecusson helps to rethink the process of studentification in a more complex way than its current theorisation as a subform of gentrification. Indeed, while this chapter has shown how in the past decade the historical neighbourhood has experienced the inflow and concentration of university students, this process has not clearly led to an increase in the social status of the area but, in fact, quite the opposite. Rather than a process of gentrification, we argue that what the Ecusson is experiencing could be conceptualised as a form of youthification, a concept that is not entirely class based and that highlights the growing share of young adults living in certain areas (Moos 2015, 4). Further research might focus on considering to what extent the recent expansion and commodification of student-oriented nightlife has contributed to urban regeneration and socio-economic revitalisation of historical neighbourhoods of university cities, and what this has meant for the relationship among the night-time economy, gentrification and demographic change.

NOTES

1. See http://www.midilibre.fr/2015/01/27/montpellier-la-population-etudiante-de-plus-en-plus-fragile,1116899.php.

2. See https://www.theguardian.com/cities/2017/mar/13/montpellier-spotlight-development-mania-france-fastest-growing-city.

3. See https://www.insee.fr/fr/statistiques/2011101?geo=COM-34172#graphi que-EMP_G1.

4. In the France Population Census Data, municipalities are divided into areas called IRIS. Yet they do not correspond to the city's neighbourhoods. In the case of the Ecusson, we considered three IRIS, Ursulines, Préfecture and Saint-Roich, that together almost correspond to the Ecusson area. Data at the IRIS scale is available only since 2006.

Chapter 11

The Transformation of Amsterdam's Red-Light District and Its Impact on Daily Life in the Area

Irina van Aalst and Ilse van Liempt

Amsterdam's red-light district (RLD), locally known as 'De Wallen' (embankment), is the oldest part of the city and dates back to the origins of Amsterdam as a port city. In the fifteenth century Amsterdam was home to the second-largest harbour in the world. The Zeedijk, a street whose name refers to the RLD's position at sea, was known as a *party street*, where numerous dancing halls provided entertainment for sailors (Brilleman 2004). During the Second World War (1939–1945) the Germans installed a ban on such activities, and the character of the area fundamentally changed. After the war, however, new bars appeared and jazz was introduced to some night bars and clubs, such as the still-operating Casablanca (Brilleman 2004). When the harbour was moved to the western part of the city in the 1960s, many bars in the Zeedijk area closed down, and again the area experienced a period of decline.

By the 1970s and 1980s the RLD, and especially the Zeedijk, became notorious for its open drug scene. The supply of heroin and tolerance for drug use also attracted international users. At that time, small neighbourhood shops and local bars shut down due to resulting crime and nuisance. Crime and migration subsequently changed the neighbourhood dynamics considerably. At that time, many local residents moved out to new towns like Purmerend and Almere (Brilleman 2004), only to be replaced by international labour migrants, including sex workers, who increasingly came from other parts of the world.

Like many of the inner-city areas discussed elsewhere in this collection, by the 1980s gentrification slowly, and somewhat spontaneously, started to shape the character of Amsterdam's RLD (Terhorst et al. 2003). Low interest rates, commercial disinvestment in the historic city centre and a relatively young population resulted in a re-appreciation of the area. At this time, gentrification in Amsterdam was contained to specific parts of the city centre and had become a clear policy goal embraced by the city council (Musterd and Van de Ven 1991). In the so-called second phase of gentrification, expensive privately owned and developed housing was built; many offices and lofts were converted into private sector apartments and fashionable bars, restaurants, galleries and exclusive shops started to enter the urban landscape.

While the RLD had not previously been affected by the first or second wave of gentrification, from the early 1990s onwards the local government started to take an active role in bringing about the restructuring of the housing market. Further transformation of the built environment was driven by ambitious city marketing policies, which included tourism, branding strategies and public–private partnerships. This wave hit the RLD in the beginning of the 2000s.

If we look at De Wallen and how this area evolved over time, it is important to note that it is one of Amsterdam's main touristic attractions and represents, for many, *the* most well-known RLD that symbolises the liberal political context of the Netherlands (Cheng 2016). It also stands as a symbol, more generally, of the image of Amsterdam as a left-wing city in relation to soft drug use, prostitution and LGBTQ rights (Neuts et al. 2014). But over the recent years the RLD has come under increasing pressure to 'upgrade' or regenerate and attract a different type of visitor. This is largely a result of the city council wanting to change the image of the city and increase tax revenue. There is, however, a further motivation, which is tension between residents and tourists.

This chapter examines the impact of recent gentrification processes and the increase in urban tourism on residents and entrepreneurs living and working in the RLD. It is based on interviews with residents, entrepreneurs (who on average have worked in the area for thirteen years or more) and a city government representative. The informants each provided in-depth information on the spatial and social effects of the current transformations and the balance between partying, working and living in this rapidly changing neighbourhood.

PROJECT 1012: *CLEANSING* DE WALLEN

Amsterdam's RLD has a unique atmosphere with its neon lights, distinctive narrow houses, canals and small alleys. There is a mix of amenities such as bars, gambling halls, sex cinemas, peep shows, massage parlours, coffee shops, foreign exchange bureaus, low-quality hotels and restaurants. In many respects, it holds a singular place in the collective imagination of many international tourists (Cheng 2016) and has a special place in the global imagination of commodified sex (Aalbers and Sabat 2012). The area is perceived as a *free zone*, a place of entertainment and excitement where its history of sex work and the visibility of sex workers create a singular, internationally known *pleasurescape*. As Nijman observes, 'The theme of the "park" is . . . drugs and sex under a pretence of normalcy' (Nijman 1999, 156). At present, it is estimated that 2.5 million tourists visit the RLD annually (Arnoldussen et al. 2016).

Of course, this has not always been the case. In the past, it was considered something of an adventure to go to the RLD. People usually did not stay long in the area and only the most *adventurous* type of tourists would go there. Today, in contrast, the area has become a popular destination for a growing number of people, not only bachelor parties, young people making use of bargain flights and drug tourists but also mass tourists on guided tours, including women and families with children (Chapuis 2016). In response, a prominent negative discourse has started to appear among Amsterdam residents about tourists and especially those visiting the RLD. Particularly vocal is a group of long-term, upper-middle-class residents of the historic city centre, who express their frustration about tourism through a continuous stream of newspaper letters, at public events and in municipal settings (see also Pinkster and Boterman 2017). As a bar owner in the area explained:

> The term tourist has gotten a really negative connotation lately and this is not entirely fair because the majority of tourists in Amsterdam, I think 95%, are just visiting the city and are culturally interested. They do not all get drunk on a beer cycle making noise along the canals. Especially on Friday you see planes full of Brits arriving. They feel that everything is allowed here. If you explain this in a positive way it is beautiful that our city can be a free zone. But this of course also has another side of the coin.[1]

Residents of Amsterdam's RLD refer to the area as a theme park, or Disneyland, to summarise what they see as tourists making too much noise or vomiting and urinating in the streets (see also Pinkster and Boterman 2017). The project that was supposed to solve some of these tensions and frictions over antisocial behaviour in Amsterdam's RLD was officially launched in 2007 by Lodewijk Asscher, alderman and then-local Labour Party leader. Project 1012,[2] named after the district's postcode or *zip code*, aims to *clean up* the city's RLD and 'restore the balance between entertainment and liveability in the area'. Project 1012 started with the launch of a report in 2007 entitled *Limits to Law Enforcement: New Ambitions for the Wallen*. This report does not refer so much to crime in the area but describes most of all how the criminal infrastructure of Amsterdam's RLD can be replaced with upscale entertainment, luxury shops, new restaurants and art projects to attract new visitors and new creative entrepreneurs who might settle in the neighbourhood. The municipality describes its vision in terms of ambitions and how the Wallen area could become 'stylish and exciting'. The main aim of this project is the refunctioning of public and private spaces and the trans-formation of the area towards upscale entertainment and nightlife that would then attract supporting creative entrepreneurs (e.g., Florida 2002, 2005).

To achieve these aims, there has been an increased number of closures of brothels, sex shops, massage salons, coffee shops and gambling halls. To understand the way the project has been put into practice, it is necessary to highlight that since the early 2000s the city of Amsterdam has been collabo-rating with private actors, including a few non-profit housing associations and a non-profit restoration company called Stadsherstel, to buy out the owners of buildings that feature window prostitution (Aalbers 2016). This fits clearly into what has been called the third wave or state-led gentrifica-tion (Hubbard 2004; Uitermark et al. 2007; Ross 2010; Aalbers and Deinema 2012). Amsterdam's RLD does not stand alone here. Similar developments have occurred in cities such as Antwerp (Loopmans and Van den Broeck 2011; Weitzer 2014) and London (Soho), where strip clubs, video shops and brothels have been transformed into high-end restaurants, bars and clubs (Sanders-McDonagh et al. 2016). Reducing the visibility of the sex industry, albeit specific elements of it, is conducted to attract more high-end consumers to the area under the auspices of preventing nuisance and eliminating crime.

At the start of Project 1012 in 2007, it was announced that the total number of windows featuring sex workers in Amsterdam's RLD would have to decrease from approximately 480 to 280, a 40 percent reduction. By 2009 the city and its official coalition partners already owned more buildings in De Wallen than all the brothel owners combined. At the time of writing (2017), 130 windows have so far been closed, as well as well-known clubs such as Yab Yum.

The discourse used to legitimise the closing of windows is twofold. First, the local government has become more sensitive to sex work and the exploita-tion that might take place in the industry. The narrative employed is typically around fighting the excesses within the business, such as coercion, exploita-tion and human trafficking (Rekenkamer Amsterdam 2011). Second, Project 1012 has sought to eradicate organised criminal networks. The rhetoric here is that this part of the city should be regained from criminogenic businesses perceived to be built on illegal profits. As well as targeting sex-on-premises establishments, on 1 June 2003 a law went into effect to curtail coffee shops, clean up the RLD more generally and even fight the well-known bike gang, the Hell's Angels. Called the Public Administration in Decision-Making Act (BIBOB), the law allows the city authority to close down companies if there is any indication that funding or criminal activities are involved. Contracts, subsidies or permits for organisations and companies that the Dutch authori-ties have doubts about may be refused. In addition to relying on their own enquiries, the authorities may use the BIBOB Bureau of the Ministry of Jus-tice to seek further advice on any applicant requesting their service.

In line with so many other urban regeneration strategies (Florida 2002), creativity and innovation feature across all the policy documents of Project 1012, and the creative industry is playing an important role in the redevelopment of Amsterdam's RLD. The promotion of *soft location factors*, vague statements about quality of life and a prestigious blend of cultural amenities and luxury consumerism is very clearly part of the policy designed to attract new residents and entrepreneurs to the area. Several former prostitution windows in the area have already been transformed into exhibition spaces and studios for clothing, shoe and streetwear designers. According to the vision of Project 1012, De Wallen area will retain its special character by re-appreciating the value of the historic city centre of Amsterdam and embrace the canals and historic buildings. Since the 2000s, the marketing of Amsterdam has focused on the city's cultural heritage to appeal to more affluent visitors who can replace the low-budget tourists. In 2010, for instance, lobbying by a broad coalition of stakeholders, including residents of the historic city centre of Amsterdam, succeeded in gaining UNESCO heritage status for Amsterdam's entire canal district.

In the vision document for Project 1012, it is argued that the neighbourhood will remain a mix of living, working and nightlife and feature an 'appealing cocktail of style and excitement, so partly "red-light district"'. At the same time, the area will become an inviting neighbourhood for everyone who wants to explore the shops, galleries, museums, restaurants, fashionable eateries and old-style *brown cafes*. How this vision is actually operationalised on the ground and experienced by people working and living in the area remains to be seen, however.

TRANSFORMING DE WALLEN

There are various areas within the RLD where sex work used to take place. Most attention has, however, been placed by Project 1012 on the Oudekerksplein, a square that was famous in the past for its concentration of Latin American women working there (see figure 11.1). It is a historic square along the canal with a fourteenth-century church in the middle, believed to be the oldest building in Amsterdam. The square is also home to *Belle*, a bronze statue installed in 2007 that serves to honour and call for respect for sex workers of the world. The Oudekerksplein is defined as one of the ten key projects (*sleutelprojecten*) in Project 1012, which in this case means that the square eventually needs to be completely free of window brothels and become home instead to a diverse range of businesses. The historic, gothic Old Church (de Oude Kerk) is already completely restored, and the public space on the square has been revamped. Various creative enterprises have settled on the square

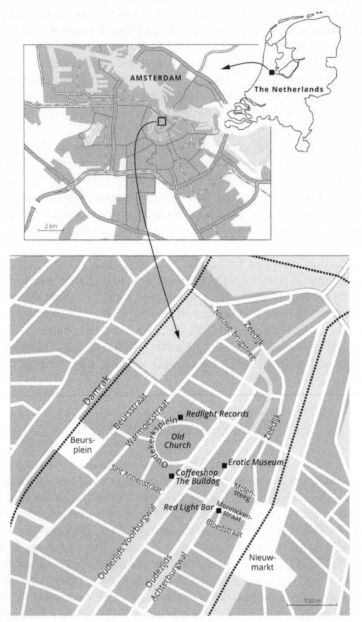

Figure 11.1.   Red-light district, Amsterdam (Wallen area). *Source*: Authors.

such as Red Light Radio, an Internet radio station that broadcasts from a former prostitution window. The broadcasts are made by various music lovers, DJs and musicians but not sex workers. The square has, since its regeneration, been described in the media as a 'new hipster stronghold'. For the rest of the RLD, some specific streets and canals around the Oudezijds Achterburgwal have been designated as a 'prostitution zone' (see figure 11.1). This small(er) area will form a cluster of sex-work establishments, which is assumed to be better controllable and manageable for the local authority.

The transformation of the RLD not only entails the closure of prostitution windows but also includes a reduction in the number of coffee shops selling cannabis in the area. Project 1012 states that twenty-six out of seventy-six coffee shops will have to close their doors in the near future. This action is legitimised through a similar line of reasoning; coffee shops are assumed to be criminogenic and can attract organised crime. The municipal council can force a coffee shop to close by revoking its exemption permit, and up to eighteen streets have now been defined as 'risky', including the Warmoesstraat and Nieuwe-brugsteeg (see figure 11.1). All coffee shops in these streets will have to be closed, and some have already been transformed into bars or restaurants. Paradoxically, the transformation has resulted in long(er) queues for the coffee shops remaining in the area. One venue, Coffee Shop Baba, recently employed doorstaff to manage the crowds. As the owner explained in the local newspaper (Brans 2014), 'One of the criteria in the new coffee shop policy is no nuisance. As such we do not prefer enormous crowds and long queues. A bouncer helps us with that'. A further paradox is that during the fight against criminogenic entrepreneurs, the local police station was closed due to budget cuts. The Warmoesstraat police station was first moved to the Beursstraat, a little further down the road, but in 2016 it was closed entirely.

THE VOICES OF RESIDENTS AND ENTREPRENEURS AROUND THE TRANSFORMATION OF RLD

The 2.5 million tourists who visit the RLD annually are not always welcomed with open arms by local residents. At night, in particular, the area is a popular nightlife district with accompanying problems such as antisocial behaviour, noise and litter. Residents often complain about noisy tourists and, especially, British bachelor parties. A woman who owns a bar and lives in the area explained:

> You don't want to know how people dress up. With an inflatable penis in front of their belly they walk around in the area. It is an embarrassing spectacle but we take it for granted now . . . but he should not urinate against the walls of our buildings on top of that. That is just too much.[3]

While recognising residents' concerns over noise and litter, it needs to be
noted that the social geography of many cities, Amsterdam in particular, is
changing. RLDs located in 'working-class' neighbourhoods are now increasingly attracting newer residents or visitors who demonstrate less tolerance to
non-normative sexual activities (Pitcher et al. 2006) and who might insist on
a 'revanchist' kind of cleansing of public space from all sorts of 'nuisance-
producing' activities (Smith 1996; Papayanis 2000; Hubbard 2004). In
Amsterdam this seems to be the case. The local government has consulted
residents and entrepreneurs in the neighbourhood, and during these meetings
there have been frequent complaints around noise, dirt and the general decline
of the area. Extra attention is now going into parking, waste collection, graffiti removal, public lighting, improvements of public space, street furniture,
the opening up of alleys that were previously closed for security reasons and
the installation of surveillance cameras.

It is often the case that in regenerating areas, newer residents are criticised for complaining about conditions that were already in existence before
they moved in. It is not, however, only the new(er) residents who complain.
Long-time residents also express concerns over noise and litter. *Verenig-
ing Vrienden van de Amsterdamse Binnenstad* is a residents' association
in Amsterdam's RLD, which argues for restoring the cultural heritage of
the inner city of Amsterdam and limiting the noise and disturbance associated with the sex industry and, most of all, with tourists. Ultimately, many
residents feel that they are losing their neighbourhood to the tourists, as one
resident explained:

> Just to going to the supermarket becomes like a whole expedition. You need
> to dive into the crowd. A simple walk through the neighbourhood becomes
> an irritation. In that sense, the hood has changed tremendously. An image that
> has been created of Amsterdam is that anything goes. And sometimes you start
> wondering who actually owns the neighbourhood?[4]

In respondents' stories about their changing relationship with their neighbourhood, it becomes clear that most have very strong place attachments.
When describing the area, they most often refer to it in aesthetic terms (like
the beauty of the canals, the old bridges and buildings), but the unique atmosphere, the dynamics, the thrill of the area and the mix of people are also
important. The cultural mix is, however, something that is under pressure,
with tourists being singled out as the group of people who now clearly dominate the area.

There is also a notable difference between daytime and night-time, with
residents expressing contrasting and ambiguous relationships with the neighbourhood at different times. At night, there is more friction between tourists

and residents because of different rhythms and noise-related nuisance. As well as tourists, residents have increasing difficulties accepting the sex workers currently working in the area and thinking of them as *belonging*. This is primarily because the workers do not speak Dutch and because there is a high turnover of workers, meaning residents have less contact with them than before. Moreover, residents, and especially the ones of the Oudekerksplein, also fear that with the arrival of creative businesses their area will become a 'yuppie neighbourhood'. They are afraid that the area will become 'boring' and like other neighbourhoods in Amsterdam. Related to this is an anxiety about increasing property prices, as one resident who grew up in the area explained: 'When I was a child it used to be a really deprived area here. Nobody wanted to live here, because it was scary with dealers and junkies. Now it is a favorite area and many people would like to live here. The housing prices are really crazy'.[5] In turn, a male resident points out that not only have housing prices gone up but the amenities in the neighbourhood have also changed tremendously. Ordinary shops like butchers, bakeries and green grocers are disappearing, and souvenir shops and chocolate stores have entered the neighbourhood, further changing the urban landscape.

> It just keeps growing. This week I cycled away in the morning and when I came back in the afternoon there was a new ice cream shop opened with rental bikes in front of it! But a bakery is nowhere to be found, because the prices for opening a shop are too high now. That is a huge disadvantage.[6]

While this transformation of the commercial landscape is caused by increasing rents, residents experience it as *downgrading* as the shops can be found in any tourist city. Even the new creative businesses that are expected to profit from the regeneration and bring something unique to the area face tough competition from the tourist industry that works with an *easy-earn model* where easy money can be made. The director of the Old Church points out that 'entrepreneurs in the area need to take a bit more risk and not go for the same easy earn model if they want to be loved by the whole neighbourhood'.[7] For some of the new creative entrepreneurs, the area is now also becoming too expensive to start a business. While they initially received start-up funds, some do not survive in the long run when the funding disappears and they cannot self-support. The director of the Old Church explains:

> In the near past there have been entrepreneurs who have not survived even when they worked really hard. A Korean restaurant for example, here across the canal. It was a very nice hip place, with entrepreneurs who did it all in a very pleasant way . . ., but they did not succeed and now a burger restaurant opened at that spot. That must be really frustrating for the people who work on Project 1012. On the one hand you are building something but then you turn around and it

already collapses. That is why the waffle shops and burger restaurants survive over and over again and not the nice boutiques and coffee bars.[8]

The city council also underestimated how difficult it would actually be to transform dark, small, narrow spaces into upmarket fashionable venues, such that the physical transformation of the area is not going as fast as first hoped or planned. There is a further problem that while the sex workers' windows have been closed, in order to increase their number of windows, brothel owners have started to use the front door as an additional window blocking access to the upper floors. It is estimated that in the entire RLD about 600 upper floors are now vacant. Property developers seek to find ways to sell these buildings, but the loss is high compared to the value the property has while running as a sex workspace (Cheng 2016).

In a further contradiction, the success of the RLD as a tourist destination now appears to actually threaten the sex industry. Potential clients walking in the area can no longer be anonymous, and most tourists come only for *visual pleasures* and taking pictures. This has the effect of deterring potential clients. In the past, it was mainly heterosexual men who walked by the windows, and the sex workers did not have to do much to attract clients. This has changed now due to the sheer volume of tourists. It is no longer desirable for people looking for sexual pleasure to peruse the windows due to fears about their privacy and indeed the number of tourists with cameras. As a male resident noted, 'In the near future there will be a thousand people taking pictures of prostitutes. As a man you will not go to visit one; you don't want it to be on Facebook! It has become like slumming. I think it will not take much time before we need crush barriers'.[9]

In 2016 a campaign was launched by artists calling for greater respect for the sex workers. Called #NoFuckingPhotos, the campaign had an accompanying mural, which aimed to educate visitors about behavioural standards. With mass tourism, new moral orders have thus been introduced to the area due to the increasing objectification and exoticisation of the women working in the area. The city council also recently, in 2017, introduced explicit guidelines for RLD tours. The main goal of these guidelines is to limit the size of groups to twenty persons and decrease nuisance for residents, entrepreneurs and road users. Tours are limited until 11:00 p.m., alcohol or drug consumption is forbidden during tours and groups are not allowed to stand still in specifically allocated 'crowd-sensitive areas', which include the alleys in the Sint Annenkwartier area, in front of the coffee shop the Bulldog, the bridges on Oudezijds Achterburgwal, in front of Casa Rosso, in front of the Condomerie, in front of the smallest house, Stoofsteeg alley, Gordijnsteeg and the corner of Monnikenstraat, Bloedstraat (see figure 11.1). In the guidelines it is also explicitly stated that taking pictures of sex workers is forbidden.[10] A sex worker who has worked in the area for more than fifteen years explains how the visitors in the area have changed over time and what those changes mean for her:

> In the past visitors thought the red-light district was a bit scary. Women on their own for example avoided the area. Today it is tighter and safer. Tourists tend to see it as one big theme park, like a Disneyland for grown ups . . . they all come to look. I sometimes feel that we are the last free attraction of the Netherlands.[11]

THE CLOSURE

The closing down of legal brothels in the Netherlands (that have been fought for so long) represents a major shift in policy and legal recognition of sex work. The closure of such establishments is especially surprising given the history of Dutch prostitution policy. In the 1980s, sex workers in the Netherlands demanded to be recognised and to receive government protection. It was argued that the criminalisation of sex work negatively affected their safety and ambiguous laws marginalised them further. An Amsterdam-based sex workers' advocacy group called *De Rode Draad* (The Red Thread) protested against the hypocrisies they saw in the system. Sex workers wanted their work to be recognised as a legal service – a type of work – and for them to be seen as legal workers and not as *fallen women* or victims (Altink et al. 2018). Due to this unique moral and legal climate in the Netherlands, Amsterdam's RLD is tied not only to notions of danger, immorality, drugs and crime but also to tolerance, excitement, freedom and self-determination.

Making sex work less visible represents a shift in how sex work is tolerated and talked about in the Netherlands. A *new* moral order around sex work has now been introduced that treats sex workers as victims and condemns this type of work rather than recognising it (van Liempt and Chimienti 2017). The anti-trafficking discourse plays an important role in the legitimisation of the closing down of workspaces across the RLD. In the official documentation of Project 1012, it has continually been stressed that prostitutes in Amsterdam's RLD tend to be in precarious and dangerous situations and that brothels are assumed to be conducive to crime (Buijs and Ivens 2012; Buijs and Duits 2015). The closing of the windows has, however, not resulted in the reduction of exploitation of sex workers; in none of the windows that have been closed so far has trafficking been proven (Buijs and Ivens 2012).

Paradoxically, a municipal brothel has opened recently, called MyRed-Light, stimulated by the city council and run by an organisation that rents out windows to sex workers so they can work without *pimps*. The board exists of high-profile people (but no representatives of sex workers), and it aims for the *normalisation* of sex work, which stands in contrast to the general trend of closing down brothels in the area. It is estimated that the city council has lost €1.7 million since stablishing the brothel, and they first had to buy the property and then sell it again. Among the sex workers of Amsterdam's RLD there is little desire to work in MyRedLight brothel, because it is no cheaper than the traditional windows or venues and sometimes even more expensive to rent there. Working hours are also limited. During the week the workers need to stop at 3:30 a.m. and close at 4:00 a.m., whereas others in the area work until 5:00 a.m.[12] Project 1012, in general, has raised frustration and anger among most sex workers. They do not feel represented and want to be treated as people who can speak for themselves rather than as victims. In April 2015 more than 200 sex workers marched through Amsterdam to protest at the demonisation of their industry and the closure of windows and brothels. This demonstration was organised by PROUD, a lobby and advocacy organisation that serves to defend the interests of sex workers in the workplace, in policies, the media and the wider society, and the Dutch sex workers union.

CONCLUSIONS

This chapter has examined the impact of gentrification processes and the increase in tourism in Amsterdam's RLD on the daily lives and experiences of residents and entrepreneurs in the area. While observing and talking to people in the area, it became clear that turning a notorious RLD into an extension of the highly expensive city centre is a delicate process that does not run smoothly and is often accompanied by certain contradictions. One contradiction we found was that while on the one hand creative start-ups were encouraged in the area, we also found many mainstream tourist shops opening up in the same district. It has turned out to be rather difficult to transform the area into an appealing cocktail of *style* and *excitement*.

The *money-making tourist business* is in direct competition with the so-called innovative creative new businesses that have been encouraged under Project 1012 to come to the area. This was illustrated by the example of a Korean restaurant that could survive only in the first years when a subsidy was given but has since been replaced by a mainstream burger restaurant. With increasing homogenisation of its retail offer, the area might lose its unique character, which will have a significant impact on the future development of the area, in general, and its nightlife, in particular.

Another contradiction identified here is that Project 1012 has spatially transformed the area that used to be *on the edge* into a mainstream space that is now accessible to all types of tourists. The fact that this has resulted in a rather mono-cultural landscape with tourist shops and themed bars means the dominant image is now in contradiction to the original aims of the project. Allowing so many entrepreneurs into the area and businesses that can be found in any touristic area is not what Project 1012 originally intended. Residents complain that the city council has decided 'to let the market do its work', and despite all the urban strategies in place, the city council is accused by residents of lacking a vision.

The transformations in the area, with many tourists disrupting the ordinary rhythm of the neighbourhood, have also resulted in many residents feeling that their neighbourhood has now been taken over by tourists. Shops and bars that were once the beating heart of the area are slowly disappearing or have become dominated by tourists. Alongside complaints about the sheer volume of people visiting the area, there are also concerns about the different way of using the space, especially at night, with little sensitivity for the fact that people also live and work in this *theme park*.

If we look at how Project 1012 has impacted sex workers in the area, it can be argued that the project has contributed to a decline in the sex workers' working conditions despite its original aim to improve their working conditions and fight exploitation. Being located in the city centre has economic advantages for sex workers. The fact that tourists always made up roughly half of the sex workers' clientele and, as such, contributed significantly to the profitability of the RLD (Flight and Hulshof 2009) is not referred to in the official documents – even though, in the 2000s the yearly profit from the RLD was estimated to be around €80 million (Arnoldussen et al. 2016). But masses of tourists are not good for the business because clients no longer feel safe and fear their privacy while walking in the area. Sex workers in the area also complain about the increasing objectification as a result of mass tourism and a changing moral landscape.

Paradoxically, while brothels and coffee shops are closing down due to the current regeneration process, tourists are still attracted to the notorious local past of the area, which is branded through guided tours and used in the marketing of themed bars such as *sailor bars*. This urban myth is far removed from residents' daily experiences, where many long-term residents express that they no longer feel at home in their own neighbourhood. Residents refer instead to experiences of their neighbourhood being taken over by tourists who are living the myth of an area that feels no longer theirs. Not only is tourists' behaviour in the area considered inappropriate by current residents, but the urban regeneration projects are perceived to be top-down. Residents' feeling, more or less powerless, has led to frustration, a loss of a sense of belonging as well as avoidance. Residents' avoiding their own area and no longer visiting bars and shops because of the dominance of tourists results in another paradox; an area marketed for its specific local past has become a place where locals no longer feel at ease.

ACKNOWLEDGEMENT

This chapter draws on qualitative research for the 'Geographies of the Urban Night' project. We would like to express our gratitude to Lieve Heijsters for her assistance in conducting the fieldwork for the project and to all respondents for their participation.

NOTES

1. Original quote in Dutch: 'De term toerist heeft een hele negatieve lading en dat is niet terecht want een heel groot deel van de toeristen – ik denk 95% – is gewoon op bezoek in de stad en is cultureel geïnteresseerd. Ze gaan niet allemaal lallend op een bierfiets over de gracht. Vooral op vrijdag zie je hier hele vliegtuigen vol Engelsen komen. Zij hebben het gevoel dat hier alles mag en kan. Als je het heel positief uitlegt, is het natuurlijk mooi dat we een vrijplaats zijn. Maar het heeft ook een keerzijde'.

2. For more information, see https://www.amsterdam.nl/projecten/project-1012/.

3. Original quote in Dutch: 'Je wilt niet weten hoe mensen zich dan uitdossen. Met zo'n "opblaaspik" voor hun buik wandelen ze door de buurt. Het is te gênant voor woorden maar wij kijken er niet meer van op . . . maar ga dan niet ook nog eens een keer tegen de gevels aan plassen. Dat is een beetje teveel'.

4. Original quote in Dutch: 'Even naar AH gaan wordt een expeditie. Je moet door die horde mensen heen. Een wandeling door je buurt is een ergernis geworden. Wat dat betreft is de buurt echt veranderd. Er een beeld ontstaan van Amsterdam dat hier alles kan en mag. Op sommige momenten denk je wel van wie is de buurt nou eigenlijk?'.

5. Original quote in Dutch: 'toen ik klein was, was het hier nog echt een achterbuurt. Niemand wilde hier wonen, omdat het eng was met dealers en junkies. Nu is het een ontzettend gewilde wijk; de huizenprijzen zijn echt gigantisch'.

6. Original quote in Dutch: '[H]et blijft maar doorgaan; ik fietste deze week 's ochtend weg en toen ik 's middags terug kwam stond er weer een nieuwe ijsjeszaak met rental bikes. Maar een bakker is nergens meer te vinden, die kan hier niet meer zitten omdat de winkelprijs veel te hoog is. Dat is een groot nadeel'.

7. Original quote in Dutch: 'Als ondernemer moet je je eigenlijk richten op een wat ingewikkelder verdienmodel wil je bevriend blijven met de hele buurt'.

8. Original quote in Dutch: 'Er zijn wel ondernemers geweest die het niet gered hebben ondanks dat ze er heel hard hun best voor deden. Bijvoorbeeld Yokio, een Koreaans restaurantje hier aan de overkant van de gracht. Dat was een hele leuke hippe zaak, met aansprekende ondernemers die dat op een hele leuke manier deden . . . maar het lukte toch niet en nu zit er weer een hamburgerrestaurant in. Dat lijkt me voor de mensen die met het 1012 project bezig zijn ook totaal frustrerend. Enerzijds bouw je wat op, maar je draait je om en het zakt alweer in elkaar. Dat zorgt er wel voor dat de wafelwinkels en hamburgerzaken het toch steeds weer winnen van de mooie boetiekjes en fijne koffietentjes'.

9. Original quote in Dutch: 'Over een tijdje staan er 1000 mensen foto's te maken van de prostituees. Als man ga je dan niet naar de hoeren. . . . je wilt niet dat het op facebook staat. Het is aapjes kijken geworden. Ik denk dat er binnenkort ook dranghekken moeten komen'.

10. For more information, see https://www.amsterdam.nl/bestuurorganisatie/best uurscommissies/bestuurscommissie-c/drukte-balans/de-wallen/.

11. Original quote in Dutch: 'Vroeger vonden bezoekers het RLD een beetje eng. Vrouwen alleen liepen met een boog om de buurt heen. Nu is het er netter en veiliger. Toeristen zien het als één groot speelparadijs, een pretpark: Disneyland voor volwassenen. Ze komen allemaal om te kijken. Soms heb ik het idee dat wij de laatste gratis attractie van Nederland zijn'.

12. For more information, see http://degroteprostitutieleugen.blogspot.nl/2017/05/de-eerste-week-van-gemeentebordeel-my.html?m=1#!/2017/05/de-eerste-week-van-gemeentebordeel-my.html.

Chapter 12

Nightlife as an Educational Setting: The Harm Reduction Perspective

Helena Valente, Cristiana Vales Pires
and Helena Carvalho

Parties work as binding events for youth and youth subcultures. While night-clubs and parties may reproduce multiple forms of inclusion and exclusion (MacRae 2006) and clubbing, in particular, is marked by distinctive forms of taste (Thornton 1997), in theory, at least, they represent fun and recreation as well as an opportunity for transgression and freedom, to overcome limits and escape social control and routine. Within the canon of nightlife studies, it is unsurprising that clubbing, in particular, is seen as a privileged moment in young people's social lives and socialisation (Hollands 1995). As well as functioning to develop and affirm social bonds, integral to many of the accounts of clubbing is the pursuit of pleasure and how pleasure models the behaviours and attitudes of participants (Riley et al. 2010, 2012). It is within this context of sociability, bonding, socialising, pleasure-seeking and trans-gression that drugs play a central role in the search for new, more pleasurable and intense experiences.

Recreational settings such as nightclubs have become, since the 1990s, privileged sites for drug use and experimentation among young people. There is evidence that drug use is higher among particular demographics and that club drugs play an important role in youth socialisation (Halkitis and Palamar 2006). The European Monitoring Centre for Drugs and Drug Addiction's (EMCDDA) annual report of 2010 states that although there is, in the general population, 'a tendency towards stabilization concerning drug use, this trend may not reflect specific drug use trends among different subpopulations' (2010, 65), in particular, partygoers. In short, it is argued that consumers who frequent nightclubs are more likely to use recreational drugs than the general population (Hoare and Flatley 2008; Measham and Moore 2009).

Recognising this reality, public authorities have developed a series of regu-latory responses. Alongside more repressive measures, others that consider the partygoer's personal choices, needs and experiences have also been developed. First created and shared between partygoers before being appropriated by professionals and governmental agencies, harm reduction HR strategies in nightlife settings have now taken place across Europe since the 1990s (Martins et al. 2015).

This chapter explores the conditions that led to the emergence of a specific mode of intervention known as *outreach teams*. We discuss the results of this type of intervention, which frames the use of drugs as an individual choice and aims to provide partygoers the necessary tools for them to use drugs responsibly (Rovira and Hidalgo 2003). The discussion is based on the experience of CHECK!N, an outreach team that has been working in different Portuguese cities for more than ten years. A comparison between two Portuguese cities is drawn here in order to understand the programme and its successes: Lisbon, the Portuguese capital, and Viseu, a smaller interior city where nightlife is focused primarily around the university. The results of a comparative study conducted between May 2014 and May 2016, which explicitly set out to examine the behaviours of partygoers and the impact CHECK!N's intervention had on them, serve as the basis for our argument.

THE CALCULATED RISK-TAKERS: DRUG USERS IN NIGHTLIFE SETTINGS

A number of researchers have paid special attention to how the use of certain drugs has become a relatively normal feature of many young people's life experiences, especially in Western post-industrial societies (e.g., Parker et al. 1998, 2002; Duff 2005; Wilson et al. 2010). These and other studies have shown that while drug users in recreational settings represent higher levels of drug use than the general population (EMCDDA 2010), they are often described as 'well-adjusted and successful goal-oriented, non-risk taking young persons, who see drug taking as part of their repertoire of life' (Parker 1997, 25). Young recreational drug users are, in other words, typically economically stable and socially integrated, and their drug-use profiles are otherwise 'normal' (ibid.). Parker and colleagues' normalisation theory has been tested by several researchers in Western countries other than the United Kingdom. In Australia, the works of Duff (2005) and Wilson et al. (2014) are notable, as are Carvalho's (2007, 2015) and Cruz and Machado's (2010) works from Portugal, where this notion of the *non-problematic drug user* is widely deployed. At the same time, drug use has also become more socially accepted by non-users; drug use and the practices associated with drug consumption are now part of everyday life in many societies and a recurrent theme in contemporary popular culture and media (Parker et al. 1998). For Parker (1997) this *normalisation* of drug consumption derives from several facts, including more liberal attitudes to the use of illicit drugs among the young people, the emergence of youth subcultures that value risk-taking and new experiences and the increasing availability of these substances. Fernandes (2009) also explores how drugs are present in day-to-day life and have become fairly *commonplace* in the media. In the 1990s, in some European countries, and later in Portugal, drug use shifted to being understood as typically associated with marginalised subcultures to becoming instead a relatively common feature of a usual night out for young adults (Manning 2013). Equally noteworthy is the fact that Parker et al. (1998) suggest that social class and gender do not appear to influence this process of normalisation. In other words, this normalisation process would be applied to people of all social backgrounds.

Partygoers and festival attendees who use psychoactive substances are typically described as non-problematic drug users, socially and personally adjusted people whose specific characteristics do not fit the problematic drug-user stereotype (Carvalho 2007; Cruz 2014). In this population, there is some indication that non-problematic drug use is marked by self-control and autoregulation further supported by self-imposed rules to manage the diverse effects of drug use as well as behaviours associated with drug use such as the type of drug, quantity, frequency and the context of consumption. Non-problematic drug users also implement strategies to avoid social and health damages (Cruz and Machado 2010; Cruz 2014) such that the majority of these users could be seen as *calculated risk-takers* (Southwell 2010). This characterisation of recreational drug users defies the traditional view of users as weak and merely victims of the drugs or of the dealers supplying them (Tammi and Hurme 2007; Southwell 2010). Within this perspective people who use drugs are instead seen as normal and accountable citizens enjoying the same rights, but also the same obligations, as all other citizens in democratic societies (Erickson et al. 1997).

The theory of normalisation is a useful perspective to frame interventions in nightlife settings and has clear implications for the type of interventions that we explore in this chapter. As Southwell (2010) points out, drug use is a complex and multifaceted reality that does not accommodate uniform solutions. These new drug-using realities call for, instead, new ways of intervening in the drug field, a field in which harm reduction strategies (HR) have appeared.

FROM THE STREET TO THE CLUB: THE HARM REDUCTION JOURNEY

According to Harm Reduction International (HRI n.d.), 'HR refers to policies, programmes and practices that aim to reduce the harms associated with the use of psychoactive drugs in people unable or unwilling to stop'. The defining features of HR are a focus on the prevention of harm, rather than on the prevention of drug use itself, and a focus on people who continue to use drugs. HR began as a collection of strategies that drug users put into practice in the 1970s in the United States, and slightly later in Europe, and developed further in response to the HIV/AIDS epidemic (Friedman et al. 2007; Fernandes 2009). People using drugs have always had a fundamental role to play in responding to drug-related harms, frequently acting more swiftly than authorities when faced with serious problems (Friedman 2007). While emphasising public health principles, HR offers both human and pragmatic interventions, trying to reduce the possible negative consequences of drug use for consumers and their communities (Marlatt 1996). By virtue of its attributes, HR strategies constituted a paradigm shift in how to approach the drug-use phenomenon, reconceptualising both the problem itself and the attitude towards it (Fernandes et al. 2006). Nevertheless, the successful implementation of these practices in the control of epidemics such as HIV/AIDS, as well as the fact that drug use has become a more pervasive issue for society, has led for HR programmes to be implemented by government agencies and non-governmental organisations (NGOs) (ibid.). Over recent decades, HR has been implemented in several countries, and especially in Europe, as a complement to other socio-sanitary approaches to the use of drugs and to sexual behaviours. Both the EMCDDA and the World Health Organization consider HR as a manifestation of mainstream public health and a fundamental part of a balanced approach to drug use (Rhodes and Hedrich 2010).

However, this dissemination of HR as a mainstream public health strategy raises questions about its nature and main objectives. Authors such as Roe (2005) or Barratt et al. (2014) argue that HR may be losing its alternative and activist nature, working to defend users' rights, namely the right to use drugs, and accepting only the medical message of how to reduce health risks. As Moore (2008, 355–56) argues:

Harm reduction policy and practice constructs a particular form of drug-using subject – a health-conscious citizen capable of rational decision-making, self-determination, self-regulation and risk management in order to minimize drug-related harm. This neo-liberal vision of the drug-using subject is a positive development in the sense that it attempts to dislodge previous understandings of drug users as irrational, and it accords them the status and attributes granted to other citizens of neo-liberal democracies. . . . But there is also a downside. Adopting a neo-liberal subject obscures the material constraints on practice that arise from inequitable social and political structures. It may also prevent drug users from developing a more politicized view of their life situation.

The emphasis on individual users' responsibility on both their drug consumption and their health assumes a fully agentic subject able to make rational choices and seems to disregard the structural factors that might cause individuals to find themselves in certain positions (Young 2000). This more institutional type of HR may also have significant implications for intervention with users. HR, which is based more on the idea of reducing health risks, often disregards people's motivations to use drugs in the first place (Race 2008). In fact, most services available to drug users are based on the essential principles of public health and have health promotion as the ultimate ideal, yet not all drug users identify with this kind of health-oriented discourse. Users consider a number of other factors besides health when deciding to use drugs, such as pleasure (Barrat et al. 2014). If people designing, promoting and implementing responses to drug use fail to acknowledge these different users' subjectivities towards drug use, they might be condemning their programmes to failure. As Lupton notes, People may resist, negotiate or ignore harm reduction imperatives 'because of a conscious sense of frustration, resentment or anger, . . . [or] because they derive greater pleasure . . . from other practices of the self' (Lupton 1995, 133, in Moore 2008, 356).

Ignoring the pleasures that are implicit to the use of drugs contributes to the failure of many messages and preventive campaigns. Preventative discourses that appeal to fear and emphasise a lack of meaning to drug use appear to be ineffective and inadequate, particularly for those who have already started their relationship with drugs (DeJong 2002; Hidalgo 2004; Ruiter et al. 2014; Marsh et al. 2017). This more-negative and harm-oriented discourse may end up being counterproductive, since once a young person starts using a drug and realises its positive effects, that person might discredit most of the preventive information received so far. Thus, the attempt to create a perception of risk that is too high may end up having effects contrary to those intended (Hidalgo 2004; Marsh et al. 2017). Thus, understanding these alternative subjectivities can be useful for services, helping them to create new strategies for involvement and develop goals with people who use drugs. Pleasure should not be seen as the antithesis of safety, control or health. It should be recognised as a valid motivation for certain behaviours and considered in official and unofficial discourses produced about drug consumption, thus avoiding resistance from a considerable range of consumers, especially young people (Race 2008).

In the light of this, it is necessary to develop interventions for all those who wish to use psychoactive substances, taking into account that different forms of use may involve different types and degrees of risk and also of pleasure. In addition, it is important to highlight the discontinuity between heavy drug use and non-problematic drug-use patterns. These non-problematic drug-use patterns are the most common among partygoers, who use psychoactive substances as a means to satisfy their desire for pleasure and play, bounded by knowledge and awareness of both risks and benefits without significant impacts for human well-being (Huizinga 2008). Race (2008) speaks about *counterpublic health*, which he understands as a set of strategies put in place by peers who assume that drugs are consumed for the purpose of pleasure. He suggests that it is possible to take drugs in a safer way while maximising pleasure and that this poses a potentially interesting set of strategies to work with drug users in party settings. The work that CHECK!N undertakes with partygoers in Portugal can be seen within this framework of a type of counterpublic health intervention, where partygoers work with other partygoers to promote not only their safety and their health but also their fun and pleasure.

CHECK!N: EDUCATING PARTYGOERS FOR THE MANAGEMENT OF PLEASURES AND RISKS IN NIGHTLIFE OF PORTUGUESE CITIES

In party settings, HR programmes were born as a bottom-up strategy shared between partygoers. Members of the dance music scene were the first to try and help their peers to manage their drug use. The first official harm reduction peer project to appear in nightlife settings in Europe was *Crew 2000* in Edinburgh in 1989. During the 1990s several others emerged, such as *Eve & Rave* in Germany in 1994, *Energy Control* in Spain and *Check iT!* in Austria in 1997 and *Techno Plus* in France in 1999 (Charlois 2009).

In Portugal, HR programmes have been included in the National Drug Strategy since 1998, and in 2001 a specific legal framework was created to accommodate HR responses (Barbosa 2009). Concerning intervention in nightlife settings, in 2001 a pilot project from *Ares do Pinhal Association* began performing colorimetric reagent pill testing in Lisbon. In 2002 the NGO *Conversas de Rua* created the first peer-based project doing intervention in nightlife settings in Lisbon and in the same year the Spirit Beverages Wholesalers National Association (ANEBE) created the first designated driver campaign, which is still active today. In 2003 Association GAF from Viana do Castelo, in northern Portugal, began doing sporadic interventions in parties and dance events. In 2006 CHECK!N was created, an intervention project in party settings promoted by APDES[1] – Piaget Agency for Development. CHECK!N began in Porto and was initially funded by the General-Directorate of Health (2006–2009). In 2009, in order to continue its work,[2] the project expanded its intervention in Viseu and Lisbon, funded by the Portuguese Institute on Drugs and Drug Addiction (currently General-Directorate for Intervention on Addictive Behaviours and Dependencies). CHECK!N works as a peer-based project, meaning 'people address their equals. So, a group of people emerging from a particular scene such as partygoers, drug users, people living with HIV, sex workers educate others who belong to the same particular context' (Charlois 2009, 5). To be peer based means that the intervention should be horizontal and inclusive, considering the partygoers' perspectives and promoting proximal and informal interventions in the environments where they move. The intention is to not recriminate and judge their behaviours but, instead, promote a comprehensive response that could provide them objective and reliable information and services to educate and support them in the adoption of safer and more pleasurable behaviours.

CHECK!N's main objective is to inform and support partygoers in the management of the pleasures and the risks that are potentially associated with partying, with a special focus on drug use. CHECK!N uses harm reduction but with a broader theoretical framework, *pleasure and risk management* (Rovira and Hidalgo 2003; Hidalgo 2004). Móro and Rácz (2013) define such an approach as 'benefit maximization', while Race (2008) sees it as 'counterpublic health'. CHECK!N assumes that behaviours, like drug taking, are influenced by a variety of factors, namely the subject's perceptions, the potential consequences, the ability to perform the behaviour, the opinions of others and the context (Fishbein and Ajzen 2010). Users' perception of risk and risk behaviour is fundamental in their decision to take or not take drugs and how to do it (Cruz 2014). However, when it comes to drugs, there is a great amount of inadequate information circulating, largely due to the illegal status of most drugs, which undergo no quality control and are frequently subjected to high levels of adulteration (Coomber 1997; Decorte 2001; Cole et al. 2011), and it is impossible for the common user to know what is the exact composition of the substance he or she intends to use, hence distorting even the most careful user's risk perception.

CHECK!N's main objective, as noted, is achieved through specific outreach strategies and participatory approaches like peer education, presence at parties and festivals, discussion groups and partnerships with local stakeholders. Through CHECK!N, people emerging from the party scene become peer educators and help other partygoers. The relationship between peers favours mutual recognition and allows the establishment of relationships of trust and the opening up of effective communication channels in the transmission of important information (Dias 2006). This is particularly important when dealing with sensitive issues like drug use. Furthermore, a series of services such as brief informative sessions and/or counselling about drugs and sexuality, condoms, earplugs, safer snorting kits, alcohol breathalysers and physiological serums are freely available for partygoers at the CHECK!N info-points. A drug-checking[3] integrated service is also provided at some events, allowing users to know the actual content of the drug they intend to use (Martins et al. 2015, 2017).

In addition to the physical space at parties, CHECK!N relies on the intervention through virtual tools. The Internet is an ever-growing tool, particularly for young people, where they can search for information on the next party, about drugs, how to use them or where to buy them, so it is important for projects working in these contexts to adapt to this new reality and migrate their outreach strategies to online (Vale et al. 2015, 2016). CHECK!N has been working together with its clients online, through a website and different social media platforms. At the same time, joining with other responses and services existing in the community is fundamental to optimise existing resources, to promote more sustainable answers and to promote health and safety in nightlife settings. In addition to the work conducted with partygoers at an individual level, CHECK!N works at a more macro-level, with party organisers, club owners and surrounding communities. Many of the risks partygoers are subjected to derive not from their individual behaviour but from the context in which they party. As Calafat et al. (2001) argue, it seems there is a growing recognition that the adverse effects of club drugs are strongly related to the environment in which they are used rather than resulting solely from the toxic properties of substances themselves.

This is the case of CHECK!N, which advises people to drink water and to take some rest period while dancing. Not all clubs have rest areas or free water, however, so this advice is not always implemented. It is also fundamental that the staff of clubs are able to recognise when a person is in distress and help him or her, or efficiently call for help. Facilitating alternatives to private transportation, controlling entrances, limiting volume levels on the dancefloor and providing condoms and earplugs are some of the strategies implemented not only by one stakeholder but by several different stakeholders in the community (Bellis et al. 2002). Only with full community engagement is it possible to achieve good health promotion results. In the next section community engagement is better illustrated through best practices implemented by the CHECK!N team.

PRESENTING CHECK!N INTERVENTION IN LISBON AND IN VISEU

CHECK!N has been working in Lisbon and Viseu since 2009, but this chapter focuses on the period between May 2014 and May 2016. The second edition of the project was promoted by APDES under co-funding provided by the Portuguese General Directorate for Intervention on Addictive Behaviours and Dependencies (SICAD). Although the theoretical background, intervention philosophy and methodology described earlier are the same in both cities, particular intervention strategies were adapted to each city specific to the local context.

Lisbon is Portugal's capital city and the largest in the country. CHECK!N's intervention here is circumscribed to some specific locations in the city's historic quarters, Bairro Alto, Cais do Sodré, Santos and Alcântara, which, over the past ten years, have become the most crowded nightlife areas in the city. Lisbon nightlife is very cosmopolitan, offering different spaces, from small bars to large clubs, with diverse consumption options in terms of cultural agendas, prices, soundscapes and audiences. If in Bairro Alto or Cais do Sodré we find mainly young adults and adults, in Santos the bars and clubs attract mainly very young adults and teenagers. In the past decade Lisbon has undergone an important transformation process that has greatly affected its nightlife (Nofre 2013; Malet Calvo et al. 2017; Mendes 2016; Nugent 2016; Malet Calvo 2017; Nofre et al. 2017a), mainly due to gentrification as a result of physical and social regeneration in the city centre, its intense touristification (Mendes 2016) and also the high number of Erasmus students temporarily living in the city (Malet Calvo 2014, 2017; Malet Calvo et al. 2017), as explored elsewhere in this anthology. These three processes are not only changing the nightscape of Lisbon but also leading to increased conflicts between different city stakeholders (Nugent 2016): partygoers, retailers, bar/ club owners, neighbours and local decision makers. Importantly, these socio-spatial changes are also impacting on the nightlife and drug-use dynamics.

In addition to the outreach intervention implemented in nightlife settings that target partygoers, CHECK!N is increasingly being involved with the community and creating specific strategies that target other actors: bartenders and other workers of nightlife venues and events, owners or promoters of bars and/or clubs, neighbours and local decision makers. The main motive is to create a holistic intervention that integrates the narratives of all the stakeholders active in the nightlife setting, involves nightlife promoters in the creation of a safer nightlife culture, creates space-times of discussion and negotiation among these different actors and, finally, is active in identifying and designing responses to solve some of the problems emerging in the local neighbourhood. In this sense, CHECK!N is very active in local networks promoted by the neighbourhoods' parish councils, namely the Social Commission of Misericórdia's Parish (which includes Bairro Alto and Cais do Sodré neighbourhoods) and the Social Commission of Estrela's Parish (which includes Santos and part of Alcântara's neighbourhood). These groups involve all the stakeholders active in the territory, including neighbours, retailers, police and professionals working in health, social care, education, arts and culture. The participation of these groups supports the team in the building of a rooted and deeper knowledge of the area's identity, dynamics and voices.

On the other hand, the CHECK!N team complements the knowledge and discussions about the territory, bringing its own unique knowledge about nightlife and its dynamics, drug-use patterns, trends and harms. In addition, from October 2015 to October 2016 the team was granted funding from Lisbon Municipality, under the programme BIPZIP (Neighborhoods and Zones for Priority Intervention), to develop and implement a safer nightlife label in

Cais do Sodré. This project was a partnership coordinated by APDES, and with the participation of the research group LXNIGHTS (from FCSH, Social Sciences and Humanities Faculty, NOVA University of Lisbon), Cais do Sodré Retailers Association and the Party+ European Network.[4] This safer nightlife label, which functioned like an award, was called SAFE!N Cais and included a certified training course for staff of bars and clubs. The involvement of the Cais do Sodré venue's owners in discussing and deciding the criteria for the label also entailed them in developing and working to specific criteria in order to be certified by the end of the project. This further led to the creation of an informal network, called Forum+, with stakeholders directly involved in nightlife, party organisers, venue owners, retailers' associations, bartenders' association, neighbourhood groups and associations, researchers and local decision makers.

Viseu, on the other hand, is a medium-sized university city, located in the northern rural region of Portugal. The city has two main nightlife areas, the city historic centre and the Jugueiros area. In the historic city centre it is still possible to find traditional cafes and bars, playing different types of music such as rock, house and pop music, and a few dance clubs. The Jugueiros area is located near Viseu's universities and is a setting that attracts mainly students, most of them moving to the city to study. In this area, there are several student parties, and usually nightlife is active from Wednesday to Saturday. In Viseu, the team also participates in partners' meetings and local networks and negotiates with the local municipality in the hope of implementing a safer nightlife label soon, much like that existing in Lisbon.

Despite the differences found in both cities, there are also some similarities that, as argued before, are transferable to party settings, in general. During our intervention and ethnographic observation, in both Lisbon and Viseu, we perceived that most of the partygoers used psychoactive substances, especially alcohol, in order to maximise positive effects of socialising such as disinhibition, stimulation and easiness to dance. But it was possible also to see and hear partygoers talking about negative consequences of their drug use, namely acute intoxication, bad trips, hangovers, violent episodes, driving under the effect of alcohol or other drugs and sexual harassment. Also in terms of the drugs used and the drug-use patterns, as explained before, in these urban settings most of the psychoactive substances used are alcohol, cannabis and stimulants such as cocaine, MDMA (3,4-methylenedioxymethamphetamine) and amphetamines. In addition, for these users, party settings were the main drug-use space-times, which was when they intended to intentionally induce altered states of mind.

The discussion until now has explored the context of HR strategies, the role of pleasure in such strategies and how they have been implemented in two contrasting cities. What we want to do now is explore how users of the service actually make use of and understand the CHECK!N programme. The aim of our study is to understand the potential benefits a project like CHECK!N provides for partygoers, particularly those who use drugs. The data was collected in Viseu and Lisbon using a questionnaire developed as a tool to access process and impact evaluation. To collect data, two different methods were used: offline and online. From a total of 305 questionnaires, over two-thirds were collected online and just under a third were conducted face-to-face at CHECK!N infostands. Slightly less than half of our questionnaires were conducted in Viseu, with the rest conducted in Lisbon.

The questionnaire was constructed in order to access (i) participants' behaviours (e.g., sex, drugs and alcohol use), (ii) drug-use patterns, (iii) harm reduction strategies, (iv) impact of CHECK!N project on its clients' knowledge, (v) impact of CHECK!N project on its clients' behaviour and (vi) clients' satisfaction with the services provided by CHECK!N. Sociodemographic dimensions, such as age, sex, country and city of origin, educational level, employment and financial situation, as well as other variables concerning the type and frequency of drug use and perception of the impact of CHECK!N intervention, were also analysed.

Of the 305 partygoers who responded to our questionnaire, 164 were women, 140 were men and 1 identified as trans. They ranged from seventeen to fifty-five years old, with a mean age of twenty-eight years, and the majority were Portuguese, with the rest of the sample from thirteen other European and non-European countries. The fact that most of the respondents were well educated (65.5 percent having professional or higher education), employed or studying, and having a fairly comfortable economic life, corroborates the idea that these types of drug users are socially integrated. In this sense, we can speculate that drug use is somehow well integrated with the rest of their daily lives, as the normalisation thesis suggests. The substance most used by the study participants in terms of prevalence was alcohol, followed by tobacco and cannabis. Ecstasy was the fourth most-used substance, with a great distance from the third place, since 42.6 percent of the sample had never tried this substance (see Figure 12.1).

Differences were also found considering sex, age and substance use, with men reporting higher levels of use than women for alcohol, cannabis, magic mushrooms, psychedelics[5] and dissociative substances. An association between age and drug-use pattern was detected. Age was positively associated with cocaine use, poppers/solvents, stimulants, psychedelics and alcohol. Once again our research corroborated the normalisation thesis, showing that many young people go from being *triers* to *current users* becoming 'post-adolescent clubbers regularly using alcohol, cannabis and "time out" drugs' (Manning 2013, 52). No association between educational level and drug use was found, and only cannabis was negatively associated with one's financial situation. This was also consistent with the normalisation thesis that speculates

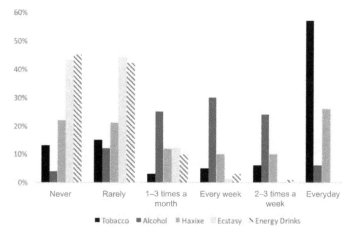

Figure 12.1. **Frequency of use of different psychoactive substances among partygoers in Viseu and Lisbon.** *Source:* **Authors.**

that there are no significant differences between educational level concerning certain type of drug use, since drug use is perceived less and less as a deviant behaviour and more a common feature of leisure, especially at night.

Concerning the impact of CHECK!N and its clients' knowledge and behaviour, a large majority of the sample stated that they had learned something from the project and, most importantly, 85 percent of the respondents considered their behaviour concerning drug use had been positively influenced by CHECK!N's intervention. When asked about how, in fact, their behaviour had changed, the respondents listed a series of harm reduction strategies they began implementing since they came in contact with CHECK!N, such as not sharing drug-use paraphernalia such as snorting tubes, avoiding mixing different drugs, seeking information prior to using a new or unknown substance or testing their drugs whenever a drug-checking service was available. In terms of satisfaction, the overwhelming majority of the participants considered 'useful' or 'very useful' the services provided by CHECK!N; the majority of the respondents considered CHECK!N's intervention philosophy 'good' or 'very good', CHECK!N's peer workers 'good' to 'very good' and the quality of the intervention provided to be 'good' to 'very good'.

CHALLENGES IN NIGHTLIFE COMMUNITY
INTERVENTION IN LISBON AND VISEU

As stated before, even though the project philosophy and methodology are the same, the project design is flexible and the intervention is adapted to the context, drug-use patterns and partygoers' profiles. In this sense, intervention strategies in Viseu are mainly focused on students' nightlife, where heavy episodic drinking is the norm. This is a very challenging intervention field for the teams and projects working in nightlife environments, since in academic events alcohol use and misuse is widely encouraged among students. In these settings, CHECK!N attempts to promote moderation and safer drinking patterns by implementing campaigns and activities, using alcohol breathalysers to demonstrate alcohol's effects and related harms. One of the more visible behavioural changes that were possible to observe during the interventions was the drinking of water during the night, alternating it with alcoholic beverages. Some of the users also reported changes in their drinking behaviour, stating that after contacting the team they avoided mixing different alcoholic beverages and actively setting out to eat during the night.

CHECK!N intervention in Lisbon is focused on nightlife districts that are being shaped and are changing due to the touristification and gentrification of the city centre. According to EMCDDA (2012), travelling is a leisure activity that is increasing among youth, who, usually, search for destinations with interesting offers in terms of nightlife and, sometimes, with more permissive drug policies. Because CHECK!N in Lisbon comes into contact with partygoers from diverse nationalities, the project felt the need to go beyond the local reality and connect with the global in order to respond to the needs of a more mobile range of consumers. For example, the team translated its leaflets to English, provided information about the Portuguese legal framework related to drug use and mapped all the teams working in party settings in other EU countries. Another challenge of increased mobility and tourism is the possibility of emerging new, more global drug-use trends happening on a local level. In 2014, the authors of this chapter implemented two focus groups in Lisbon,[6] one with professionals working in the drug field and the other with recreational drug users. These focus groups intended to assess the local reality in what concerns new drug-use trends. In these focus groups, both professionals and users stated that international mobility (tourism, migration and Erasmus) was related to emerging drug-use trends, since when people travel they come into contact with other drugs and other drug-use patterns. In this sense, the project needed to be aware and have the means to identify emerging trends in drug use or in the informal drug markets.

Despite these challenges, CHECK!N is accomplishing its principal objectives, which are to increase knowledge and to promote positive behaviour change in partygoers in terms of their recreational drug use. It can also be inferred that the majority of CHECK!N clients, although using drugs, care about their health and when given accurate information are more likely to implement behaviours that promote their well-being.

CONCLUSIONS

This chapter confirms the validity and efficacy of the implementation of harm reduction responses in nightlife environments. As shown earlier, the offering of education for the management of pleasures and risks related to recreational drug use and sexuality is effective and appreciated by partygoers. However, it is important to highlight that nightlife environments are often dynamic and experimental settings that are constantly reinvented by different actors. In addition, every year several new psychoactive substances appear (EMCDDA 2015), and some of them are used in party settings. Globalisation, touristification and advances in information and communication technologies, like the Internet, mean the emergency not only of new substances but also of new drug and party practices. These mutable processes are very challenging for the projects, peers and professionals working in nightlife settings, who must then update constantly to guarantee the suitability and pertinence of their information and services. This is a difficult task because it implies ongoing needs assessments, research and evaluation procedures, and often there are no means to implement them since these activities, although considered necessary by project funders, are not considered in the project's budget. Though now technically in a post-recession scenario, we are witnessing political disinvestment and a lack of financial support for this type of intervention despite an intense growth of the city's cultural and leisure activities, particularly those related to nightlife.

As argued in this chapter, drug use is an important aspect of a *night out* not only for young people but also for adults, and it is fundamental to give people the necessary tools to enjoy their party experiences in more pleasurable and safer ways. The data presented in this chapter reinforces the idea that, in the current scenario, using nightlife venues as educational settings can be an effective way of minimising the risks of alcohol and drug use, while respecting users' subjectivities and desire to party. The possibility of managing many of the problems of nightlife settings without relying on prohibitive measures is good not only for partygoers but also for nightlife staff and owners and the municipalities dealing with these issues. The introduction or further development of harm reduction responses in party settings should therefore be prioritised by public or private funding agencies with an interest in nightlife, namely government institutions, municipalities, clubs and bars.

NOTES

1. APDES is a Portuguese NGDO (non-governmental development organisation) that intends to promote the integrated development of vulnerable and stigmatised

individuals, groups and communities. For more information, see http://www.apdes.pt/en/apdes/about-us.html.

2. Since 2009 the Portuguese city of Porto has not received governmental funding to promote specific interventions in its nightlife districts and venues.

3. A drug-checking integrated service is a place where people who use drugs can have their drugs chemically analysed along with some brief interventions and counselling when needed.

4. Party+ is the European network for safer party labels. More information about this network is available at http://www.safernightlife.org/partyplus.

5. In order to analyse the group of drugs' family/typology, three additional variables were created: stimulants, psychedelics and dissociatives. For stimulants, we compute the variables: cocaine, speed, ecstasy and other stimulants. For psychedelics we compute magic mushrooms, tryptamines, phenethylamines, 2C-B and other hallucinogens. For dissociative substances, we compute ketamine and GHB (γ-hydroxybutyric acid).

6. These focus groups were an activity of a rapid assessment and response implemented in the scope of the European Project 'New Psychoactive Substances among People Who Use Drugs Heavily' (JUST/2013/DPIP 4000004774). These data were not published but a contribution for the five-country RAR Report available at http://npsineurope.eu/images/pdf/publication/NPS_5_country_rar_report.pdf.

Chapter 13

Policies for Nightlife and the Democratic City: From Urban Renewal to Behaviour Control in Rio de Janeiro, Brazil

Marcos Paulo Ferreira de Góis

Terms such as 'creative culture', the 'cultural industries' and the 'night-time economy' have become increasingly used in public speeches by business people, politicians and urban planners. They are deployed as the latest answers to urban decay in both developed and developing cities. Together, nightlife, creativity and culture promise profit, social order and redevelopment by promoting new sites for entertainment and leisure activities. In Brazil, cities like Rio de Janeiro have invested in projects and plans to promote the construction of stadiums, heritage and recreational centres and urban monuments to attract tourists, mobilise entrepreneurs and renew public spaces for leisure activities (Gaffney 2010; Curi et al. 2011). These places are built to remain active long into the evening and extend consumption through the night. Nightlife itself seems to have become a new commodity for attracting urban capital and is a central feature in the expansion of many urban economies. The night has thus become as much a political as an economic issue for city planners and investors, involving both the public realm and the use of public and private services and infrastructure.

The current night scene of Rio de Janeiro is notably varied, mixing aspects of a more traditional nightlife with elements from abroad, mostly from European cities. The nightscape of Rio de Janeiro is a composition of renewed and regenerated venues in the form of bars, restaurants and nightclubs alongside old-fashioned bars and liquor warehouses, cultural centres, museums, theatres and *cafeterias* and entertainment centres that group together cinemas, department stores, supermarkets and food halls. These brightly lit places are intersected by residential neighbourhoods, where traffic and street life slowly fade away after sunset. Rio's nightscape also includes dark points and obscure places where, as it is commonly said, 'one should never go after the sun goes down'. Practices, mobilities, habits and imaginaries in the night are organised around a regime of invisibility and visibility.

The increased role of the government in organising nightlife resulted from changes to its constitutional duties. Democratic decentralisation in Brazil at the end of the 1980s played a vital role in allowing local governments to directly participate in urban redevelopment and fiscal collection. Until then, the urban environment was often described as simply *tragic*, due to reduced investment during the period of high inflation in the 1980s and 1990s. At the beginning of the 1990s, however, the City Council approved a new Comprehensive Plan, which established key policies for urban development. The plan served as a public guide for urban projects and, in a broad sense, helped local governments to stimulate nightlife. Municipal investment in urban projects in Rio de Janeiro has increased since the 1990s and reached a peak in recent years, especially with the Olympic Games and the urban restructuring of the seaport area.

In this chapter, I discuss the role of public policies for nightlife, especially the actions taken by public officials to renew and regulate public spaces in Rio de Janeiro. I also investigate specific sites and behaviours in Rio's nightlife and aim to demonstrate the role of nightlife in the redevelopment of the urban economy, especially in terms of how discourses of visibility, order and conflict organise the perception of the city before and after dark. The first part of the chapter focuses on the more general aspects of the relationship between public policies and the night-time economy. Rio de Janeiro is later analysed according to three revitalisation projects developed for downtown, coastal and suburban areas. Finally, the chapter ends with some thoughts on how Rio de Janeiro compares to the global phenomenon of expanding nocturnal activities and night leisure spaces.

URBAN POLICIES AND SOCIAL LIFE

The emergence of public and commercial leisure activities in South America in the early nineteenth century typically occurred in 'downtown' areas in capitals such as Rio de Janeiro, Buenos Aires, Bogotá or Montevideo. Street lighting, police departments, leisure palaces, theatres, restaurants, cabarets and street life emerged in the colonial period along with new technologies, behaviours and social spaces (Baldwin 2012). The night-time became a period of leisure as well as work-related activities, making visible practices formerly hidden from view and creating public places for sociability at night (see also Otter 2008). Today, we are witness to an expansion of night-time activities and a demand for twenty-four-hour services, including markets, gas stations and public transportation (Melbin 1987; Gwiazdzinski 2005).

In the past thirty years there has been a gradual increase in sociological, historical and geographical research about nightlife, especially dedicated to the study of the urban economy (Bianchini 1995; Chatterton 2002; Roberts and Eldridge 2009). Studies of the night have also focused on gentrification and social struggles between different classes, especially in relation to post-industrial and deindustrial cities of the United Kingdom and the United States (Hollands 1995, 2002; Thornton 1996; Dixon et al. 2006). Equally, the expansion of social life in the night has been examined in relation to social inequalities and spatial process of gentrification and segregation (Chatterton and Hollands 2003) as well as discrimination related to gender, race and sexuality (Talbot 2006). Many of these accounts start from a sense of crises: first, an economic crisis that broke the growth of investment in developed countries in the 1970s; second, a political crisis related to the new role of states and the birth of new political groups, identities and communities including those centred around ethnicity, race, sexuality and gender to interregional competitiveness. Third, urban nightlife is typically framed as having partially emerged due to an exodus to suburban and wealthier areas and a limited investment in public spaces in urban centres.

In Rio, the idea of an urban crisis was defined by local politicians as a product of public disinvestment and economic decay in the 1980s. During this decade, part of the traditionally urban population moved (or were moved by the local government) from downtown to neighbourhoods located at the edge of the urbanised area (Gondim 1987). Decades before, wealthier neighbours had also moved from downtown to middle-class areas such as Copacabana. The further abandonment of the city centre is also recognised as resulting from the economic crisis or 'lost decade' of the 1980s that swept across South America. Downtown nightscapes were described at this time as mundane, silent, dangerous and precarious, with enclosed shopping centres created to meet the public demand for leisure and entertainment, albeit in closed spaces. An increasing sense of insecurity and fear of being in public spaces at night contributed to the development of these semiprivate places in the 1980s. While the urban crisis and urban decay left behind undervalued land and buildings, these became profitable businesses by the end of the 1980s. Local stakeholders, including politicians, landowners, architects, engineers, historians, impresarios and artists, joined together in executing plans to redevelop the downtown area. Renewing the centre was designed to manage the crisis and, more important, 'entertainment' was the key word in a range of urban projects. Some plans to renew Rio's urban landscape and street life adopted ideas from urban renewal projects from other cities, especially those that emphasised the significant role of culture in regenerating city centres. A comparison can be drawn here between the processes explored by Lovatt and O'Connor (1995) in the United Kingdom and the case of the

Cultural Corridor in Rio as discussed by Pinheiro and Del Rio (1993); both demonstrate the significance of cultural centres to urban regeneration and the promotion of nightlife.

The European model of regeneration, which is often associated with the creation of heritage sites and various cultural developments, indicates that the way people see and use the city has changed in recent decades (Choay 2001; Jeudy 2005). Local stakeholders have attempted to create a new image of the urban centre, promoting history and culture as attractions to tourists, residents and local investors. Heritage has had to be reimagined, incorporating cultural centres, museums, theatres, entertainment centres, nightclubs and movie theatres. This process of urban renewal has affected cities, as a whole, and the experience of nightlife, in particular.

In the case of Rio, urban renewal can be evaluated as having had both positive and negative consequences. For a certain segment of the public, it implies improvements in facilities, urban infrastructure and access to places for nightlife. For others, it may be identified with the removal and erasure of practices regarded as transgressive or contrary to the dominant hegemonic culture. Resistance to urban redevelopment in Rio exists in places such as the *botequins* (small old-fashioned bars), liquor stores, traditional restaurants and street vending of food and drinks. But nightlife has become an important economic issue to local government and developers who have now increasingly sought to 'manage' activities commonly associated with the city at night, such as violence, drug dealing, illegal commerce and sex work.

Gentrification, much like in the West, has been understood in Brazil as a process in which the renovation of built spaces and changes in social activities result in changes to the social composition of an area as well as patterns of consumption. The adaptation of the term to Brazilian cities faces important theoretical and empirical challenges, however, as a result of the economic structure of Brazilian society, existing settlement patterns of cities, forms of cultural consumption and so forth. Thus, when the term is brought to the discussion of Brazilian cities, it draws upon debates launched by the English-speaking literature but is not always clearly applicable to the local context where there are significant differences in both the urban form and urban behaviours. In Rio de Janeiro, the process of gentrification is not so clearly associated with downtown areas or the urban core, for example. As noted earlier, wealthy inhabitants moved from the core area to suburban sites at the turn of the twentieth century in a progressive search for status and urban amenities, following the coastline and going towards the west side of the municipal territory. Meanwhile, working-class, blue-collar and other groups (migrants from different regions of the country) moved to new lands close to industrial sites where properties were less expensive. These processes accelerated after the 1940s, when several actions transformed the downtown area into a space largely for business centres and commercial stores. In the 1970s and 1980s, the margins of the city centre continued to be inhabited by people who had no relatives in the city and by older residents who did not or could not relocate. In general, they lodged in two-storey, twenty-foot-wide buildings, old tenement houses around the central business district, usually sharing rooms in boarding houses or cheap hotels (Lago 2015; Monteiro 2015).

Downtown nightlife in the 1970s was mostly moribund, and crime and vice dominated newspaper headlines (*Revista Cruzeiro*, 4 April 1973). In earlier times, nightlife in Rio occurred in spaces at the margin of the downtown centre, where popular and elite activities took place side by side. Even people from distant neighbourhoods used to go to these places to have fun at night, visiting operas, plays and vaudeville shows. Carnival celebrations used to occur during the daylight in public spaces and would extend into masquerades that took place in private clubs at night. The loss of such nightlife activities in Rio emerged during a conservative period where the privileging of specific behaviours led to new practices emerging far from downtown. Between the 1940s and the 1980s, nightlife migrated to Copacabana, and the centre of the city remained for those who could not afford to relocate (Góis 2015).

Moving the capital to Brasília in 1960 further damaged the urban environment of Rio, and a significant financial investment was undertaken to improve public spaces. However, the economic crisis further deeply affected the city in the 1980s, and high rates of inflation stalled public resources and private capital investment. The city simply could not pay for the urban regeneration projects that developers had been trying to achieve since the end of the 1970s. If the downtown area was exposed to a decline in investment, suburban streetscapes were no better. Wealthier neighbourhoods suffered from fragile urban infrastructure. Sanitation and street lighting problems were common, and public spaces were further muted by dictatorial enforcements (Mendonça 2004). Working-class neighbourhoods were abandoned to their own fate, and unplanned settlements, both favelas and housing built by residents, grew adjacent to train stations and railways (Perlman 1976). Urban development projects for the whole city were created in the beginning of the 1990s in an attempt to reset the economy of suburban neighbourhoods. *Rio Cidade* and *Favela Bairro* were examples of such redevelopment projects that aimed to recover the urban form and therefore encourage local investment.

Global processes and global models of redevelopment have affected Rio de Janeiro but in a very particular way. The local government has had to deal with three main problems over the years: the loss of its political centrality since the capital moved to Brasília in 1960, a dictatorial government established in 1964 that repressed some forms of public expression and the aforementioned economic crisis in the 1980s that slowed and even stalled efforts at urban renewal. The 1990s became a time when democracy and capital held the urban projects together to change the city's nightscape, a process that has since become crucial to the image and economy of the city.

The post-dictatorship period began to emerge in 1984 with the election, by an electoral college, of President Tancredo Neves. A new constitution was created in 1988, redistributing federal powers to states and municipalities. At the same time, this period was defined by the introduction of neo-liberalism to the Brazilian economy, a rising inflation rate and the decentralisation of tax liability (Amann and Baer 2002). As a proposed solution to various economic dilemmas, the Brazilian government privatised public industries, created a new currency and gave municipalities a significant role in urban development.

Rio de Janeiro was initially run by a populist governor in the 1980s. Leonel Brizola (1922–1994), head of the Democratic Labour Party, endorsed structural transformations in urban design. Assisted by Oscar Niemeyer (1907–2012), the architect best known for his work in Brasília, Brizola attempted to redesign the landscape of Rio de Janeiro, proposing projects to remodel unplanned settlements and local infrastructure. The governor introduced many political agents to the local government; the first two mayors were Brizola's disciples: Marcello Alencar (1925–2014) and Cesar Maia (1945–), and both of them offered a different view of the city and its urban planning.

Alencar and Maia were especially concerned with public space renewal and private investment. They took advantage of the new constitution and the new economic context to introduce neo-liberal enterprises to the city through local investors and opening public–private partnerships in consortium operations. Banks, construction companies, real estate developers and the local government played a crucial role in developing urban space from the beginning of the 1990s. While Alencar had to deal with uncertain public revenue and a fragile institutional background, Maia had a stronger institutional and political base from which to develop these projects.

The Brazilian Federal Constitution established guidelines for urban policies and foundations that local governments had to abide by to collect taxes and develop urban projects. The main instrument of urban policy was the Comprehensive Plan, used for planning urban sprawl and development management, a problem that had increased only since the 1940s. Nightlife was absent from public discussion in the Comprehensive Plan, but between the lines the plan for redevelopment of the city contained instruments for night planning. First, street lighting became a part of public infrastructure and an element of urban zoning, a matter that had been absent from previous projects. Second, urban facilities were referred to in accordance with individual neighbourhoods' unique identities in order to reactivate street life, especially in traditionally commercial areas. Third, public–private partnerships were established as a mechanism for urban transformation, divvying the costs of urban renewal between different stakeholders. Fourth, heritage sites were preserved as cultural spaces dedicated to addressing the needs of various audiences. Also, in the 1992 Comprehensive Plan, it is implicit that areas classified as sites of permanent preservation could not be repurposed (Article 51); cultural areas were defined to enhance land values (Article 124); and criteria were stipulated to define heritage sites (Article 131).

These features were crucial to the renewal of Rio de Janeiro's nightlife in at least three areas: the downtown centre, the seaside touristic sites and the commercial areas at the core of residential suburbs. Those areas were progressively improved: first the downtown, then the seaside and finally the suburbs. Urban projects were created for specific neighbourhoods and led to major transformations in the cityscape. As discussed later, all of them entailed an aspect of nightlife and attempted to stimulate the night-time economy.

GOING DOWNTOWN

The first urban project, *Corredor Cultural* (Cultural Corridor), was a plan coordinated by local stakeholders and involved artists, politicians, academics and urban planners. The project was concerned with heritage preservation through architectural renewal of nineteenth-century buildings (Pinheiro and Del Rio 1993). To encourage owners and potential buyers to renew or invest in its properties, the local government offered tax exemptions. Nonetheless, the project encountered several hurdles. First, some buildings were in an advanced state of physical decay, discouraging owners or buyers from improving them. Second, part of the heritage site was in the Central Business District (CBD), which made them more valuable as sites for entirely new buildings. Third, the local government did not take on the costs of public space renewal due to the economic and institutional crisis in the 1970s.

By the end of the 1980s the project returned to the local government's agenda. The political and economic contexts were by then 'friendlier', and peripheral areas of the centre were granted specific urban legislation. The main argument was that a historical and cultural landscape of nineteenth-century Rio de Janeiro mixed with investment in modern technology, in both private and public spaces, could revitalise social life in the city centre. Restaurants, coffee shops, museums and cultural centres were promoted by the local impresarios, who expected to revive the urban atmosphere by filling streets with new practices, and maybe their business with new patrons (*Jornal O Globo*, 4 September 1988). The investment was substantial, and national banks, chambers of commerce and other public institutions and private entrepreneurs created an urban scape crossing the CBD area. Between 1984 and 2010, 150 cultural sites had been inaugurated, and more than 500 bars and restaurants opened in the area between the neighbourhoods of Praça XV, Lapa and Saara. Street lighting was improved by creating street-level poles, and special modern lamps that created scenic views of the nineteenth-century streets were installed.

By the beginning of the 2000s, the continuing investment in the area attracted a new audience composed of not only downtown workers but also university students interested in cheap liquor and a variety of musical genres. Initially, white-collar workers occupied chairs and tables on the sidewalks outside bars and restaurants, where music (usually Brazilian popular music) was played by a solo artist with a guitar or keyboard. Students changed the night environment, adding new practices by increasing the sale of alcohol and then by demanding new spaces for their practices and music tastes (*Jornal O Globo*, 25 March 2001). *Circo Voador*, a popular concert house inaugurated in 1982 under Lapa's aqueduct, was the first stage for alternative music that opened in the area. Since then, new music houses and nightclubs have started to present new artists and a diverse cultural language. At the same time, new alcohol-related venues have opened and spread elsewhere, including restaurants, bars, pizzerias, pubs, liquor stores and alcohol street vendors. It appears that this was the first time that public institutions joined together with local investors to regenerate the central area and stimulate nightlife. In fact, it was the first time that the night had been part of an urban redevelopment project.

A NIGHT AT THE SHORE

While downtown nightlife flourished, seaside neighbourhoods began to be remodelled by the project *Rio Orla*, approved in 1990, during the administration of Mayor Marcello Alencar. The central aim of *Rio Orla* was to increase the value of the beach as an image and realm of carioca sociability. Expanding tourism was also considered for its potential to raise money for the city and to open urban 'frontiers' to the private sector. Interventions were planned to be finished in time for the 1992 United Nations Conference on Environment and Development, held in the city of Rio de Janeiro.

Rio Orla was an extensive project in terms of its scale (approximately 35 km or 22 miles) but was very limited in terms of its design. All the beaches were renewed following the same pattern: a vehicular lane, a bicycle path, a larger promenade, kiosks to sell beverages and appetisers and a new set of lights focusing on the sand strip. However, the promenades were designed to respect traditional sidewalks made in Portugal, and they became a powerful image for tourism advertisements. Patrons transformed kiosks into sites of sociability at night, and local businesses saw it as an opportunity to convert them into restaurants. As the changes in physical space took place, the public also changed, becoming even more socially segmented and middle class oriented.

Sporting activities and kiosks created an environment where other kinds of activities took place or expanded. Nightlife became more vivid, with new upmarket restaurants, hotels, table dance clubs and LGBTQ+ nightclubs occupying the edge of the coastal neighbourhoods. Legal practices were followed by illegal activities like sex work, street vending and drug dealing. Tourism also increased, following the growth of these local facilities. Low- and high-economic circuits joined and created a complex network of legal and illegal practices, most of them tourist oriented. A common scene in the Copacabana nightscape showed a few people walking, running, skating or biking; a small number of people hanging out in the beach; many kiosks occupied by groups or couples; and dozens of people cheering at bars and nightclubs.

Rio Orla spread the formula along the coastal area, including the bay area, in neighbourhoods near downtown. These places became part of the night circuit for the people who practised sports or met friends at night. However, the example of Copacabana reproduced the best on the edge of neighbourhoods like Ipanema, Leblon and Barra da Tijuca, including its touristic aspects, sports and nightly entertainment. This was also due to the characteristics of these neighbourhoods, which remain mostly inhabited by the middle class.

URBAN RENEWAL AND NIGHTLIFE EVERYWHERE

While these examples demonstrate the growth of development and government nightlife in Rio de Janeiro in a fairly conventional manner, the idea of nightlife in the European and North American contexts differs from that in Latin American cities. The pivotal point is about the *places* of nightlife. References to the use of *private spaces*, nightclubs, restaurants, casinos, shopping centres and so on are relatively common in European and North American studies (Thornton 1996; Hobbs et al. 2000; Monaghan 2002; Chatterton and Hollands 2003). In the case of Latin American cities, there is greater interest in understanding the activities that take place in public spaces. In such spaces, activities, problems and conflicts resulting from different uses and forms of appropriation of place arise. Therefore, when it comes to research on nightlife in Latin American cities, the analysis tends to value spaces of greater social visibility at night: the street.

At the end of the 1980s academics agreed that the city was facing hard times (Ribeiro and Lago 1995). According to their claims, and as indicated earlier, the urban environment needed to be reorganised to deal with the urban and economic restructuring of Rio and its metropolitan area. It was argued that new urban models should be adopted to reset the relationship between the public and spaces they used. In the Strategic Plan of 1996, for example, the city was presented as a complex whole with specific demands for public goods. In that context, Mayor Cesar Maia proposed the urban project *Rio Cidade* in 1993. Inspired by European urban projects (like Barcelona's Olympics-led urban regeneration), the central idea was to reinstitute the urban order by returning public space to citizens. Strategic points of the city were chosen by technical teams, architecture firms and urban planners in a process referred to by Jaime Lerner (2014) as *urban acupuncture*, that is, the city was compared to an ill human body, which needs treatment to become healthy. The proposed cure came from small interventions in neural areas, and the expected result was to be the stimulation of certain points of the body, spreading the cure from one specific point to the rest of the city.

Rio Cidade was a controversial project of urban *revitalisation*, which achieved substantial approval by local citizens (68 percent in a survey conducted by *Jornal O Globo* in 1996). Depressed suburbs in the north and west sides of the city such as Madureira and Campo Grande saw their commercial sites flourish and grow after years of neglect. Middle-class neighbourhoods around the downtown centre like Copacabana and Ipanema saw the rise of commercial centres and public life (*Jornal O Globo*, 20 May 1997). However, citizens complained about the design-oriented policies of developing the environment, stating that the redevelopment was committed to aesthetic purposes instead of social ones. Fancy obelisks, painted streets, expensive sidewalk pavements or useless walkways were considered a waste of public money. Yet a new technical and intellectual discourse moulded the project, enhancing the unique neighbourhoods' histories and creating commercial spaces to redevelop the local economy.

Clearly, the nightscape of Rio beyond downtown and the coast has changed in the past thirty years as a result of the project. The areas inhabited by workers were referred to in the 1980s as commuter or dormitory suburbs. There were few references to nightlife in working-class neighbourhoods, with ill-lit streets and scenes of violence the only reference to the night (Mendonça 2004). This is an aspect that still needs to be better studied, but it indicates that much of the night-time leisure available in these areas was restricted to community life. Workers found few nocturnal amusements in their neighbourhoods, having to travel vast distances to find them in other parts of the city. The situation at night would typically be a quiet neighbourhood, with only a few cheap bars and pubs running after 8:00 p.m., serving beers and appetisers, a couple of people hanging outside their houses, talking to neighbours and watching children playing and a mass of workers returning to their homes from their workday. This is a scene that can be described as a *genospace* (Gomes 2004), a space marked by familiar and communitarian places, different from the cosmopolitan view of nightlife usually attached to the city centre. Meanwhile, a cultural movement based on the Afro-American movement Black is Beautiful called funk was born in the favelas of Rio de Janeiro; this was a form of nocturnal leisure, which became part of the social life of the residents of the poorest areas of the city from the beginning of the 1990s (Lessa 2005).

Urban interventions transformed the commercial centres of many such neighbourhoods, changing the physical space and encouraging commercial activities. Local government altered social practices by constructing public spaces and reformulating the night environment. Sidewalks in residential neighbourhoods were commonly used as spaces for taking in fresh air and greeting neighbours. These practices faded during the 1980s and 1990s due to increased violence and declining urban maintenance. Investments result-ing from *Rio Cidade* in suburban areas, however, relocated social space to commercial centres, where sidewalks in front of restaurants, bars, pizzerias, food trucks or appetiser tents became occupied not only by neighbours but also by people from different areas of the city, tied together by public interest in social encounters. Nightlife thus became concentrated in these neighbour-hoods' commercial centres, or more accurately, as planned, the *acupoints*.

REGULATING NIGHTLIFE

After a decade of urban projects and public policies aimed at changing the urban environment of Rio, actions have shifted from urban renewal to behav-iour control. At the same time, urban renewal policies have migrated in the direction of areas that had not been focused on in previous actions, especially sites associated with the Summer Olympic Games held in 2016. The first years of public investment focused on public spaces and the physical realm; nightlife was not at the centre of public policies but has earned a space in the more general process of redevelopment, becoming part of the programmes' objectives. In the past ten years, after changes in physical and social spaces have been undertaken, the local government has now turned its actions towards unruly and transgressive practices, in general, and acted specifically on illegal vending of beverages, drinks and beers, drug dealing, sex work, public performances on public space and other popular practices that usually occur at night.

The first act of the new mayor, Eduardo Paes, in office from 2009 to 2016, was to enact a decree regulating street vendors of Lapa, a traditional district for nightlife in Rio's centre.[1] The idea was to designate an area for their commercial practices and to establish a pattern of actions that could be reproduced in other areas of the city. In doing so, Lapa became an 'urban laboratory' for municipal officers, an example for the whole city and citizens to follow. The programme called Lapa Legal was the first effort to control unwanted behaviour in the streets of the neighbourhood. Not only street vendors but also drug dealers and users, owners of restaurants and bars, nightlife entrepreneurs and all sorts of patrons began to sense a more intensive presence of officers in the streets of Lapa at night.

The experience was managed by the Municipal Public Order Bureau in a strategic policy called *Choque de Ordem* – Clash of Order – and aimed to control public spaces and their uses by police enforcement. By regulating nightlife, the government planned to protect the site from unruly behaviours and to offer a venue for touristic and cultural activities. The motivation was to preserve the work undertaken by previous governments and to establish the Lapa area as a potential centre for tourism, especially at night, as shown in the strategic and government plans for the period.

Changes in regulations and control patterns sometimes require changes in physical spaces, and the Lapa Legal project, created in the context of Eduardo Paes's administration, expressed that idea by proposing three different interventions held by the municipality: (i) an aesthetic redesign of small buildings and public monuments, (ii) a rearrangement of spatial objects and repairs on sidewalks and (iii) a temporary conversion of streets into walkable pathways at night, otherwise known as pedestrianisation. These actions aimed to reorganise night-time behaviours and practices and to boost the night-time economy, but owners of local businesses and dwellers and regulars of Lapa questioned the actions of the local government and reversed some of them, such as the opening of streets for pedestrians. This meant that the regulation of nightlife also became part of a set of shared actions between public authorities, users and local businesses that aimed to control behaviour as a key measure of assuring sustainability of the Lapa neighbourhood.

Changes in the physical space, behaviour regulation and management of street vending reveal the conflicted processes that underlined the development of the area. Proposed interventions did not come about without being challenged by social agents; changes in the form and content of sociability in Lapa's night were criticised, and urban policies had to be rethought. A fall in the number of patrons visiting the area seems to have shown that the amount of control applied needed to be more moderate to maintain and develop nightlife. The decision to control behaviour by policing street life also led to the relocation of people from the centre of nightlife to new areas, marginalising them further. The heavy-handed actions, as a result, only worked as a stimulus for the creation of other night places, protected from the eyes of authority.

Overall, what can be seen is that the process of *returning* to the city centre has been extensively negotiated since the 1980s and occurred against the backdrop of intense political debate and a constant clash of economic interests with public engagement in night-time activities. At the same time, it appears that the process required an adaptation of traditional local interests to global imperatives, especially linked to tourism, associating the traditional carioca image to a set of modern and regulated services. No doubt this process led to the emergence of a new audience for local nights, but it also allowed for the whole city to come together in one place (Lapa) at the same moment (Friday nights).

AFTERMATH: STREET LIFE AND NIGHT FEVER

Although valuable, there are still few studies about Rio that focus on nightlife as a research topic. In general, there is a greater commitment to studying the social groups that express their identities, patterns of consumption and behaviour in the nocturnal period (Almeida and Tracy 2003). There have been few advances on a political discussion about the actions of urban agents for developing the night-time economy and more general night culture (for São Paulo, see the Night Manifesto 2014). In addition, there is relative disinterest over the setting of nightlife, that is, the spaces that actually emerge or come alive at night due to specific social practices. In this chapter, my motivation has been to present an extensive overview of the relation among the nightlife of the city, the actions of political agents and stakeholders and the role of democracy in the configuration of nocturnal public spaces: places of encounter, conflicts and negotiations of actions in society. I have examined the political context of Rio de Janeiro, observing the urban planning of the city and its consequences for nightlife in three areas: downtown, the coastal zone and the suburbs. This observation was guided by the urban projects created in the 1980s.

These projects shaped three types of urban environments, downtown, the coast and the suburbs, leading to diverse activities, behaviours and designs. In Rio, nightlife is a result of public planning but is wrapped up in the practices of common people and private investments. Different actions compose the nightscape, and they do it in a manner that reflects the disputes, tensions and negotiations between different social agents, sometimes leading to a reorientation of official practices. Negotiation is a strategy to resist in a scenario of ongoing conflicts between conservative initiatives and new venues and practices for the night-time economy.

Places change over time, assimilating the demands of public agents, citizens and private investors. Shifts in policies also reflect changes in the way that people understand their environment. Usually these transformations occur on the back of old practices and simply reproduce them. Rio's nightlife has been transformed, but one can still find elements of past times, adaptations to new scenarios, political resistance against controversial projects and negotiations about places and the activities that occur within them. Resistance can also be observed in the absorption of popular genres of music or architecture, in urban plans and practices and in the use of old business and houses as heritage sites for new venues dedicated exclusively to entertainment at night. The commitment of social groups, non-profit organisations, chambers of commerce and neighbourhood associations has improved the original projects and increased demand for direct participation. The nightscape is a political arena, and urban projects must deal with the demands of local groups, local history, law enforcement and the economic context, be that in crisis or otherwise. Although the projects discussed here have ostensibly valued and sought to better manage or develop these places, they have also contributed to controlling social practices with varying degrees of success.

Between the 1980s and today, ideas about nightlife and how it is planned for and understood have been constantly revisited. *Safety* has become the keyword to defend the creation of leisure/consumer centres in a context of increasing criminality and abandonment of public spaces. In this scenario, one can understand the creation of new projects as a political programme to redevelop Rio's street life through commercial stimulation. *Mobility* also becomes a central issue as urban sprawl leads to economic stagnation. The need for decentralisation and multiple economic clusters seems to be crucial in dealing with the spread of urbanisation in the past seventy years and has motivated the *redevelopment discourse* to spread to new areas, engaging with local demands for public spaces and urban infrastructure. *Organisation* has been considered a *revolutionary trope* to contain crime, vice and illegal practices. Controlling behaviour by redesigning places was commonly associated with gentrification in Rio, but, in fact, it was demanded by local residents and business owners to reduce the apparent chaos promoted by the concentration of too many people in the same area.

In conclusion, I can point to some wider problems common to other contexts. First, new urban projects such as those discussed here can save some areas from urban decay, but they can also play a different role in other areas, transforming them into *no-go places* or places segregated from the legal or *legitimated* city. The bright venues became a powerful image of the city and can represent a new feature for urban tourism, being part of a *lightscape*, well lit and visible from anywhere. On the other hand, there will be places hidden from some citizens, marginalised because of their transgression from the master plan and obscured by the clouds of the neo-liberal, socially sanitised night-time economy. This process can shape a visibility regime where some kinds of behaviours and activities become unknown or out of the focus, not representing the desired image of the city.

Second, excessive investment in tourist venues does not always promote a profitable nightlife and, in this sense, profit can be understood as a less-prominent issue. If we establish that nightlife can contribute to social life, democracy and a sense of equality, social practices must be understood as attached to space and place. It means that there must be life on the streets at night, a kind of life that resembles the diversity of practices that exist in the city. A more inclusive nightlife should be open not only to mass culture but also to alternative and popular interventions. Public space can be a realm for sociability and a place in the sense that it can allow people from diverse back-grounds to congregate, not only to consume but also to expand their sense of the city in its many forms.

Third, it is difficult to balance the actions between freedom and control. State concerns usually shift towards order and control of behaviours and prac-tices. The idea of regulation is at the core of public policy, but why must it always be conservative? Innovative ideas can reintroduce a more revolution-ary way of thinking about night-time: not the usual concern about violence and transgression nor the gentrified view of *great white ways* but something compared to a dimmed light, absorbing the variations in the rhythms of the city and its spatial organisation over the days of the week and the hours of the day. A more sensible urbanism for cities and their citizens at night will focus more on places to be and less on places to see.

NOTE

1. Municipal Decree no. 30798, 1 February 2009.

Part 4

AFTERWORD

Afterword: Night Mayors, Policy Mobilities and the Question of Night's End

Will Straw

As I write this afterword, reports on two developments involving the culture of night have arrived at my inbox, retrieved by the daily Google searches I set up a few years ago for this purpose. One of these developments is an event – France's first-ever 'Conférence Nationale de la Vie Nocturne' (14–15 September 2017). The roster of speakers at this high-profile meeting, held in Paris, includes Mirik Milan (leading spokesman for the Night Mayor movement and himself the *nachtburgemeester* or 'night mayor' of Amsterdam) and Amy Lamé (appointed earlier this year as Night Czar for London). The long list of issues to be addressed at the event suggests something of the burden which discussions of the night are now called upon to assume: culture, tourism, security, public tranquillity, transportation, health, risk reduction, the economy and training. Like an earlier landmark event held in the same city, the 2010 'Estates General' on the Parisian night (Mairie de Paris 2010), the 2017 conference brings together city officials; official or informal representatives of night-time entertainment sectors; and an assortment of academic sociologists, anthropologists, urbanists and geographers.

The other news to arrive on this day was more modest in its journalistic eventfulness but no less symptomatic of the night's new status as an object of collective attention. This was notification of the launch of 'Politiques de la Nuit', a thematic new issue of the interdisciplinary French academic journal *Cultures et Conflits*. This volume assembled a group of sociologists, anthropologists and others to explore the multitude of ways in which the night is a site of political conflict. While some of the struggles analysed might seem minor and tame (like the efforts of night concierges in luxury hotels to overcome the stigmatisation to which they are subject) (Menoux 2017), others were marked by more obvious kinds of political urgency (such as the complex work by a wide range of Parisian social agencies to ensure the survival of the homeless at night) (Bruneteaux 2017). The special issue of *Cultures et conflicts* is the latest in a series of recent periodical issues, most of them in French, devoted to the theme of night.[1] What this issue made clear was the extent to which the night now serves as an effective point of thematic convergence for a variety of research projects studying such phenomena as social marginality, urban work and gendered leisure practices.

At one level, the notion that the night is a recent object of attention and analysis seems absurd. The night has always been with us, of course. In the history of urban governance, night has served for centuries as the pretext for regimes of policing, structures of social exclusion and complex systems for the regulation of moralities both public and private. In the realm of ideas, the night has been invoked within the aesthetic sensibilities of important artistic movements, from romanticism through surrealism and on to the cultures of house and rave music. The academic social sciences have long studied the night, even when they have not always acknowledged that they are doing so. Early twentieth-century sociologies of dance hall ritual or histories of urban theatre form part of a prehistory of current scholarship on the night, even when the *nightness* of these phenomena has gone unexplored.

Nevertheless, it seems clear that, over the past fifteen years or so, the ascension of the night as a focus for urban policymakers has run parallel to the growth of an interdisciplinary academic field I have elsewhere called 'night studies' (Straw 2017). The 'Night Mayor' phenomenon, with high journalistic appeal, is the most obvious cause of the former;[2] more broadly, as several articles in this volume show, the night has become a key site around which struggles over urban gentrification, public safety and the survival of a lively urban culture have gathered. The growth of an academic field studying the night not only occasionally intersects with these policy developments but has also followed its own, multiple logics. A scattered and incomplete list of these logics might include the following: the emergence and ongoing development of the notion of the night-time economy, as traced by Eldridge and Nofre in their introduction to this volume; the rise, in the discipline of history, of an attention to popular experiences of time (e.g., Delattre 2003); a growing interest in the cultural practices of urban subcultures and minoritarian (often LGBTQ+) communities (e.g., Yuzna 2013); the growth of urban cultural studies, often faithful to the work of Walter Benjamin and marked by an interest in *flâneurie* (i.e., in the practices of the urban strowler), illumination and other hallmarks of urban modernity (e.g., Montandon 2009; Beaumont 2015); a philosophical interest in the night, rooted in the work of Foucault and others, which embraces those elements of nocturnal behaviour and experience banished from the realms of daytime reason (e.g., Bronfen 2013; Dunn 2016); the 'affectual turn' in cultural analysis, which has nourished interest in the ways in which the night shapes political sentiment and forms of social solidarity (e.g., DeGuzmán 2014; Sharma 2014); and, across several disciplines, an interest in the ecological dimensions of night-time urban lighting (e.g., Bogard 2013; Hasenöhrl et al. 2014). Alongside these currents, and interacting with them in different moments, are the more specialised, local case studies of urban nightlife represented in this volume.

POLICY MOBILITY AND THE NIGHT

If the current academic interest in the night can be traced back along these multiple threads, the growth of the night as policy sector has involved very different patterns. Rather than attempting a straight genealogy of policy initiatives directed at the night, it is more useful to briefly trace the processes that have surrounded one particular policy initiative, that of the naming of Night Mayors, Night Czars or other officials charged with protecting and developing the culture of night.

In briefly sketching these processes, we may follow two guiding principles offered within what are called policy mobility studies – that is, studies concerned with the ways in which policies move across time and space and with the transformations undergone in this movement. One of these is the notion of policy mobility as bound up with circulatory systems, a principle that may be interpreted at different levels of complexity, as Russell Prince suggests:

> Circulatory system descriptions might imagine policy in very narrow terms as just policy documents travelling across electronic networks and being 'applied' in different places, while descriptions that emphasize the way policy travels in a variety of forms might see policy as involving more than words on a page to include the relationships that get arranged around it. (Prince 2012, 318)

In the international take-up of the Night Mayor phenomenon, for example, we see multiple systems of circulation producing distinct clusters of actors and relationships. By 2015, it had become common for city governments in many parts of the world (or consultants advising them) to call for the naming of a city administrator dedicated to the protection and advancement of night-life. The reports and statements in which this call was made followed one circulatory system, typically that of professionals within the policy process or quasi-professional observers (like myself) who followed and collected them online. The proposal for a Night Mayor was typically included in the lists of recommendations, which are a conventional concluding section of consultancy reports.

Alongside this system, news media interested (and bemused) by the notion of a Night Mayor sent profiles of Mirik Milan or Clément Léon (Night Mayor

of Paris since 2013) along other circuits, where they were picked up by journalistic feature writers and shared widely on social media. The youthful pho-
togeneity of these figures, and their avowed connection to grassroots cultural
activities, enhanced their newsworthiness and furthered the circulation of their
profiles. Through these circuits, the notion of a Night Mayor was absorbed
within the thinking of urban cultural activists and civil society groups seeking
new tools with which to pursue their agendas vis-à-vis city governments.

The rapidly developing celebrity of Amsterdam's Night Mayor, Mirik
Milan, helped to personalise the Night Mayor phenomena. His increasingly
frequent visits to other cities, where he met with variable combinations of
governmental and civil society actors, appeared to disseminate the concept of
Night Mayor outside of the conventional pathways of urban policy mobility.
In Canada, for example, we may trace the process through which personal
visits by Milan, journalistic reports and local expert opinion interacted to put
the notion of Night Mayor on the agenda of every major city in the country.
In Toronto, a journalist who had learned of Milan's role through international
press coverage questioned local municipal politicians as to their opinions of
the Night Mayor phenomenon, pushing the concept into the terrain of public debate, where it has come closer to fruition. In Edmonton, where Milan
himself spoke at a hospitality industry function, media used his presence as
the pretext for raising the question of whether that city needed such a role.
In Vancouver, a city resident who had recently returned from a visit to his
native Holland was interviewed about the Night Mayor phenomena, translating Milan's actions into the language of local politics.[3]

In each of these cases, Milan's name and profile became the pivot around
which discussion of the Night Mayor role was introduced, but the policy
contexts for which that role might be imagined varied widely. In Toronto, the
problem of nightlife has been framed as one in which gentrification is kill-
ing off live music venues; in Edmonton, it is the broader question of how a
lively night-time culture might be brought into being. In the first, the night is
a zone of conflict, while in the second it is more a terrain of promise. For the
former, the Night Mayor is imagined as the champion of a threatened sector
of cultural activity, for the latter, a visionary capable of remaking the city's
cultural fabric.

The difference between these two visions of the Night Mayor confirms
the utility of the second of the precepts offered by specialists working in the
field of policy mobility studies: that we 'avoid the temptation to understand
policy transfer through a straightforward import–export metaphor' (McCann
and Ward 2012, 327). In cases where the notion of Night Mayor (or some
variant thereof) has been considered or adopted, it has been shaped by
local, political and administrative traditions. In France, Night Mayors have
emerged as figures of civil society or in relation to associative groups and

often received only quasi-official recognition from city administrations. In Amsterdam, the position of the Night Mayor has been formalised, but the holder himself is chosen in a special election from within the nightlife sector. The most high profile of such appointments recently, that of London's Night Czar Amy Lamé, was made by the Mayor's Office, and most proposals for similar positions within Canadian or American governments imagine the role as akin to that of a manager of a limited economic or social sector within city government.

Like other elements of a new urbanism, such as pedestrian-only streets and bicycle-friendly development, the Night Mayor phenomenon has been marked by the temporal lag between European and North American initiatives. The ubiquitous discussion of the Night Mayor phenomenon in North America in 2017 is evidence that this lag is being narrowed. While the question of its implementation in Canada and the United States was marked, in its early stages, by the sentiment that the Night Mayor is an eccentric, typically European phenomenon out of place in North American cities, it is now more common to see North America as simply behind in its adoption. It is perhaps revealing of the initial difficulties of adaptation that the first such position in the United States was marked by obscurity – it was that of Night Mayor of downtown Iowa City, a position created by a non-profit business association and given to one of its board members.[4] The proposed Nightlife Ambassador of New York City, on the other hand, will be appointed by the Mayor to work within the Mayor's Office for Media and Entertainment.[5]

NIGHT POLICIES, NIGHT STUDIES

Policy initiatives directed at the night have their own, limited terrain of implementation, but they are rarely able to remain purely administrative in character. This is because they cannot help but raise the conceptual question of what kind of category 'night' might name. If the night is more than just a period of time – if it is a set of practices and behaviours, of pathways and places, of values and affects – then a fuller conceptual engagement with the very category of 'night' is required. Even the driest of policy documents about the night waver between calling it a block of time, an economic sector and a population. The uncontrolled accumulation of metaphors for the night ensures that invitations to a more theoretical engagement issue forth from every announcement of a new policy tool. Nowhere is this more obvious than in the current proliferation of official or quasi-official administrative roles intended to ensure the representation of the night within city government.

If we are to have Night Mayors (Amsterdam), Night Czars (London) or Night Ambassadors (New York), each of these terms casts the night as a particular kind of space. At the same time, the models of governance implicit in each of these titles presume distinct kinds of authority. 'Night Mayor' suggests an alternative city invisible within the daytime city and in need of representation. 'Night Ambassador' evokes the model of a foreign land sending emissaries to another political entity in order to make its wishes known. 'Night Czar' builds on the sense, most common within Western governments, of a figure given atypical levels of authority and independence in order to confront a sector marked by challenges – like the 'drug czars' of American governments since at least the 1930s.

Studies of these figures may attempt to remain at the level of the purely administrative. Observers may compare the respective mandates and resources of Night Mayors and Night Czars and evaluate the extent to which they fulfil (or combine) such traditional roles as those of lobbyist, sectoral manager or representative of minority populations. An administrative analysis, however, will have difficulty avoiding a more conceptual, even theoretical understanding of these political roles. At what point, in the emergence of the Night Mayor or Night Czar, have we come to see the night in terms that are almost entirely spatial and territorial rather than temporal and cyclical? During the 2017 presidential election campaign in France, Christophe Vidal (the Night Mayor of Toulouse) asked all candidates how they intended to represent 'the 10 million people in our country who are active in the evening and the night in our country, those engaged in night-time leisure and those who suffer in the night' (my translation). The image offered here was that of the night as a political constituency (a riding or *circonscription*) with its own populations and need for representation (Ladepeche.fr 2017). At this point, we are already deep within an enterprise of fanciful political theorising, one that links backwards to earlier, more speculative ideas about night-worlds or nocturnal species.

THE END OF THE NIGHT?

In 2015, two British journalists published articles arguing that nightlife, at least for a younger generation, was dying (Burrell 2015; Mangan 2015). These claims invited (and only partially offered) a multitude of qualifications. The alleged death of nightlife was, in fact, the death of the nightclub and of the rituals of club-going among British youth, in particular. What was significant in these claims, however, was that they went beyond the familiar diagnoses of the decline of nightlife in once-prominent nightlife capitals. Obituaries for nightlife in Manhattan, London and Paris have been a recurring journalistic genre throughout the past 100 years and particularly common in the past decade or two. As the introduction to this volume by Adam Eldridge and Jordi Nofre argues, anxieties over the imminent decline of nightlife in this or that city reveal a broader recognition of the vulnerability of the night and those who venture into it.

The articles by Burrell and Mangan did not lay the blame for the demise of the nightclub mostly (or at all) on the battles over gentrification, which continue to drive nightlife politics in so many cities. The problem was not that nightlife was being forced out of cities but that broad changes in sensibility and behaviour among young populations meant that the night-time outing to music clubs was no longer a viable or attractive option. The reasons had more to do with the shifting priorities and financial resources of a younger generation than with external forces weakening the nightclub sector. Social media, it was argued, sharply reduced the need for clubs as a means of meeting people; streaming services made them no longer necessary as a means of learning about new music. Inflated drink prices in bars and declining salaries for young people encouraged the purchase of alcohol in retail stores for home consumption. Could it be the case that, amid the appointment of Night Mayors and innumerable panels on saving night-time culture, the latter's most sacrosanct form (the nightclub) was in a period of irreversible decline?

This account of the contemporary world runs counter to those images of drunken crowds and noisy club districts, which still push municipal governments to enact measures to control or transform their nights. It contradicts, as well, the claim of cultural theorists such as Jacques Rancière, to the effect that what drives cultural participation in the contemporary world is less the scarcity of meaning (of expression, of style) than that of social connection (Rancière 2006, 89). It must be noted as well that, if a certain kind of nightlife might indeed be in decline, this has not slowed the worldwide spread of *nuit blanche* art events, extended museum nights, bookstore nights, nocturnal bicycle rides and the general rush of so many social and cultural actors to occupy the night.

NOTES

1. Others include issues: no. 3 (2013) of *Le magasin du xixe siècle*, no. 11 (2015) of *Articulo: Journal of Urban Research*, no. 453 (July–August 2015) of *L'Ena hors les murs: Magazine des Anciens Elèves de l'ENA* and no. 26 (2015) of the Quebec journal *Intermédialités*.

2. See, for coverage of Night Mayors and their equivalents, actual or proposed, in many cities, the following: Martin Pinguet, 'NEW YORK : BIENTÔT UN MAIRE DE LA NUIT POUR CALMER LES TENSIONS ENTRE POLICE ET RIVERAINS?' *Traxmag*, 5 May 2017, http://fr.traxmag.com/article/41693-new-york-bientot-un-maire-de-la-nuit-pour-calmer-les-tensions-entre-police-et-riverains; 'Christophe

Vidal, maire de la nuit 2014, interpelle les candidats sur l'économie de la nuit', *Ladepeche.fr,* 18 April 2017, http://www.ladepeche.fr/article/2017/04/18/2558456-chris tophe-vidal-maire-nuit-2014-interpelle-candidats-economie-nuit.html; 'New York, Edinburgh Mull Appointing Night Mayors', *IQ News,* 15 May 2017, https://www. iq-mag.net/2017/05/new-york-edinburgh-mull-appointing-night-mayors/#.WVGkM mjyuM; John Thistleton, 'How a Night Mayor Can Solve Tuggeranong's Nightmare', *Riot Act!* 23 May 2017, https://the-riotact.com/how-a-night-mayor-can-solve-tug geranongs-nightmare/204222; Emma Kennedy, 'The Stuff of Night Mayors – Why Dublin Needs One', *Independent* (Ireland), 22 March 2016, http://www.indepen dent.ie/life/the-stuff-of-night-mayors-why-dublin-needs-one-35757327.html; 'New York City to Create New "Nightlife Ambassador" Position', *Washington Times,* 16 June 2017, http://www.washingtontimes.com/news/2017/jun/16/new-york-city-to-create-new-nightlife-ambassador-p/; Washington Fajardo, 'Prefeito da Noite', *O Globo,* 16 June 2017, https://oglobo.globo.com/cultura/prefeito-da-noite-21478690.

3. Petti Font, 'A Night Mayor Is a Great Dream for Vancouver', *Ottawa Metro,* 24 May 2016, http://www.metronews.ca/views/vancouver/urban-compass/2016/05/24/ a-night-mayor-is-a-great-dream-for-vancouver.html; Kevin Maimann, 'Does Edmonton Need a Night Mayor?' *Metro,* 13 May 2016, http://www.metronews.ca/news/ edmonton/2016/05/13/amsterdam-night-mayor-gives-edmonton-advice.html; Alex Ballingall, '"Night Mayor" Promotes Peace between Day and Night Interest', *Toronto Star,* 30 April 2016, https://www.thestar.com/news/gta/2016/04/30/night-mayor-promotes-peace-between-day-and-night-interests.html.

4. Liz Zabel, 'New Liaison Says Iowa City Offers More "besides Its Reputation"', *Gazette,* 18 June 2017, http://www.thegazette.com/subject/life/people-places/ new-liaison-says-iowa-city-offers-more-besides-its-reputation-20170617.

5. Jem Aswad, 'New York City to Name a "Nighttime Ambassador" to Advocate for Music, Nightlife', *Variety,* 16 June 2017, http://variety.com/2017/biz/news/ new-york-city-to-name-nighttime-ambassador-1202469125/.

Bibliography

Aalbers, Manuel B. 2016. 'Amsterdam'. In *Red Light City*, edited by Tsaiher Cheng, 84–89. Westmount: The Architecture Observer.

Aalbers, Manuel B., and Michaël Deinema. 2012. 'Placing Prostitution'. *City* 16(1–2): 129–45.

Aalbers, Manuel B., and Magdalena Sabat. 2012. 'Re-making a Landscape of Prostitution: The Amsterdam Red Light District'. *City* 16(1–2): 112–28.

Aftab. 2011. 'Saat Kari Edaraat Afzayesh Yaft'. http://www.aftabnews.ir/vdcgwt9 qxak9xu4.rpra.html.

Aftab. 2012. 'Vazyiat Cinema ha az Eftar ta Sahar'. http://aftabnews.ir/vglfxjdycw 6dv1p..gwwiai,0.html.

Agrama, Hussein Ali. 2012. 'Reflections on Secularism, Democracy, and Politics in Egypt'. *American Ethnologist* 39(1): 26–31.

Agriantoni, Christina, and Maria-Christina Hatziioannou. Eds. 1995. *The Metaxourgeio of Athens*. Athens: NRC.

Al Faruqi, Ismail Raji, and Lois Ibsen Al Faruqi. 1993. *The Cultural Atlas of Islam*. New York: Macmillan.

Alcohol Policy Team. 2016. 'How to Keep Health Risks from Drinking Alcohol to a Low Level Government Response to the Public Consultation'. London: Department of Health. https://www.gov.uk/government/uploads/system/uploads/attach ment_data/file/545911/GovResponse2.pdf.

Alexandri, Georgia. 2013. 'Spatial and Social Changes in the Centre of Athens: The Case of Metaxourgeio'. PhD Thesis, Harokopeio University (in Greek). http://estia. hua.gr/file/lib/default/data/10719/theFile.

Alexandri, Georgia. 2015. 'Reading between the Lines: Gentrification Tendencies and Issues of Urban Fear in the Midst of Athens' Crisis'. *Urban Studies* 52(9): 1–16.

Allame-Majlesi. 2000 (1698). *Bihar-al-Anwar, 110 vol*. Beirut, Lebanon: Dar Ihya Turath al Arabi.

Almas-e-Sharq. 2012. 'Saat Kari Mojtamae Tejari Almas-e Sharq'. http://ns1.almas shargh.com/fa/2012-06-12-07-14-21/95.

Almeida, Maria, and Kátia Tracy. 2003. *Noites Nômades: Espaço e Subjetividade nas Culturas Jovens Contemporâneas*. Rio de Janeiro: Rocco.

Altink, Siestke, Ilse van Liempt and Marjan Wijers. 2018. 'From Regulated Tolerance to Control: Prostitution Policy in the Netherlands'. In *Assessing Prostitution Policies in Europe*, edited by Hendrik Wagenaar and Synnøve Økland Jahnsen. Milton Park: Routledge.

Alves, Rute, Mariana Pereira and Mariana Rafeiro. 2015. 'O Memorando de Entendimento e as Reformas no Mercado de Arrendamento e na Reabilitação Urbana'. In *Governar com a Troika: Políticas Públicas em Tempo de Austeridade*, edited by Maria de Lurdes Rodrigues and Pedro Adao de Silva, 237–59. Coimbra: Almedina.

Amann, Edmund, and Werner Baer. 2002. 'Neoliberalism and Its Consequences in Brazil'. *Journal of Latin American Studies* 34(4): 945–59.

Ambrust, Walter. 1996. *Mass Culture and Modernism in Egypt*. Cambridge, UK: University of Cambridge Press.

Amid, Atepheh. 2013. *Night, Space and Urban Design: Case Study of Mashhad, Iran*. London: University of Westminster.

Amin, Ash, and Nigel Thrift. 2002. *Cities: Reimagining the Urban*. Cambridge: Polity.

Anderson, Ben. 2009. 'Affective Atmospheres'. *Emotion, Space and Society* 2(2): 77–81.

Anderson, Jon. 2004. 'Talking whilst Walking: A Geographical Archaeology of Knowledge'. *Area* 36: 254–61.

Appleyard, Donald. 1981. *Livable Streets*. Berkeley: University of California Press.

Arapoglou, Vassilis, and John Sayas. 2009. 'New Facets of Urban Segregation in Southern Europe Gender, Migration and Social Class Change in Athens'. *European Urban and Regional Studies* 16(4): 345–62.

Arnoldussen, Paul, Peter Paul De Baar, Bert Nap, Piet de Rooij and Marian van de Veen. Eds. 2016. *Aan de Amsterdamse Wallen*. Amsterdam: Boom.

Ashworth, Gregory, and Stephen J. Page. 2011. 'Urban Tourism Research: Recent Progress and Current Paradoxes'. *Tourism Management* 32(1): 1–15.

Association of Town & City Management and TBR & MAKE Associates. 2013. *Lambeth after Dark: Getting Serious about the Night Time Economy*. London: London Borough of Lambeth.

Atherton, John, Chris Baker and Elaine Graham. 2005. 'A "Genius of Place"?' In *Pathways to the Public Square: Proceedings of the 2003 IAPT Conference*, edited by Elaine Graham and Anna Rowlands, 63–83. Vit Verlag: Münster.

Atkinson, Rowland, and Hazel Easthope. 2009. 'The Consequences of the Creative Class: The Pursuit of Creativity Strategies in Australia's Cities'. *International Journal of Urban and Regional Research* 33(1): 64–79.

Australian Broadcasting Corporation. 2016. 'ICAC: NSW Liberal Figures and Businessmen Tried to Evade Political Funding Laws, Report Finds'. ABC News. 31 August. http://www.abc.net.au/news/2016-08-30/independent-commission-against-corruption-icac-spicer-report/7796928.

AWP and Armengaud, Marc. 2013. *Paris la Nuit: Chroniques Nocturnes*. Paris: Pavillon de l'Arsenal.

Ayubi, Nazih N. 1999. *Over-Stating the Arab State: Politics and Society in the Middle East*. London: Tauris and Co.

Azad-Del, M. 2012. 'Barresi Vazyiat Tarh Eftar ta Sahar dar Sal 1391'. http://www. mardomsalari.com/template1/News.aspx?NID=141805.

Bahun, Sanja. 2010. 'The Semblance of Materiality: Review of Brigitte Peucker, *The Material Image: Art and the Real in Film* (Cultural Memory of the Present)'. *Other Voices* 4(1). http://www.othervoices.org/4.1/sbahun/index.php.

Baird, Mike. 2016. Facebook Post. https://www.facebook.com/mikebairdMP.

Baldwin, Peter. 2012. *In the Watches of the Night: Life in the Nocturnal City, 1820–1930*. Chicago: University of Chicago Press.

Bancroft, Angus. 2012. 'Drinking with and without Fun: Female Students' Accounts of Pre-drinking and Club-Drinking'. *Sociological Research Online* 17(4): 1–11.

Bancroft, Angus, Mariah Jade Zimpfer and Orla Murray. 2014. 'Working at Pleasure in Young Women's Alcohol Consumption: A Participatory Visual Ethnography'. *Sociological Research Online* 19(3): 1–14.

Barbosa, Jorge. 2009. 'A Emergência da Redução de Danos em Portugal: Da "clandestinidade" à Legitimação Política'. *Revista Toxicodependências* 15(1): 33–42.

Barnett, Jonathan. 2011. *City Design: Modernist, Traditional, Green, and Systems Perspectives*. New York: Routledge.

Barratt, Monica J., Matthew Allen and Simon Lenton. 2014. '"PMA Sounds Fun": Negotiating Drug Discourses Online'. *Substance Use & Misuse* 49(8): 987–998.

Barrett, Raymond. 2010. *Dubai Dreams: Inside the Kingdom of Bling*. London; Boston: Nicholas Brealey.

Barrie, Matt. 2016. 'Would the Last Person in Sydney Please Turn the Lights Out?' LinkedIn. 3 February. https://www.linkedin.com/pulse/would-last-person-sydney-please-turn-lights-out-matt-barrie.

Bastians, Kate. 2016. 'Controversial Six-Storey Development in Heart of Double Bay Gets Green Light'. Wentworth Courier. 29 July. http://www.dailytelegraph. com.au/newslocal/wentworth-courier/controversial-sixstorey-development-in-heart-of-double-bay-gets-green-light/news-story/497dc46af26de127a6078ad7af 681fcf.

Bayat, Asef. 2013. *Life as Politics: How Ordinary People Change the Middle East*. Stanford: Stanford University Press.

Bayat, Asef. 2017. 'Is There A Youth Politics?'. *Middle East – Topics & Arguments*. 9: 16–24. https://doi.org/10.17192/meta.2017.9.7219.

Beall, Jo, Owen Crankshaw and Sue Parnell. 2002. *Uniting a Divided City: Governance and Social Exclusion in Johannesburg*. London Sterling, VA: Earthscan Publications.

Beaumont, Matthew. 2015. *Nightwalking: A Nocturnal History of London*. London and New York: Verso.

Beavon, Keith, and Sidney Orrock. 2004. *Johannesburg: The Making and Shaping of the City*. Pretoria: Unisa Press.

Belev, Boyan. 2001. 'Privatization in Egypt and Tunisia: Liberal Outcomes and/or Liberal Policies?' *Mediterranean Politics* 6(2): 68–103.

Belhassen, Yaniv, and Carla Almeida-Santos. 2006. 'An American Evangelical Pilgrimage to Israel: A Case Study on Politics and Triangulation'. *Journal of Travel Research* 44: 431–41.

Bellis, Mark A., Gerry Hale, Andy Bennett, Mohammad Chaudry and Mary Kilfoyle. 2000. 'Ibiza Uncovered: Changes in Substance Use and Sexual Behaviour amongst Young People Visiting an International Night-Life Resort'. *International Journal of Drug Policy* 11: 235–44.

Bellis, Mark A., Karen Hughes and Helen Lowey. 2002. 'Healthy Nightclubs and Recreational Substance Use'. *Addictive Behaviours* 27(6): 1025–35.

Bentley, Ian, Alan Alcock, Paul Murrain, Sue McGlynn and Graham Smith. 1985. *Responsive Environments: A Manual for Designers*. Oxford: Butterworth Architecture.

Bernstein, Elizabeth. 2007. *Temporarily Yours. Intimacy, Authenticity, and the Commerce of Sex*. Chicago: University of Chicago Press.

Bianchini, Franco. 1990. 'The Crisis of Urban Public Social Life in Britain: Origins of the Problem and Possible Responses'. *Planning Practice and Research* 5(3): 4–8.

Bianchini, Franco. 1995. 'Night Cultures, Night Economies'. *Planning Practice & Research* 10(2): 121–26.

Bille, Mikkel, Peter Bjerregaard and Tim F. Sørensen. 2015. 'Staging Atmospheres: Materiality, Culture, and the Texture of the In-Between'. *Emotion, Space and Society* 15: 31–38.

Birdsall, Carolyn. 2013. '(In)audible Frequencies: Sounding Out the Contemporary Branded City'. In *Paris-Amsterdam Underground: Essays on Cultural Resistance, Subversion, and Diversion*, edited by Christoph Lindner and Andrew Hussey, 115–32. Amsterdam: Amsterdam University Press.

Bissell, David. 2010. 'Passenger Mobilities: Affective Atmospheres and the Sociality of Public Transport'. *Environment and Planning D: Society and Space* 28(2): 270–89.

Blanks, Stephen, and Jaimee Burke. 2016. 'Removal of Rights in New South Wales'. YouTube video, 34:03, posted by 'BenchTV'. 30 August 2016. https://www.you tube.com/watch?v=hmpjV0lgQtw&t=23s.

Blokland, Talja, and Gwen van Eijk. 2010. 'Do People Who Like Diversity Practice Diversity in Neighborhood Life? Neighborhood Use and the Social Networks of "Diversity-Seekers" in a Mixed Neighborhood on the Netherlands'. *Journal of Ethnic and Migration Studies* 36(2): 313–32.

Blum, Alan. 2010. 'The Imagination of Self-Satisfaction: Reflections on the Platitude of the "Creative City"'. In *Circulation and the City: Essay on Urban Culture*, edited by Alexandra Boutros and Will Straw, 64–95. Montreal, Quebec: McGill-Queen's University Press.

BMI. 2010. 'Elaam Saat Kar-e Jadid Shoab Bank Meli Iran az Aval-e Mehr Mah'. http://www.bmi.ir/Fa/ShowNews.aspx?nwsId=5710.

Bochner, Stephen, Nimmi Hutnik and Adrian Furnham. 1985. 'The Friendship Patterns of Overseas and Host Students in an Oxford Student Residence'. *The Journal of Social Psychology* 125(6): 689–94.

Bogard, Paul. 2013. *The End of Night: Searching for Natural Darkness in an Age of Artificial Light*. Boston, MA: Little, Brown and Company.

Böhme, Gernot. 2013. 'The Art of the Stage as a Paradigm for an Aesthetics of Atmospheres'. *Ambiances*. http://ambiances.revues.org/315.

Boichot, Camille, and Pauline Guinard. 2013. 'L'Esthétisation des Espaces Publics à Berlin (Allemagne) et Johannesburg (Afrique du Sud): L'Art pour Vendre les

Espaces Publics ou pour Rendre les Espaces à Leurs Publics?'. In *Art et Espaces Publics*, edited by Marc Veyrat, 151–77. Paris: L'Harmattan.

Boogaarts, Drs Simone. 2008. 'Claiming Your Place at Night: Turkish Dance Parties in the Netherlands'. *Journal of Ethnic and Migration Studies* 34(8): 1283–300.

Bottenberg, Marieke, and Marie-Louise Janssen. 2012. *De Positie van Chinese Masseuses in de Chinese Beautybranche in Nederland. Onderzoeksrapport Fenomeenonderzoek Mensenhandel en Mensensmokkel in de Chinese Beautybranche.* Woerden: KLPD.

Bouhdiba, Abdelwahab. 2004. *La sexualité en Islam*, Paris: Presses Universitaires de France.

Bouillon, Florence. 2000. 'Des Escales Dans la Nuit: Les Snacks Égyptiens à Marseille'. *Les Annales de la Recherche Urbaine* 87: 43–51.

Bounds, Michael, and Alan Morris. 2006. 'Second Wave Gentrification in Inner-City Sydney'. *Cities* 23(2): 99–108.

Bourdieu, Pierre. 1979. *La Distinction*. Paris: Éditions de Minuit.

Bourdieu, Pierre. 1980. *The Logic of Practice*. Stanford: Stanford University Press.

Bourdieu, Pierre. 1984. *Distinction: A Social Critique of the Judgement of Taste*. Cambridge, MA: Harvard University Press.

Bouzarovski, Stefan. 2011. 'Skopje'. *Cities* 28: 265–77.

Brands, Jelle, Tim Schwanen and Irina van Aalst. 2015. 'Fear of Crime and Affective Ambiguities in the Night-Time Economy'. *Urban Studies* 52(3): 439–55.

Branley, Alison. 2016. 'Leaked Documents Show Star Casino Under-Reporting Violence'. *PM with Mark Colvin,* ABC Radio. 31 October. http://www.abc.net.au/pm/content/2016/s4566342.htm.

Brans, Lennart. 2014. 'Wallen Blijven Voorlopig de Wietbuurt'. *Het Parool.* 16 November. https://www.parool.nl/amsterdam/-wallen-blijven-voorlopig-de-wietbuurt~a3791192/.

Bremner, Lindsay. 2010. *Writing the City into Being: Essays on Johannesburg, 1998–2008.* Johannesburg: Fourthwall Books.

Briggs, Daniel, Tim Turner, Kerri David and Tara De Courcey. 2011. 'British Youth Abroad: Some Observations on the Social Context of Binge Drinking in Ibiza'. *Drugs and Alcohol Today* 11(1): 26–35.

Brilleman, Eveline. 2004. *De Zeedijk*. Bussum: Uitgeverij THOTH.

Bronfen, Elizabeth. 2013. *Night Passages: Philosophy, Literature, and Film*. New York: Columbia University Press.

Brown, Wendy. 2005. *Edgework: Critical Essays on Knowledge and Politics*. Princeton, NJ: Princeton University Press.

Brown, Wendy. 2006. 'American Nightmare: Neoliberalism, Neoconservatism, and De-democratization'. *Political Theory* 34(6): 690–714.

Brun, Alexandre, and Stéphane Coursière. 2014. 'Faire Converger Projet Métropolitain et Stratégies Universitaires: L'Autre Grand Chantier de Montpellier?' *Espaces et Sociétés* 159: 37–57.

Bruneteaux, Patrick. 2017. 'La prise en charge nocturne des sous-prolétaires à la rue: Du hors-droit à la profilisation humanitaire de l'urgence sociale (1980–2015)'. *Cultures & Conflits* 105–6: 45–162.

Brunt, Lodewijk. 2003. 'Between Day and Night, Urban Time Schedules in Bombay and Other Cities'. In *Night-Time and Sleep in Asia and the West: Exploring the Dark Side of Life*, edited by Brigitte Steger and Lodewijk Brunt, 171–90. London: Routledge.

Budd, Tracey. 2003. 'Alcohol Related Assault: Key Findings from the British Crime Survey. Home Office Online Report 35/03'. http://www.dldocs.stir.ac.uk/documents/alcassault.pdf.

Buijs, Laurens, and Linda Duits. 2015. 'Amsterdam's Plan to Save Prostitutes Is a Billion Euro Gentrification Project'. *Medium*. 30 January. https://medium.com/@lalalalinder/amsterdams-plan-to-save-prostitutes-is-a-billion-euro-gentrification-project-375183088650.

Buijs, Laurens, and Laurens Ivens. 2012. 'Asscher heeft met wallenproject weinig successen kunnen claimen'. *de Volkskrant*. 23 May. https://www.volkskrant.nl/magazine/-asscher-heeft-met-wallenproject-weinig-successen-kunnen-claimen~a3259401/.

Burke, Thomas. 1943. *English Night-Life: From Norman Curfew to Present Black-Out*. London: Collins.

Burrell, Ian. 2015. 'Not Going Out: Why Millennials Are No Longer Going to Night Clubs'. *Independent*. 10 August 2015. http://www.independent.co.uk/arts-entertainment/music/features/not-going-out-why-millennials-are-no-longer-going-to-night-clubs-10449036.html.

Buvik, Kristsin, and Bergjlot Baklien. 2016. ' "Girls Will Be Served until You Have to Carry Them Out": Gendered Serving Practices in Oslo'. *Addiction Research & Theory* 24(1): 17–24.

Cabannes, Yves, Silvia Guimarães-Yafai and Cassidy Johnson. 2010. *How People Face Evictions*. London: Development Planning Unit, University College London.

Cabinet Office. 2003. *Alcohol Misuse: How Much Does It Cost?* London: Prime Minister's Strategy Unit.

Cabinet Office. 2004. *Alcohol Harm Reduction Strategy for England*. London: Prime Minister's Strategy Unit.

Calafat, Amador, Cesáreo Fernández, Montserrat Juan, Mark A. Bellis, Karl Bohrn, Pekka Hakkarainen, Mary Kilfoyle-Carrington, Anna Kokkevi, Nicole Maalsté, Fernando Mendes, Ioanna Siamou, Joseph Simon, Paolo Stocco and Patrizia Zavatti. 2001. *Risk and Control in the Recreational Drug Culture*. Palma de Mallorca, Spain: IREFREA.

Callinan, Ian. 2016. 'Review of Amendments to the Liquor Act 2007 (NSW)'. Sydney: Independent Liquor Law Review. 16 September. http://www.liquorlawreview.justice.nsw.gov.au/Documents/report/LiquorLawReviewReport.pdf.

Campkin, Ben, and Marshall, Laura. 2017. *LGBTQ+ Infrastructure in London: Night Venues, 2006–Present*. London: UCL Urban Laboratory.

Cameron, Samuel. 2004. 'Space, Risk and Opportunity: The Evolution of Paid Sex Markets'. *Urban Studies* 41(9): 1643–57.

Campo, Daniel, and Brent D. Ryan. 2008. 'The Entertainment Zone: Unplanned Nightlife and the Revitalization of the American Downtown'. *Journal of Urban Design* 13(3): 291–315.

Carmo, Renato M., Rita Cachado and Daniela Ferreira. 2015. 'Desigualdades em Tempos de Crise: Vulnerabilidades Habitacionais e Socioeconómicas na Área Metropolitana de Lisboa'. *Revista Portuguesa de Estudos Regionais* 40: 5–22.

Carmona, Matthew. 2010. 'Contemporary Public Space: Critique and Classification, Part One: Critique'. *Journal of Urban Design* 15: 123–48.

Carmona, Matthew, Tim Heath, Taner Oc and Steve Tiesdell. 2010. *Public Places – Urban Spaces: The Dimensions of Urban Design*. Oxford: Architectural Press.

Carvalho, Maria Carmo. 2007. *Culturas Juvenis e Novos Usos de Drogas em Meios Festivos: O Trance Psicadélico como Analisador*. Porto: Campo de letras.

Carvalho, Maria Carmo. 2015. 'Ambientes recreativos noturnos-as dimensões ambientais e os fenómenos do uso de substâncias psicoactivas, do risco e da proteção'. Porto: Faculdade de Psicologia e Ciências da Educação da Universidade do Porto. Tese de Doutoramento.

Caulfield, Jon. 1989. 'Gentrification and Desire'. *Canadian Review of Sociology and Anthropology* 26(4): 617–32.

Čengić, Nihad. 2013. 'Urban Form and Urban Ethics in Changing Socialistic Democracy'. *The Importance of Place* 2(2): 91–93.

Čengić, Nihad, and Armin Hodo. 2018. *Sistem gradski centara i funkcionalna atraktivnost mjesnih zajednica Sarajeva, 2014: razvoj metode mjerenja*. Sarajevo: Arhitektonski Fakultet Sarajevo.

Chabrol, Marie. 2011. 'De Nouvelles Formes de Gentrification? Dynamiques Résidentielles et Commerciales à Château-Rouge (Paris)'. PhD Thesis, Université de Poitiers.

Chapuis, Amandine. 2016. 'Touring the Immoral. Affective Geographies of Visitors to the Amsterdam Red-Light District'. *Urban Studies* 54(3): 616–32.

Charlois, Thierry. 2009. 'Safer Nightlife in Europe'. Fifth Meeting of EXASS Network in Budapest, Hungary, 4–6 May 2009.

Chatterton, Paul. 1999. 'University Students and City Centres – The Formation of Exclusive Geographies'. *Geoforum* 30(2): 117–33.

Chatterton, Paul. 2002. 'Governing Nightlife: Profit, Fun and (Dis)Order in the Contemporary City'. *Entertainment Law* 1(2): 23–49.

Chatterton, Paul. 2010. 'The Student City: An Ongoing Story of Neoliberalism, Gentrification, and Commodification'. *Environment and Planning A* 42(3): 509–14.

Chatterton, Paul, and Robert Hollands. 2002. 'Theorising Urban Playscapes: Producing, Regulating and Consuming Youthful Nightlife City Spaces'. *Urban Studies* 39(1): 95–116.

Chatterton, Paul, and Robert Hollands. 2003. *Urban Nightscapes: Youth Cultures, Urban Spaces and Corporate Power*. London: Routledge.

Cheng, Tsaiher. 2016. *Red Light City*. Westmount: The Architecture Observer.

Choay, Françoise. 2001. *The Invention of the Historic Monument*. New York: Cambridge University Press.

Citizens' Ombudsman. 2013. 'Special Report: The Phenomenon of Racist Violence in Greece and How It Is Combated'. Athens: The Greek Ombudsman. https://www.synigoros.gr/resources/docs/sronracistviolencesummary2013.pdf.

City of Sydney. 1994. *Living City: Sydney City Council's Blueprint for Sydney*. Sydney: City of Sydney.

City of Sydney. 2008. *Sustainable Sydney 2030, the Vision*. Sydney: City of Sydney.
City of Sydney. 2011. 'Open Late for Everyone. Time to Have Your Say: Night Time Economy Phase Two'. 11 October. http://sydneyyoursay.com.au/nighteconomyphase2.
City of Sydney. 2012. 'Summary of Online Submissions for OPEN Sydney Discussion Paper'. 18 June. http://meetings.cityofsydney.nsw.gov.au/council/about council/meetings/documents/meetings/2012/Committee/Cultural/180612/120618_CCSC_ITEM08_ATTACHMENTC.PDF.
City of Sydney. 2013. *OPEN Sydney, Future Directions for Sydney at Night: Strategy and Action Plan 2013–2030*. Sydney: City of Sydney.
Clarke, Patrick. 2009. 'Urban Planning and Design'. In *Sustainable Urban Design – An Environmental Approach*, edited by Adam Ritchie and Randall Thomas, 12–20. London: Taylor & Francis.
Clarke, Terry Nichols. 2004. *The City as an Entertainment Machine*. Oxford: Elsevier.
Clerval, Anne. 2008. 'La Gentrification à Paris Intra-Muros: Dynamiques Spatiales, Rapports Sociaux et Politiques Publiques'. PhD Thesis, Université Panthéon-Sorbonne – Paris I.
Clerval, Anne. 2010. 'Les Dynamiques Spatiales de la Gentrification à Paris: Une Carte de Synthèse'. *Cybergeo: European Journal of Geography*. 20 July. http://cybergeo.revues.org/23231.
Cócola-Gant, Agustín. 2015. 'Tourism and Commercial Gentrification'. Paper presented at the RC21 International Conference – The Ideal City: Between Myth and Reality. Representations, Policies, Contradictions and Challenges for Tomorrow's Urban Life'. Urbino, Italy, 27–29 August 2015.
Cohen, Erik. 1979. 'A Phenomenology of Tourist Experiences'. *Sociology* 13(2): 179–201.
Cohen, Stanley. 1972. *Folk Devils and Moral Panics: The Creation of the Mods and Rockers*. London: MacGibbon and Kee.
Colaboratória, Grupo Interdisciplina. 2014. *Night Manifesto – Manifesto da Noite*. São Paulo: Invisíveis Produções.
Cole, Claire, Lisa Jones, Jim McVeigh, Andrew Kicman, Qutub Syed and Mark Bellis. 2011. 'Adulterants in Illicit Drugs: A Review of Empirical Evidence'. *Drug Testing and Analysis* 3(2): 89–96.
Comedia. In association with the Calouste Gulbenkian Foundation. 1991. *Out of Hours: A Study of Economic, Social and Cultural Life in Twelve Town Centres in the U.K.* London: Comedia.
Comelli, Cécilia. 2015. 'Mutations Urbaines et Géographie de la Nuit à Bordeaux'. PhD Thesis, University of Bordeaux Montaigne.
Cook, Matthew, and Tim Edensor. 2017. 'Cycling through Dark Space: Apprehending Landscape Otherwise'. *Mobilities* 12(1): 1–19.
Coomber, Ross. 1997. 'The Adulteration of Illicit Drugs with Dangerous Substances—The Discovery of a "Myth"'. *Contemporary Drug Problems* 24(2): 239–71.
Crankshaw, Owen, and Caroline White. 1995. 'Racial Desegregation and Inner City Decay in Johannesburg'. *International Journal of Urban and Regional Research* 19: 622–38.
Crary, Jonathan. 2013. *24/7: Late Capitalism and the Ends of Sleep*. London: Verso.

Crawford Adam, and John Flint. 2009. 'Urban Safety, Anti-social Behaviour and the Night-Time Economy'. *Criminology and Criminal Justice* 9(4): 403–14.

Crivello, Silvia. 2009. 'Torino di Notte: Politiche Urbane, Consumo e Dinamiche Spaziali nel Playscape della Città'. *Archivio di Studi Urbani e Regionali.* doi:10.3280/ASUR2009-095006.

Cruz, Olga S. 2014. 'Nonproblematic Illegal Drug Use: Drug Use Management Strategies in a Portuguese Sample'. *Journal of Drug Issues* 45(2): 133–50.

Cruz, Olga S., and Carla Machado. 2010. 'Consumo Não Problemático de Drogas Ilegais'. *Toxicodependências* 16(2): 39–47.

Cuervo, Hernán, and Johanna Wyn. 2014. 'Reflections on the Use of Spatial and Relational Metaphors in Youth Studies'. *Journal of Youth Studies* 17(7): 901–15.

Cullen, Gordon. 1961. *The Concise Townscape.* London: Architectural Press.

Ćurak, Nerzuk. 2015. 'Kriza ljevice u dejtonskoj močvari'. In *Razgovor o ljevici: Identitet, kriza i izazovi u Bosni i Hercegovini danas*, edited by Emina Abrahamsdotter and Besima Borić, 9–20. Sarajevo: Friedrich-Ebert-Stiftung (FES).

Curi, Martin, Jorge Knijnik and Gilmar Mascarenhas. 2011. 'The Pan American Games in Rio de Janeiro 2007: Consequences of a Sport Mega-Event on a BRIC Country'. *International Review for the Sociology of Sport* 46(2): 140–56.

Daalde, Annelies L. 2007. *Prostitutie in Nederland na opheffing van het Bordeelverbod.* The Hague: WODC.

Darlinghurst Business Partnership. 2015. 'Economic Effects of Sydney's "Lockout" Laws'. 14 May. http://www.dbp.org.au/lockout-survey-results.

Davidson, Rob, and Robert Maitland. 1997. *Tourism Destinations.* London: Hodder & Stoughton.

Davies, Paul, and Hannah Mummery. 2006. *NightVision: Town Centres for All.* London: The Civic Trust.

Day, Katy, Brendan Gough and Majella McFadden. 2003. 'Women Who Drink and Fight: A Discourse Analysis of Working Class Women's Talk'. *Feminism and Psychology* 13(2): 141–58.

DCLG. 2012. *National Planning Policy Framework.* London: GLC.

De Madariaga, Inés S. 2013. 'From Women in Transport to Gender in Transport: Challenging Conceptual Frameworks for Improved Policy Making'. *Journal of International Affairs* 67(1): 43–65.

DeCorte, Tom. 2001. 'Quality Control by Cocaine Users: Underdeveloped Harm Reduction Strategies'. *European Addiction Research* 7(4): 161–75.

DeGuzmán, Maria. 2014. *Buenas Noches, American Culture: Latina/o Aesthetics of Night.* Bloomington: Indiana University Press.

DeJong, William. 2002. 'The Role of Mass Media Campaigns in Reducing High-Risk Drinking among College Students'. *Journal of Studies on Alcohol* 14: 182–92.

Delattre, Simon. 2003. *Les Douze heures Noires: La Nuit à Paris au Xixe Siècle.* Paris: Albin Michel.

Delgadillo, Natalie. 2017. 'The Rose of the "Night Mayor" in America'. *Governing: The States and Localities.* http://www.governing.com/topics/urban/gov-night-mayor-economy-america.html.

Demant, Jakob, and Sara Landolt. 2014. 'Youth Drinking in Public Places: The Production of Drinking Spaces in and Outside Nightlife Areas'. *Urban Studies* 51(1): 170–84.

Department for Culture, Media & Sport, The Home Office and the Office of the Deputy Prime Minister. 2005. 'Drinking Responsibly: The Government's Proposals'. http://alcoholresearchuk.org/wp-content/uploads/2014/01/odpm-drinking-responsibly-january-2005.pdf.

Department of Urban and Regional Planning. 1995. 'Researching the Possibilities of a Specialised Housing Policy in the Context of Urbanization – Urban Regeneration of Historical Areas of the Centre of Athens: The Case of Metaxourgeio'. Final Report of the Research Programme. Athens: NTUA.

DeVerteuil, Geoffrey. 2015. *Resilience in the Post-Welfare Inner City: Voluntary Sector Geographies in London, Los Angeles and Sydney*. Bristol: Policy Press.

Dević, Ana. 1997. 'Redefining the Public-Private Boundary: Nationalism and Women's Activism in Former Yugoslavia'. *The Anthropology of East Europe Review* 15(2): 45–61.

Dias, Sónia. 2006. *Educação pelos Pares: Uma Estratégia na Promoção da Saúde*. Lisboa: Universidade Nova de Lisboa.

Dirsuweit, Teresa. 2002. 'Johannesburg: Fearful City?' *Urban Forum* 13: 3–19.

Dirsuweit, Teresa. 2007. 'Between Ontological Security and the Right Difference: Road Closures, Communitarianism and Urban Ethics in Johannesburg, South Africa'. *Autrepart* 42(2): 53–71.

Dixon, John, Mark Levine and McAuley. 2006. 'Locating Impropriety: Street Drinking, Moral Order, and the Ideological Dilemma of Public Space'. *Political Psychology* 27(2): 187–206.

Dlamini, Jacob. 2009. *Native Nostalgia*. Auckland Park, South Africa: Jacana Media.

Donnelly, Neil, Suzanne Poynton and Don Weatherburn. 2017. 'The Effect of Lockout and Last Drinks Laws on Non-domestic Assaults in Sydney: An Update to September 2016'. *Crime and Justice Bulletin* 201: 12.

Drake, Cathryn. 2014. 'How a Derelict Athens District Was Turned into a Vibrant Arts Hub'. *Financial Times*. 21 February. https://www.ft.com/content/95a574fa-9567-11e3-8371-00144feab7de#axzz2uET8d4MI.

Duany, Andrés. 2003. 'Neighbourhood Design and Practice'. In *Urban Villages and the Making of Communities*, edited by Peter Neal, 112–48. New York: Spon Press.

Duff, Cameron. 2005. 'Party Drugs and Party People: Examining the "Normalization" of Recreational Drug Use in Melbourne, Australia'. *International Journal of Drug Policy* 16(3): 161–70.

Duff, Cameron. 2012. 'Accounting for Context: Exploring the Role of Objects and Spaces in the Consumption of Alcohol and Other Drugs'. *Social & Cultural Geography* 13(2): 145–59.

Duff, Cameron, and David Moore. 2015. 'Going out, Getting about: Atmospheres of Mobility in Melbourne's Night-Time Economy'. *Social & Cultural Geography* 16(3): 299–314.

Dunn, Nick. 2016. *Dark Matters: A Manifesto for the Nocturnal City*. London: Zero Books.

Eckardt, Frank. 2003. *Consumption and the Post-Industrial City*. New York: Peter Lang.

Edensor, Tim. 2013. 'Reconnecting with Darkness: Gloomy Landscapes, Lightless Places'. *Social & Cultural Geography* 14(4): 446–65.

Edensor, Tim. 2015a. 'Light Design and Atmosphere'. *Visual Communication* 14(3): 321–50.

Edensor, Tim. 2015b. 'The Gloomy City: Rethinking the Relationship between Light and Dark'. *Urban Studies* 52(3): 422–38.

Edensor, Tim. 2016. 'Aurora Landscapes: Affective Atmospheres of Light and Dark'. In *Conversations with Landscape*, edited by Karl Benediktsson and Karin Anna Lund, 227–40. London: Routledge.

Edensor, Tim, and Emily Falconer. 2014. '*Dans Le Noir?*: Eating in the Dark: Sensation and Conviviality in a Lightless Place'. *Cultural Geographies* 22(4): 601–18.

Eder, Mine, and Özlem Öz. 2015. 'Neoliberalization of Istanbul's Nightlife: Beer or Champagne?' *International Journal of Urban and Regional Research* 39(2): 284–304.

Ehrenfeucht, Renia, and Anastasia Loukaitou-Sideris. 2007. 'Constructing the Sidewalks: Municipal Government and the Production of Public Space in Los Angeles, California, 1880–1920'. *Journal of Historical Geography* 33: 104–24.

Ekirch, Roger A. 2006. *At Day's Close: Night in Times Past*. London and New York: W.W. Norton and Company.

El Messiri, Sawsan. 1977. 'The Changing Role of the Futuwwa in the Social Structure of Cairo'. In *Patrons and Clients in Mediterranean Societies*, edited by Ernest Gellner and John Waterbury, 239–54. London: Duckworth.

Eldridge, Adam. 2010. 'The Urban Renaissance and the Night-Time City: Who Belongs in the City at Night?' In *Social Sustainability in Urban Areas: Communities, Connectivity and the Urban Fabric*, edited by Tony Manzi, Karen Lucas, Tony Lloyd Jones and Judith Allen, 183–98. Abingdon: Earthscan.

Eldridge, Adam, and Marion Roberts. 2008. ' "A Comfortable Night Out?": Alcohol, Drunkenness and Inclusive Town Centres'. *Area* 40(3): 365–74.

EMCDDA. 2010. *2010 Annual Report on the State of the Drugs Problem in Europe*. Lisbon: European Monitoring Centre of Drugs and Drug Addiction.

EMCDDA. 2012. *Travel and Drug Use in Europe: A Short Review*. Lisbon: European Monitoring Centre of Drugs and Drug Addiction.

EMCDDA. 2015. *New Psychoactive Substances in Europe. An Update from the EU Early Warning System (March 2015)*. Lisbon: European Monitoring Centre of Drugs and Drug Addiction.

Emmanouil, Dimitris. 2013. 'The "Crisis" in the Centre of Athens and the Housing Market: Re-examining Hypotheses of "Decline" and "Abandonment" '. In *The Centre of Athens as a Political Stake*, edited by Thomas Maloutas, George Kandylis, Michalis Petrou and Nikos Souliotis, 53–87. Athens: NCSR (in Greek).

Emmanouil, Dimitris. 2014. 'The Greek System of Home-Ownership and the Post-2008 Crisis in Athens'. *Région et Développement* 39: 167–82.

Encyclopædia-Iranica. 1996a. 'Čahāršanba-Sūrī'. http://www.iranicaonline.org/articles/search/keywords:caharsanba-suri.

Encyclopædia-Iranica. 1996b. 'Čella'. http://www.iranicaonline.org/articles/search/keywords:%C4%8Cella.

Encyclopædia-Iranica. 1996c. 'Nowruz'. http://www.iranicaonline.org/articles/search/keywords:Nowruz.

Enjavi, Sayyed Abolqasem. 1973. *Jashnha va Adab va Moataghedaat Zemestaan.* Tehran: Amir Kabir.

Erenberg. Lewis. A. 1984. *Steppin' Out: New York Nightlife and the Transformation of American Culture, 1890–1930.* Chicago and London: University of Chicago Press.

Erickson, Patricia, Diane Riley, Yuet Cheung and Patrick O'Hare. 1997. *Harm Reduction: A New Direction for Drug Policies and Programs.* Toronto: University of Toronto Press.

European Union. 1997. *Treaty of Amsterdam.* Luxembourg: Office for Official Publications of the European Communities.

Evans, Graeme. 2001. *Cultural Planning: An Urban Renaissance?* London: Routledge.

Evans, Graeme. 2012. 'Hold Back the Night: Nuit Blanche and All-Night Events in Capital Cities'. *Current Issues in Tourism* 15(1–2): 35–49.

Evans, Graeme. 2017. 'Keynote 1'. Paper presented at Tourism and the Night Symposium. University of Westminster, London, 14–15 July 2017.

Evans, James, and Phil Jones. 2011. 'The Walking Interview: Methodology, Mobility and Place'. *Applied Geography* 31(2): 849–58.

Fakoori, Haji Yar. 2010. *Gozaresh-e Nazarsanji az Zaeran Imam Reza dar Ayam-e Norooz.* Mashhad, Iran: Omran-va Maskan-Sazan Samen.

Farrelly, Elizabeth. 2016. 'There's Never Been a Better Time to Protest in the Streets'. *The Sydney Morning Herald.* 30 October. http://www.smh.com.au/comment/theres-never-been-a-better-time-to-protest-in-the-streets-20161027-gsbxwx.html.

Feixa, Carles, and Jordi Nofre. Eds. 2013. *#GeneraciónIndignada: Topías y utopías del 15M.* Lleida: Milenio.

Fernandes, Luis. 2009. 'O que a Droga Faz à Norma'. *Toxicodependências* 15(1): 3–18.

Fernandes, Luis, Marta Sousa Pinto and Mariana Oliveira. 2006. 'Caracterização e Análise Critica das Práticas de Redução de Riscos na Área das Drogas em Portugal'. *Revista Toxicodependências* 12(2): 71–82.

Fernández, Miquel. 2014. *Matar al Chino: Entre la Revolución Urbanística y el Asedio Urbano en el Barrio del Raval de Barcelona.* Barcelona: Virus Editorial.

Ferras, Robert. 1978. *'Ecusson et Polygone': Enfants et Retraités dans le Centre de Montpellier.* Montpellier, France: Société Languedocienne de Géographie.

Fileborn, Bianca. 2016. 'Doing Gender, Doing Safety? Young Adults' Production of Safety on a Night Out'. *Gender, Place & Culture* 23(8): 1107–20.

Filipović, Muhamed. 2003. 'Kritika pojma tranzicije i pitanje njegovih implikacija'. *Pregled – časopis za društvena pitanja* 44(1–2): 31–51.

Finney, Andrea. 2004a. *Alcohol and Sexual Violence: Key Findings from the Research,* 215. London: The Home Office.

Finney, Andrea. 2004b. *Violence in the Night-Time Economy: Key Findings from the Research,* 214. London: The Home Office.

Finney, R. Zachary, Robert A. Orwig and Deborah F. Spake D. 2009. 'Lotus-Eaters, Pilgrims, Seekers, and Accidental Tourists: How Different Travellers Consume the Sacred and the Profane'. *Services Marketing Quarterly* 30: 148–73.

Fishbein, Martin, and Icek Ajzen. 2010. *Predicting and Changing Behaviour: The Reasoned Action Approach*. New York: Psychology Press.

Flight, Sander, and Paul Hulshof. 2009. *Klanten van Raamprostitutie: De Vraag naar Raamprostitutie in Amsterdam Onderzocht*. Amsterdam: DSP-groep.

Florida, Richard. 2002. *The Rise of the Creative Class and How It's Transforming Work, Leisure, Community and Everyday Life*. New York: Basic Books.

Florida, Richard. 2005. *The Flight of the Creative Class*. New York: Harper Business.

Florida, Richard. 2012. *The Rise of the Creative Class, Revisited*. New York: Basic Books.

Forsyth, Alasdair. 2009. ' "Lager, Lager Shouting": The Role of Music and DJs in Nightclub Disorder Control'. *Adicciones* 21(4): 327–45.

Forsyth, Alasdair, and Martin Cloonan. 2008. 'Alco-Pop? The Use of Popular Music in Glasgow Pubs'. *Popular Music and Society* 31(1): 57–78.

Foucault, Michel. 1972. *The Archaeology of Knowledge and the Discourse on Language*. London: Tavistock.

Foucault, Michel. 1991. *The Foucault Effect: Studies in Governmentality*, edited by Graham Burchell, Colin Gordon and Peter Miller. Chicago: University of Chicago Press.

Fowler, David. 2008. *Youth Culture in Modern Britain, c.1920–c.1970: From Ivory Tower to Global Movement – A New History*. Basingstoke: Palgrave Macmillan.

Fragkos Markos. 'In the Centre of Athens You Don't Only Find Ghettos'. *VIMA*. 15 March 2011. http://www.tovima.gr/blogs/article/?aid=389999.

Friedman, Samuel R., Wouter de Jong, Diana Rossi, Graciela Touzé, Russel Rockwell, Don C. Des Jarlais and Richard Elovich. 2007. 'Harm Reduction Theory: Users' Culture, Micro-Social Indigenous Harm Reduction, and the Self-Organization and Outside-Organizing of Users' Groups'. *International Journal of Drug Policy* 18(2): 107–17.

Frishkopf, Michael. 2001. 'Tarab in the Mystic Sufi Chant of Egypt'. In *Colors of Enchantment: Visual and Performing Arts of the Middle East*, edited by Sherifa Zuhur, 233–70. Cairo: The American University in Cairo Press.

Frith, Simon. 1993. 'Popular Music and the Local State'. In *Rock and Popular Music: Policies, Politics, Institutions*, edited by Tony Bennett, Simon Frith, Lawrence Gossberg, John Shepherd and Graeme Turne, 14–24. London: Routledge.

Gaffney, Christopher. 2010. 'Mega-Events and Socio-spatial Dynamics in Rio de Janeiro, 1919–2016'. *Journal of Latin American Geography* 9(1): 7–29.

Gallan, Ben. 2015. 'Night Lives: Heterotopia, Youth Transitions and Cultural Infrastructure in the Urban Night'. *Urban Studies* 52: 555–70.

Gallan, Ben, and Christopher R. Gibson. 2011. 'New Dawn or New Dusk? Beyond the Binary of Day and Night'. *Environment and Planning A* 43: 2509–15.

Galloway, Josie, Alasdair Forsyth and David Shewan. 2007. *Young People's Street Drinking Behaviour: Investigating the Influence of Marketing & Subculture*. Glasgow: Glasgow Centre for the Study of Violence.

Garside, Jayne. 1993. 'Inner City Gentrification in South Africa: The Case of Woodstock, Cape Town'. *GeoJournal* 30(1): 29–35.

Gehl, Jan. 1996. *Life between Buildings: Using Public Space*. Copenhagen: Danish Architectural Press.

Gehl, Jan, and Lars Gemzoe. 2001. *New City Spaces*. Copenhagen: Danish Architectural Press.

Gervais-Lambony, Philippe. 2012. 'Nostalgies Citadines en Afrique Sud'. *Espaces Temps*. https://www.espacestemps.net/articles/nostalgies-citadines-en-afrique-sud/.

Gindroz, Ray. 2002. 'City Life and New Urbanism'. *Fordham Urban Law Journal* 29: 1419–37.

Giordano Emanuele, Dominique Crozat, Ana Albuquerque and Daniel Bartement. 2017. 'Vivre sa nuit à Montpellier'. [Rapport de recherche] UMR 5281 ART-Dev; Université Paul Valéry - Montpellier 3. https://halshs.archives-ouvertes.fr/halshs-01539033.

Gladstone, David, and Jolie Préau. 2008. 'Gentrification in Tourist Cities: Evidence from New Orleans before and after Hurricane Katrina'. *Housing Policy Debate* 19(1): 137–75.

Glass, Ruth Lazarus. 1964. *London: Aspects of Change*. London: MacGibbon & Kee.

Glazebrook, Diana, and Mohammad Jalal Abbasi-Shavazi. 2007. 'Being Neighbors to Imam Reza: Pilgrimage Practices and Return Intentions of Hazara Afghans Living in Mashhad, Iran'. *Iranian Studies* 40(2): 187–201.

Góis, Marcos. 2015. 'Na Calada da Noite: Modernidade e Conservadorismo na Vida Noturna Carioca (1760–1950)'. *Espaço Aberto* 5(2): 45–60.

Gomes, Paulo. 2004 'Nomospace and Genospace: A Spatial Matrix'. *Geojournal* 60(4): 339–44.

Gondim, Linda. 1987. 'The Poor, the Periphery, and the State in Metropolitan Rio de Janeiro'. *Journal of Planning Education and Research* 6(3): 178–86.

Gough, Katherine V., and Monica Franch. 2005. 'Spaces of the Street: Socio-spatial Mobility and Exclusion of Youth in Recife'. *Children's Geographies* 3(2): 149–66.

Goulding, C., and A. Shankar. 2011. 'Club Culture, Neotribalism and Ritualised Behaviour'. *Annals of Tourism Research* 38(4): 1435–53.

Grabovac, Nikola. 2015. *Privreda Bosne i Hercegovine pred kolapsom: Zbirka eseja i drugih dokumenata*. Fojnica: Štamparija Fojnica.

Grayson, Rollo A. S., and Lisa S. McNeill. 2009. 'Using Atmospheric Elements in Service Retailing: Understanding the Bar Environment'. *Journal of Service Marketing* 23(7): 517–27.

Grazian, David. 2007. 'The Girl Hunt: Urban Nightlife and the Performance of Masculinity as Collective Activity'. *Symbolic Interaction* 30: 221–43.

Grazian, David. 2008. *On the Make: The Hustle of Urban Nightlife*. Chicago: University of Chicago Press.

Greed, Clara. 2003. *Inclusive Urban Design: Public Toilets*. Abingdon: Architectural Press.

Greene, Solomon J. 2003. 'Staged Cities: Mega-Events, Slum Clearance, and Global Capital'. *Yale Human Rights and Development Law Journal* 6: 161.

Griffiths, Ron. 1998. 'Making Sameness: Place Marketing and the New Urban Entrepreneurialism'. In *Cities, Economic Competition, and Urban Policy*, edited by Nick Oatley, 41–57. London: Paul Chapman Publishing.

Guillaume, Philippe. 2000. 'Johannesburg: Géographies de l'Exclusion'. PhD Thesis, University of Reims.

Guillaume, Philippe. 2004. 'La Violence Urbaine à Johannesburg. Entre Réalité et Prétexte'. *Geographica Helvetica* 59: 188–98.

Gwiazdzinski, Luc. 2005. *La Nuit, Dernière Frontière de la Ville*. La Tour d'Aigues: Éditions de l'Aube.

Gwiazdzinski, Luc. 2014. 'The Sustainable Metropolis: When Night Enlightens Day'. Métropolitiques.eu, Métropolitiques. https://hal.inria.fr/halshs-01074019/document.

Gwyther, Gabrielle. 2008. 'Once Were Westies'. *Griffith Review* 20: 81.

Hadfield, Phil. 2006. *Bar Wars: Contesting the Night in Contemporary British Cities*. Oxford: Oxford University Press.

Hadfield, Phil. 2015. 'The Night-Time City. Four Modes of Exclusion: Reflections on the Urban Studies Special Collection'. *Urban Studies* 52(3): 606–16.

Hadfield, Phil. 2017. 'Hackney Evening and Night-Time Economy Public Behaviour Study: Project to Inform the London Borough of Hackney Licensing Policy Review 2017: Final Technical Report (and Summary Report)'. http://www.phil hadfield.co.uk.

Hae, Laam. 2011a. 'Dilemmas of the Nightlife Fix: Post-Industrialisation and the Gentrification of Nightlife in New York City'. *Urban Studies* 48(16): 3449–65.

Hae, Laam. 2011b. 'Gentrification and Politicization of Nightlife in New York City'. *ACME: An International E-Journal for Critical Geographies* 10(3): 564–84.

Hae, Laam. 2012. *The Gentrification of Nightlife and the Right to the City: Regulating Spaces of Social Dancing in New York*. New York: Routledge.

Halilović, Semir. 2014. 'Dossier: Sve sarajevske ratne gazde i kafane – živio podrum!' http://semirhalilovicc.blogspot.ba/2014/11/dossier-sve-sarajevske-ratne-gazde-i.html.

Halkitis, Perry N., and Joseph J. Palamar. 2006. 'GHB Use among Gay and Bisexual Men'. *Addictive Behaviours* 31(11): 2135–39.

Hall, Stuart. Ed. 1997. *Representation: Cultural Representations and Signifying Practices*. Milton Keynes: The Open University.

Hall, Tom, Amanda Coffey and Howard Williamson. 1999. 'Self, Space and Place: Youth Identities and Citizenship'. *British Journal of Sociology of Education* 20(4): 501–13.

Hamnett, Chris. 1984. 'Gentrification and Residential Location Theory: A Review and Assessment'. In *Geography and the Urban Environment. Progress in Research and Applications*, edited by David T. Herbert and Ron J. Johnston, 283–319. London: John Wiley.

Hamnett, Chris. 1991. 'The Blind Men and the Elephant: The Explanation of Gentrification'. *Transactions of the Institute of British Geographers, New Series* 16: 173–89.

Hannigan, John. 1998. *Fantasy City: Pleasure and Profit in the Postmodern Metropolis*. London: Routledge.

Hargreaves, Alan. 1996. 'A Deviant Construction: The French Media and the "Banlieues"'. *New Community* 22(4): 607–18.

Harmpis, Aimilios. 2014. 'Metaxougeio, the Last Neighbourhood'. *Kathimerini*. 2 November. http://www.kathimerini.gr/789970/article/politismos/polh/meta3oyr geio-h-teleytaia-geitonia.

Harris, Amy. 2016. 'Kings Cross Faces Permanent Transformation in Face of Massive Tower Property Deal'. *Daily Telegraph.* 23 October 2016. http://www.dailytelegraph.com.au/news/nsw/kings-cross-faces-permanent-transformation-in-face-of-massive-tower-property-deal/news-story/414fb365677b7a20ce34e170a2c7e954.

Harris, Andrew. 2012. 'Art and Gentrification: Pursuing the Urban Pastoral in Hoxton, London'. *Transactions of the Institute of British Geographers* 37(2): 226–41.

Hartog, François. 2003. *Régimes d'Historicité: Présentisme et Expériences du Temps.* Paris: Seuil.

Harvey, David. 1989. 'From Managerialism to Entrepreneurialism: The Transformation in Urban Governance in Late Capitalism'. *Geografiska Annaler. Series B. Human Geography* 71(1): 3–17.

Harvey, David. 2006. *Paris, Capital of Modernity.* London: Routledge.

Hasenöhrl, U., Katharina Krause, Josiane Meier and Merle Pottharst. Eds. 2014. *Urban Lighting, Light Pollution and Society.* London and New York: Taylor & Francis.

Hatziotis, Kostas. 1999. *Neighbourhoods of Old Athens. The Metaxourgeio.* Athens: Municipality of Athens Cultural Centre.

Haydock, William. 2014. 'The Rise and Fall of the "Nudge" of Minimum Unit Pricing: The Continuity of Neoliberalism in Alcohol Policy in England'. *Critical Social Policy* 34(2): 260–79.

Haywardy, Keith, and Dick Hobbs. 2007. 'Beyond the Binge in "Booze Britain": Market-Led Liminalization and the Spectacle of Binge Drinking'. *British Journal of Sociology* 58(3): 437–56.

He, Shenjing. 2015. 'Consuming Urban Living in "Villages in the City": Studentification in Guangzhou, China'. *Urban Studies* 52(15): 2849–73.

Heath, Tim. 1997. 'The Twenty-Four Hour City Concept – A Review of Initiatives in British Cities'. *Journal of Urban Design* 2(2): 93–204.

Henckel, Dietrich. 2016. 'Opening Session: Conference Intro'. Paper presented at Stadt Nach Acht. Stadt Nach Acht, Berlin, 24–25 November 2016.

HESA [Higher Education Statisitics Agency]. 2016). 'Non-UK Domicile Students and General Student Numbers'. https://www.hesa.ac.uk/stats#non-uk.

Hidalgo, Eduardo. 2004. *Hacia la Percepción de Riesgo Basada en la Evidencia.* Barcelona: Asociación Bienestar y Salud & Energy Control.

Hil, Richard, and Judith Bessant. 1999. 'Spaced-Out? Young People's Agency, Resistance and Public Space'. *Urban Policy and Research* 17(1): 41–49.

Hills, Brendon. 2011. 'Kings Cross Crackdown'. *Sunday Telegraph.* 29 May 2011. http://www.dailytelegraph.com.au/kings-cross-crackdown/news-story/d37f9fd9eed1a1b9cc7d535ed22caa8c.

HM Government. 2007. *Safe, Sensible, Social. The Next Steps in the National Alcohol Strategy.* London: The Stationery Office.

HM Government. 2012. *The Government's Alcohol Strategy.* London: The Stationery Office.

Hoare, Jacqueline, and John Flatley. 2008. 'Drug Misuse Declared: Findings from the 2007/08 British Crime Survey'. London: Home Office Statistics Unit of the Science and Research Group. http://webarchive.nationalarchives.gov.uk/20110220110345/ http://rds.homeoffice.gov.uk/rds/pdfs08/hosb1308.pdf.

Hobbs, Dick, Philip Hadfield, Stuart Lister and Simon Winlow. 2003. *Bouncers: Violence and Governance in the Night-Time Economy*. Oxford: Oxford University Press.

Hobbs, Dick, Stuart Lister, Phil Hadfield, Simon Winlow and Steve Hall. 2000. 'Receiving Shadows: Governance and Liminality in the Night-Time Economy'. *British Journal of Sociology* 51: 701–17.

Hobbs, Dick, Kate O'Brien and Louise Westmarland. 2007. 'Connecting the Gendered Door: Women Violence and Doorwork'. *British Journal of Sociology* 58(1): 21–38.

Hobbs, Dick, Simon Winlow, Philip Hadfield and Stuart Lister. 2005. 'Violent Hypocrisy Governance and the Night-Time Economy'. *European Journal of Criminology* 2(2): 161–83.

Hodžić, Kadrija. 2013. 'Utjecaj neoliberalizma na zatečenost ekonomske misli Bosne i Hercegovine pred recesijom'. In *Proceedings Book of the Third International Scientific Conference on Economy of Integration: Using Knowledge to Move from Recession to Prosperity*, edited by University of Tuzla, Bosnia and Herzegovina, OFF-SET Tuzla: Univerzitet u Tuzli, Ekonomski fakultet, Bosna i Hercegovina, 123–47.

Hollands, Robert. 1995. *Friday Night, Saturday Night: Youth Cultural Identification in the Post-Industrial City*. Newcastle: University of Newcastle.

Hollands, Robert. 2002. 'Divisions in the Dark: Youth Cultures, Transitions and Segmented Consumption Spaces in the Night-Time Economy'. *Journal of Youth Studies* 5(2): 153–71.

Hollands, Robert, and Paul Chatterton. 2003. 'Producing Nightlife in the New Urban Entertainment Economy: Corporatization, Branding and Market Segmentation'. *International Journal of Urban and Regional Research* 27(2): 361–85.

Holloway, Sarah L., Mark Jayne and Gill Valentine. 2008. ' "Sainsbury's Is My Local": English Alcohol Policy, Domestic Drinking Practices and the Meaning of Home'. *Transactions of the Institute of British Geographers* 33(4): 532–47.

Holloway, Sarah, Gill Valentine and Mark Jayne. 2009. 'Masculinities, Femininities and the Geographies of Public and Private Drinking Landscapes'. *Geoforum* 40: 821–31.

Homan, Shane. 2003. *The Mayor's a Square: Live Music and Law and Order in Sydney*. Newtown: Local Consumption Publications.

Homan, Shane. 2017. 'Lockout Laws or "Rock Out" Laws? Governing Sydney's Night-Time Economy and Implications for the "Music City"'. *International Journal of Cultural Policy* 1–15. doi:10.1080/10286632.2017.1317760.

The Home Office. 2008. 'Launch of New Multi-million Binge Drinking Advertising Campaign'. http://www.cjp.org.uk/news/archive/launch-of-new-multi-million-binge-drinking-advertising-campaign-17-06-2008/.

Home Office and KPMG. 2008. *Review of the Social Responsibility Standards for the Production and Sale of Alcoholic Drinks*. London: Home Office.

Homer, Sean. 2009. 'Retrieving Emir Kusturica's Underground as a Critique of Ethnic Nationalism'. *Jump Cut: A Review of Contemporary Media* 51. https://www.ejumpcut.org/archive/jc51.2009/Kusterica/.

Hornberger, Julia. 2008. 'Nocturnal Johannesburg'. In *Johannesburg: The Elusive Metropolis*, edited by Sarah Nuttall and Achille Mbembe, 285–96. Durham, NC: Duke University Press.

House of Commons. 2012. *Science and Technology Committee: Alcohol Guidelines*. HC1536. London: The Stationery Office.

Houssay-Holzschuch, Myriam. 2010. 'Crossing Boundaries. Tome 1: Itinéraire Scientifique; Tome 2: Publications; Tome 3: Vivre ensemble dans l'Afrique du Sud post-apartheid'. Habilitation à Diriger des Recherches, Geography, Université Panthéon-Sorbonne – Paris I.

HRI. n.d. 'What Is Harm Reduction? A Position Statement from Harm Reduction International'. https://www.hri.global/what-is-harm-reduction.

Hubbard, Phil. 2004. 'Cleansing the Metropolis: Sex Work and the Politics of Zero-Tolerance'. *Urban Studies* 41(9): 129–40.

Hubbard, Phil. 2008. 'Regulating the Social Impacts of Studentification: A Loughborough Case Study'. *Environment and Planning A* 40(2): 323–41.

Hubbard, Phil. 2009. 'Geographies of Studentification and Purpose-Built Student Accommodation: Leading Separate Lives?' *Environment and Planning A* 41(8): 1903–23.

Hubbard, Phil. 2012. *Cities and Sexualities*. Abingdon: Routledge.

Hubbard, Phil, and Rachel Colosi. 2015. 'Taking Back the Night? Gender and the Contestation of Sexual Entertainment in England and Wales'. *Urban Studies* 52(3): 589–605.

Huisman, Wim, and Hans Nelen. 2014. 'The Lost Art of Regulated Tolerance? Fifteen Years of Regulating Vices in Amsterdam'. *Journal of Law & Society* 41(4): 604–26.

Huizinga, Johan. 2008. *Homo Ludens: Proeve Eener Bepaling van het Spel-Element der Cultuur*. Amsterdam: Amsterdam University Press.

Hutton, Fiona. 2010. 'Up for It, Mad for It? Women, Drug Use and Participation in Club Scenes'. *Health, Risk and Society* 6(3): 223–37.

Human Rights Watch. 2012. *Hate on the Streets. Xenophobic Violence in Greece*. New York: Human Rights Watch.

Hyra, Derek. 2017. *Race, Class, and Politics in the Cappuccino City*. Chicago: University of Chicago Press.

Ibrahim, Hilmi. 1982. 'Leisure and Islam'. *Leisure Studies* 1(2): 197–210.

INE. 2011. *Censos 2011 Resultados Definitivos – Portugal*. Instituto Nacional de Estatística [National Institute for Statistics – Portugal].

INSEE. 2012. 'Montpellier Agglomération: Un Territoire Attractif pour les Étudiants et les Jeunes dans un Contexte Immobilier Tendu'. https://www.insee.fr/fr/statistiques/1286026.

INSEE. 2017. 'Population en 2013 Recensement de la population - Base infracommunale' (IRIS). https://insee.fr/fr/statistiques/2386737.

IRNA. 2011. 'Ta Payan Sal-e 90 Record Zaerin Mashhad be 28 Million Miresad'. http://www.irna.ir/fa/News/101683/زائری_تعداد_رکورد_90_سال_تاپایان/سایر ن_مشهد_به_28_میلیون_نفر_می_رسد.

Ismailidou, Elli. 2010. 'They Push Us to a Civil War'. *Vima*. 24 October. http://www.tovima.gr/politics/article/?aid=362720.

Iveson, Kurt. 2014. 'Building a City for "The People": The Politics of Alliance-Building in the Sydney Green Ban Movement'. *Antipode* 46(4): 992–1013.

Izadi, Mohammad Saeid. 2008. 'A Study on City Centre Regeneration: A Comparative Analysis of Two Different Approaches to the Revitalization of Historic City Centre in Iran'. PhD Thesis, Faculty of Humanities and Social Sciences, School of Architecture, Planning and Landscape. Newcastle University, Newcastle.

Jabareen, Yosef Rafeq. 2006. 'Sustainable Urban Forms: Their Typologies, Models and Concepts'. *Journal of Planning Education & Research* 26: 38–52.

Jacobs, Jane. 1961. *The Death and Life of Great American Cities*. New York: Random House.

James. 2015. 'Since Lockout Laws, Newtown Has Been a Hideous Place to Be at Night'. 10 June 2016. http://www.sneakymag.com/life/since-the-lockouts-laws-newtown-has-been-a-hideous-place-to-be-at-night.

Jancar, Barbara. 1988. 'Neofeminism in Yugoslavia: A Closer Look'. *Women & Politics* 88(1): 1–30.

Janoschka, Michael, and Jorge Sequera. 2016. 'Gentrification in Latin America: Addressing the Politics and Geographies of Displacement'. *Urban Geography* 37(8): 1175–94.

Janoschka, Michael, Jorge Sequera and Luis Salinas. 2014. 'Gentrification in Spain and Latin America: A Critical Dialogue'. *International Journal of Urban and Regional Research* 38(4): 1234–65.

Janssen, Bram. 2012. 'Place of Light – Maboneng Precinct'. https://vimeo.com/44611197.

Jayne, Mark. 2006. *Cities and Consumption*. London: Routledge.

Jayne, Mark, Chris Gibson, Gordon Waitt and Gill Valentine. 2012. 'Drunken Mobilities: Backpackers, Alcohol, "Doing Place"'. *Tourist Studies* 12(3): 211–31.

Jayne, Mark, Gill Valentine and Sarah L. Holloway. 2008. 'The Place of Drink: Geographical Contributions to Alcohol Studies'. *Drugs: Education, Prevention and Policy* 15(3): 219–32.

Jeudy, Henri-Pierre. 2005. *La Machinarie Patrimoniale*. Belval, France: Circé.

Johnston, Ron J., Derek Gregory, Geraldine Pratt and Michael Watts. 2000. *The Dictionary of Human Geography*. Hoboken, NJ: Wiley.

Jones, Owen. 2011. *Chavs: The Demonization of the Working Class*. London: Verso.

Judd, Dennis R., and Susan S. Fainstein. 1999. *The Tourist City*. New Haven, CT, and London: Yale University Press.

Kaminer, Tahl, Marc Schoonderbeek, Jaap Jan Berg and Joost Zonneveld. Eds. 2009. *Houses in Transformation: Interventions in European Gentrification*. Rotterdam: NAi Utigevers Publishers.

Kandylis George, Maloutas Thomas and Sayas John. 2012. 'Immigration, Inequality and Diversity: Socio-ethnic Hierarchy and Spatial Organization in Athens, Greece'. *European Urban and Regional Studies* 19(3): 267–86.

Kanton Sarajevo. 1999. *Statistički Bilten: decembar 1999*. Sarajevo: Zavod za informatiku i statistiku Kantona.

Kaouni, Dimitra. 2009. *Metaxourgeio's Redevelopment: Spatial and Social Approach of a Multicultural Neighbourhood of Athens*. Undergraduate Thesis, Department of Regional Planning and Development, Aristoteleio University of Thessaloniki.

Katsaouni, Stavroula. 2014. 'ReMap: When a Platform for Contemporary Art Become a Platform for Displacement and "Gentrification"'. Undergraduate research paper, School of Architecture, University of Crete.

Keep Sydney Open. 2016a. 'About'. *Keep Sydney Open*. http://www.keepsydneyo pen.com/#about.

Keep Sydney Open. 2016b. 'Submission by Keep Sydney Open (KSO) Review of the Liquor Amendment Act 2014 by the Hon. IDF Callinan AC QC'. 4 April. http://www.keepsydneyopen.com/assets/160404-Keep_Sydney_Open_Submission.pdf.

Kelling, George L. and James Q. Wilson. 1982 'Broken Windows: The Police and Neighborhood Safety'. *The Atlantic,* March Issue. http://www.theatlantic.com/magazine/archive/1982/03/broken-windows/4465/.

Kheirabadi, Masoud. 1991. *Iranian Cities, Formation and Development*. Austin: University of Texas Press.

Khemsurov, Monica. 2010. 'The 2.0 Report'. *New York Times Magazine* 13 May. http://tmagazine.blogs.nytimes.com/2010/05/13/the-2-0-report/?_r=0.

Kidd, Kenneth. 2008. 'What If It's Not Really Gentrification?' TheStar.Com. 8 November. https://www.thestar.com/news/2008/11/08/what_if_its_not_really_gentrification.html.

Kleftogianni, Ioanna. 2010. 'The Ghetto of the Centre Forces Theatres and Galleries Away'. *Eleutherotypia*. 1 October. http://www.enet.gr/?i=news.el.article&id=208886.

Knafou, Rémy. 2012. *Les Lieux du voyage*. Paris: Editions Le Cavalier Bleu.

Koh, Tyson. 2016. 'Callinan's Report Has Locked Us Out of the Debate'. *Daily Telegraph*. 19 September. http://www.dailytelegraph.com.au/news/opinion/justic-callinans-report-has-locked-us-out-of-the-debate/news-story/d9c588141c290 af68b6adde1a25690aa.

Kolko, Jed. 2007. 'The Determinants of Gentrification'. doi:10.2139/ssrn.985714.

Kornberger, Martin, and Stewart Clegg. 2011. 'Strategy as Performative Practice: The Case of Sydney 2030'. *Strategic Organization* 9(2): 136–62.

Koslofsky, Craig. 2011. *Evening's Empire: A History of the Night in Early Modern Europe*. Cambridge: Cambridge University Press.

Kounadi, Iro. 2012. 'Metaxourgeio: Dangerously . . . Attractive'. *In2Life*. 23 March. http://www.in2life.gr/delight/goingout/article/221283/metaxoyrgeio-epikindyna-gohteftiko.html.

Koutrolikou, Penny. 2015. 'Socio-spatial Stigmatization and Its "Incorporation" in the Centre of Athens'. *City* 19(4): 503–14.

Koutrolikou, Penny. 2016. 'Governmentalities of Urban Crises in Inner-City Athens, Greece'. *Antipode* 48(1): 172–92.

Koziol, Michael. 2015. 'Newtown Bars to Trial 3am Lockout and Shots Ban'. *Sydney Morning Herald*. 31 July 2015. http://www.smh.com.au/nsw/newtown-bars-to-trial-3am-lockout-and-shots-ban-20150731-giomj5.html.

Krätke, Stefan. 2012. 'The New Urban Growth Ideology of "Creative Cities"'. In *Cities for People, Not for Profit*, edited by Neil Brenner, Peter Marcuse and Margit Mayer, 138–49. New York: Routledge.

Kreitzman, Leon. 1999. *The 24 Hour Society*. London: Profile Books Ltd.

Kronja, Ivana. 2004. 'Turbo Folk and Dance Music in 1990s Serbia: Media, Ideology and the Production of Spectacle'. *Anthropology of East Europe Review* 22(1): 103–114.

Ladepeche.fr. 2017. 'Christophe Vidal, Maire de la Nuit 2014, Interpelle les Candidats sur l'Économie de la Nuit'. 18 April 2017. http://www.ladepeche.fr/article/ 2017/04/18/2558456-christophe-vidal-maire-nuit-2014-interpelle-candidats-eco nomie-nuit.html.

Lago, Luciana. 2015. *Desigualdades e Segregação na Metrópole: O Rio de Janeiro em Tempo de Crise*. Rio de Janeiro: Letra Capital.

Laughey, Dan. 2006. *Music and Youth Culture*. Edinburgh: Edinburgh University Press.

Laville, Sandra. 2017. 'Police Appeal against Ruling in Favour of Worboys Rape Survivors'. *Guardian*. 10 March 2017. https://www.theguardian.com/uk-news/2017/ mar/10/police-appeal-against-ruling-in-favour-of-worboys-survivors.

Law, Chrstopher M. 1993. *Urban Tourism: Attracting Visitors to Large Cities*. London: Mansell.

Lawler, Stephanie. 2005. 'Disgusted Subjects: The Making of Middle-Class Identities'. *The Sociological Review* 53(3): 429–46.

Le Corbusier. 1973. *The Athens Charter*. New York: Grossman Publishers.

Leach, Brittany. 2013. 'Slutwalk and Sovereignity: Transnational Protest as Emergent Global Democracy'. MA dissertation, University of Georgia, Atlanta.

Leach, Edmund R. 1971. *Replanteamiento de la Antropología*. Barcelona: Seix Barral.

Lees, Loretta. 2004. 'Urban Geography: Discourse Analysis and Urban Research'. *Progress in Human Geography* 28(1): 101–7.

Lees, Loretta, Tom Slater and Elvin Wyly. 2008. *Gentrification*. London: Routledge.

Lees, Loretta, Tom Slater and Elvin Wyly. 2010. *The Gentrification Reader*. London: Routledge.

Lefevbre, Henri. 1968. *Le Droit à la ville*, Paris: Ed. du Seuil, Collection Points.

Lefebvre, Henri. 1974. *La production de l'espace*. Paris: Éditions Anthropos.

Lefebvre, Henri. 1991. *The Production of Space*. Oxford: Blackwell.

Lennox, Gordon. 2002. 'Dancing on Drugs: Risk, Health, and Hedonism in the British Club Scene'. *Family Practice* 19(2): 215–16.

Leppäkari, Maria, and Kevin Griffin. 2017. *Pilgrimage and Tourism to Holy Cities: Ideological and Management Perspectives*. Wallingford, UK: CABI.

Lerner, Jaime. 2014. *Urban Acupuncture: Celebrating Pinpricks of Change That Enrich City Life*. Washington, DC: Island Press.

Lesjak, Miha, Emil Juvan, Elisabeth M. Ineson, Matthehw H. T. Yap and Eva Podovšovnik-Axelsson. 2015. 'Erasmus Student Motivation: Why and Where to Go?' *Higher Education* 70(5): 845–65.

Lessa, Carlos. 2005. *O Rio de Todos os Brasis*. Rio de Janeiro: Record.

Levi, Pavle. 2007. *Disintegration in Frames: Aesthetics and Ideology in the Yugoslav and Post-Yugoslav Cinema*. Stanford, CA: Stanford University Press.

Ley, David. 1980. 'Liberal Ideology and Post-Industrial City'. *Annals of the Association of American Geographers* 70: 238–58.

Leyshon, Michael. 2008. ' "We're Stuck in the Corner": Young Women, Embodiment and Drinking in the Countryside'. *Drugs: Education, Prevention and Policy* 15(3): 267–89.

Lialios, Giorgos. 2010. 'Metaxourgeio, an Area Emitting a Sense of Decline'. *Kathimerini*. 2 October. http://www.kathimerini.gr/406547/article/epikairothta/ellada/meta3oyrgeio-mia-perioxh-poy-anadidei-ais8hsh-parakmhs.

Lieberg, Mats. 1995. 'Teenagers and Public Space'. *Communication Research* 22(6): 720–44.

Lister, Stuart, Dick Hobbs, Steve Hall and Simon Winlow. 2000. 'Violence in the Night-Time Economy; Bouncers: The Reporting, Recording and Prosecution of Assaults'. *Policing and Society: An International Journal of Research and Policy* 10(4): 383–402.

Llewellyn-Smith, Catherine, and Vivienne McCabe. 2008. 'What Is the Attraction for Exchange Students: The Host Destination or Host University? Empirical Evidence from a Study of an Australian University'. *International Journal of Tourism Research* 10(6): 593–607.

Llewelyn-Davies. 2000. *Urban Design Compendium.* London: English Partnerships.

Lloyd, Richard. 2010. *Neo-Bohemia. Art and Commerce in the Post-Industrial City.* New York: Routledge.

London Assembly Police and Crime Committee. 2015. 'Investigation into the Impact of Alcohol on Policing London's Night-Time Economy'. https://www.london.gov.uk/sites/default/files/policing_the_night-time_economy_-_written_submissions.pdf.

London Borough of Southwark. n.d. 'Let's Talk about . . . Women's Safety'. 30 April 2017. http://www.2.southwark.gov.uk/info/200030/community_safety_and_enforcement/3585/lets_talk_about_womens_safety.

Loopmans, Maarten, and Pieter Van den Broeck. 2011. 'Global Pressures, Local Measures: The Re-regulation of Sex Work in the Antwerp Skipper's Quarter'. *Tijdschrift voor Economische en Sociale Geografie* 102(5): 548–61.

Louvet, Pascaline. 2010. 'La problematique du bruit à Montpellier: Acterus, Gestions et Représentations'. MA dissertation, Université Paul Valéry-Montpellier 3.

Lovatt, Andrew, Justin O'Connor, John Montgomery and Paul Owens. 1994. *The 24-Hour City: Selected Papers from the First National Conference on the Night-Time Economy.* Manchester, UK: Manchester Institute for Popular Culture.

Lovatt, Andy. 1996. 'The Ecstasy of Urban Regeneration: Regulation of the Night-Time Economy in the Transition to a Post-Fordist City'. In *From the Margins to the Centre: Cultural Production and Consumption in the Post-Industrial City,* edited by Justin O'Connor and Derek Wynn, 141–68. Farnham: Ashgate.

Lovatt, Andy, and Justin O'Connor. 1995. 'Cities and the Night-Time Economy'. *Planning Practice and Research* 10(2): 127–33.

Lucas, Karen, Sophie Tyler and Georgina Christodoulou. 2009. 'Assessing the "Value" of New Transport Initiatives in Deprived Neighbourhoods in the UK'. *Transport Policy* 16: 115–22.

Lynch, Kevin. 1984. *Good City Form.* London: Cambridge.

MacDonald, Heather. 2015. ' "Green, Global, and Connected": Can Sydney Solve Its Metropolitan Governance Problems?' In *Transforming Distressed Global*

Communities: Making Inclusive, Safe, Resilient, and Sustainable Cities, edited by Fritz Wagner, Riad Mahayni and Andreas Piller, 211–29. Burlington: Ashgate.

Maček, Ivana. 2000. *Everyday Life in Sarajevo under Siege*. Uppsala: Acta Universitatis Upsaliensis.

Mackinnon, Olivia. 2017. 'NSW Premier Reveals What She's Doing about the Lockout Laws'. *Kiis 1065*. 24 January. http://www.kiis1065.com.au/shows/ kyle-jackie-o/new-nsw-premier-reveals-what-she-s-doing-about-the-lockout-laws.

MacLean, Sarah. 2016. 'Alcohol and the Constitution of Friendship for Young Adults'. *Sociology* 50(1): 93–108.

MacLean, Sarah, and David Moore. 2014. ' "Hyped Up": Assemblages of Alcohol, Excitement and Violence for Outer-Suburban Young Adults in the Inner City at Night'. *International Journal of Drug Policy* 25(3): 378–85.

MacRae, Rhoda. 2006. 'Notions of "Us" and "Them": Markers of Stratification in Clubbing Lifestyles'. *Journal of Youth Studies* 7(1): 55–71.

Madriaga, Manuel. 2010. ' "I Avoid Pubs and the Student Union Like the Plague": Students with Asperger Syndrome and Their Negotiation of University Spaces'. *Children's Geographies* 8(1): 39–50.

Mairie de Paris. 2010. 'Les nuits de Paris: Etats généraux. Paris, Mairie de Paris'. https://drive.google.com/file/d/0B7WOfZJICAvFNFQyR1lDcG1idXM/view.

Malbon, Ben. 1999. *Clubbing: Dancing, Ecstacy and Vitality*. London: Routledge.

Malet Calvo, Daniel. 2014. ' "Tornar-se Outra Pessoa": Narrativas de Transformação Subjetiva e Processos de Distinção entre os Jovens Estudantes Erasmus em Lisboa'. *Antropolítica: Revista Contemporânea de Antropologia* 37: 51–77.

Malet Calvo, Daniel. 2017. 'Understanding International Students beyond Studentification: A New Class of Transnational Urban Consumers. The Example of Erasmus Students in Lisbon (Portugal)'. *Urban Studies* (online first). doi:10.1177/0042 098017708089.

Malet Calvo, Daniel, Jordi Nofre and Miguel Geraldes. 2017. 'The Erasmus Corner: Place-Making of a Sanitised Nightlife Spot in the Bairro Alto (Lisbon, Portugal)'. *Leisure Studies* 36(6): 778–92.

Maloutas, Thomas, George Kandylis, Michalis Petrou and Nikos Souliotis (eds). 2013. 'The Decline of the City Centre and the Residential Choices by Higher and Middle Income Strata'. In *The Centre of Athens as a Political Stake*, edited by Thomas Maloutas, George Kandylis, Michalis Petrou and Nikos Souliotis, 29–51. Athens: NCSR (in Greek).

Maloutas, Thomas, and Nikos Karadimitriou. 2001. 'Vertical Social Differentiation in Athens: Alternative or Complement to Community Segregation?' *International Journal of Urban and Regional Research* 25(4): 699–716.

Manchester Bars. 2017. 'Manchester Bars – Chorlton Bars'. http://www.manchester bars.com/location-chorlton.htm.

Mangan, Lucy. 2015. 'The End of the Nightclub Will Mark an End to Murder on the Dancefloor'. https://www.theguardian.com/commentisfree/2015/aug/12/ death-nightclub-murder-dancefloor-teenagers-triumph-nerd-culture.

Manning, Paul. 2013. *Drugs and Popular Culture: Drugs, Media and Identity in Popular Culture*. London: Routledge.

Markham, Francis, Bruce Doran and Martin Young. 2016. 'The Relationship between Electronic Gaming Machine Accessibility and Police-Recorded Domestic Violence: A Spatio-temporal Analysis of 654 Postcodes in Victoria, Australia, 2005–2014'. *Social Science & Medicine* 162: 106–14.

Marlatt, G. Allan. 1996. 'Harm Reduction: Come as You Are'. *Addictive Behaviours* 21(6): 779–88.

Marsh, Whitney, Heith Copes and Travis Linnemann. 2017. 'Creating Visual Differences: Methamphetamine Users Perceptions of Anti-meth Campaigns'. *International Journal of Drug Policy* 39: 52–61.

Martin, Deborah. 2000. 'Constructing Place: Cultural Hegemonies and Media Images of an Inner-City Neighbourhood'. *Urban Geography* 21(5): 380–405.

Martin, William H., and Sandra Mason. 2004. 'Leisure in an Islamic Context'. *World Leisure Journal* 46(1): 4–13.

Martín-Díaz, Jordi. 2014. 'Urban Restructuring in Post-War Contexts: The Sarajevo Case'. *Hungarian Geographical Bulletin* 63(3): 303–17.

Martinić, Tena. 1965. 'Socijalizam kao negacija dihotomije "radno" i "slobodno" vrijeme'. *Politička misao* 283: 104–13. http://hrcak.srce.hr/115643.

Martins, Daniel, Monica J. Barratt, Cristiana Vale Pires, Helena Carvalho, Mireia Ventura Vilamala, Iván Fornís Espinosa and Helena Valente. 2017. 'The Detection and Prevention of Unintentional Consumption of DOx and 25x-NBOMe at Portugal's Boom Festival'. *Human Psychopharmacology: Clinical and Experimental* 32(3). doi:10.1002/hup.2608.

Martins, Daniel, Helena Valente and Cristiana Vale Pires. 2015. 'CHECK!IN: The Last Frontier for Harm Reduction in Party Settings'. *Saúde e Sociedade* 24(2): 646–60.

Marwick, Arthur. 2011. *The Sixties: Cultural Revolution in Britain, France, Italy and the United States, c.1958–c.1974*. Oxford: Oxford University Press.

Massey, Doreen. 2007. *Space, Place and Gender*. Cambridge: Policy Press.

Mattson, Greggor. 2015. 'Style and the Value of Gay Nightlife: Homonormative Placemaking in San Fransisco'. *Urban Studies* 52(16): 3144–59.

May, Reuben A. Buford. 2014. *Urban Nightlife: Entertaining Race, Class, and Culture in Public Space*. New Brunswick, NJ: Rutgers University Press.

May, Reuben A. Buford, and Kenneth Sean Chaplin. 2008. 'Cracking the Code: Race, Class, and Access to Nightclubs in Urban America'. *Qualitative Sociology* 31(1): 57–72.

Mayer, Margit. 2012. 'The "Right to the City" in Urban Social Movements'. In *Cities for People, Not for Profit*, edited by Neil Brenner, Peter Marcuse and Margit Mayer, 63–86. New York: Routledge.

Mayor of London. 2017a. 'Press Release July/24. Night Czar Hosts First Women's Night Safety Summit'. https://www.london.gov.uk/press-releases/mayoral/night-czar-hosts-first-womens-night-safety-summit-0.

Mayor of London. 2017b. 'From Good Night to Great Night: A Vision for London as a 24-Hour City'. https://www.london.gov.uk/sites/default/files/24_hour_london_vision.pdf.

McCann, Eugene, and Kevin Ward. 2012. 'Policy Assemblages, Mobilities and Mutations: Toward a Multidisciplinary Conversation'. *Political Studies Review* 10: 325–32.

McGuirk, Pauline, and Phillip O'Neill. 'Planning a Prosperous Sydney: The Challenges of Planning Urban Development in the New Urban Context'. *Australian Geographer* 33(3): 301–16.

McKenzie. Marcia. 2017. 'Affect Theory and Policy Mobility: Challenges and Possibilities for Critical Policy Research'. *Critical Studies in Education* 58(2): 187–204.

McNab, Heather. 2017. 'Newtown Liquor Accord Disputes BOCSAR Assault Statistics'. *Central Sydney.* 8 March. http://www.dailytelegraph.com.au/newslocal/cen tral-sydney/newtown-liquor-accord-disputes-bocsar-assault-statistics/news-story/ 5a06d726adbd42ca9eb97bd50dd021f1.

McNeill, Donald. 2011. 'Fine Grain, Global City: Jan Gehl, Public Space and Commercial Culture in Central Sydney'. *Journal of Urban Design* 16(2): 161–78.

McRobbie, Angela. 2009. *The Aftermath of Feminism: Gender, Culture and Social Change.* London: Sage.

Measham, Fiona, Judith Aldridge and Howard Parker. 2001. *Dancing on Drugs: Risk, Health and Hedonism in the British Club Scene.* London: Free Association Books.

Measham, Fiona, and Kevin Brain. 2005. ' "Binge" Drinking, British Alcohol Policy and the New Culture of Intoxication'. *Crime, Media, Culture* 1(3): 262–83.

Measham, Fiona, and Karenza Moore. 2009. 'Repertoires of Distinction: Exploring Patterns of Weekend Polydrug Use within Local Leisure Scenes across the English Night Time Economy'. *Criminology & Criminal Justice* 9(4): 437–64.

Melbin, Murray. 1978. 'Night as Frontier'. *American Sociological Review* 43: 3–22.

Melbin, Murray. 1987. *Night as Frontier: Colonizing the World after Dark.* New York: Free Press.

Mele, Christopher. 2000. 'The Materiality of Urban Discourse: Rational Planning in the Restructuring of the Early Twentieth-Century Ghetto'. *Urban Affairs* 35(5): 628–48.

Mendes, Luis. 2016. 'What Can Be Done to Resist or Mitigate Tourism Gentrification in Lisbon? Some Policy Findings & Recommendations'. In *City Making and Tourism Gentrification*, edited by Marc Glaudemans and Igor Marko, 34–41. Tilburg, The Netherlands: Stadslab European Urban Design Laboratory.

Mendonça, Leila. 2004. *Reflexos da Cidade: A Iluminação Pública no Rio de Janeiro.* Rio de Janeiro: Centro de Memória da Eletricidade no Brasil.

Menéndez, Patricia, Don Weatherburn, Kypros Kypri and Jacqueline Fitzgerald. 2015. 'Lockouts and Last Drinks: The Impact of the January 2014 Liquor Licence Reforms on Assaults in NSW, Australia'. *Crime and Justice Bulletin* 183: 12.

Menoux, Thibault. 2017. 'La Face Cachée d'un Groupe Professionnel'. *Cultures & Conflits* 105–6: 61–82.

Midwinter-Pitt, Victoria. 2007. *Rampant: How a City Stopped a Plague.* Produced by Penny Chapman. Ultimo: ABC Commercial (film), 57 min.

Milestone, Katie. 1996. 'Regional Variations: Northernness and New Urban Economies of Hedonism'. In *From the Margins to the Centre: Cultural Production and Consumption in the Post-Industrial City*, edited by Justin O'Connor and Derek Wynne. Aldershot: Arena.

Mitchell, Kristine. 2012. 'Student Mobility and European Identity: Erasmus Study as a Civic Experience?' *Journal of Contemporary European Research* 8(4): 490–518.

Mitchell, Timothy. 1988. *Colonising Egypt.* Cambridge, UK: Cambridge University Press.

Mlabon, Ben. *Clubbing: Dancing, Ecstasy and Vitality*. London: Routledge.

Monaghan, Lee F. 2002. 'Regulating "Unruly" Bodies: Work Tasks, Conflict and Violence in Britain's Night-Time Economy'. *British Journal of Sociology* 53(3): 403–29.

Montandon, Alain. Ed. 2009. *Promenades Nocturnes*. Paris: L'Harmattan.

Monteiro, João Carlos. 2015. 'Habitação de Interesse Social em Cenários de Revalorização Urbana: Considerações a Partir da Experiência Carioca'. *Cadernos Metrópole* 34: 441–59.

Montgomery, John. 1994. 'The Evening Economy of Cities'. *Town and Country Planning* 63: 302.

Montgomery, John. 2003. 'Cultural Quarters as Mechanisms for Urban Regeneration. Part 1: Conceptualising Cultural Quarters'. *Planning, Practice & Research* 18(4): 293–306.

Moore, Clover. 2013. 'Arts & Culture: A Flourishing Cultural Life Enriches Our City and Community'. http://www.clovermoore.com.au/workingfor-sydney/issues/arts-culture.

Moore, David. 2008. 'Erasing Pleasure from Public Discourse on Illicit Drugs: On the Creation and Reproduction of an Absence'. *International Journal of Drug Policy* 19(5): 353–58.

Moore-Ede, Martin. 1993. *The Twenty Four Hour Society: Understanding Human Limits in a World That Never Stops*. Wokingham, UK: Addison-Wesley.

Moos, Markus. 2016. 'From Gentrification to Youthification? The Increasing Importance of Young Age in Delineating High-Density Living'. *Urban Studies* 53(14): 2903–20.

Moran, Jonathon. 2014. 'Kings Cross Club Owners Look outside CBD to Avoid Lockout Laws'. *Daily Telegraph*. 14 March. http://www.dailytelegraph.com.au/kings-cross-club-owners-look-outside-cbd-to-avoid-lockout-laws/news-story/843c590f48e68e5473b81ab92b57921c.

Móró, Levente, and Jozsef Rácz. 2013. 'Online Drug User-Led Harm Reduction in Hungary: A Review of "Daath"'. *Harm Reduction Journal* 10(1): 18.

Morris, Nina J. 2011. 'Night Walking: Darkness and Sensory Perception in a Night-Time Landscape Installation'. *Cultural Geographies* 18(3): 315–42.

Moser, Caroline O. N. 2016. 'Gender Transformation in a New Global Urban Agenda: Challenges for Habitat III and Beyond'. *Environment and Urbanization* 29(1): 221–36.

Murphy-Lejeune, Elizabeth. 2002. *Student Mobility and Narrative in Europe. The New Strangers*. New York: Routledge.

Murray, Martin J. 2011. *City of Extremes: The Spatial Politics of Johannesburg*. Durham, NC: Duke University Press.

Musgrove, Frank. 1963. *The Migratory Elite*. London: Heinemann.

Musterd, Sako, and Jac Van de Ven. 1991. 'Gentrification and Residential Revitalization in Amsterdam'. In *Urban Housing for the Better-Off: Gentrification in Europe*, edited by Jan van Weesep and Sako Musterd, 89–97. Utrecht: Stedelijke Netwerken.

Nakazawa, Takashi. 2017. 'Expanding the Scope of Studentification Studies'. *Geography Compass* 11(1) (online first). doi:10.1111/gec3.12300.

Nayak, Anoop. 2003. 'Last of the "Real Geordies"? White Masculinities and the Subcultural Response to Deindustrialisation'. *Environment & Planning D: Society and Space* 21(1): 7–25.

Neuts, Bart, Tim Devos and Toon Dirckx. 2014. 'Turning Off the Red Lights: Entrepreneurial Urban Strategies in "De Wallen" Amsterdam'. *Applied Geography* 49: 37–44.

Nevin, Alice. 2014. 'Instant Mutuality: The Development of Maboneng in Inner-City Johannesburg'. *Anthropology Southern Africa* 37: 187–201.

Nicholls, Emily. 2016. 'What on Earth Is *She* Drinking? Doing Femininity through Drink Choice on the Girl's Night Out'. *Journal of International Women's Studies* 17(2): 77–91.

Nicholls, Sean. 2014. 'Onward Christian Soldier: A Premier's Faith'. *Sydney Morning Herald.* 26 April. http://www.smh.com.au/nsw/onward-christian-soldier-a-premiers-faith-20140425-379pp.html.

Nijman, Jan. 1999. 'Cultural Globalization and the Identity of Place: The Reconstruction of Amsterdam'. *Cultural Geographies* 6: 146–64.

Nofre, Jordi. 2011. 'Youth Policies, Social Sanitation, and Contested Suburban Nightscapes'. In *Everyday Life in the Segmented City (Research in Urban Sociology, Volume 11)*, edited by Camilla Perrone, Gabriele Manella and Lorenzo Tripodi, 261–81. Bingley, UK: Emerald Publishing.

Nofre, Jordi. 2013. '"Vintage Nightlife": Gentrifying Lisbon Downtown'. *Fennia: International Journal of Geography* 191(2): 106–21.

Nofre, Jordi. 2015. 'Barcelona de Noche: Unas Primeras Notas sobre Geopolítica de la Higienización Social, Moral y Política de la Ciudad Neoliberal'. *Working Papers of the Institute of Sociology, University of Porto* 3(3): 1–25.

Nofre, Jordi, Emanuele Giordano, Adam Eldridge, João C. Martins and Jorge Sequera. 2017b. 'Tourism, Nightlife and Planning: Challenges and Opportunities for Community Liveability in La Barceloneta'. *Tourism Geographies.* doi.org/10.1080/14616688.2017.1375972

Nofre, Jordi, Iñigo Sánchez-Fuarros, Joao Carlos Martins, Daniel Malet Calvo, Patricia Pereira, Isabel Soares, Miguel Geraldes and Ana López Díaz. 2017a. 'Exploring Nightlife and Urban Change in Bairro Alto'. *City & Community* 16(3): 330–44.

Nottingham, Chris. 2003. 'What Time Do You Call This? Change and Continuity in the Politics of the City Night'. In *Night-Time and Sleep in Asia and the West: Exploring the Dark Side of Life*, edited by Brigitte Steger and Lodewijk Brunt, 191–214. London: Routledge.

NSW Government. 2009. 'Planning Circular: Planning for Entertainment'. 26 October 2009. http://www.planning.nsw.gov.au/Policy-and-Legislation/~/media/C1F528B3BC0043C9B6691CC012795240.ashx.

NSW Government. 2014. 'Plan of Management for the Sydney CBD Entertainment Precinct'. 3 June 2014. http://www.liquorandgaming.nsw.gov.au/Documents/liquor/law-and-policy/sydney-CBD-plan-of-management.pdf.

NSW Government. 2016. 'Sydney Lockout and Last Drink Laws to Remain'. 8 December. https://www.nsw.gov.au/news-and-events/news/sydney-lockout-and-last-drink-laws-to-remain.

Nugent, Ciara. 2016. 'Lisbon Is a City Famed for Its Nightlife – And the Residents Hate It'. *New Statesman – CityMetric*. 6 October. http://www.citymetric.com/ business/lisbon-city-famed-its-nightlife-and-residents-hate-it-2478.

O'Connor, Justin, and Derek Wynne. 1996. 'Left Loafing: City Cultures and Postmodern Lifestyles'. In *From the Margins to the Centre: Cultural Production and Consumption in the Post-Industrial City*, edited by Justin O'Connor and Derek Wynne. Aldershot: Arena.

Oloukoï, Chrystel. 2016a. 'La Marche Urbaine: Un Outil pour Appréhender les Émotions a Johannesburg?' *Carnets de Géographes* 9. https://cdg.revues.org/576.

Oloukoï, Chrystel. 2016b. 'Nuits, Objets de Peurs et de Désirs à Maboneng (Johannesburg, Afrique du Sud)'. *Sociétés Politiques Comparées* 38. http://www.fasopo. org/sites/default/files/charivaria2_n38.pdf.

Oloukoï, Chrystel, and Pauline Guinard. 2016. 'La Nuit à Maboneng (Johannesburg, Afrique du Sud): Un Front Urbain entre Sécurisation, Marchandisation et Contestation'. *L'Espace Politique* 30. doi:10.4000/espacepolitique.3977.

Omeragić, A. 1998. 'Delozacije u vrijeme blagdana'. *Oslobodjenje*. 26 December.

Otter, Chris. 2008. *The Victorian Eye: A Political History of Light and Vision in Britain, 1800–1910*. Chicago: University of Chicago Press.

Page, Stephen. 1995. *Urban Tourism*. London: Routledge.

Papatsiba, Vassiliki. 2006. 'Study Abroad and Experiences of Cultural Distance and Proximity: French Erasmus Students'. In *Living and Studying Abroad: Research and Practice*, edited by Michael Byram and Anwei Feng, 108–33. Toronto: Multilingual Matters Ltd.

Papayanis, Marylin Adler. 2000. 'Sex and the Revanchist City: Zoning out Pornography in New York'. *Environment and Planning D: Society and Space* 18(3): 341–53.

Parker, Howard. 1997. 'Adolescent Drugs Pathways in the 1990s'. In *Tackling Drugs Together: One Year On*, edited by Julia Braggins. The Centre for Crime and Justice Studies. London: Institute for the Study and Treatment of Delinquency.

Parker, Howard, Lisa Williams and Judith Aldridge. 2002. 'The Normalization of "Sensible" Recreational Drug Use: Further Evidence from the North West England Longitudinal Study'. *Sociology* 36(4): 941–64.

Parker, Howard J., Judith Aldridge and Fiona Measham. 1998. *Illegal Leisure: The Normalization of Adolescent Recreational Drug Use*. London: Routledge.

Parker, Richard, and Peter Aggleton. 2003. 'HIV and AIDS-Related Stigma and Discrimination: A Conceptual Framework and Implications for Action'. *Social Science & Medicine* 57(1): 13–24.

Peach, Ceri. 2009. 'Slippery Segregation: Discovering or Manufacturing Ghettos?' *Journal of Ethnic and Migration Studies* 35(9): 1381–95.

Peck, Jamie. 2005. 'Struggling with the Creative Class'. *International Journal of Urban and Regional Research* 29(4): 740–70.

Peck, Jamie. 2010. *Constructions of Neoliberal Reason*. Oxford: Oxford University Press. http://trove.nla.gov.au/version/50991146.

Pennay, A., Elizabeth Manton and Michael Savic. 2014. 'Geographies of Exclusion: Street Drinking, Gentrification and Contests over Public Space'. *International Journal of Alcohol Policy* 25(6): 1084–93.

Pennay, Amy, and Robin Room. 2012. 'Prohibiting Public Drinking in Urban Public Spaces: A Review of the Evidence'. *Drugs: Education, Prevention and Policy* 19(2): 91–101.

Perez-Fragero, Andrés B. 2008. 'Case Study: *Botellón* in Spain'. In *Swimming with Crocodiles: The Culture of Extreme Drinking*, edited by Marjana Martinic and Fiona Measham, 183–218. New York: Routledge.

Perlman, Janice. 1976. *The Myth of Marginality: Urban Poverty and Politics in Rio de Janeiro*. Berkeley and Los Angeles: University of California Press.

Phillips, Walter. 1980. ' "Six O'Clock Swill": The Introduction of Early Closing of Hotel Bars in Australia'. *Historical Studies* 19(75): 250–66.

Pinheiro, Augusto, and Vicente Del Rio. 1993. 'Cultural Corridor: A Preservation District in Downtown Rio de Janeiro, Brazil'. *Traditional Dwellings and Settlements Review* 4(2): 51–64.

Pinkster, Fenne, and Willem R. Boterman. 2017. 'When the Spell Is Broken: Gentrification, Urban Tourism and Privileged Discontent in the Amsterdam Canal District'. *Cultural Geographies* 24(3): 457–72.

Pitcher, Jane, Rosie Campbell, Phil Hubbard, Maggie O'Neill and Jane Scoular. 2006. *Living and Working in Areas of Street Sex Work*. London: Joseph Rowntree Foundation.

Pitnam, Juliet. 2013. 'Maboneng Precinct: Jonathan Liebman. An Entrepreneurial Spirit Revitalises Downtown Joburg'. *Entrepreneur* (magazine). 27 March 2013.

Plateforme Nationale de la Vie Nocturne. 2017. 'Conférence Nationale de la Vie Nocturne'. http://pnvn.org/wp-content/uploads/2017/09/PlaquetteCNVN.pdf.

Portman Group. 2015. *Code of Practice on the Naming, Packaging and Promotion of Alcoholic Drinks*. London: Portman Group. http://www.portmangroup.org.uk/codes/alcohol-marketing/code-of-practice/code-of-practice.

Postman, Neil. 1985. *Amusing Ourselves to Death: Public Discourse in the Age of Show Business*. New York: Penguin Press.

Prichard Craig, Boon Bronwyn, Bill Amanda and Jones Deborah. 2006. 'Creativity and Class'. *Ephemera* 6(4): 517–25.

Prince, Russell. 2012. 'Metaphors of Policy Mobility: Fluid Spaces of "Creativity" Policy'. *Geografiska Annaler: Series B, Human Geography* 94(4): 317–31.

Prince, Russell. 2016. 'Neoliberalism Everywhere: Mobile Neoliberal Policy'. In *The Handbook of Neoliberalism*, edited by Simon Springer, Kean Birch and Julie MacLeavy, 397–406. New York: Routledge.

Pubs of Manchester. 2012. *Pubs of Manchester: Past and Present*. http://pubs-of-manchester.blogspot.co.uk/2012/11/wythenshawe.html.

Puhalo, Srđan. 2009. *Etnička distanca i (auto)stereotipi građana Bosne i Hercegovine*. Sarajevo: Friedrich Ebert Stiftung.

Punter, John. 2005. 'Urban Design in Central Sydney 1945–2002: Laissez-Faire and Discretionary Traditions in the Accidental City'. *Progress in Planning* 63(1): 11–160.

Quilter, Julia. 2016. 'Callinan Review Largely Backs Sydney Lockout Laws, but Alcohol's Role in Family Violence Is a Blind Spot'. *The Conversation*. 16 September 2016. https://theconversation.com/callinan-review-largely-backs-sydney-lockout-laws-but-alcohols-role-in-family-violence-is-a-blind-spot-65404.

Race, Kane. 2008. 'The Use of Pleasure in Harm Reduction: Perspectives from the History of Sexuality'. *International Journal of Drug Policy* 19(5): 417–23.

Race, Kane. 2016. 'The Sexuality of the Night: Violence and Transformation'. *Current Issues in Criminal Justice* 28(1): 105–10.

Ramet, Pedro. 1988. 'The Rock Scene in Yugoslavia'. *East European Politics & Societies* 2(2): 396–410.

Ramet, Sabrina P. 2003. 'Shake, Rattle and Self-Management: Rock Music and Politics in Socialist Yugoslavia, and After'. In *Kazaaam! Splat! Ploof!: The American Impact on European Popular Culture since 1945*, edited by Sabrina P. Ramet and Gordana Crnkovic, 173–97. London: Rowman & Littleflied Publishers.

Rancière, Jacques. 2006 (2004). 'Problems and Transformations in Critical Art'. In *Participation*, edited by Claire Bishop, 83–93. London and Cambridge, MA: MIT Press.

Ravetz, Alison. 1983. *Remaking Cities*. London: Croom Helm.

Razi, Hashem. 1992. *Gaah Shomari va Jashnhay-e Iran, Bastan*. Tehran: Behjat.

Reckwitz, Andreas. 2012. 'Affective Spaces: A Praxeological Outlook'. *Rethinking History: The Journal of Theory and Practice* 16(2): 241–58.

Reclaim the Streets. 2016a. 'Keep Newtown Weird and Safe'. Facebook Event. 23 April 2016. https://www.facebook.com/events/228027434229609/.

Reclaim the Streets. 2016b. 'About: Story'. Facebook page. https://www.facebook.com/pg/RTSsydney/about.

Reclaim the Streets. 2016c. Facebook Post. 4 April. https://www.facebook.com/RTSsydney.

Reclaim the Streets. 2016d. 'Reclaim the Streets'. Facebook Event. 19 March 2016. https://www.facebook.com/events/237327156602371/.

Rekenkamer Amsterdam. 2011. *Onderzoeksrapport Coalitieproject 1012. Grip op ambitie?* Amsterdam: Rekenkamer Amsterdam.

Rezvani, Alireza. 2005. *Mashhad Dar Jostejooye Hoviat-e Shahri*. Mashhad: Housing and Urban Planning Ministry.

Rezvani, Alireza. 2010. Olgooyabi Fazayi-Kalbodi-e Eghamat-e Aghshar-e Kamdaramad, Baft-e Piramoon-e Haram Motahar. Mashhad: Vezarat-e Maskan va Shahrsazi.

Rhodes, Tim, and Dagmar Hedrich. 2010. 'Harm Reduction and the Mainstream'. In *EMCDDA MONOGRAPHS – Harm Reduction: Evidence, Impacts and Challenges*, edited by Tim Rhodes and Dagmar Hedrich, 19–36. Luxembourg: Publications Office of the European Union.

Ribeiro, Luiz, and Luciana Lago. 1995. 'Restructuring in Large Brazilian Cities: The Centre/Periphery Model'. *International Journal of Urban and Regional Research* 19(3): 369–82.

Riley, Sarah, Christine Griffin and Yvette Morey. 2012. 'The Rise of the "Pleasure Citizen": How Leisure Can Be a Site for Alternative Forms of Political Participation'. In *Democracy in Transition: Political Participation in the European Union*, edited by Kyriakos N. Demetriou, 61–76. Berlin: Springer.

Riley, Sarah, Yvette Morey and Christine Griffin. 2010. 'The "Pleasure Citizen": Analyzing Partying as a Form of Social and Political Participation'. *Young: Nordic Journal of Youth Research* 18(1): 33–54.

Roberts, Marion. 2004. *Good Practice in Managing the Evening and Late Night Economy: A Literature Review from an Environmental Perspective*. London: Central Cities Institute, University of Westminster and the Office of the Deputy Prime Minister.

Roberts, Marion. 2006. 'From "Creative City" to "No-Go Areas": The Expansion of the Night-Time Economy in British Town and City Centres'. *Cities* 23(5): 331–38.

Roberts, Marion. 2014. 'A Helping Hand? The Contribution of the Night-Time Economy to the Evolving High Street'. In *Evolving High Streets: Resilience and Reinvention - Perspectives from Social Science*, edited by Neil Wrigley and Erin Brookes, 25–29. Southampton: ESRC/University of Southampton.

Roberts, Marion. 2016. 'What a "Night Czar" Can Do to Help Nightlife Survive'. *The Conversation*. 19 October. https://theconversation.com/what-a-night-czar-can-do-to-help-nightlife-survive-67253.

Roberts, Marion, and Adam Eldridge. 2009. *Planning the Night-Time City*. London: Routledge.

Roberts, Marion, Tim Townshend, Ilaria Pappalepore, Adam Eldridge and Mulyawan Budhi. 2012. *Local Variations in Youth Drinking Culture*. York: Joseph Rowntree Foundation.

Roberts, Marion, and Chris Turner. 2005. 'Conflicts of Liveability in the 24-Hour City: Learning from 48 Hours in the Life of London's Soho'. *Journal of Urban Design* 10(2): 171–93.

Robertson, James. 2016. 'Poll Shows Voters Favour Extending Lockout Laws'. *Sydney Morning Herald*. 29 August. http://www.smh.com.au/nsw/majority-back-broader-lockout-laws-across-the-state-20160828-gr31t9.html.

Rodrigues, Walter. 2010. *Cidade em Transição. Nobilitação Urbana, Estilos de Vida e Reurbanização em Lisboa*. Oeiras: Celta Editora.

Rodríguez, Xosé A., Fidel Martínez-Roget and Ewa Pawlowska. 2012. 'Academic Tourism Demand in Galicia, Spain'. *Tourism Management* 33(6): 1583–90.

Roe, Gordon. 2005. 'Harm Reduction as Paradigm: Is Better Than Bad Good Enough? The Origins of Harm Reduction'. *Critical Public Health* 15(3): 243–50.

Rogers, Anne, Peter Huxley, Sherrill Evans and Claire Gately. 2008. 'More Than Jobs and Houses: Mental Health, Quality of Life and the Perceptions of Locality in an Area Undergoing Urban Regeneration'. *Social Psychiatry and Psychiatric Epidemiology* 43: 364–72.

Rokni, Mohamad Mahdi. 2007. *Shogh-e Didar, Mabahesi Piramoon-e Ziarat*. Mashhad: Astan-Quds-Razavi.

Room, Robin. 1988. 'The Dialectic of Drinking in Australian Life: From the Rum Corps to the Wine Column'. *Australian Drug and Alcohol Review* 7(4): 413–37.

Rose, Damaris. 1984. 'Rethinking Gentrification: Beyond the Uneven Development of Marxist Urban Theory'. *Environment and Planning D: Society and Space* 2(1): 47–74.

Ross, Becki L. 2010. 'Sex and (Evacuation from) the City: The Moral and Legal Regulation of Sex-Workers in Vancouver's West End, 1975–1985'. *Sexualities* 13(2): 197–218.

Rovira, Josep, and Eduardo Hidalgo. 2003. 'Gestión del placer y del riesgo o como enseñar a disfrutar la noche y no morir en el intento'. *VIII Jornadas sobre*

Prevención. de Drogodependencias. https://pt.scribd.com/document/44671396/ Gestion-de-placeres-y-riesgos-en-el-uso-de-drogas.

Rowe, David, and Nathaniel Bavinton. 2011. 'Tender for the Night: After-Dark Cultural Complexities in the Night-Time Economy'. *Continuum: Journal of Media & Cultural Studies* 25: 811–25.

Rowe, David, and Rob Lynch. 2012. 'Work and Play in the City: Some Reflections on the Night-Time Leisure Economy of Sydney'. *Annals of Leisure Research* 15(2): 132–47.

RTPI. 2007. *Gender and Spatial Planning: Good Practice Note 7.* London: Royal Town Planning Institute.

Ruiter, Robert A. C., Loes T. E. Kessels, Gjalt-Jorn Y. Peters and Gerjo Kok. 2014. 'Sixty Years of Fear Appeal Research: Current State of the Evidence'. *International Journal of Psychology* 49(2): 63–70.

Russell, Andrew, Sue Lewis, Mathilde Matthijsse and K. Masson. 2011. *'Revealing Alcohol Narratives': A Qualitative Study of Young People's Relationships with Alcohol: In County Durham & Darlington.* London: Public Health England.

Ryder, Andrew. 2004. 'The Changing Nature of Adult Entertainment Districts: Between a Rock and a Hard Place or Going from Strength to Strength'. *Urban Studies* 41(9): 1659–86.

Safi, Michael. 2015. 'Stop the Bets! Morrison's Focus on Offshore Betting Won't Help Problem Gamblers'. *Guardian.* 7 September. https://www.theguardian.com/commentisfree/2015/sep/07/stop-the-bets-morrisons-focus-on-offshore-betting-wont-help-problem-gamblers.

Sage, Joanna, Darren Smith and Phil Hubbard. 2012. 'The Rapidity of Studentification and Population Change: There Goes the Studenthood'. *Population, Space and Place* 18(5): 597–613.

SAHWA 2016. 'Youth Survey 2016 Descriptive Report'. Barcelona Center for International Affairs. http://sahwa.eu/Media/Sahwa/Youth-Survey.

Sánchez de Madariaga, Inés, and Marion Roberts. Eds. 2013. *Fair Shared Cities: The Impact of Gender Planning in Europe.* Abingdon: Ashgate.

Sánchez García, José. 2010. 'De las celebraciones para los santos a la Mulid Music Dance: utopia, identidad y juventud en espacios comunitarios en Egipto'. *Revista Trans de Etnomusicología. Revista Transcultural de Música* 14: 1697-0101. http://www.redalyc.org/html/822/82220947018/.

Sánchez García, José, and Carles Feixa. 2016. *Musicians, Artists and Players: Leisure Education as a Source for Job Opportunities in Arab Mediterranean Countries.* Barcelona: SAHWA Policy Reports Series. doi.org/10.24241/swpr.2017.4.1.

Sánchez, Iñigo. 2017. 'Mapping Out the Sounds of Urban Transformation: The Renewal of Lisbon's Mouraria Quartier'. *Toward an Anthropology of Ambient Sound.* Nova Iorque: Routledge.

Sanders-McDonagh, Erin, Magali Peyrefitte and Matt Ryalls. 2016. 'Sanitising the City: Exploring Hegemonic Gentrification in London's Soho'. *Sociological Research Online* 21(3): 1–6.

Sazman-Mojri-Tarh. 2010. *Dovomin Neshast Takhasosi Sazman Mojri.* Mashhad: Shahrdari Mashhad.

Schatz, Laura, and Dallas Rogers. 2016. 'Participatory, Technocratic and Neoliberal Planning: An Untenable Planning Governance Ménage À Trois'. *Australian Planner* 53(1): 37–45.

Schielke, Samuli. 2003. 'Habitus of the Authentic, Order of the Rational: Contesting Saints' Festivals in Contemporary Egypt'. *Middle East Critique* 12(2): 155–72.

Schielke, Samuli. 2006. 'Snacks and Saints: Mawlid Festivals and the Politics of Festivity, Piety and Modernity in Contemporary Egypt'. PhD Thesis, University of Amsterdam, Faculty of Social and Behavioural Sciences, PDF document.

Schielke, Samuli. 2015. *Egypt in the Future Tense: Hope, Frustration, and Ambivalence before and after 2011 (Public Cultures of the Middle East and North Africa)*. Indianapolis: Indiana University Press.

Schivelbusch, Wolfgang. 1988. *Disenchanted Night: The Industrialisation of Light in the Nineteenth Century*. Oxford: Berg.

Schlör, Joachim. 1998. *Nights in the Big City, Paris. Berlin. London 1840–1930*. London: Reaktion.

Schnepel, Burkhard. 2006. 'Strangers in the Night: The Making and Unmaking of Differences from the Perspective of an Anthropology of the Night'. In *The Making and Unmaking of Differences: Anthropological, Sociological and Philosophical Perspectives*, edited by Richard Rottenburg, Burkhard Schnepel and Shingo Shimada, 123–44. New Brunswick, NJ: Transaction Publishers.

Schwanen, Tim, Irina van Aalst, Jelle Brands and Tjerk Timan. 2012. 'Rhythms of the Night: Spatiotemporal Inequalities in the Nighttime Economy'. *Environment and Planning A* 44(9): 2064–85.

Scott, Allen J. 2006. 'Creative Cities: Conceptual Issues and Policy Questions'. *Journal of Urban Affairs* 28(1): 1–17.

Scott, Allen John. 2014. 'Beyond the Creative City: Cognitive – Cultural Capitalism and the New Urbanism'. *Regional Studies* 48(4): 565–78.

Scott, James C. 1998. *Seeing Like a State: How Certain Schemes to Improve the Human Condition Have Failed*. New Haven, CT: Yale University Press.

Scott, Susie. 2009. *Making Sense of Everyday Life*. Cambridge: Polity Press.

Scraton, Sheila, and Beccy Watson. 1998. 'Gendered Cities: Women and Public Leisure Space in the "Postmodern City"'. *Leisure Studies* 17(2): 123–37.

Seekings, Jeremy. 2008. 'The Continuing Salience of Race: Discrimination and Diversity in South Africa'. *Journal of Contemporary African Studies* 26(1): 1–25.

Seekings, Jeremy, and Nicoli Nattrass. 2008. *Class, Race, and Inequality in South Africa*. New Haven, CT: Yale University Press.

Sellars, Alethea. 1998. 'The Influence of Dance Music on the UK Youth Tourism Market'. *Tourism Management* 19(6): 611–15.

Sennett, Richard. 1974. *The Fall of Public Man*. London: Faber.

Sevilla-Buitrago, Álvaro. 2012. Debating Contemporary Urban Conflicts: A Survey of Selected Scholars. *Cities* 31: 454–68.

Shakourzadeh, Ebrahim. 1984. *Aqayed va Rosoom-e Mardom-e Khorasan*. Tehran: Soroosh.

Sharafi, Ali. 2006. *Sanjeshe-e Entezarat-e Zaeran-e Noroozi, Dar Rabeteh ba Khadamat-e Shahri va Mizan-e Rezayatmandi-e Anha az Amalkard-e Shahrdari-e Mashhad*. Mashhad: Shardari Mashhad.

Sharma, Sara. 2014. 'Because the Night Belongs to Lovers: Occupying the Time of Precarity'. *Communication and Critical/Cultural Studies* 11(1): 5–14.

Shaw, Robert. 2010. 'Neoliberal Subjectivities and the Development of the Night-Time Economy in British Cities'. *Geography Compass* 4(7): 893–903.

Shaw, Robert. 2014. 'Beyond Night-Time Economy: Affective Atmospheres of the Urban Night'. *Geoforum* 51(1): 87–95.

Shaw, Robert. 2015a. 'Controlling Darkness: Self, Dark and the Domestic Night'. *Cultural Geographies* 22(4): 585–600.

Shaw, Robert. 2015b. 'Night as Fragmenting Frontier: Understanding the Night That Remains in an Era of 24/7'. *Geography Compass* 9(12): 637–47.

Sheard, Laura. 2011. ' "Anything Could Have Happened": Women, the Night-Time Economy, Alcohol and Drink Spiking'. *Sociology* 45(4): 639–53.

Sherkat-e-Omran-va-Behsazi-e-Shahri. 1999. *Tarh-e Nosazi va Bazsazi dar Markaz-e Shahr-e Mashhad*. Mashhad: Shahrdari Mashhad.

Shirlow Peter, and Rachel Pain. 2003. 'The Geographies and Politics of Fear'. *Capital & Class* 27(2): 15–26.

Simic, Andrei. 1973. *The Peasent Urbanities: A Study of Rural-Urban Mobility in Serbia*. London: Seminar Press.

Simpson, Ludi. 2007. 'Ghettos of the Mind: The Empirical Behaviour of Indices of Segregation and Diversity'. *Statistics in Society Series A* 170(2): 405–24.

Skeggs, Beverly. 1999. 'Matter Out of Place: Visibility and Sexualities in Leisure Spaces'. *Leisure Studies* 18(3): 213–32.

Skeggs, Beverly, and Vik Loveday. 2012. 'Struggles for Value: Value Practices, Injustice, Judgment, Affect and the Idea of Class'. *The British Journal of Sociology* 63(3): 472–90.

Slater, Tom. 2006. 'The Eviction of Critical Perspectives from Gentrification Research'. *International Journal of Urban and Regional Research* 30(4): 737–57.

Slater Tom, and Ntsiki Anderson. 2012. 'The Reputational Ghetto: Territorial Stigmatization in St Paul's, Bristol'. *Transactions of the Institute of British Geographers* 37(4): 1–17.

Slobodna Bosna. 2012. 'Alternativna historija Sarajeva se pisala u kafićima'. 4 September. https://www.slobodna-bosna.ba/vijest/2220/alternativna_historija_sarajeva_se_pisala_u_kaficima.html.

Smith, Darren P. 2005. 'Studentification: The Gentrification Factory?' In *Gentrification in a Global Context: The New Urban Colonialism*, edited by Rowman Atkinson and Gary Bridge, 72–89. London: Routledge.

Smith, Darren P. 2008. 'The Politics of Studentification and (Un)balanced Urban Populations: Lessons for Gentrification and Sustainable Communities?'. *Urban Studies* 45(12): 2541–64.

Smith, Darren P. 2009. ' "Student Geographies", Urban Restructuring, and the Expansion of Higher Education'. *Environment and Planning A* 41(8): 1795–804.

Smith, Darren P., and Louise Holt. 2007. 'Studentification and "Apprentice" Gentrifiers within Britain's Provincial Towns and Cities: Extending the Meaning of Gentrification'. *Environment and Planning A* 39(1): 142–61.

Smith, Neil. 1996. *The New Urban Frontier. Gentrification and the Revanchist City*. New York: Routledge.

Smith, Neil. 2002. 'New Globalism, New Urbanism: Gentrification as Global Urban Strategy'. *Antipode* 34(3): 427–50.

Smith, Oliver. 2014. *Contemporary Adulthood and the Night-Time Leisure Economy*. Basingstoke: Palgrave Macmillan.

Smith, Valene L. 1989. *Hosts and Guests: The Anthropology of Tourism*. Philadelphia: University of Pennsylvania Press.

Smith, Zoe, Karenza Moore and Fiona Measham. 2009. 'MDMA Powder, Pills and Crystal: The Persistence of Ecstasy and the Poverty of Policy'. *Drugs and Alcohol Today* 9(1): 13–19.

Sorkin, Michael. 1992. *Variations on a Themepark: The New American City and the End of Public Space*. New York: Hill and Wang.

Soussan, Christophe, and Anette Kjellgren. 2016. 'The Users of Novel Psychoactive Substances: Online Survey about Their Characteristics, Attitudes and Motivations'. *International Journal of Drug Policy* 32: 77–84.

Southwell, Mat. 2010. 'People Who Use Drugs and Their Role in Harm Reduction'. In *EMCDDA MONOGRAPHS – Harm Reduction: Evidence, Impacts and Challenges*, edited by Tim Rhodes and Dagmar Hedrich, 101–3. Luxembourg: Publications Office of the European Union.

Souto-Otero, Manuel. 2008. 'The Socio-economic Background of Erasmus Students: A Trend towards Wider Inclusion?' *International Review of Education* 54(2): 135–54.

Springer, Simon. 2016. *The Discourse of Neoliberalism: An Anatomy of a Powerful Idea*. London: Rowman & Littlefield International.

Springer, Simon, Kean Birch and Julie MacLeavy. 2016. *The Handbook of Neoliberalism*. New York: Routledge.

Staehell, Lynn, and Don Mitchell. 2016. *The People's Property? Power, Politics, and the Public*. New York: Routledge.

Start Magazin. 2016. 'Nedim Nedo Kapetanović, stari šmeker i osnivač kafića Evergreen'. 2 October. http://www.startbih.info/Aktuelnost.aspx?id=83302.

Stefansson, Anders. 2007. 'Urban Exile: Locals, Newcomers and the Cultural Transformation of Sarajevo'. In *The New Bosnian Mosaic: Identities, Memories and Moral Claims in a Post-War Society*, edited by Xavier Bougarel, Elissa Helms and Ger Duijzings, 59–77. Aldershot: Ashgate.

Straw, Will. 2015a. 'Night as Fragmenting Frontier: Understanding the Night That Remains in an Era of 24/7'. *Geography Compass* 9(12): 637–47.

Straw, Will. 2015b. 'The Urban Night'. In *Cartographies of Place: Navigating the Urban*, edited by Michael Darroch and Janine Marchessault, 185–200. Montreal, Quebec: McGill-Queens University Press.

Straw, Will. 2017. 'Penser la Nuit Urbaine' (Preface). In *La Nuit: Dernière frontière de la ville* (new edition), edited by Luc Gwiazdzinski, 7–10. Paris: Rhuthmos.

Sturma, Michael. 1983. *Vice in a Vicious Society: Crime and Convicts in Mid-nineteenth-century New South Wales*. St. Lucia: University of Queensland Press.

Su-Jan, Yeo, and Chye Kiang Heng. 2013. 'An (Extra)ordinary Night Out: Urban Informality, Social Sustainability and the Night-Time Economy'. *Urban Studies* 51(4): 712–26.

Su-Jan, Yeo, Hee Limin and Chye Kiang Heng. 2012. 'Urban Informality and Everyday (Night)life: A Field Study in Singapore'. *International Development Planning Review* 34: 369–90.

Sumartojo, Shanti. 2015. 'On Atmosphere and Darkness at Australia's Anzac Day Dawn Service'. *Visual Communication* 14(3): 267–88.

Sutton, Liz. 2009. ' "They'd Only Call You a Scally If You Are Poor": The Impact of Socio-economic Status on Children's Identities'. *Children's Geographies* 7(3): 277–90.

Tabnak. 2012. 'Elaam Saat Kari Edaraat dar Mah Ramazan'. http://www.tabnak.ir/fa/news/258940/.

Talbot, Deborah. 2004. 'Regulation and Racial Differentiation in the Construction of Night-Time Economies: A London Case Study'. *Urban Studies* 41(4): 887–901.

Talbot, Deborah. 2006. 'The Licensing Act 2003 and the Problematization of the Night-Time Economy: Planning, Licensing and Subcultural Closure in the UK'. *International Journal of Urban and Regional Research* 30(1): 159–71.

Talbot, Deborah. 2007. *Regulating the Night: Race, Culture and Exclusion in the Making of the Night-Time Economy*. New York: Ashgate.

Talen, Emily. 2006. 'Design for Diversity: Evaluating the Context of Socially Mixed Neighbourhoods'. *Journal of Urban Design* 11: 1–32.

Talen, Emily. 2008a. *Design for Diversity: Exploring Socially Mixed Neighborhoods*. Oxford: Architectural Press.

Talen, Emily. 2008b. 'The Unbearable Lightness of New Urbanism'. In *New Urbanism and Beyond: Designing Cities for the Future*, edited by Tigran Haas, 77–79. New York: Rizzoli International.

Talen, Emily. 2009. 'Bad Parenting'. In *Urban Design*, edited by Alex Krieger and William S. Saunders, 183–85. Minneapolis: University of Minnesota Press.

Tammi, Tuukka, and Toivo Hurme. 2007. 'How the Harm Reduction Movement Contrasts Itself against Punitive Prohibition'. *International Journal of Drug Policy* 18(2): 84–87.

Tarbatt, Jonathan. 2012. *The Plot: Designing Diversity in the Built Environment. A Manual for Architects and Urban Designers*. London: RIBA.

Tash-Consultant-Engineers. 2008. *Tarh-e Nosazi va Behsazi-e baft-e Piramoon-e Haram-e Motahar-e Hazrat-e Reza*. 3rd ed. Mashhad: Shahrdari Mashhad.

Taylor, Yvette, and Emily Falconer. 2015. ' "Seedy Bars and Grotty Pints": Close Encounters in Queer Leisure Spaces'. *Social & Cultural Geography* 16(1): 43–57.

Terhorst, Pieter, Jacques van de Ven and Leon Deben. 2003. 'It's All in the Mix'. In *Cities and Visitors: Regulating People, Markets and City Space*, edited by Lily M. Hoffman, Susan Fainstein and Denis R. Judd, 75–90. London: Wiley-Blackwell.

TfL. 2006. *Safer Travel at Night (STaN)*. London: Transport for London.

Thomas, Colin, J., and Rosemary D. F. Bromley. 2000. 'City-Centre Revitalisation: Problems of Fragmentation and Fear in the Night-Time City'. *Urban Studies* 37(8) 1403–29.

Thornton, Sarah. 1996. *Club Cultures: Music, Media, and Subcultural Capital*. Cambridge, UK: Polity Press and Blackwell Publishers.

Thornton, Sarah. 1997. 'The Social Logic of Subcultural Capital'. In *The Subcultures Reader*, edited by Ken Gelder, 184–92. Oxon: Routledge.

Tierney, John. 2006. ' "We Want to Be More European": The 2003 Licensing Act and Britain's Night-Time Economy'. *Social Policy and Society* 5(4): 453–60.

Tiesdell, Steve, and Anne-Michelle Slater. 2006. 'Calling Time: Managing Activities in Space and Time in the Evening/Night Time Economy'. *Planning Theory and Practice* 7: 137–57.

Tomsen, Stephen. 2014. 'Identity Wars. Crime, Safety and Conflict in Sydney's Night-Time Economy'. *Etnografia e ricerca qualitativa* 3: 463–80.

Townshend, Tim G. 2013. 'Youth, Alcohol and Place-Based Leisure Behaviours: A Study of Two Locations in England'. *Social Science & Medicine* 91: 153–61.

Townshend, Tim G., and Marion Roberts. 2013. 'Affordances, Young People, Parks and Alcohol Consumption'. *Journal of Urban Design* 18(4): 494–516.

Tsantaki, Sandy. 2012. 'Only a Bomb Can Save This City'. *Kathimerini*. 2 February. http://www.kathimerini.gr/450961/article/politismos/arxeio-politismoy/mono-vomva-swzei-ayth-thn-polh.

Tse, Justin K. H., and Johanna L. Waters. 2013. 'Transnational Youth Transitions: Becoming Adults between Vancouver and Hong Kong'. *Global Networks* 13: 535–50.

Tulumello, Simone. 2016. 'Reconsidering Neoliberal Urban Planning in Times of Crisis: Urban Regeneration Policy in a "Dense" Space in Lisbon'. *Urban Geography* 37(1): 117–140.

Turner, Frederick Jackson. 1921. 'The Significance of the Frontier in American History'. In *The Frontier in American History*, 1–38. New York: Henry Holt & Co.

Tutenges, Sébastien. 2015. 'Pub Crawls at a Bulgarian Nightlife Resort: A Case Study Using Crowd Theory'. *Tourist Studies* 15(3): 283–99.

Tyler, Imogen. 2008. 'Chav Mum Chav Scum'. *Feminist Media Studies* 8(1): 17–34.

Uitermark, Justus, Jan Willem Duyvendak and Reinout Kleinhans. 2007. 'Gentrification as a Governmental Strategy. Social Control and Social Cohesion in Hoogvliet, Rotterdam'. *Environment and Planning A* 39(1): 125–41.

Upton, Suzanne. 2016. 'Tilly Devine & the Razor Gang Wars, 1927–31'. https://gallery.records.nsw.gov.au/index.php/galleries/people-of-interest/tilly-devine-the-razor-gang-wars-1927-31.

Vaiou, Dina. 2007. *Intersecting Everyday Lives and Space-Time Transformations in the City: Migrant and Local Women in the Neighbourhoods of Athens. PYTHAGORAS II Final Report*. Athens: National Technical University of Athens.

Vale Pires, Cristiana, Marta Borges and Helena Valente. 2015. 'Netreach Work in Europe: Responses to Developments on the Dark Web and the Use of New Psychoactive Substances'. In *Between Street and Screen. Traditions and Innovations in the Drugs Field*, edited by Marije Wouters and Jane Fountain. Lengerich: Pabst Publishers.

Vale Pires, Cristiana, Fernando Caudevilla Gálligo and Helena Valente. 2016. 'Netreach Work: Implementing Web-Based Harm Reduction Interventions with Online Drug Users'. *Adiktologie* 2(16): 182–87.

Valentine, Gill, and Katherine Harris. 2014. 'Strivers vs Skivers: Class Prejudice and the Demonisation of Dependency in Everyday Life'. *Geoforum* 53: 84–92.

Valentine, Gill, Sarah Holloway, Charlotte Knell and Mark Jayne. 2008. 'Drinking Places: Young People and Cultures of Alcohol Consumption in Rural Environments'. *Journal of Rural Studies* 21(4): 28–40.

Valentine, Gill, Tracey Skelton and Deborah Chambers. 1998. 'Cool Places: An Introduction to Youth and Youth Cultures'. In *COOL PLACES: Geographies of Youth Cultures*, edited by Gill Valentine and Tracey Skelton, 1–32. London: Routledge.

Van den Nouwelant, Ryan. 2017. 'Place, Identity and Community Conflict in Mixed-Use Neighbourhoods: The Case of Kings Cross, Sydney'. PhD dissertation, University of New South Wales.

Van den Nouwelant, Ryan, and Christine Steinmetz. 2013. 'Concentration vs. Dispersal of a Late-Night Economy'. *Spaces and Flows: An International Journal of Urban and ExtraUrban Studies* 3(4): 31–43.

van Liempt, Ilse, and Milena Chimienti. 2017. 'The Gentrification of Progressive Red Light Districts and New Moral Geographies: The Case of Amsterdam and Zurich'. *Gender, Place and Culture* 24(11): 1569–86.

van Liempt, Ilse, and Irina van Aalst. 2012. 'Urban Surveillance and the Struggle between Safe and Exciting Nightlife Districts'. *Surveillance & Society* 9(3): 280–92.

van Liempt, Ilse, Irina van Aalst and Tim Schwanen. Eds. 2015. 'Introduction: Geographies of the Urban Night'. *Urban Studies* 52(3): 407–21.

van Mol, Chirstof, and Joris Michielsen. 2015. 'The Reconstruction of a Social Network Abroad. An Analysis of the Interaction Patterns of Erasmus Students'. *Mobilities* 10(3): 423–44.

van't Klooster, Erik, Jeroen van Wijk, Frank Go and Johan van Rekom. 2008. 'Educational Travel: The Overseas Internship'. *Annals of Tourism Research* 35(3): 690–711.

Varna, George, and Steve Tiesdell. 2010. 'Assessing the Publicness of Public Space: The Star Model of Publicness'. *Journal of Urban Design* 15: 575–98.

Vassal, Serge. 1969. 'Les Nouveaux Ensembles Universitaires Français. Eléments de Géographie Urbaine'. *Annales de Géographie* 78: 131–57.

Vezarat-Maskan-va-Shahrsazi. 1971. *Shakhes hay-e Tosey-e Shahri, Tehran: Vezarat-e Maskan va Shahrsazi*. Mashhad: Vezarat-e Maskan va Shahrsazi.

Vezarat-Maskan-va-Shahrsazi. 1992. *Tarh-e Nosazi va Omran Harim-e Haram-e Motahar-e Imam Reza*. Mashhad: Vezarat-e Maskan va Shahrsazi.

Visser, Gustav, and Nico Kotze. 2008. 'The State and New-Build Gentrification in Central Cape Town, South Africa'. *Urban Studies* 45(12): 2565–93.

Volčič, Zala, and Karmen Erjavec. 2010. 'The Paradox of Ceca and the Turbo-Folk Audience'. *Popular Communication: The International Journal of Media and Culture* 8(2): 103–19.

Volle, Jean-Paul, Laurent Viala, Emmanuel Négrier and Catherine Bernié-Boissard. 2010. *Montpellier, La Ville Inventée*. Marseille: Parenthèses Editions.

Volterra & TfL. 2014. 'The Impact of the Night Tube on London's Night Time Economy'. http://content.tfl.gov.uk/night-time-economy.pdf.

Vuletic, Dean. 2011. 'The Making of a Yugoslav Popular Music Industry'. *Popular Music History* 6(3): 269–85.

Wacquant, Loic. 2007. 'Territorial Stigmatization in the Age of Advanced Marginality'. *Thesis Eleven* 91: 66–77.

Wadds, Phillip. 2013. 'Policing Nightlife: The Representation and Transformation of Security in Sydney's Night-Time Economy'. PhD dissertation, University of Western Sydney.

Wadds, Phillip. 2015. 'Crime, Policing and (In)Security: Press Depictions of Sydney's Night-Time Economy'. *Current Issues in Criminal Justice* 27(1): 95–112.

Waitt, Gordon, and Chris Gibson. 2009. 'Creative Small Cities: Rethinking the Creative Economy in Place'. *Urban Studies* 46(5&6): 1223–46.

Waitt, Gordon, Loretta Jessop and Andrew Gorman-Murray. 2011. '"The Guys in There Just Expect to Be Laid": Embodied and Gendered Sociospatial Practices of a "Night Out" in Wollongong, Australia'. *Gender Place and Culture* 18(2): 255–75.

Wang, Ning. 1999. 'Rethinking Authenticity in Tourism Experience'. *Annals of Tourism Research* 26(2): 349–70.

Waters, Johanna, and Rachel Brooks. 2011. '"Vive la Différence?": The "International" Experiences of UK Students Overseas'. *Population, Space and Place* 17(5): 567–78.

Watson, Vanessa. 2009. '"The Planned City Sweeps the Poor Away . . .": Urban Planning and 21st Century Urbanisation'. *Progress in Planning* 72: 151–93.

Weitzer, Ronald. 2014. 'The Social Ecology of Red-Light Districts: A Comparison of Antwerp and Brussels'. *Urban Affairs Review* 50(5): 702–30.

White, Rob. 1993. 'Youth and the Conflict over Urban Pace'. *Children's Environments* 10(1): 85–93.

Whyte, William H. 1980. *The Social Life of Small Urban Spaces*. New York: Project for Public Places.

Whyte, William H. 1988. *City, Rediscovering the Centre*. New York: London Doubleday.

Wilkinson, Marian, Peter Cronau and Anne Davies. 2017. 'Crown Confidential – Packer's Losing Hand'. *Four Corners,* ABC TV. 6 March.

Wilkinson, Samantha. 2016. 'Hold the Phone! Culturally Credible Research "with" Young People'. *Children's Geographies* 14(2): 232–38.

Wilkinson, Samantha. 2017. 'Drinking in the Dark: Shedding Light on Young People's Alcohol Consumption Experiences'. *Social and Cultural Geography* 18(6): 739–57.

Williams, Robert. 2008. 'Night Spaces: Darkness, Deteritorrialization, and Social Control'. *Space and Culture* 11(4): 514–32.

Willis, Paul. 1990. *Common Cultures. Symbolic Work at Play in the Everyday Cultures of the Young*. Boulder, CO: Westview Press.

Wilson, Hannah, Joanne Bryant, Martin Holt and Carla Treloar. 2010. 'Normalisation of Recreational Drug Use among Young People: Evidence about Accessibility, Use and Contact with Other Drug Users'. *Health Sociology Review* 19(2): 164–75.

Windle, Joel, and Maria Alice Nogueira. 2015. 'The Role of Internationalisation in the Schooling of Brazilian Elites: Distinctions between Two Class Fractions'. *British Journal of Sociology of Education* 36(1): 174–92.

Winkler, Tanja. 2009. 'Prolonging the Global Age of Gentrification: Johannesburg's Regeneration Policies'. *Planning Theory* 8(4): 362–81.

Winlow, Simon, and Steven Hall. 2006. *Violent Night: Urban Leisure and Contemporary Culture*. London: Bloomsbury Academic.

Bibliography

Wolifson, Peta. 2016. 'Encountering the Night with Mobile Methods'. *Geographical Review* 106(2): 174–200.

Wolifson, Peta, and Danielle Drozdzewski. 2016. 'Co-opting the Night: The Entrepreneurial Shift and Economic Imperative in NTE Planning'. *Urban Policy and Research*. 35(4): 486–504.

Young, Helen. 2011. *Manchester: Responsible Alcohol Sales Project*. London: Alcohol Learning Centre.

Young, Julian Buchanan Lee. 2000. 'The War on Drugs or a War on Drug Users?' *Drugs: Education, Prevention and Policy* 7(4): 409–22.

YPEKA. 2011. *Actions of the Ministry of Environment & Energy, Government of Greece for the Centre of Athens*. Athens: Ministry of Environment & Energy.

Yuzna, Jake. Ed. 2013. *The Fun: The Social Practice of Nightlife in NYC*. New York: Powerhouse Books.

Zgodić, Esad. 2015. 'Najamni rad i socijaldemokratija'. In *Razgovor o ljevici: Identitet, kriza i izazovi u Bosni i Hercegovini danas*, edited by Emina Abrahamsdotter and Besima Borić, 21–52. Sarajevo: Friedrich-Ebert-Stiftung (FES).

ZPUPPS. 1977. *Sarajevo – sistem gradskih centara: programski projekat*. Sarajevo: Zavod za prostorno i urbanističko planiranje i programiranje Sarajeva.

Zukin, Sharon. 1991. *Landscapes of Power: From Detroit to Disney World*. Berkeley: University of California Press.

Zukin, Sharon. 1995. *The Cultures of Cities*. Oxford: Blackwell.

Index

Aalbers, Manuel, B., 178, 180
Aalst, Irina van, 14, 177–91
alcohol, 7, 8, 37–38, 49, 51, 56, 62–63,
    87–88, 104, 107, 130, 152, 157,
    165, 166, 202, 214, 231; gender, 39,
    56, 131, 132–33, 138, 202; health
    concerns, 37, 38, 40, 45, 134, 136,
    137, 138, 201, 204, 205; public
    drinking, 114–27. *See also* licensing
alternative nightlife, 45–46, 56, 131,
    148, 152–53, 156–61, 162
Amsterdam, the Netherlands, 2, 7, 14,
    58, 129, 130, 141, 177–82, 184, 185,
    187, 188, 189, 190n4, 191n10, 225,
    228, 229, 232n3
Anglophone. *See* Eurocentricism
anti-social behaviour, 1, 4, 7, 8, 10, 50,
    115, 179, 183. *See also* violence
asylum seekers. *See* refugees
Athens, Greece, 7, 8, 12, 67–69, 71–78
atmosphere, 9, 13, 51, 61, 63, 103, 106,
    107, 113n10, 115, 118, 119, 120,
    121, 122, 123, 125, 127, 131–34,
    138, 165, 178, 184, 213
austerity, 10, 74, 142, 149, 158,
    167, 209
authenticity, 8, 9, 103, 104, 106, 157,
    236, 271

authorities, 1, 61, 76, 77, 79, 80, 90, 93,
    105, 108, 124, 134, 135, 137, 138,
    142, 162, 173, 180, 192, 195, 218
authority, 52, 135, 137–39, 141, 180,
    183, 218, 230

bachelor parties, 179, 183
Barcelona, Spain, 8, 97, 166, 167,
    170, 216
bars, 3, 4, 6, 7, 8, 9, 12, 14, 28, 36,
    40–42, 45, 55–59, 61–63, 65, 69,
    73–75, 78, 92, 97, 114–16, 118–22,
    124, 126, 130, 131, 132, 134,
    137–39, 141, 147, 151–54, 156,
    158, 164, 167, 177–80, 183, 186,
    188, 189, 200, 201, 205, 207, 210,
    213–18, 231
bars, theming of, 188, 189
Belgrade, Serbia, 5, 54
belonging, 4, 46, 51, 158, 185, 189
Berlin, Germany, 5, 97, 98
Bianchini, Franco, 5, 6, 37, 165, 209
binge drinking, 137, 138. *See also*
    drunkenness
Bosnia. *See* Sarajevo, Bosnia and
    Herzegovina
botellón, 118, 124, 155. *See also* alcohol
bouncers, 131, 138, 152, 183

Bourdieu, Pierre, 54, 62, 156, 170.
    See also distinction
branding, 3, 5, 41, 69, 72, 79, 149, 165,
    167, 178
Brazil, 14, 150, 158, 159, 207, 208, 210.
    See also Rio de Janeiro, Brazil
Brazilians, 150, 210, 212, 214
Brown, Wendy, 4, 8, 14, 70. *See also*
    neoliberalism

cafes, 28, 55, 66n2, 73, 74, 75, 78, 81,
    207, 11, 29, 36, 55, 56, 69, 88, 92,
    166, 181, 201. *See also* restaurants
Cairo, Egypt, 7, 12, 99–102, 104, 105,
    107–12
casinos, 37, 42–45, 47, 215
Chatterton, Paul, 118, 155, 162,
    168, 209
Chatterton Paul and Hollands, Robert,
    27, 38, 70, 114, 116, 131, 164, 166,
    209, 215
class, 7, 8–9, 10, 11, 12, 13, 15, 19–34,
    39, 47–50, 53, 61–66, 70–72, 85,
    97, 99–113, 115, 117, 121, 123, 125,
    127, 128n5, 150, 151
clubbing, 3, 192. *See also* nightclubs
clubs. *See* nightclubs
Comedia Consultancy, 5, 37
community liveability, 167, 179
cosmopolitanism, 3, 8, 20, 102, 104,
    105, 109, 149, 158, 160, 165–66,
    170, 200, 216–17. *See also*
    globalisation
Crary, Jonathan, 2, 3, 11, 85
creative industries, 8, 22, 24, 37–38, 41,
    42, 47, 50, 51, 70, 73, 77–79, 160,
    169–70, 179–80, 181, 185, 207,
    209–10
creativity, 5, 15, 38, 48, 49, 51, 69, 78,
    79, 141, 160, 181, 207
crime, fear of, 19, 24, 30–31, 69, 70,
    76, 95, 125, 207–8, 209, 210. *See
    also* safety
czars, night. *See* night mayors

dancing, 56, 66n4, 105, 106, 113n8,
    122, 123, 133, 138, 152, 158,
    177, 199
disability, 10, 15, 130
discotheque. *See* nightclubs
distinction, 61, 62, 63, 66, 75, 123, 148,
    156–57, 159, 160, 168, 170, 192
DJs, 100, 103, 106, 107, 109, 138,
    183, 245
Drinkscapes, 114–16, 120–26
drug checking, 197, 198, 199, 203,
    206n3
drugs, 44, 107, 177, 183, 192–206, 210,
    215. *See also* harm reduction
drug use, 11, 12, 39, 74, 76–79, 132,
    165, 177, 178, 192–206
drunkenness, 120, 124, 128n4, 131–33,
    136, 179, 201, 231. *See also* alcohol
Duff, Cameron, 118, 119

economic crisis. *See* austerity
education. *See* Studententification;
    students
Ekirch, Eric, 1, 90
Eldridge, Adam, 1–15, 37, 85, 87, 134,
    151, 163, 164, 167, 174, 209,
    226, 230
elites, 1, 15, 20, 103, 109, 150, 169,
    211, 258
employment, 2, 4, 5, 14, 47, 71, 104,
    111, 115, 151
entertainment, 3, 6, 20, 40, 42, 43, 46,
    47, 52, 55, 58, 69, 70, 75, 101, 117,
    130, 131, 134, 138, 139, 143, 167,
    171, 177–80, 207, 209, 210, 215,
    220, 225, 229
entrepreneurs, 3, 6, 14, 22, 24, 68, 75,
    77, 78, 92, 170, 178–81, 183–86,
    188, 189, 207, 213, 218
Erasmus students, 147–62, 169,
    200, 204
ethnicity, 4, 60, 73, 104, 134, 151, 166,
    168, 169, 209, 236, 237, 249, 260
Eurocentrism, 5, 31, 85–86, 98, 102

Europe, 5, 8–10, 40, 85, 141, 147, 148, 163–67, 169, 193, 195, 197, 234, 239, 242, 243, 252, 253, 258, 264, 269

European cities, 1, 65, 118, 141, 147, 150, 155, 163, 166, 167–69, 171, 172, 174, 207

evening and night-time economy, 5, 53, 136

everyday life, 19, 65, 72, 73, 86, 99, 100, 106, 112, 107, 164, 193

exclusion, 1, 2, 10, 19, 20, 33, 48, 95, 100, 101, 117, 123, 127, 131, 151, 192, 209, 226. *See also* segregation

families, 9, 30, 87, 149, 153, 174, 179

fashion, 55, 60, 104, 109, 118, 131, 157

fear, 1–3, 9, 10, 15, 19, 33, 48, 64, 68–70, 76–80, 117, 125, 136, 185, 186, 189, 196, 209. *See also* safety

female. *See* women

femininity, 131, 134, 143

feminism, 56, 131, 133, 140

festivals, 3, 54, 60, 73, 89, 90, 92, 111, 141, 194, 198

Florida, Richard, 6, 37, 38, 50, 69, 70, 78–79, 180, 181. *See also* creativity

food, 28, 31, 58–60, 74, 81, 88, 89–91, 93, 119, 134, 159, 207, 210, 217

Foucault, Michel, 36, 49, 80, 226

France, 13, 55, 164, 166, 169, 170, 172–74, 176, 197, 225, 228, 230

frontier, the night as, 11, 20, 21, 31, 33, 85, 97, 161

fun, 1, 3, 10, 54, 60, 68, 91, 107, 121, 124, 126, 132, 154, 192, 196–98, 205, 211

galleries, 12, 62, 73, 74, 75, 178, 181. *See also* creativity

gambling, 3, 36, 41, 45, 49, 50, 88, 178, 180. *See also* casinos

gay. *See* LGBTQ

gender, 1, 10, 13, 15, 28, 85, 89, 103, 107, 110, 123, 129–32, 134, 136–43, 152, 166, 194, 209

gentrification, 2, 7, 9, 11–15, 19–23, 29–33, 41, 42, 44, 47, 49–51, 69, 70, 73, 74, 79, 80, 86, 95, 97, 120, 148, 149, 156, 160, 161, 163, 166–70, 172–178, 180, 188, 200, 204, 209, 210, 220, 226–28, 231

gentrifiers, 14, 79, 80, 168, 173–76

globalisation, 13, 48, 54, 148, 205, 207, 211

global nightlife, 10, 35

governance, 3, 15, 36–39, 40, 42, 49–51, 100–102, 135, 145, 208, 225–32

Grazian, David, 132, 164

Greece, 73, 74. *See also* Athens, Greece

Gwiazdzinski, Luc, 2, 208

Hadfield, Phil, 6, 7, 13, 37, 38, 58, 70, 92, 97, 130, 135, 138

Hae, Laam, 7, 33, 37, 38, 39, 41, 47, 51, 92, 97, 153, 165, 174

harm reduction, 44, 194–98, 202, 203, 205. *See also* drugs

Harvey, David, 21, 37, 96

health risks, 192–206, 225. *See also* harm reduction

Henckel, Dietrich, 14

heteronormative, 130, 131, 141, 142, 152

heterosexuality, 13, 130–41, 132, 152, 186

Hobbs, Dick, 7, 37, 136, 138, 215

Hollands, Robert, 7, 38, 70, 114, 116, 131, 151, 164, 166, 192, 209, 215

homosexuality. *See* LGBTQ

housing, 4, 6, 21, 30, 44, 49, 50, 71, 72, 76, 115, 139, 149, 150, 153, 154, 161, 164, 171, 172, 174, 175, 178, 180, 185, 211

Hubbard, Phil, 99, 129, 134, 168, 171, 180, 184

hyper-masculinity, 64, 130, 131, 138
hypernights, 105, 107, 112n7

identity, 9, 10, 24, 39, 46, 57, 64, 75, 103, 105, 111, 112, 123, 132, 159, 162, 200
impacts, spatial, social, economic, or public health, 10, 14, 20, 35, 37, 40, 41, 45–48, 51, 55, 56, 94, 96, 136, 141, 147–49, 177, 178, 188, 193, 202, 203
Imran Reza Shrine. *See* Mashhad, Iran
inclusion, 1, 9, 10, 41, 46, 123, 127, 138, 167, 192
inclusive nightlife, 2, 9, 10, 30, 36, 53, 57, 61, 66, 124, 127, 129, 141, 143, 197, 221
informal economy, 28, 70, 72, 75, 104, 106, 110, 155, 204
innovative nightlife, 36, 63, 109, 188, 221. *See also* alternative nightlife
insecurity. *See* fear; safety
intoxication. *See* drunkenness
investors, 21, 22, 23, 26, 34n2, 71, 80, 149, 160, 162, 171, 207, 210, 212, 214, 219
Iran, 7, 12, 85–92, 94, 97
Islam, 51, 63, 71, 73, 87–91, 102, 105–6, 109, 111n1, 111n2, 112n5, 113n9

Jayne, Mark, 115, 119, 126, 166
Jeppestown, South Africa, 19, 21, 22, 24–31
Johannesburg, South Africa, 8, 11, 19, 20, 22–25, 34

Keep Sydney Open, 37, 40, 41–42, 46–48, 50
Kerameikos, 71, 75, 76, 81. *See also* Athens, Greece
Kings Cross, Sydney, 35, 39, 42–45, 50. *See also* Sydney, Australia
Koslofsky, Kraig, 1, 85, 88, 90, 164
Kreitzman, Leon, 3, 85, 86

late-night, 1, 2, 4, 8, 12, 86, 87, 89, 139, 140
Latin American cities, 215
Lees, Loretta, 30, 35, 69, 80, 96
Lefebvre, Henri, 54, 110
legislation, 44, 129, 130, 136, 137, 142, 163, 213. *See also* licensing
leisure, 1, 4–6, 8–11, 13–15, 20, 21, 30, 31, 38, 39, 41, 50, 53, 54, 56, 57, 61, 67, 69, 72, 80, 86, 88–91, 99–102, 108–11, 114, 119, 124, 147–53, 155, 157–60, 162–65, 167, 173, 203–5, 207–9, 216, 217, 220, 226, 230
leisure, right to, 9, 48, 110
LGBTQ, 4, 15, 38, 39, 44, 46, 48, 119, 129, 131, 152, 178, 215, 226
licensing, 6, 38, 40, 52n2, 70, 129, 130, 134–36, 138, 166
Liebmann, Jonathan, 21, 22, 23, 26, 34n2
Liempt, Ilse van, 1, 3, 14, 19, 33, 69, 70, 153, 165, 177–90
lifestyle(s), 13, 64, 70, 111, 155–58, 161, 162, 166, 168–71, 176
lighting, 1, 4, 13, 21, 27, 28–29, 90, 98, 113, 122, 123, 125, 127, 178, 184, 208, 211, 212, 214, 220, 227
liquor licensing. *See* licensing
liquor stores, 28, 207, 210, 214
Lisbon, Portugal, 5, 7, 8, 13, 14, 147–53, 155–59, 161, 162, 166, 167, 169, 171, 172, 193, 197, 199–204
live music, 40, 42, 46, 47, 50, 58, 228. *See also* music
lockout laws, 11, 35–37, 40, 42–48, 50, 52
London, United Kingdom, 1, 5, 58, 87, 98, 100, 129, 135, 139–41, 158, 180, 225, 229, 230
loss, of nightlife, 1–15, 37, 42, 45, 47, 48, 95, 115, 177, 180, 230–31
loss, of space, 23–24, 48
Lovatt, Andy, 5, 6, 114, 165, 209
LXNIGHTS, 201

Maboneng, 1, 19–31, 33, 34. *See also* Johannesburg, South Africa

mahragan, 12, 13, 99, 100, 102–5, 107–11

mainstream, 8, 13, 38, 57, 64, 68, 100, 103, 104, 110, 111, 131, 132, 147, 148, 151–53, 155–59, 162, 166, 188, 195

Manchester, United Kingdom, 6, 7, 13, 58, 92, 97, 114–27

Mashhad, Iran, 7, 12, 85–87, 91–94, 97, 98. *See also* Iran

media, 12, 42, 54, 68, 69, 76, 77, 79, 100, 104, 108, 110, 111, 137, 140, 152, 154, 158, 162, 183, 188, 193, 194, 199, 227–29, 231

Melbin, Murray, 11, 85, 86, 97, 98, 208

men, 12, 29, 35, 100–102, 106–8, 110, 123, 124, 131, 132, 133, 134, 136, 137, 142, 186, 202; and masculinity, 13, 39, 130–32, 134, 142, 143

Metaxourgeio, Athens, 12, 68, 69, 71–80. *See also* Athens, Greece

migration, 10, 38, 46, 60, 65, 71, 72, 74, 76, 77, 79, 158–60, 171, 177, 204, 210

Milestone, Katie, 6, 7, 92

modernity, 3, 23, 54, 103, 110, 226

Montpellier, France, 7, 8, 13, 163, 164, 169, 170, 172–75, 176n1, 176n2

Moore, Clover, 36, 40, 42, 50, 52

morality, 8, 36, 38–40, 41, 42, 44, 45, 49, 50, 63, 68, 86, 87, 102, 106, 108, 109, 111, 113, 127, 136, 166, 186, 187, 189, 226

moral panic, 8, 38, 39, 40, 42, 44, 50, 136

mulid, 99, 105–9, 110, 111

music, 12, 40, 42, 46, 47, 50, 54–60, 63, 64, 99, 100, 102–11, 112n3, 113n10, 115–18, 122, 124, 127, 134, 152, 155, 159, 165, 183, 197, 201, 214, 217, 220, 226, 228, 231, 232; as resistance, 99, 105. *See also* mahragan

Muslims. *See* Islam

neighbourhood, 9, 12, 14, 19, 21, 23, 25, 31, 34, 63, 64, 68, 71–78, 96, 99, 102, 105–8, 110, 111, 115, 121, 153, 158–66, 168–79, 181, 184, 185, 189, 200, 201, 207, 209, 216–18, 220

neighbours, 2, 28, 104, 200, 209, 216, 217

neoliberalism, 4, 8, 9, 11, 12, 31, 33, 35–38, 41, 42, 44, 47, 49–52, 60–61, 64, 67n10, 97, 100, 104, 107, 110, 130, 136–37, 143, 149, 152, 162, 195, 212, 220

Netherlands, the, 133, 178, 187

New York, United States of America, 1–3, 5, 7, 15, 92, 99, 165, 229, 231n2, 232n5

night and day, boundaries between, 24–25, 27, 28, 30, 33, 85–86, 97

nightbus. *See* transport

nightclubs, 9, 45, 55, 88, 97, 115, 118, 119–20, 130, 131, 139, 154, 192, 207, 210, 214, 215, 230, 231

night czar. *See* night mayors

nightlife, 1–8, 10–15, 17, 35–41, 44–71, 73–75, 78–80, 86–89, 91, 92, 94, 95, 97, 98, 111, 114, 116, 120, 126, 127, 129–32, 134–38, 140–42, 148–55, 159–70, 172–76, 180, 181, 183, 188, 192–94, 197, 199–201, 203–21, 227–32

nightlife, promotion of, 20, 47, 137, 138, 143, 156, 161, 210

nightlife, regulation of, 1, 5, 7, 10, 11, 14, 35, 36–51, 52n12, 58, 68, 70, 77, 86, 92, 97, 116, 130, 134, 135, 165, 192, 194, 208, 217–19, 221, 226. *See also* licensing

nightlife and displacement, 71, 73, 74, 80, 95, 118, 167, 169–71, 175

nightlife facilities, 53, 58–62, 65, 66, 79. *See also* bars; cafes; nightclubs; restaurants

nightlife venues. *See* bars; cafes; nightclubs; restaurants night mayors, 2, 5, 129, 141, 225, 227–31, 231n2

night-time, definition of, 2, 4, 8–10, 60, 229

night-time economy, history of, 165; expansion of, 1–15, 35, 40, 53, 54, 57, 225–30

night-time economy, 3, 5, 20, 35, 39, 53, 58–69, 116, 122, 129–33, 135, 136, 138, 139, 140–41, 151, 153, 161, 163–67, 170, 173–75, 207, 208, 213, 215, 218–220, 226. *See also* loss, of nightlife

Nofre, Jordi, 1–15, 44, 153, 161, 163, 166, 167, 200, 226, 231

noise, 2, 7, 8, 39, 69, 117, 118, 163, 173–74, 179, 183, 184, 185, 231

objectification, of women, 131, 133, 186, 189

Olympics, 36, 40, 57, 72, 216, 217

opening hours, 28, 39, 57, 85, 88–90, 163. *See also* twenty-four-hour

Paris, France, 2, 5, 58, 105, 141, 225, 227, 228, 230

parks, drinking in, 116–17, 124–26

parties, 12, 14, 59, 60, 64, 89–91, 100, 107, 110, 118, 148, 152–57, 160, 171, 178, 179, 192, 197–201, 204, 205, 206n4

pilgrimage: in Iran, 91–94, 98; in Egypt, 111n2

place, 4, 20, 22–24, 26–28, 31, 33, 40, 55–58, 62, 68, 76, 79, 80, 90, 98, 106, 111n2, 120, 124–27, 130, 139, 159, 178, 189, 218–21, 227, 229

place-making, 37, 38, 41, 62

planning, 10, 35–37, 39–42, 50–52, 58, 61, 65, 66, 69, 80, 93–95, 98, 129, 134, 135, 138, 139, 212, 219

pleasure. *See* fun

police, 37, 40, 44, 60, 70, 76–78, 85, 116, 130, 132, 135, 139, 142, 164, 183, 200, 208, 218, 231

policy, urban, 9, 69, 70, 135, 138, 139, 149, 152, 208, 212, 218, 226, 228

policymakers, 41, 51, 53, 58, 130, 142, 226

policy mobilities, 225–31

Porto, Portugal, 14, 150, 197, 206n2

Portugal, 148, 150, 155, 158, 162, 167, 193, 194, 197, 201, 214. *See also* Lisbon, Portugal; Porto, Portugal

post-industrialisation, 6–9, 11, 37, 39, 70, 75, 80, 97, 152, 163–65, 175, 193, 209

private space, 19, 32, 180, 215

prostitution. *See* sex work(ers)

psychoactive substances, 194, 196, 201, 203, 205, 206. *See also* alcohol; drugs

public space, 14, 29, 30, 48, 55, 58–59, 61–62, 96, 97, 116, 117, 124, 132, 181, 207, 208, 209, 211, 212–16, 218, 220, 221

public space, regulation of, 14, 31, 61, 66, 96, 118, 129, 184, 208, 211, 217–19

pubs, 39–41, 45, 58, 63, 114–17, 120, 121, 126, 130, 131, 151, 158, 214, 216

race, 4, 10, 11, 15, 20, 31, 76, 80, 85, 110, 130, 151, 166, 168, 209. *See also* ethnicity

racism, 9, 141. *See also* refugees

rave, 100, 103, 105, 108, 165, 197, 226

Reclaim the Streets, 37, 46–48. *See also* Keep Sydney Open

refugees, 10, 12, 74, 77–78

religion, 7, 10, 12, 15, 85, 89, 90, 98, 102, 103, 105, 106–10, 112–13, 166. *See also* Islam

residents, 8, 10, 12, 14, 19–31, 23, 33, 47, 71–73, 75–79, 86, 90, 91, 93–97, 133, 148, 149, 160, 163, 164, 166, 167, 170, 173, 174, 177–79, 181, 183–86, 188, 189, 200, 210, 211, 217, 220. *See also* neighbours resistance, 15, 38, 39, 51, 53, 59, 63–65, 99, 196, 210, 220. *See also* transgression

restaurants, 9, 36, 45, 55, 57, 59, 60, 61, 62, 69, 73–75, 88–90, 93, 115, 118, 164, 167, 178–81, 183, 185, 186, 207, 208, 210, 213–15, 217, 218. *See also* bars; cafes

revitalisation, 11, 53, 70, 71, 75, 95, 160, 164–66, 176, 208, 216. *See also* urban redevelopment; urban regeneration

Rio de Janeiro, Brazil, 14, 207–17, 219, 220

risk. *See* health risks

Roberts, Marion, 2, 6, 7, 8, 10, 13, 37, 85, 87, 116–17, 125, 129–43, 151, 164, 166, 167, 174, 209

Rome, Italy, 6, 8, 90

safety, 12, 28, 29, 33, 36, 37, 40, 44, 69, 71, 73, 77, 78, 95, 97, 116, 125, 129, 132, 133, 135, 136, 137, 140, 141, 143, 149, 163, 166, 187, 196, 197, 199, 205, 209, 220, 226, 231

Sarajevo, Bosnia and Herzegovina, 7, 8, 11, 53–67

Schivelbusch, Wolfgang, 4, 85

security, in nightlife settings, 21, 22, 28, 29, 33, 69, 70, 75, 79, 116, 168, 184, 225

segregation, 61, 66, 72, 148, 155, 160, 171, 209. *See also* exclusion

sexuality, 10, 112, 132, 198, 205, 209. *See also* heterosexuality; LGBTQ

sex work(ers), 12, 38, 39, 44, 52, 60, 75–77, 78, 79, 133, 134, 153, 165, 177, 178, 179, 180, 181, 183, 186, 189, 197, 210, 215, 217

Shaw, Rob, 7, 9, 11, 21, 31, 97, 120, 123, 126, 127, 152

shopping, 6, 28, 61, 85–86, 87, 88, 91, 94, 96, 104, 209

smoking, 62, 89, 117, 127

socialisation, in nightlife settings, 4, 5, 15, 59, 60, 152, 155, 192, 201

social media, 101, 154, 186, 198–99, 205

socio-spatial segregation. *See* segregation

soundscapes, 127, 200

South Africa. *See* Johannesburg, South Africa

Spain, 118, 124, 158, 167, 197

spatial displacement, 44, 46, 70, 71, 73, 74, 77, 80, 95, 118, 167, 169–71, 175. *See also* gentrification

staff, nightlife venues, 131, 132, 138, 140, 151, 154, 199, 201, 205. *See also* bouncers; workers

stakeholders, 9, 38, 39, 69, 76, 77, 79, 80, 135, 153, 164, 181, 199, 200, 201, 209, 210, 213, 219

Straw, Will, 3, 14, 53, 153, 225–32

streets. *See* public space

Studententification, 14, 155, 165, 167–76; in the United Kingdom, 171

students, 55, 87, 117, 147, 149–51, 153, 155–57, 162, 167–72, 175, 201, 214

subcultures, 13, 38, 51, 53, 54, 56, 57, 65, 66, 148, 157, 159, 162

suburbia, 13, 20, 22–24, 30, 31, 34, 46, 49, 57, 64, 71, 87, 114–27, 149, 165, 208, 211, 213, 217

surveillance, 70, 125, 127, 184. *See also* security, in nightlife settings

Sydney, Australia, 1, 5, 8, 11, 35–52

Tahrir, Cairo, Egypt, 12, 105, 108–10

Talbot, Deborah, 4, 20, 37–39, 209

tension, in urban nightscapes, 9, 39, 64, 97, 149, 161, 166, 174–76, 179, 219

time management, 54, 59–60, 86, 88, 97

Tokyo, Japan, 2, 3, 5, 15

tourism, 2, 3, 4, 6, 8, 14, 36, 39, 47, 69, 94, 96, 129, 141, 149, 152, 153, 155, 157, 167, 178, 179, 185, 186, 188, 189, 204, 214, 215, 218–20, 221, 225; and tension with residents, 94,

96, 167, 178, 183–87, 189. *See also* pilgrimage, in Iran

touristification, 149, 163, 167, 200, 204, 205

tourists, 4, 9, 47, 90, 149, 151–53, 156, 157, 161–64, 166, 169, 170, 174, 178, 179, 181, 183–89, 207, 210, 244

traditional nightlife, 15, 148, 166, 167, 207

transgression, 1, 10, 37, 38, 39, 59–60, 99, 107, 108, 132, 192, 201, 217, 220, 221. *See also* drugs; resistance

transport, 5, 44, 89, 91, 101, 129, 134, 135, 139–41, 153, 171, 172; public transport, 3, 91, 101, 129, 139–40, 141, 153, 171, 172, 208

24-hour. *See* twenty-four-hour

twenty-four-hour, 2, 11, 12, 37, 40, 85–87, 94, 96–98, 141, 164, 167, 208

uncivilised behaviour. *See* anti-social behaviour

underground venues. *See* alternative nightlife

United Kingdom, 5, 6, 8, 13, 115–18, 129–31, 133, 135, 139, 142, 155, 165, 166, 168, 171, 193, 209

United Kingdom, history of nightlife, 1, 5–8, 165

urban night, 2, 3, 5, 7, 10, 20, 52, 53, 54, 63, 64, 65, 68, 69, 75, 100, 101, 109, 114, 115, 117, 119, 121, 123, 125, 127, 145, 162–65, 167, 169, 176, 190, 209, 227

urban nightscapes, sanitation of, 38, 76, 77, 79, 109, 111, 211, 220

urban redevelopment, 4, 11, 24, 72, 75, 93, 95, 96, 98, 181, 207, 208, 210–12, 214, 216, 217, 220

urban regeneration, 3, 5–8, 11, 14, 21, 24, 26, 37, 69–71, 78, 93, 94–97, 98, 120, 149, 163–65, 172, 176, 181, 183, 185, 189, 200, 208, 210, 211, 213–17. *See also* gentrification

venues. *See* bars; cafes; nightclubs; restaurants

vibrant nightlife, 11, 12, 37, 39, 46–48, 53, 55, 57, 58, 65, 86, 115, 150, 160, 166, 169, 173

violence, 8, 13, 24, 37, 40, 41, 42, 44, 45, 46, 50, 52, 51, 59, 64, 131–33, 136, 137, 142, 163, 170, 201, 210, 216, 217, 221

Viseu, Portugal, 14, 193, 199, 201–4

visitors. *See* tourists

Wacquant, Loïc, 77, 80, 100

Wilkinson, Samantha, 13, 45, 114–28

Williams, Rob, 10, 68, 75, 124

women, 13, 38, 56, 63, 101, 107, 116–17, 119–20, 122, 124, 125, 129–34, 136–39, 140, 142, 143, 154, 179, 181, 187, 202. *See also* femininity

Women's Safety Charter, 140–41

work. *See* employment

workers, 5, 93, 95, 97, 112, 131, 138, 149, 165, 167, 169, 174, 200, 214, 216. *See also* bouncers; sex work(ers)

working class, 7, 8–9, 12, 13, 39, 50, 64, 71, 97, 123, 125, 127, 131, 132, 149, 153, 158, 167, 168, 170, 173, 174, 184, 210, 211, 216

Wythensahwe and Chorlton, England, 13, 114–16, 120, 121, 123, 125, 126, 128. *See also* Manchester, United Kingdom

youth, 7, 8, 10, 11, 13, 37, 38, 40, 41, 54, 55, 60, 62, 63, 64, 65, 70, 99, 100–103, 107–11, 114–27, 131–33, 136, 137, 147–62, 170–73, 175, 192–94, 200, 204, 231

youth-oriented nightlife, 57, 62, 102, 107, 116, 151, 152, 163, 167, 169

Yugoslavia, 11, 53–57, 63, 65, 66

zero-tolerance policies, 140

Zukin, Sharon, 6, 22, 96

About the Editors and Authors

ABOUT THE EDITORS

Jordi Nofre holds a PhD in human geography from the University of Barcelona (2009). Since 2010 he has been enrolled as an FCT (Portuguese Foundation for Science and Technology) Postdoctoral Research Fellow at the Interdisciplinary Centre of Social Sciences at the New University of Lisbon. His research includes two main areas, namely nightlife and urban transformations in south European cities and social geographies of youth in Euro-Mediterranean countries. In 2014, Nofre created LXNIGHTS (http://lxnights.hypotheses.org/), an informal scientific network on nightlife encompassing twenty-two scholars across ten countries (the United Kingdom, France, the Netherlands, Germany, Italy, Romania, Spain, the United States, Canada and Portugal) in order to widen and spread knowledge and good practice, exchange research experiences and promote and launch new win-win joint initiatives between international scientific partners. Nofre is also co-founder and Director of the recently created Observatory of Nightlife in Lisbon.

Adam Eldridge holds a PhD from the Department of Gender and Cultural Studies at the University of Sydney, Australia. He is currently Senior Lecturer in the Department of History, Sociology and Criminology at the University of Westminster. He is the co-author of *Planning the Night-Time City* (2009) with Marion Roberts and has published on different aspects of nightlife, including hen parties, the urban renaissance and discourses of belonging. He is currently exploring debates about diversity in urban centres at night and the relationship between nightlife and gentrification.

Atepheh Amid is an independent scholar, architect and urban designer. She is currently working in London with AECOM. She holds a PhD from the

Department of Architecture and the Built Environment at the University of Westminster. Her research examines the relationship between nightlife and regeneration in pilgrimage sites.

Helena Carvalho holds a PhD in psychology from the Faculty of Psychology and Educational Sciences of the University of Porto. She is Assistant Professor in the Higher Education School of Porto and is also a researcher on counselling, drugs, social exclusion and human rights. She is a member of the Research in Education and Community Intervention and of the Center of Psychology at the University of Porto.

Nihad H. Čengić is a Docent of Urban Design, Urban Planning and Spatial Planning at the Faculty of Architecture, the University of Sarajevo, where he received a PhD in 2008. He has been working closely with the Universities of Graz, Barcelona, Trondheim, Oslo, Skopje and Trabzon since 1994 and has been engaged in a number of workshops, summer schools and research projects. Nihad is currently exploring and writing about post-war urban transition from planning towards self-organisation, real rights and illegal building, development ethics and conflicts of public and private domain, deregulation and privatisation and urban planning and urban meaning in Bosnia and Herzegovina. Nihad is Head of Urban Design and is Planning Chair at the Faculty of Architecture, Sarajevo.

Dominique Crozat is Professor in social and cultural geography at the University Paul Valéry Montpellier 3, France. He is Head of the 'Master of Territories, Corporate Planning and Development' programme hosted at the UPVM and is founder and Director of the Interuniversity Program 'Cultures and Territories'. Crozat led the program 'Metropolitan Peripheries Running. Mobilities. Innovations. Urbanities' (2004–2008), which focused on examining social and spatial changes in Bordeaux, Madrid, Barcelona and Lisbon. His research focuses on tourism and theories of modernity, the construction of spatial identities and forms of spatial segregation. In 2009 Professor Crozat created the Observatory of the Urban Tranquility in Montpellier, in partnership with various key actors of the city.

Emanuele Giordano holds a PhD in Geography and Urban Planning at the University Paul Valéry Montpellier 3. He is currently a research fellow at the University Côte d'Azur, Nice. Most of his research can be positioned at the intersection of urban, social and cultural geography, focusing on urban lighting practices and their political implications, and the role the nighttime economy plays in processes of urban change, including gentrification, studentification and touristification.

Marcos Paulo Ferreira de Góis is Associate Professor in the Department of Geography and Public Policy at the Universidade Federal Fluminense, UFF, Brazil, holding a PhD in geography from Universidade Federal do Rio de Janeiro, UFRJ, Brazil. His dissertation, on nightscapes of Rio de Janeiro, examined the relationship between public policy, urban renewal and behaviour control in public spaces over the past thirty years. He is the author of *Paisagens Luminosas e Cenários Noturnos: Formas, Práticas e Significados da Noite na Cidade do Rio de Janeiro* (2017), among other publications in Portuguese about the nightlife of Rio de Janeiro. He is currently exploring how urban mobility shapes the 'night out' phenomenon and the policies of segregation in Rio and is working on comparative methodologies for future research on nightlife in Latin American cities.

Penny-Panagiota Koutrolikou is Senior Lecturer at the School of Architecture, NTUA. She is an architect/planner, with an MA in sociology (Goldsmiths College, UK) and a PhD in planning studies (UCL, UK). Her PhD research focused on 'Ethnocultural Relations in East London's Multiculturalism'. More recently she has been working on processes of stigmatisation and racism in inner-city Athens, conducting a discourse analysis of politics, media and policies, on questions of hegemony, crisis and governance and on socio-spatial justice.

Daniel Malet Calvo holds a PhD in social anthropology (2011) from the University of Barcelona. He is currently enrolled as an FCT Postdoctoral Research Fellow at the Centre for Research and Studies in Sociology, University Institute of Lisbon (CIES-IUL). He has conducted ethnographic work in Barcelona (Spain), Lisbon (Portugal) and Santiago Island (Cape Verde). His research examines Erasmus students, youth mobility and urban change. He is a member of the Research Group on Exclusion and Social Control (GRECS) and of the Observatory for the Anthropology of Urban Conflict (OACU) in the Anthropology Department at the University of Barcelona in partnership with the Catalan Institute of Anthropology (ICA). Malet Calvo is also co-founder and member of the research networks LXNIGHTS and Turismografias, respectively.

Jordi Martín-Díaz holds a PhD in geography from the University of Barcelona. His research focuses on geopolitical and urban change in post-socialist Sarajevo in Bosnia and Herzegovina. His thesis took the Bosnian capital city as a case study to carry out a cross-cutting analysis of the factors and actors that shaped the performance and influence of the international community in the urban transformation of Sarajevo during the post-war period. His research has been published in such journals as *Cities*, *Area* and *Hungarian Geographical Bulletin*.

João Carlos Martins holds an MA in urban anthropology at the ISCTE-IUL and a PhD in urban and tourism sociology at the New University of Lisbon. Martins has conducted qualitative and quantitative research on the touristification of seaside areas, urban leisure promotion and labour seasonality in the Algarve in southern Portugal. He is currently the management assistant of LXNIGHTS, a network focusing on nightlife studies, and is also an independent research and management consultant on urban tourism, nightlife and community sustainability.

Chrystel Oloukoï studied at the university Paris 1 Panthéon-Sorbonne and at the Ecole Normale Supérieure of Paris (ENS), where she received a BA in geography and planning and an MA in geography of the global south. She is currently pursuing a PhD in African Studies at Harvard University, with a specialisation in urban anthropology and critical media practice, and is exploring the politics of leisure, sexuality and security at night in Johannesburg (South Africa) and Lagos (Nigeria).

Marion Roberts is internationally recognised as a researcher in two specialisms within the broad field of urban design and planning. She has led many funded research projects on the night-time economy since 2002 and has published widely on the topic, as well as carrying out advisory roles for central and local governments and NGOs. Marion's PhD was an interdisciplinary project on gender and the built environment, a topic that she has pursued in scholarly research throughout her academic career, recently co-chairing a working group for the European Commission–funded COST network Gender STE from 2012 to 2016. Her teaching activities have supported the expansion and consolidation of the urban design programmes within the Faculty of Architecture and the Built Environment at the University of Westminster, where she is Emeritus Professor of urban design. She continues to carry out research and consultancy in both fields.

Iñigo Sánchez-Fuarros holds a PhD in cultural anthropology from the University of Barcelona and is currently enrolled as a researcher at the Queen's Belfast University. He was enrolled as a postdoctoral researcher in the Institute of Ethnomusicology at the New University of Lisbon between 2011 and 2016, where he also taught on popular music studies and was a co-founder of LXNIGHTS. His research mainly focuses on music, migration and the city and the anthropology of the senses. Among many other works, his publications include *Made in Spain. Studies in Popular Music* (2013) and *Musical Performance and the Changing City* (2013). He is Director of the journal *Transcultural Music Review*.

José Sánchez García holds a PhD in social anthropology from the University of Barcelona. He is currently Assistant Lecturer in the Department of Social and Cultural Anthropology at the Autonomous University of Barcelona (UAB). Sánchez's research has focused on, among other areas, the relationship between piety and music in Pakistani collectives in Barcelona, gender identities in Gulf countries and youth political movements after 2011 in Spain and Egypt. His publications include 'Revolution against Youth: Youth Political Movements and Discursive Productions in Egyptian Insurrection', in the edited volume *The System Is against Us*, and 'From "Hara" to "Midam": Urban Politic Spaces of Youth in Cairo', in the edited volume *Youth, Space and Time: Agoras and Chronotopes in the Global City*.

Will Straw is James McGill Professor of urban media studies in the Department of Art History and Communication Studies at the McGill University in Montréal. He is the author of *Cyanide and Sin: Visualizing Crime in Fifties America* (2006) and more than 150 articles on popular music, cinema, newspapers and urban culture. His blog, www.theurbannight.com, tracks developments in night-time culture around the world.

Helena Valente is a Psychologist with a post-graduate degree in human rights law. Helena has been working in the NGO APDES since 2007 and has extensive experience in coordinating national and European projects related to nightlife, drug use in party settings, drug checking and new psychoactive substances. She is also a member of the executive board of the NEW NET network.

Cristiana Vales Pires holds an MA in anthropology and is currently completing a PhD, also in anthropology. Her focus is on multiculturalism, migration and globalisation. She has worked with APDES since 2009, collaborating on local and European harm reduction projects with teams that target nightlife settings.

Irina van Aalst is an urban geographer at the University of Utrecht in the Department of Human Geography and Spatial Planning. Most of her research can be positioned at the intersection of urban, cultural and economic geography. She has published on urban nightlife, public spaces, surveillance, the creative industries and youth, and has supervised PhD students on projects, including art in public space, the Dutch publishing sector and dynamics in nightlife districts. In 2009 she received a four-year grant (NWO, Netherlands Organisation for Scientific Research) for a research project on 'Surveillance in Urban Nightscapes', which examined public spaces in night-time

entertainment districts and the socio-spatial effects of surveillance (www.
stadsnachtwacht.nl). She is Director of the Master programme in human
geography and is a Geography Fellow at the University College Utrecht.

Ilse van Liempt is Assistant Professor in urban geography and qualitative
research at the University of Utrecht in the Department of Human Geography and Spatial Planning. Her research is centred around migration and in/
exclusion in urban space. She has published on the urban night in several
journals and edited volumes. Her publications include 'The Gentrification of
Progressive Red-Light Districts and New Moral Geographies: The Case of
Amsterdam and Zurich' in *Gender, Place and Culture*; 'Reclaiming Civility
in Urban Nightlife Districts' in *Urban Space* (2016); a special journal issue
titled 'Geographies of the Night' for *Urban Studies* (2015); and 'Urban Surveillance and the Struggle Between Safe and Exciting Nightlife Districts' in
Surveillance & Society.

Samantha Wilkinson is currently Research Associate in the School of
Sociology and Social Policy at the Nottingham University, working on the
BOUGH project, which aims to broaden understandings of care for people
with dementia. Prior to this, she undertook a PhD in human geography on
young people, alcohol and urban life.

Peta Wolifson is a PhD candidate in human geography at the University
of New South Wales, Australia. Her doctoral thesis examines experiences,
representations and governance in Sydney's nightlife. Peta's research interests span from gentrification, retailing and the cultural economy to urban
ethnography, neo-liberal discourse and the regulation of consumption spaces.
She has published on the use of mobile methods and the significance of bio-
graphical narratives in experiences of nightlife in the inner Sydney suburb
of Surry Hills where she grew up and still lives. Peta has also published
research on the implementation of mobile night-time economy discourses in
Sydney's nightlife planning. Peta's research is grounded in qualitative mobile
methods and discourse analysis. She has also written for *The Conversation*
in Australia.

Lightning Source UK Ltd.
Milton Keynes UK
UKHW041902121218
333898UK00001B/50/P